MEMOIRS
OF
THEODORE THOMAS

Theodore Thomas

MEMOIRS

OF

THEODORE THOMAS

BY

ROSE FAY THOMAS

Author of
"Our Mountain Garden"

Illustrated

NEW YORK

MOFFAT, YARD AND COMPANY

1911

𝕯𝖊𝖉𝖎𝖈𝖆𝖙𝖊𝖉

TO

CHARLES NORMAN FAY

THE BEST AND TRUEST FRIEND OF THEODORE THOMAS
AND THE CHIEF PROMOTER OF HIS ART

PREFACE

In writing the following chronicle of the life and art work of my husband, Theodore Thomas, I have endeavored to confine my own part of the narrative to a simple relation of the sequence of events in his career, and to occasional touches such as might reveal something of the deeper and more intimate side of his nature which was known only to those who shared his home. In describing his achievements I have used, as far as possible, the words of others—chiefly of eminent professional critics or musicians, who personally attended the great musical events under his leadership and wrote the articles I have quoted, while the impression created by them was still fresh and vivid in their minds.

Mr. Thomas never conducted a concert in Europe, or sought to advertise himself or his work there in any way. Nevertheless, he was regarded by the foremost European musicians as their peer, and his letter files contain personal expressions of gratitude and honor from the contemporary composers and executant artists of every land in which the art of music holds an honored place. At the request of my publishers, and others, I have inserted a number of these letters, as adding to the general interest of the book, and showing the importance which even the greatest foreign composers attach to the performance of their works in America.

In conclusion let me say that it has been my faithful endeavor to make this record correct in every detail, but Mr. Thomas preserved very few letters or papers except those of a purely business character and the letters from musicians, above mentioned. For the first thirty years of his life even these are almost wholly lacking, and had he not, fortunately, written a short auto-biographical sketch as an introduction to a work edited and collaborated by Mr. George P. Upton in 1905,* which included a volume of his concert programmes, I should have had to leave the record of these formative years of his career almost a blank. This sketch, however, enabled me to place such additional material as I have been able to collect from other sources in its proper sequence. As for the rest, it has been no easy matter to piece together—from pro-grammes and prospectuses, from the scrap-books of friends, from old magazine articles and musical encyclopedias, and from a hundred other nonde-script sources—the continuous narrative of his life. If, therefore, some inaccuracies have crept in, despite my earnest care, and the six years of research I have devoted to the work, I must crave indulgence because of the great difficulty of the task. ROSE FAY THOMAS.

"FELSENGARTEN," *October* 11, 1910.

* "Theodore Thomas, a Musical Autobiography," Edited by George P. Upton. A. C. McClurg & Co., publishers.

CONTENTS

CHAPTER XX

1895—1904

CHAPTER XXI

1904

APPENDIX

LIST OF ILLUSTRATIONS

MEMOIRS OF
THEODORE THOMAS

CHAPTER I

1835-1860

CHILDHOOD—HIS FIRST VIOLIN—PLAYS BEFORE THE KING
—EMIGRATES TO AMERICA 1845—PLAYS IN THE ENG-
LISH THEATER ORCHESTRA—PLAYS IN A MARINE' BAND
—FIRST CONCERT TOUR—RETURNS TO NEW YORK AND
JOINS THE GERMAN THEATER ORCHESTRA—BECOMES A
MEMBER OF THE ITALIAN OPERA COMPANY UNDER ECKERT
1851—MEMBER OF JULLIEN'S ORCHESTRA—ELECTED
MEMBER OF THE NEW YORK PHILHARMONIC SOCIETY
1854—MEMBER OF THE MASON-THOMAS QUARTETTE
1855—FIRST TWO VISITS TO CHICAGO, 1855 AND 1859

THEODORE THOMAS rarely spoke about the past,
almost never about his childhood. For this period
of his life, therefore, the material at the command
of his biographer is very limited. He was the
son of educated and refined parents; his father,
Johann August Thomas, was a musician of good
standing, in the town of Esens, Ost Friesland;
and his mother the daughter of a physician. He
was born on October 11, 1835, and christened, in
the Lutheran church of Esens, " Christian Fried-
rich Theodore Thomas." The first two names,
however, he seems never to have used, and, even
in early childhood, when he appeared in public as

1

a " *Wunder-kind*," his name was printed, as we know it now, simply " Theodore Thomas."

Theodore was the eldest of a large family of children, none of whom but himself inherited any unusual musical ability, or subsequently adopted music as a profession. His genius, however, showed itself while he was still so young that, in later life, he had no memory of a time when he was not already an artist before the public. While he was still a baby of two years old, he began to tease his father for a violin, and so persistent were his entreaties that at last his father hunted up a cast-off old instrument and gave it to him, expecting that the baby would soon tire of the strange plaything. To the surprise and amusement of his parents, however, the little chap took the violin very seriously, and would sit all day on the front door-steps of the house, scraping away on his big fiddle as hard as he could, and when he had played until his baby hands could no longer hold up the instrument, he would lay it aside for awhile and say, " Mamma, I am going away—far away," and would tell long tales of how he meant to journey to distant lands.

He must have been a fascinating little fellow, and as full of life as a young colt—a headstrong, dominating boy, withal, and not always easy for his gentle mother to manage. He used to tell a story of his German grandmother, who seems to have been a terrible old lady, with whom he was not on the best of terms in those days. On one occasion she had been to the funeral of the child of a neighbor, and when she returned little Theodore was playing on the floor behind the tall porcelain stove. I know not what mischief he was engaged in, but it highly exasperated her and she grimly shook a long, black-gloved finger at the small culprit, remarking, " It is a pity it had not been YOU! " On another occasion, it is said, this same redoubtable grandmother discovered that thieves were visiting her apple orchard. In this emergency she promptly loaded a gun, and taking a pillow out into the orchard every night, she slept under her trees until the rest of the apples were garnered, hoping for a chance to capture the marauder.

No doubt it was from this determined ancestor that Theodore inherited his own tremendous will power, for his mother's face expresses only sweetness and dignity, and his father seems to have followed, rather than guided, the brilliant career of his gifted son. The relations of Theodore Thomas to his parents were always very close and tender. From his early childhood he worked hard that his earnings might help them, and after his father's death he took his mother into his home and provided for her declining years during the remainder of her life under his own roof.

As a young boy Theodore was not fond of going to school, and his teachers made many a complaint because he would spend his time writing music instead of studying his lessons. Indeed, he soon became so proficient in musical writing that his father often said to his wife, " If Theodore continues as he has begun he will be a great musician one of these days, and the time will come when we shall be proud of him." Meantime, the old violin of his baby days had given place to a better one, and his father had begun to teach him seriously. From the very start, music—that most subtle and difficult of arts— presented no difficulties to him, and it seemed, as his musical training progressed, as if he were simply recalling something he had already mastered in a previous state of existence, rather than learning something new; and so rapid was his progress that at seven years of age he could read and execute, at sight, any piece of music put before him, and had already made his *début* as a concert artist. On one occasion, when the blind King George of Hanover heard him play, he offered to take the young prodigy under the royal patronage, and provide for his education. Why this brilliant offer was declined I do not know, but it came at the time the Thomas family was about to emigrate to America, and probably his mother was not willing to leave her boy behind. So he was brought to the New World in 1845, a boy of ten, to educate himself and carve out his own career as best he might.

It cannot be said that the outlook for a great musical career in America was promising at that time. In 1845 New York, its most important city, was a provincial town of two-story houses, and the pigs ran around Broadway and ate the refuse thrown out for their benefit. The only resource open to an instrumentalist was to join a brass band and play for street parades or dancing. The orchestra, as we have it to-day, was an almost unknown quantity, the nearest approach to it being the Philharmonic Society, which had made a feeble beginning three years previously, and the small so-called orchestras of a dozen musicians, more or less, which played in the theaters. Nor were there any facilities for musical education to be found in this crude young city, as yet, or any music teachers except for the piano and cornet. In matters of general education the conditions could not have been much better; for, although the parents of Theodore Thomas were themselves well educated for that day, they did not attach enough importance to it to force the unwilling footsteps of their musical son into school, but allowed him to devote all his time and talents to music alone, and to earning money with his violin, in order to help with the family expenses. And so this wonderful boy, with his magnificent intellect reaching eagerly in all directions for knowledge, was left at ten years old to his own guidance, to grope about blindly in the effort to develop himself with the slender means at his command as best he could.

The father of young Thomas was but little more prosperous in America than he had been in Europe, and Theodore was not only expected to take care of himself, during his first years in America, but also to contribute towards the family maintenance. In a country where, as yet, there

was almost no demand for music, except as a
background for social or civic functions, this was
a difficult thing to do, and he was often hard
pressed to find any means of livelihood. Once,
in an emergency more pressing even than usual,
he took his fiddle into a saloon and played and
passed around the hat, as we still see the little
Italian beggars doing on the streets of the New
York of to-day. " I thought," he afterwards
said, in alluding to the incident, " that it was
better to play in a saloon for half an hour than
to be in debt for my board."

At other times he was glad to get engagements
to play all night for dancing, at balls and parties.
But his artist's soul revolted at the common
musical work he was thus obliged to do for a
living; he realized, child though he was, that he
must not let it demoralize his art, and resolved to
turn the long monotonous hours during which
he played for dancing to good account, by imag-
ining that he was practicing studies and exercises.
Every note was played pure and true, every
rhythm well defined, every shade of expression
drawn with care and delicacy, through the long
watches of these wearisome nights, and when, at
last, the dance was done, and the tired boy packed
his violin and went home by the light of early
dawn, he felt with satisfaction that his time had
at least not been thrown away.

Probably it was these very ballroom performances which developed in him the remarkable
sense of rhythm which was such a striking char-

acteristic of his later work; and the training he imposed upon himself there, by playing with beauty of tone and accuracy of phrasing, while still conforming to the strict rhythm of the dance, perhaps laid the foundation of certain qualities of his orchestral conducting in after life, whereby he was able to sway thousands of performers with absolute ease and certainty through the changing rhythms of the most intricate scores.

In addition to these desultory performances, Theodore also secured a regular engagement in the orchestra of the English theater. And here, at last, he found some intellectual food; for it was here that he heard, for the first time, the works of Shakespeare and Beethoven, two intellectual giants whose names were ever afterwards linked together in his mind, and became beacon lights in his career. There were great actors in the Shakespearean performances of those days, and the works they gave made a profound impression on our twelve-year-old boy, and the musical selections which accompanied them, though probably poorly performed, were often from the works of the masters, so that his association with this theater was not without some educational results.

When Theodore was fourteen years old, his father secured an engagement for himself and his son to play the first and second horns in a marine band on shipboard. This engagement was continued for a year, and was an important factor in Theodore's education, for here he be-

came thoroughly familiar with the brass choir
of the orchestra; although when someone asked
him in after years what sort of a horn player he
had been, he promptly replied, " Damn bad! "

At the expiration of this engagement, the whim
seized our young musician to make a concert tour
through the Southern States. So he secured a
horse, had a few concert posters printed, announcing the coming appearance of the wonderful boy
violinist T. T., packed his few belongings in a
valise, and purchased a large pistol for use in case
of a much-hoped-for attack by brigands. To further enhance the adventurous atmosphere of the
journey, he determined to ride on a straight line,
over fences and ditches, through streams and for-
ests, regardless of how the road ran. Like young
Lochinvar, he " stopped not for brake and stayed
not for stone, he swam the Esk river where ford
there was none," and, as may be supposed, the
adventures thus carefully planned for were many
and varied. In one town he was called upon by
a deputation from the city fathers with the request that he leave at once, as they were convinced that the devil was in his violin.

Boy-like he would ride until he reached some
pleasant place, and amuse himself there until his
money was spent, then he would take out some
of his posters and tack them up around the town,
and engage the dining-room of his hotel for a
concert. When the time for the concert arrived
he would stand at the door and sell tickets until
he thought his audience was all in, after which

Theodore Thomas at 14

he would hastily run up to his room, don his concert clothes, seize his violin, and presently appear at the stage end of the room and give the concert. In this romantic fashion he whiled away a year, but even as a child Theodore Thomas could not be satisfied long in idleness, and the fall found him once more back in New York.

The two years of his absence had wrought a remarkable change in the musical outlook of that city, and now he found that some educational advantages were open to him and some prospect of an artistic career. His first step was to join the little orchestra of the German theater, and he often said in later life that it was here that he received his first real intellectual impetus through hearing the plays of Goethe, Schiller, and the others master minds of German literature. He was now fifteen, and remarkably mature in mind for that age. He felt keenly that he needed more education, but no one suggested to him that what he lacked was general knowledge, and that he ought to go to school. So his only thought was to broaden his knowledge of art. At this time it was his intention to become a composer and violin virtuoso, and with this end in view he began those exhaustive musical researches which ended only with his life, and eventually made him one of the most profound scholars of his day.

Equally thorough were his self-imposed studies in the technical department of his art, and no opportunity was neglected which brought him improvement in executive knowledge of the violin. In this connection nothing was more helpful to young Thomas than his engagement as one of the first violins of the Italian Opera company of New York, which began when he was sixteen, in the year 1851. At this time the greatest singers the world has ever heard were singing in New York. Thomas was not slow to perceive that they—especially Jenny Lind and Henrietta Sontag —possessed the true secret of tone-quality, and it occurred to him that the same kind of tone which they produced with the voice could also be created on the violin. Acting on this theory, as he listened to these great artists in concert or opera, night after night, he endeavored to reproduce their singing, tone for tone, on his beloved instrument, and thus established his ideal of tone-quality on a totally different basis from that generally in use, for the best German violinists of that time used a loud, somewhat harsh tone, wholly lacking in the rich, velvety softness so familiar to us now. From these singers, also, he learned the pure Italian style which was such a striking characteristic of his interpretations of the classic masters. In after years he was wont to advise singers to study the violin, and violinists to study singing, saying that by violin practice the singer would perfect the ear, while the violinist would learn from vocal studies a pure and musical quality of tone. Thomas always seemed to rank Jenny Lind and Henrietta Sontag as in a class by themselves, and considered them as the most perfect and greatest exponents of their art that the world has ever seen.

Carl Eckert, a distinguished European musician, spent the winter of 1851 in New York as conductor of the Italian Opera Company. He recognized immediately the ability of young Thomas, and appointed him leader of the second violins. This was a very responsible position for one so young, and brought him at once into close contact with an experienced and able musician. His work under Eckert was of the greatest value to him, for it taught him to maintain order and system in the orchestra, and to manage musicians with tact and justice. It also opened his eyes to the possibilities of the "many-headed instrument" under favorable conditions. Eckert was one of the few conductors for whom Thomas retained, through life, a genuine respect and admiration, and whom he characterized as a master of his art. Eckert did not remain long in this country and was succeeded by Arditi in 1852. Under this conductor Thomas was again promoted, this time to the stand of the Concert-meister, the highest position in the orchestra, and one which in his case was peculiarly important because Arditi placed in his hands the engaging of all the other members of the orchestra, and many other matters not ordinarily included in the duties of the Concert-meister. This work taught him the practical business side of orchestral management, and all the necessary details of contracts, salaries, etc., and was important to him in this way, although he gained no fresh artistic impetus from his association with Arditi, whom he held in slight esteem as a conductor.

In 1853 Thomas, now a youth of eighteen, for the first time heard and played in a large and complete orchestra. Jullien, the famous European conductor, came to America and organized a large orchestra in New York, with which he gave popular concerts at Castle Garden during the season of 1853-1854. Jullien, whom Thomas has characterized as " The Charlatan of all ages," was a curious mixture of absurd affectations and a genuine love of art. His orchestra was always very large, and composed of the best players, and he worked very honestly, according to his lights, to popularize symphonic music by playing it on all his programmes, interspersed with light numbers, in much the same way that Thomas himself adopted in after years. But the music he associated with it was common and incongruous, and he made even the symphonies themselves absurd by his fantastic method of conducting. Clothed with elaborate care, his coat thrown widely open to display a white waistcoat and an embroidered shirt with wristbands of extravagant length, turned back over his cuffs, and wearing a moustache and a wealth of long black hair, he was a startling figure. He wielded his baton, encouraged his forces, and repressed the turbulence of his audience with indescribable gravity and magnificence; went through all the pantomime of the British Army or Navy Quadrille, seized a violin or a piccolo at the moment of climax, and at last sank exhausted into his gorgeous velvet chair. All compositions of Beethoven he conducted with a jeweled baton, and in a clean pair of gloves, handed him at the moment on a silver salver! *

As may be imagined, an artist of this kind did not impress Theodore Thomas very favorably, even at that age, but his engagement with Jullien was nevertheless of great benefit to him, for, amongst the musicians brought over for this orchestra, were a number of wood-wind players of whom Thomas said, " New York never saw the like, before or since." From these men he gained a thorough knowledge of this important class of orchestral instruments. It is probable that he gained from Jullien some valuable hints, which he made use of afterwards, as to popularizing symphonic music in Garden Concerts, and he certainly learned also how *not* to do it!

Thomas was elected a member of the Philharmonic Society of New York—now in the twelfth year of its existence—in 1854, and continued in close association with it, first as a violin player and afterwards as its conductor, for thirty-six years, almost consecutively.

The year 1855 was an important one for Thomas, for it brought him under one of the best influences of his life, both in music and friendship. It was in this year that William Mason, a refined, sincere, and highly-educated musician, organized a quartette of string players,

* See Grove's " Dictionary of Music "; art. Jullien.

to give a series of chamber concerts in New York, and invited Thomas to be its first violin. A man of his caliber naturally selected for his musical associates men who were not only fine musicians, but who were also refined and sincere in character. Thomas was the youngest member of the quartette, and had probably had fewer educational advantages than any of the others, but his genius soon dominated in all musical matters. In his interesting book, " Memoirs of a Musical Life," Mason thus writes of him, " It became apparent, almost from the start, that Theodore Thomas had in him the genius of conductorship. He possessed by nature a thoroughly musical organization, and was a born conductor and leader. . . . From the time he took the leadership, free and untrammeled, the quartette improved rapidly. His was the dominating influence, felt and acknowledged by us all." But if Thomas took the lead in the musical work of the quartette, on the other hand, he yielded himself in many ways to the influences of his gifted colleagues. The other members of this famous organization, which Thomas often called the " cornerstone of American music," were J. Mosenthal, Carl Bergmann, and G. Matzka. Mason played the piano, and later the place of Bergmann was taken by F. Bergner. The friendships made with these eminent men were continued through life, and, beginning as they did just at the formative period of his character, the influence they exerted was of great value to Thomas, both as man and musician.

Theodore Thomas at 22

By nature Thomas was an idealist. In spite of his splendid physique, his strong passions, his abounding vitality, and the unrestrained liberty which had been his from early childhood, he was, in mind and heart, as delicate and sensitive as a girl. In his youthful amusements he was rollicking and boisterous—sometimes a regular dare-devil—but he was never common or vicious. Speaking of this, he once said, " In my youth, I threw away every twenty-four hours enough vitality to have supplied six men, and never went to bed if I could help it. But I never did anything which I would be ashamed to tell my boys about now." Many a wild story is told of his midnight escapades, amongst them one which ended by his being chased by an angry policeman. Quick as thought, Thomas swung himself up into a convenient tree, and when the policeman shouted to him to come down, he pulled his violin out of its case and played such infectiously merry tunes that the policeman began to grin, and walked off, muttering something about " Only that Thomas boy," and molested him no further! At another time he, one day, went into the piano warerooms of the Steinway firm, just as William Steinway was about to conclude the sale of a fine grand piano to a lady customer. Thomas listened a few moments to Steinway's eulogium on the piano, and suddenly, to the dismay of the dealer, he turned to the lady very seriously, and said, " Madame, I advise you not to listen to what Mr. Steinway is telling you, he merely wishes

to fool you into buying a very inferior instrument,
you had better have nothing to do with him."
Steinway turned upon the incorrigible youth in
a rage, whereupon Thomas uttered a war-whoop
of delight and, jumping over each of the pianos
which stood in a long row down the length of
the wareroom, disappeared out of the back door,
and left the irate Steinway to conclude his sale
as best he might.

But in spite of all kinds of wild pranks and
daring escapades, he, nevertheless, held himself
with such a strong hand through youth and early
manhood, that he never lost his ideality, or tar-
nished the purity of his soul, and as he matured
in years and experience, he became sedulously
careful not only in regard to his words and actions,
but even in regard to his thoughts. He would not
listen to vulgar talk, go to questionable plays,
or read immoral, or even trashy books, for fear
of poisoning his mind with demoralizing ideas
which would impair the purity of his interpretation
of the music of the classic masters. "I avoid
trashy stuff," he said, "otherwise, when I come
before the public to interpret master-works, and
my soul should be inspired with noble and impressive emotions, these evil thoughts run around
in my head like squirrels and spoil it all. A
musician must keep his heart pure and his mind
clean if he wishes to elevate, instead of debasing
his art. And here we have the difference between
the classic and the modern school of composers.
Those old giants said their prayers when they

wished to write an immortal work. The modern man takes a drink."

For a young man with a nature like this to come into constant and intimate association with the refined and scholarly men of the Mason-Thomas Quartette, must have brought out all that was best and truest in himself, and done much to form and strengthen those high standards to which his after life was dedicated. Nor was it in character-building alone that Thomas was benefited by his work in the Quartette. It was Dr. Mason's object to make its performances conform to the highest standard of similar organizations in Europe—notably those which he had heard in the *salon* of Liszt, of whom he was a pupil. This idea found an enthusiastic echo in the breast of Thomas, in whom the love of perfection was a dominating trait of character. The programmes were at first of a somewhat miscellaneous character, containing even solo numbers for singers, etc. But gradually they became more and more æsthetic, until at last they reached a point where even Thomas could carry them no higher. After this, solos of every kind were generally strictly debarred, and nothing but chamber music, pure and simple, was given a place. The programmes generally consisted of three numbers, of which the first and last were for the string quartette, and the second was either a sonata or trio, in which the piano took part. The first programme of the first season is appended, as well as all the programmes of the final season. It was to these chamber concert programmes that Tausig referred more especially, when he wrote, on the back of a photograph of himself, which he gave Thomas, " To Theodore Thomas, the maker of the best and most authoritative programmes in the world."

MASON-THOMAS CHAMBER CONCERTS

First Concert
November 27, 1855
Programme

Quartet in D minor, *œuvre posthume* . . . . Schubert
Romanze from Tannhaeuser, " O du mein holder
  Abendstern " . . . . Wagner
Otto Feder
(a) Fantaisie Impromptu . . . . Chopin
(b) Deux Préludes in D flat and G, op. 24 . . . . . . Heller
William Mason
Variations Concertantes for 'cello and piano . Mendelssohn
Song, " Feldwaerts flog ein Voegelein " . . . . Nicolai
Otto Feder
Trio in B major, op. 8 . . . . Brahms

Thirteenth Season—1868
Programmes
I

Quintet in G minor . . . . Mozart
Sonata in A, op. 47 . . . . Beethoven
Quartet in D minor, posthumous . . . . Schubert

II

Quartet in A minor, op. 9 . . . . Volkmann
Trio in B flat, op. 99 . . . . Schubert
Quartet in E minor, op. 59, No. 2 . . . . Beethoven

III

Quartet in D minor......................Haydn
Trio in B flat, op. 97.....................Beethoven
Quartet in A, op. 41, No. 3...............Schumann

IV

Quartet in D minor, op. 77...................Raff
Quintet in E flat, op. 44...................Schumann
Quartet in B, op. 18, No. 6...............Beethoven

V

Octet, op. 32..............................Spohr
" Faschingsschwank aus Wein," for piano...Schumann
Quartet in B flat, op. 130................Beethoven

VI

Quartet in D minor (K. 421)...............Mozart
Sonata for piano and 'cello, in G minor, op. 5,
    No. 2................................Beethoven
Sonata for piano and 'cello, in G minor, op. 22. Schumann
Sonata for piano, in G minor, op. 22.......Schumann
Octet in E flat, op. 20.. ....Mendelssohn

In order that the performance might be worthy
of the compositions rendered, the Quartette gave
three mornings a week to rehearsing the six programmes which made up the repertoire of the
year, although they did not make enough money
from the concerts to pay the expenses of giving
them, and Mason quietly made good the annual
deficit from his own pocket, without even saying
anything about it to the rest. It was this exhaustive study of master-works, especially those
of Beethoven, continued through fourteen years,
which gave Thomas his mastery of the string

choir of the orchestra, and his profound insight into the classic school of music.

Nor was he satisfied with even the severe training he had so far imposed upon himself; but from this time on, throughout his whole life, every moment which could be snatched from his daily duties was devoted to the study of, not only the art, but also the so-called science of music. Harmony, fugue, counterpoint, thorough-bass, acoustics—any and every thing that had to do with his art, he absorbed as sand absorbs water, and still was never satisfied, but always reaching out with passionate eagerness for more and more knowledge as long as he lived. " I still progress in my art," he said a few weeks before his death, " because I am still studying and learning."

As a virtuoso, Thomas was now rapidly rising to pre-eminence, and the following notice from *Dwight's Journal of Music,* printed in 1856, describes his violin playing at this period:

" Decidedly the most wonderful performance of the concert, which closed the Mason-Thomas series this season, was Mr. Thomas' playing of the celebrated Chaconne by Bach. This young artist (and very young he is, although the stamp of genius matures his almost boyish face), bids fair to rise high in the musical world. . . . Young Thomas played the whole unfalteringly, without notes, and consequently with all the more freedom and abandon. His technic, too, gives proof of untiring industry in practice, but more than all, his evident enjoyment of what he was playing, and his thorough entering into the spirit of the music, showed the true artist in him.

His choice of pieces also betokens real love of art and reverence. He never plays any but good music. Such men are, or ought to be, the true missionaries of art in this country."

The years between 1855 and 1860 passed in quiet but busy uneventfulness for the young musician, and the only unusual happenings were his first two visits to Chicago—then a brisk little Western city, already beginning to take an interest in things musical. These trips were made in 1856 and 1859, respectively, and on both tours Thomas was a member of a troupe of which Carl Formes, the basso, was the star. At the concert of 1859, Thomas played the Kreutzer Sonata of Beethoven, and the *Illinois Staats-Zeitung* ended its notice of the performance thus, "During the last two years Thomas has become America's most accomplished violinist."

CHAPTER II

1860-1867

FIRST EXPERIENCE AS CONDUCTOR—APPOINTED CONDUCTOR OF THE ITALIAN OPERA—FIRST ORCHESTRAL CONCERT—FOUNDS THE THEODORE THOMAS ORCHESTRA 1864—MARRIES MISS RHODES—CONDUCTS SUMMER CONCERTS AT BELVEDERE LION PARK—SYMPHONY SOIRÉES—INAUGRATES SUMMER NIGHT CONCERTS AT TERRACE GARDEN 1866—APPOINTED CONDUCTOR OF THE BROOKLYN PHILHARMONIC SOCIETY—BUILDING OF STEINWAY HALL—FIRST EUROPEAN TRIP—VON BUELOW—TAUSIG—BERLIOZ

THOMAS was now a man of twenty-two, and never was musician better equipped for his future career than this self-trained product of a new, and as yet, unmusical country. There was not a branch of his art, either technical or theoretical, of which he was not a master, and, as yet, the only master in America; and it followed, as a perfectly natural sequence, that destiny should soon assign to him the rôle of national educator. He still retained his position as Concert-meister in Ullman's opera company, which was now under the conductorship of Carl Anschuetz. But the time had come, at last, when he was himself to be promoted to the conductor's stand. This important advancement came, as often happens, very

22

unexpectedly, and is thus described by William Mason: *

"One evening (December 7, 1860) Thomas came home tired out from his work, and after dinner had settled himself in a comfortable chair for a good rest, when a message came to him from the Academy of Music, about two blocks away. An opera season was in progress there. The orchestra was in its place and the audience seated, when word was received that Anschuetz, the conductor, was ill. . . . Would Thomas come to the rescue and conduct the opera? He had never conducted opera before and the work for the evening (Halévy's 'Jewess,') was unfamiliar to him. . . . He thought for a moment, and then said, 'I will.' He arose quickly, got himself into his dress suit, hurried to the Academy, and conducted the opera as if it were a common experience. Thomas was not the man to say, 'Give me until next week,' he was always ready for every opportunity."

The position thus suddenly achieved proved to be a permanent one, and the correspondent of *Dwight's Journal of Music* sketched the young musician as he appeared in this new and important rôle, in the following words:

"The place of Carl Anschuetz is taken by Theodore Thomas, the young violinist, who looks ' severe in youthful beauty,' as he wields the baton—rather nervously it must be confessed—and directs the performances of venerable, spectacled, and bald-headed 'cellists and trombonists old enough to be his grandfathers. It is always a treat to see

* See "Memories of a Musical Life," William Mason, p. 200.

him in the orchestra. He plays the violin with such careless grace that even his elevation to the conductorship does
not reconcile me to the loss of his violin performance."

At the time Thomas was elected to the Philharmonic Society, in 1854, the chief musical
authority in New York was Carl Bergmann, a
talented musician who had come to this country as
'cello player in a small orchestra named the
" Germania," of which he afterwards became the
conductor. When the " Germania " orchestra disbanded, Bergmann at first accepted an engagement in Chicago, where he was the conductor of
the Chicago Philharmonic Society during the winter of 1854-55. In 1855, however, the conductor
of the New York Philharmonic Society having
been taken ill, the position was offered to him and
he accepted it and, returning to the East, settled
permanently in New York. Many years later,
when Thomas was asked to write a brief sketch
of Bergmann as a musician, he found it difficult
to formulate any satisfactory estimate of this
peculiar character, and wrote and rewrote his
remarks many times before he let them stand.
Thomas and Bergmann were associated very
closely in their musical work, for Thomas played
under Bergmann in the Philharmonic orchestra;
while Bergmann played under Thomas in the
Mason-Thomas Quartette. Thomas had a high
respect for Bergmann's ability, but while he
acknowledged his talent he, nevertheless, found
him lacking in thoroughness, nor was his standard

of performance in keeping with the ideals of
Thomas. In writing of him, Thomas said:

" He gave the impression that he never worked much,
nor cared to do so. He lacked most of the qualities of a
first-rank conductor, but he had one great redeeming
quality for those days, which soon brought him into prominence, he possessed an artistic nature and was in sympathy
with the so-called ' Zukunft Musik.' He did not have force
enough, however, to make an impression, and had no standard. As a 'cello player, he was only a moderate performer, but he did everything with a certain grace. . . . I
always felt that under favorable circumstances, Bergmann might have been of greater service to his adopted
country." *

A nature like that of Thomas could not long
be satisfied with either the restricted field of
quartette music, or the mediocre standard of the
Philharmonic orchestra. Nor was the opera a
wholly congenial branch of art to him. In 1862
therefore, he began to extend his field of action,
and we find for the first time amongst his records
the announcement of an orchestral concert under
his own direction. The programme of this first
" Thomas Concert " was as follows:

ORCHESTRAL CONCERT—MAY 13, 1862

Theodore Thomas, Conductor

Programme

Overture, " The Flying Dutchman," (First time in
    America)................................... Wagner
Hymn, " Lord, be Thou with Us ".............. Apel
The Teutonia Choral Society

* See " Theodore Thomas, a Musical Autobiography," p. 36.

Aria, " Bel raggio ".........................Rossini

Mme. de Laussan

Violin Concerto, A minor.......................Molique

B. Wollenhaupt

Quartette for two pianos, " Les Contrastes "..Moscheles

Messrs. Mills, Goldbeck, Hartmann, and Mason

Aria, " Ernani ".................................Verdi

Mme. de Laussan

Overture and incidental music to " Streuensee "

(First time in America)..................Meyerbeer

Orchestra, Chorus, and Harp Obligato

In this modest venture the orchestra numbered
but little more than forty players, and Thomas
confined his own part of the programme to the
opening and closing numbers. But it was characteristic of him that these two numbers were
compositions which had never been played in
America before, and especially characteristic that
one of them, the Overture to the " Flying Dutchman," should have been music of a school so
progressive that it was then ironically called " The
music of the future." Thus early in his career
did Thomas begin to provide that America should
be abreast of the Old World in hearing the
current musical literature.

The first Thomas Concert was sufficiently successful to encourage its young promoter to more
efforts in the same line, and he has given, in the
following words, his own account of what one
may call his dedication to his life work:

" In 1862 I concluded to devote my energies to the cultivation of the public taste for instrumental music. Our

chamber concerts had created a spasmodic interest, our programmes were reprinted as models of their kind, even in Europe, and our performances had reached a high standard. As concert violinist, I was at that time popular, and played much. But what this country needed most of all to make it musical, was a good orchestra, and plenty of concerts within reach of the people. The Philharmonic Society, with a body of but sixty players, and only five yearly concerts, was the only organized orchestra which represented symphonic music in this country. . . . The orchestra was often incomplete. If a member had an engagement elsewhere he would go to it instead of to the rehearsal. When one of the wind choir was absent, his place would be filled as best it could. A clarinet or oboe part would be played on a violin, or a bassoon on a 'cello, etc. The conductor could not, therefore, rehearse as he ought. . . . Under these circumstances justice could not be done to the standard, much less to the modern and contemporary works. Such conditions barred all progress. I had been prominent before the public in chamber concerts, and as concertmeister of the opera since 1855, and during later years as conductor also of opera and concerts, and I thought the time had come to form an orchestra for concert purposes. I therefore called a meeting of the foremost musicians of New York, told them of my plans to popularize instrumental music, and asked for their coöperation. I began by giving some orchestral concerts at Irving Hall, and conducted some of the Brooklyn Philharmonic concerts, alternating with Theodore Eisfelt." *

For two years Thomas gave occasional orchestral concerts in New York, as opportunity offered; but he soon discovered that he could not reach

* See "Theodore Thomas, a Musical Autobiography," p. 50.

the high standard he was aiming for by this kind of desultory work, and he decided that he must have an orchestra of his own. Having reached this decision, he did not stop to ask where a penniless youth, like himself, was to get the money to pay the salaries of a large body of musicians, or to meet the other large expenses of the organization, but he simply engaged his men and announced his concerts, in perfect confidence that he could carry his gigantic scheme to a successful consummation. To-day, in the same city, now become musical through half a century of culture, the promoters of a similar plan for a permanent orchestra, found it necessary to raise a guarantee fund of ninety thousand dollars per annum before they could venture to start such an institution. But Thomas had no guarantee fund, either then or at any other time in New York, and consequently he organized his orchestra without it and assumed the whole financial responsibility himself.

The orchestra, thus organized, was called the " Theodore Thomas Orchestra," and gave its first concert in Irving Hall, on December 3, 1864, with the following programme:

Symphony, No. 8, F major. . . . . .Beethoven
Scena and Aria, " Non piu di fiore ". . . . . .Mozart
Miss Fanny Raymond
Concerto in F major, op. 21, Larghetto and Finale. Chopin
Mr. S. B. Mills
Suite, op. 113, in D. . . . . .F. Lachner

Cavatina, " Ah, S'estinto "..............Mercadante
                Miss Fanny Raymond
Dramatic Symphony, " Romeo and Juliet," Second
    part................................... Berlioz

This concert was the first of a regular series of
Symphony " Soirées," as evening performances
were called in those days. They were very successful artistically, but only moderately so financially. This, however, did not discourage our
young enthusiast, for he knew that, as yet, only
a very small percentage of the American public
understood, or enjoyed symphonic music; and already he had resolved that his mission in life should
be to teach the people to know and love the
highest form of music, and to give it to them in
the most perfect manner. In short, he wished to
raise his beloved art from the low level of a mere
amusement, to its rightful place beside its sister
arts of painting, sculpture, and architecture. It
was his belief that as soon as this should be
accomplished, and the public should learn the true
value and importance of music, as an art,
the wealthy men and women of New York would
come forward and endow a permanent orchestra,
and engage him as its conductor, thus relieving
him from the great financial burden of its maintenance and enabling him to devote his whole time
and attention to making the orchestra as complete and its performances as perfect as any in
the world. A few years of sacrifice and hard work
would accomplish this, he thought, and so he en-

tered, with hope and confidence, upon one of the longest and most arduous careers that was ever dedicated to the cause of art and humanity.

The year 1864 was an epoch-making period in the life of Thomas for more than one reason. Not only was it the year in which he founded the Thomas Orchestra, but it was also the year in which he married his first wife. Minna L. Rhodes was the brilliant and highly educated daughter of an old New York family. At the time Thomas met her she was a pupil at Miss Porter's famous school in Farmington. Amongst the educational advantages which Miss Porter considered essential for her scholars was the opportunity to become familiar with the best music, both by studying it and hearing it performed. In pursuance of this idea she engaged, for the professor of music at Farmington, Carl Klauser, one of the best theoretical musicians and teachers America has ever had. In speaking of him, Thomas said,

" He had much influence in this country in cultivating the taste for everything that is noble in music. He created an artistic and refined atmosphere for his pupils, and the young women who studied under him at Farmington, and who came from all parts of the country, took away with them genuine love and respect for the art of music, and were active in promulgating this spirit all their lives. I have often met with instances of this, most unexpectedly, and in widely separated localities." *

Klauser was at that time also a young man, and an intimate friend of Thomas, and he was

* See " Theodore Thomas, a Musical Autobiography," p. 43.

instrumental in bringing the Mason-Thomas Quartette to Farmington for an annual series of chamber concerts at Miss Porter's school, from 1856 until the Quartette was finally disbanded. It was during these repeated visits that Thomas and Miss Rhodes formed the attachment which united their lives in 1864.*

This marriage probably exerted a very strong influence in the development of the young musician's character, for through it he was brought into a new atmosphere—the atmosphere of intellectual culture. Mrs. Thomas, even at that early age, was a remarkably brilliant woman, and had received the most thorough educational training of the day. It was, no doubt, her fine mind and accurate knowledge which attracted Thomas, for he was always an admirer of intellectuality rather than beauty, in women. " I do not care for so-called 'pretty women,' " he said. " What I admire is character and intelligence. If a woman has these, she does not need beauty, but I will confess that if a woman of character and intellect has beauty in addition, it is like a lamp shining through an alabaster vase. But this is a rare combination."

Unlike many intellectual women, Mrs. Thomas was a notable *Hausfrau*. Her home was always a model of order, her table delicately and bountifully served, and her children carefully reared. It is said that as her sons grew to manhood, she made it a point to keep always ahead of them in

* The author regrets that she has been unable to procure a good likeness of Mr. Thomas' first wife.

their studies, and that when they entered Yale and Columbia universities, she could have written their examination papers as well as themselves. A wife of this character was a healthy stimulus to a mind like that of Thomas, and prevented him from becoming one-sided through the exclusive contemplation of his own specialty.

It was always a source of deep regret to Thomas that he had not had a university education, and he did what he could do to supply his lack in this direction by reading, always carrying with him on his travels some book of history, philosophy, or the like, as long as he lived. His memory was so retentive that he never forgot what he read, and thus he became, without realizing it himself, a very well informed man on a wide range of subjects, and it is a curious fact that his intimate friends through life were physicians, architects, writers, or business men, rather than musicians. He knew, personally, nearly every eminent musician of both America and Europe, but was intimate with but very few.

The first season of the Thomas Orchestra was not very remunerative, but Thomas felt that he had, at least, made a fair beginning, and when summer came, he continued his work by accepting an engagement to play three afternoons a week, from June until September, in Belvedere Lion Park, at 110th Street. These open-air concerts in a park were the forerunners of the popular Summer Night Concerts which he gave during so many subsequent years in different cities of the

East and West. Thomas recognized at the outset
that he could make them serve an educational
purpose, and determined to utilize them in
familiarizing the public with symphonic works.
The programme of the first concert was very light,
but on the second and third programmes, respectively, he gave the first and second symphonies of
Beethoven and a Mozart overture, while the fourth
included a Mozart symphony and the overture to
" Fidelio." Apparently the experiment was not a
success. No doubt the public complained, and the
manager objected to a symphonic repertoire from
a park band stand. It was probably the first of
a long series of occasions when his audience turned
a deaf ear to the musical feast he set before it,
and clamored for popular programmes. So he
changed his tactics, but without ever losing sight
of his ultimate object, and abandoned for a time
giving whole symphonies, administering them, instead, in small doses, one movement at a time,
as he thought the people could digest them.

By means of this engagement, inferior though it
was, Thomas managed to keep half of his orchestra
together through the summer season, and when
winter came, he enlarged it once more to sixty men,
and gave Symphony Soirées as he had done the
two previous winters.

During the summer of 1866, Thomas inaugurated his real Summer Night Concerts, and gave
over a hundred of them on consecutive nights at
Terrace Garden, between June 11 and September
29. But the programmes were, as yet, of the

lightest character compatible with his standards, and symphonic works were sparingly introduced. This engagement was, however, a great advance on that of the previous summer, because the orchestra was larger and the concerts given daily, thus permitting him to keep the players of the orchestra under his exclusive and constant direction, and it followed naturally that their artistic progress was rapid, and that when fall came, they were in excellent shape for their winter's work.

The season of 1866 and 1867 was memorable to Thomas for two reasons. The first of these was his appointment as the conductor of the Brooklyn Philharmonic Society, an office which he held continuously as long as he lived in New York. The Brooklyn Philharmonic Society was not composed of orchestral musicians, like that of New York, but of private citizens, music lovers, who were organized to provide an annual series of symphony concerts for that city. Hence, in accepting this appointment, Thomas was able to utilize his own orchestra, thus securing to his men an extra engagement of twenty performances. His Symphony Soirées were resumed, and the opening of Steinway Hall, which was the other important event of the winter for him, provided him with a large number of miscellaneous concerts in addition, so that his professional outlook began, at last, to appear really promising.

This hall had been built by the piano firm of Steinway and Sons, over their warerooms in Fourteenth Street, presumably as a business venture,

but the firm was always very generous in regard
to the use of the hall by others, and it soon became the musical center of America, and the
place where all the most important concerts of
New York were given during the winter season.
It was not large, and would be reckoned now-a-
days as a cramped and inconvenient auditorium
for orchestral purposes. Nevertheless it was the
only hall which the metropolitan city possessed
during all Thomas' residence there, and he often
said that the city of New York owed much to the
Steinways for building and maintaining for so
many years a hall where, although it was by no
means ideal, it was, nevertheless, possible to give
the best music. Nor has any hall of as satisfactory
size and stage capacity been built in that city
from the time it was closed to the present writing
(1910). The Thomas Orchestra could not have
been maintained in New York so many years
without this hall in which to do its work and store
its belongings, and when the growth of the city
took the concert-going public so far away from
its location that concerts could no longer be profit-
ably given there, the lack of a " home " for his
orchestra lost it to New York, while the building of such a " home " in Chicago won it in perpetuity for the Western city.

Thomas had been so entirely a self-educated
man that he felt very doubtful in regard to his
own acquirements. There was no standard of
musical art in this country yet, nor were there
conductors or orchestras of established reputation

by which to measure himself or his work. So he determined, in the spring of 1867, to take a short vacation for the first time in his life, and spend about two months in Europe, hearing everything he could in that brief time and impressing the highest standards of orchestral, quartette, and solo violin performances on his mind, in order that he might thereby improve his work at home.

His little journal * of this trip—consisting of only a few lines, jotted down daily in pencil—gives in a nutshell an expert's criticism of the best musical performances of Europe at that time. The greater part of it is quoted below:

" April 29, 1867.   Arrived in London at ten o'clock. In the evening heard ' Faust ' in Covent Garden. Garcia and Lucca, very good. Orchestra extraordinary. Costa conducting.

" April 30, London.   Matinée at St. James.   Ella conducting—a monkey. In the evening opera at Her Majesty's Theater. Titiens—great! Orchestra middling good, chorus very strong and good. Arditi conducting. Bad, everything bad.

" May 2, London.   Opera at Covent Garden, ' Marriage of Figaro.' A very good performance. Cherubino (Lucca) very beautiful. Yesterday I heard a Philharmonic concert. Second class. Dr. Wylde, conductor, very bad. They gave the Fifth Symphony and Mozart's Clarinet Concerto. Tedious.

" May 6, Paris.   Heard Pasdeloup. In the Haydn Symphony and Septet, Beethoven, the whole orchestra

* The original diary is written in German.

Theodore Thomas and His Orchestra at Steinway Hall, New York

was good. The Overture to Genoveva, Schumann, was bad. Conducting middling.

"May 8, Paris. Grand opera, 'Don Carlos.' Only seven contra-basses, but they played for twenty! Extraordinary—wonderful—For the first time I heard a contra-bassoon, the effect was wonderful. Verdi sounds better in the Grand Opera of Paris than in New York.

"Spent a delightful hour with Berlioz, in which we talked over all his larger compositions. It seems he had heard already that I played his music, and, as I was leaving, he asked me if there was anything of his that I would like which I did not already have in my library. I told him yes, there was one thing that I wanted very much, and that was his great 'Requiem Mass.' Hearing this, Berlioz went to the music case, took down his own copy of the score and inscribed it, 'To Theodore Thomas in remembrance of the grateful author, Hector Berlioz,' and presented it to me."

"May 16, Munich. Reached Munich at four this afternoon and went to the opera this evening. Performance not very good. Afterwards heard Gungl's orchestra. No comparison with mine.

"May 18, Vienna. Reached here this morning and drove out to the graves of Beethoven and Schubert. Later in the day I heard 'Traviata.' Went also to the Prater. The whole four miles were illuminated, and bands playing all along. I paid especial attention to the performance of Johann Strauss.

"May 20, Vienna. Heard 'The Huguenots.' Bad. Violins good, but the basses scratched. Seems to be always the German style.

"May 21, Vienna. In the Volksgarten to hear Strauss again. In the afternoon the orchestra of the

Conservatoire played for my benefit the Unfinished Symphony of Schubert. Beautiful.

"May 23, Dresden. Arrived at three and called on Rietz at five. He received me most cordially. I found in him the first conductor who really knows something.

"May 28, Berlin. Grand opera. ' Prophète.' Johanne Wagner as Fides. Orchestra under Radicke very scholastic.

"May 30, Berlin. Opera again. In the afternoon Liebig in ' Orpheus.' In the evening Beethoven's ' Fidelio.' Taubert conducted—an old machine, but no precision. The opera itself made a great impression on me. Met Dvörak afterwards.

"At last I have met Tausig. He is the ninth wonder of the world! He played for me everything imaginable, and became very confidential during our interview.

"June 1, Hanover. A Beethoven concert. Violin concerto, played by Joachim. He is the most noted violinist of the time. Bott directed the Seventh Symphony. A man of no talent, and no conductor. We would not dare to play so in America.

"June 9. Performance of ' Judas Maccabeus,' Rietz conducting. A fine performance, especially in the choral work. The Bach Suite was also well played. Beautiful effects."

On this little European tour, Thomas traveled at high pressure, visiting only such cities as afforded him the best musical performances, or brought him into personal relations with the most noted musicians in his own specialties of orchestra, opera, quartette, or violin. While listening critically to their performances, he compared them with his own, hoping to glean new and valuable suggestions from them. To his surprise, he found himself, not only abreast, but ahead of the first European musicians in conducting, while in quartette and solo playing, he had little to learn, even from the great Joachim himself. Nor could his severest self-criticism show him any essential of musicianship in which he was lacking. But, although he did not learn much that was new, musically, the trip was nevertheless an important one to him, for it brought him in touch with the great art centers of Europe, broadened his mental horizon, and gave him confidence in himself. He now knew that he was on the right road, and no longer worked in the dark. One valuable bit of musical information he gained which was of great service to him, and this was a thorough knowledge of the dance music of Johann and Josef Strauss. The days were long past when Thomas' services were needed in the ballroom, but he recognized that the dance music of the Strauss family had a distinct value in the concert room, and that it was worthy of its own place on his lighter programmes. He, therefore, went many times to hear it under the leadership of Strauss himself, and carefully noted his best effects, for reproduction in the Summer Night Concerts at home. When he returned he brought with him pretty much everything the Strausses had ever written, adding to his collection of their works, later, all their subsequent publications, until his library contained the scores and parts of nearly two hundred dances and marches by these celebrated composers of light

music. No one knew the value of a good piece
of popular music so well as Thomas, and he was
always on the lookout for such dainty musical
tid-bits, and would take infinite pains to make
them effective. An instance of the kind, which
belongs to this period, was his adaptation of
Schumann's little piano compositions " Traumerei "
and " Romanza " to orchestra. The idea did not
originate with him, as the two compositions, linked
together, had already been orchestrated by a New
York musician named George Matzka, but the
arrangement was not satisfactory to Thomas.
He therefore rearranged them for the string
choir only, omitting the basses, and playing the
final portion with muted instruments, ending with
a diminuendo *" piano, pianissimo, pianississimo,"*
as he said. To still further heighten the effect, he
would have the violinists of the orchestra continue to draw their bows over the strings after
the music had in reality ceased, and the audience,
watching the moving bows in breathless silence,
were actually unable to distinguish when it became inaudible, but continued to hear it, in imagination, floating off to an immeasurable distance,
until Thomas broke the spell by quietly laying
down his baton. Later, when Thomas began to
travel with his orchestra, this little arrangement
of the " Traumerei " created such a sensation with
the public everywhere that it might almost be
called the cornerstone of his success.

On his return from Europe in July, his Summer Night Concerts were already in progress

under the conductorship of Matzka and Eben,
who had started the season for him in his absence.
He at once assumed his old place at the conductor's desk, and the rest of the season was
carried out so successfully that, at its close, some
business men offered to build a hall for his use in
the summer seasons of the future—a very important matter for Thomas, as we shall see.

One of the pleasant features of his European
trip, had been the courteous attentions of the
famous musician Hans von Buelow. Buelow
was at that time one of the musical autocrats of
Europe, and, in particular, an authority on the
important subjects of Beethoven and conducting.
He had watched the work of Thomas in America
with the interest of a connoisseur, and when he
came to Munich, Buelow gave him a very cordial
welcome, and took a great deal of trouble to make
his stay there agreeable. A pleasant friendship
sprang up between the two musicians, and after
the return of Thomas to America he played one
of Buelow's compositions in New York. Buelow
—however great as a student and executant
musician—was not much of a composer, and the
" Ballade " for orchestra which Thomas performed,
had been a dismal failure in the European concerts
where it had been given. Perhaps for this reason
Thomas brought his best effort to bear upon its
American performance, with the result that he was
able to write to Buelow the comforting news that it
had scored a success. At the same time he sought
his advice on certain points in the interpretation

of some Beethoven works, in which he had made
what seemed to him necessary changes, which he
wished to have endorsed by the highest authority
then living. In reply he received the following
interesting letter:

MUNICH, *June,* 1868.

MR. THEODORE THOMAS,

Honored Sir:

Accept my sincerest thanks for your kind letter and
the communications accompanying it, which were of deep
interest to me. . . . The news of the "*non-fiasco*" of my
orchestral "*Ballade*" delighted me, especially because,
Honored Sir, it proved that you found it worth while to
give to my little composition the careful preparation necessary to produce an impression upon the audience with it.
This, in itself, is so flattering to me that it would have
compensated me even for a failure.

Not less agreeable to me was the news that Liszt's
"*Ideale*" has found favor with New York music-lovers,
through your intelligent interpretation. I place special
value upon this work among the symphonic poems. Have
you produced the "*Hunnenschlacht*" yet? I consider
this composition almost as pleasing to the audience as the
"*Festklange*," "*Tasso*," and "*Preludes*." Besides, it is
not especially difficult.

Your description of the sorrows of a conductor who
has to concern himself with the gymnastics of taming a
diva to suit the public, amused me immensely. I regret
that you, who know how to wield the pen so cleverly, do
not publish such accounts in the "*Signale*." I would
humbly advise, in such a case, that even the *recitative* of
this *Cabaletta* should be directed with a revolver! You
are mistaken, however, if you imagine that similar delights
are unknown to us poor European conductors. Here in

Munich, for instance, we have to suffer even more unbearable trials, especially from *soi-disant* "musical"
male singers, whom the devil should take first of all.
They do not accept any suggestion, and make the same
demands as the Italian "throat-beast." For instance,
one must double the *tempo* in a Mozart aria, if the "musical" singer does not know how to breathe properly, or
how to hold the note the requisite time. But enough of this.

My time is so very limited (on the 21st of this month
comes the first representation, and this time really a
model performance of Wagner's "*Meistersinger*") that
I cannot think of a cozy chat with the pen or the tongue,
and therefore I will devote my scant measure of time to
answering your questions in regard to the Ninth Symphony, quoting from the new octavo edition of Schott,
which is cheaper, and in some details, more correct than the
pretentious edition of Haertel, which I have not at hand.

One important mistake is, as you correctly state, at the
end of the 2-3 measure in D in the *Allegro ma non tanto*
(*Finale*). The C♮ in the wood-winds, as a melodious tone,
is correct, therefore in the viola and contralto voices must
be resolved. I agree thoroughly with your action in
strengthening the *Canto fermo* in the trumpets and horns
in the above mentioned 2-3 *tempo*. Two years ago I
added this in the orchestral parts here. In the finale of
the Eighth Symphony, development of 2-2, I had the two
trumpets enter at the beginning of the theme in A
major, to strengthen the feeble wood-winds in the sustained tone E, and also at the fourth section at D major
on A. My piety extends even farther. In the C
minor symphony, first movement, third section, I do not
have this passage

played by the bas-
soons, but by the

horns, as in the analogous passage in E♭ (I do not let the

bassoons enter before the G). Experience has taught me, furthermore, that even with the most efficient orchestras, the beginning of this movement never goes perfectly, if the leader does not beat three measures before, whereby the first measure acquires a rhythmical position as the fourth of a period of four measures. Something similar is needed in the *Scherzo* of the "*Eroica*," where the twice intervalled period of two beats may easily cause uncertainty if the players do not introduce a slight accent. Your completing the flute passages in the *Scherzo* (*alla ottava*) I also find permissible. . . .   *

The second mistake you have also correctly verified (in the first movement). I consider it very essential, as it disturbs the harmonic structure and lessens the effect of the ascending passages of the bassoon and clarinet. The oboes must double the parts of the second violins and violas in the higher octave, therefore it should be,

and not

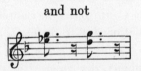

That you preserve such pleasant memories of your too brief stay in Munich, and my humble self, only increases my sincere regret that you cannot be present at our musical festival in Munich, which is soon to occur. I cherish the ambition that on June 21, Munich will provide the very best specimen of the musical ability

---

* Here a piece is torn out of the letter, and the next few lines are missing. The original is in German.

that old Europe can produce. And therefore a trans-Atlantic listener of your caliber would be doubly valuable. Well, our motto—yours and mine—is "Onward." I hope within two years we here shall arrive at the point always to have something ready of which we need not be ashamed for unexpected guests.

For to-day, allow me now to say good-by.

Very truly yours,

HANS VON BUELOW.

CHAPTER III

1868-1870

THE building of the new hall at Central Park
Garden was an event of great importance to
Thomas, for, be it remembered, he was aiming for
a *permanent* orchestral institution, and for this the
first essential is a suitable building in which to
work—a building which shall have not only a
convenient hall and stage for concerts and daily
rehearsals, but also a large library, ample storage
capacity for the instruments, chairs, platforms,
music stands, and all the rest of its paraphernalia, and convenient offices for the transaction
of its business. The Central Park Garden did
not, it is true, realize all of these requirements;
but it, at least, provided a good home for the
Summer Night Concerts, and insured their continuance indefinitely.

Thomas evidently felt its erection to be a great
step in advance, for he celebrated its opening,
on the evening of May 25, 1868, by composing a
march for the first number of the programme—

46

a most unusual act for him. Throughout his entire life he was singularly reluctant to compose music, although the few times when he did take pen in hand and write, show him to have been gifted with a creative talent which was both beautiful and original. He once said, in this connection, "As a young man I wished to be a composer, but circumstances forced me into the executant's career. My creative vein was worthy of development, had I had the time for it, but it fell short of genius, and I believed I could do more for my art and my country by familiarizing the people with the literature already created than by adding to it myself. The exacting nature of my work in the orchestra required all my time and strength, and made any other kind of serious work impossible, and as long as I could not give the time necessary to produce compositions which would be satisfactory to myself, I preferred to let it alone altogether." For the same reason he early gave up both his solo and quartette playing, for he would not touch anything which he could not perfect, and was severely critical of his own work. " Mediocrity is the curse of art," he was wont to say, " It should be *wiped out,* not encouraged."

The Summer Night Concerts in the new hall were even more popular than those of the preceding years, and experience had now shown him how to make them at once attractive and educational to the public. In after years he gave similar concerts in many other cities, but he always ad-

hered to the same system as that which characterized the original Central Park Garden series in
1868. Subsequent series differed in degree but
not in kind. The halls in which this class of concerts were given were always very large, cool, and
airy; evergreen trees in tubs, palms, and potted
plants standing about, gave a suggestion of an
open-air garden, often a fountain splashed
pleasantly in the center. The front section was
railed off, and served as an auditorium for those
who came for the music only; here the price of
admission was fifty cents. In the rear section, to
which the admission was only twenty-five cents,
the formal rows of chairs gave place to small
tables with chairs around them. Here the men
could have a quiet smoke while listening to the
music, or, during the two long intermissions of
the programme, could order refreshments. The
whole atmosphere of the place was one of in-
formality and restful enjoyment.

In making the programmes Thomas followed a
system of his own. They were divided into three
short parts, with long intermissions between. The
first part consisted of short, brilliant numbers, such
as would not be disturbed by the entrance of late
comers. During the second part the audience
was quiet, and therefore here we find symphonic
movements, or classic gems of one kind or another.
By the time the last part of the programme was
reached, it was late and the audience tired, so this
part consisted of marches, waltzes, or other music
having rich orchestral color and strongly marked

rhythms, to wake the people up and send them home happy. This was the general plan on which the Summer Night Concert programmes were constructed for many years, and the following, selected from the series of 1868, is a good example:

CENTRAL PARK GARDEN
August 7, 1868

Coronation March...........................Strauss
Overture, " Heimkehr aus der Fremde "....Mendelssohn
Waltz, " Masaniello "........................Auber
Intermission
Overture, " Tannhaeuser ".....................Wagner
Andante from Symphony No. 8.............Beethoven
Scherzo from Symphony in C...............Schubert
Intermission
Schiller March.............................Meyerbeer
Overture, " Mignon "..............Ambrose Thomas
Ave Maria.............................Bach-Gounod
Waltz, " Sphaeren Klange ".................Strauss
Turkish March.............................Mozart

But although Thomas never changed his method of making the programmes, nevertheless, he rarely played the same one twice. It was one of his lifelong customs to make a fresh programme for every concert, for he thought that it soon became perfunctory to the orchestra, and lost its vitality if it were repeated literally. Consequently, in all the ten thousand or more programmes which he has left as the record of his work, there are hardly any duplicates.

As may be imagined, concerts of the foregoing character appealed strongly to the general public, and tired business or professional men, especially, found the Central Park Garden a most restful place in which to forget the cares and worries of the day, and gain fresh inspiration for the next. Thomas often said, " What our over-worked business and professional men most need in America, is an elevating mental recreation which is not an amusement." It not infrequently happened that after one of his concerts, some entire stranger would make his way into the dressing-room and say, " Mr. Thomas, I have come to thank you for the benefit I have derived from the concert to-night. I came here very tired and worried about some professional perplexities of my own from which I have been unable to free my mind of late. I am not a musical man, but while listening to your fine orchestra, I was able to forget my own anxieties for the time, and I shall go home so refreshed in mind that I believe I shall sleep well and be in better condition to solve my problems in the morning." This sort of personal testimony came to him from time to time in many distant cities, but the men who spoke these pleasant words would have been surprised if they had known how much courage and inspiration they were, in turn, giving to him by so doing.

Thomas had now achieved his original aim of having an orchestra of his own whose members should play exclusively under his baton all the

year. The new hall assured him of a regular
summer engagement for himself and his men, and
during the winter his Symphony Soirées, the
Brooklyn Philharmonic, and a large number of
miscellaneous concerts provided enough work to
keep them together and pay the salary list.
Nevertheless there was, after all, no real permanency to the orchestra, and it was merely his
private organization for which he alone was financially responsible, and which he maintained at the
cost of constant risk and never ceasing anxiety.
Thomas was a very scrupulous man about all
matters of business. When he engaged musicians
to play in his orchestra, he felt in honor bound
to pay their salaries whether the concerts were
financially successful or not. And as he had no
private property of his own to draw upon, in
case of disaster, he was obliged to manage so that
the losses of one concert should be made good by
the profits of another, and thus bring them out
even in the end. This he contrived to do, but it
was very difficult, and the worry and anxiety it
involved were so harassing to a man already over-
burdened by the musical work of the organization that he early perceived the necessity of some
form of financial endowment for the orchestra—
preferably a well-equipped building in a central
location—and planned for that end. At that day,
however, the public, even in the metropolitan
city of New York, was not ripe for the art institution which was gradually taking shape in his
mind, and he recognized that he must do much

missionary work yet, before the popular demand
for symphonic music would be general enough for
the creation of a great orchestra as an endowed
institution. The problem before him was, therefore, how to keep his orchestra together and
pay its expenses during the years while he was
gradually creating that demand. The long season
of summer concerts in New York was now provided for, as we have seen, but the winter engagements still fell short of what was needed, and
at the close of the season of 1868-69 Thomas decided to give up all his winter concerts in New
York and play in that city only in summer. For
the rest of the year he planned to travel to the
larger cities of the East and West, and in this
way secure the money needed to carry on his
orchestra until the Utopian time should come when
New York music-lovers were numerous and enthusiastic enough to endow it permanently, and
leave him free to give all his time and attention to its artistic side.

The route which Thomas sketched out for his
first tour with the orchestra in 1869, might be
called the great musical highway of America, for
it included all the large cities which Thomas
thought might become musical centers in time. It
was as follows:

OUTWARD	HOMEWARD
New York.	St. Louis.
New Haven.	Indianapolis.
Hartford.	Louisville.

OUTWARD	HOMEWARD
Providence.	Cincinnati.
Boston.	Dayton.
Worcester.	Springfield, O.
Springfield, Mass.	Columbus.
Albany.	Pittsburg.
Schenectady.	Washington.
Utica.	Baltimore.
Syracuse.	Philadelphia.
Rochester.	New York.
Buffalo.	
Cleveland.	
Toledo.	
Detroit.	
Chicago.	

During the twenty-two years between 1869 and 1891, Thomas traveled over this " highway " a number of times every year. In the larger of its cities he gave concerts on every trip, arranging the intermediate stops in accordance with the engagements offered. But there was not a city on the list which was not visited more or less often, and given its own opportunity for musical culture. In addition to the regular route just specified, and which I have designated as the " highway," Thomas had a number of others over which he traveled at less frequent intervals. One of these led through the Southern States; another through New England to Montreal, and thence through Canada to the far Northwest; another straight across the continent to San Francisco, returning through Texas.

The task of his biographer, from now on, therefore becomes very complex, for, during these twenty-two years of incessant traveling, Thomas ceased to be a mere New York musician, and became a national educator in the broadest sense of the term and was identified with the musical life of every large city in America in a greater or less degree.

On his first tour over the "highway," in the fall of 1869, Thomas gave his opening concert in Boston on November 5. Then, as now, Boston was the most cultivated city of America, and Thomas did not find it necessary to do much musical missionary work there, for the people were ripe for the best he had to offer. Indeed, one may say that Boston "discovered" Thomas, for the press notices of the concerts he gave there in 1869 show a discriminating appreciation of the peculiar qualities of his musical work one does not find in those of New York until some years later. I quote these notices, as well as those from the leading journals of some of the other large cities visited on this tour, somewhat at length, because they give, collectively, a complete description of the orchestra, and of Thomas as a conductor, as well as of the general musical conditions in the principal American cities at that period.

"The visit of this famous orchestra," said the critic of *Dwight's Journal of Music*, " has given our music-lovers a new and quick sensation. Boston has not heard such performances before; and Boston, in the frankest humor, gave itself up to the complete enjoyment and unstinted praise of what it heard. . . . We rejoice in the coming of this orchestra. It is just the kind of thing we, for years, have longed for in view of our own progress here. . . . We thank Mr. Thomas for setting palpably before us a higher ideal of orchestral execution. We shall demand better of our own in future. They cannot witness this example without a newly-kindled desire, followed by an effort to do likewise."

The critic of the *Advertiser* wrote: "A fine precision and accuracy is one manifestation of the artistic unity of this orchestra, but that is very little when compared with the wonderful *vitality* which fills and permeates all its performances. And this we conceive to be the peculiar and remarkable characteristic of the Thomas orchestra. A spirit of intense life seems to animate it in every part, and as a result, the works of the great masters glow and flame under its touch, and the hearts of those who hear burn within them."

The tour, thus happily begun in Boston, was continued westward as far as Chicago, where its performances made an equally strong impression. In describing the first concert, the critic of the *Tribune* said: "The performance of the Theodore Thomas orchestra on Saturday evening was without exception the finest musical event Chicago has ever known. . . . We doubt if there is an orchestra in the world more admirably arranged. . . . The light and shade of this orchestra are something marvelous. . . . It is not alone that it plays in time and tune, but it plays with delicious expression, and, for a great orchestra to take a theme *pianissimo* and literally deceive you to be-lieving that the tone comes from a great distance, as if it were wafted over the water, and then diminish it still further so perfectly that it is impossible to tell when the tone ends, shows a training and handling almost incredible."

The critic of the *Post* wrote in a more personal way about the conductor himself: ". . . What magic or mesmeric power is it by which the di-rector, with his slight baton, winds to the utmost tension the senses, passions, and nerves of every-one in his audience and holds them sensitive and powerless beneath his spell? It is the power of music—pure, unalloyed, ideal. And right here we may sum up in one little sentence the signal achievement of this orchestra. *It makes real and perceptible to the hearer the composer's subtlest ideal."*

At that time the musical critic of the *Tribune* was George P. Upton, to whom a mutual friend had given a letter of introduction to Thomas. Mr. Upton gives the following account of his re-ception, when he presented it: "Mr. Thomas greeted me most cordially, with a strong grip of his powerful hand, and then with that peculiar smile of his, which had so many different meanings, said in a brusque way, 'I am glad to meet any friend of Mr. Dohn's, and will be pleased to have you come and see me while I am here. You must not expect me to call upon you, for I am too busy, and besides I never go into newspaper offices. I have no need to cultivate the critics, for I know my work. I do not care to read what they write, and would not have time if I did care.'"* This prickly greeting would have discouraged or offended most men, but Mr. Upton rather enjoyed it, and the subsequent call which he made upon Thomas was the beginning of a warm and lifelong friendship between these two men, so different in temperament and yet so congenial. Thomas made many friends in the course of his long and varied career, but never one more stanch and true, from first to last, than George P. Upton.

Journeying onward from Chicago, Thomas and his men presently made their début in Cincinnati. Here, as in Boston, Thomas found the field already prepared for his work, for music had been an important factor in the life of the city for some years. Nevertheless, the performances of the Thomas Orchestra were a revelation here as they had been in every previous place. The critic of the *Enquirer* wrote, "We have not seen at any time audiences so wrought upon as those that attended the concerts of Theodore Thomas." And the comment of the *Gazette* after the first performance was, "The audience at Mozart Hall last night heard the finest orchestral music that has ever been given in this city. . . . The evening

* See "Theodore Thomas, A Musical Autobiography," edited by George P. Upton, p. 118, vol. i.

was one, for those who heard this orchestra for the first time, to remember as the night when they were lifted up and inspired as never before." This was the beginning of his long association with the musical life of Cincinnati.

St. Louis and many other cities also heard the Thomas Orchestra for the first time on this important tour, but I will quote only one more of the many enthusiastic notices it inspired, namely, that which appeared in the Pittsburg *Evening Chronicle,* and which speaks more especially of the influence of Thomas in elevating the local standards everywhere. " In regard to Theodore Thomas and his orchestra," wrote the critic of this paper, " the fiat of the press and music-loving public is one. . . . Thomas infuses music and poetry into an orchestra, and we observe with a rare sense of pleasure the precision, delicacy, and mastery with which the music is controlled, lifted up into gorgeous volumes of sound, or refined away into impalpable realms where the least faint sound lingers trembling on the ear, and begin to comprehend why it is that the genius which evokes such spells is hailed with the acclamations of enraptured audiences. . . . Our people will ever owe a debt to the artists who have given us so rare an exposition of the loftiest orchestral music. We will now have *a standard by which we can judge critically hereafter.* This is the chief excellence of true art. It so elevates the taste that whoever once comes within its ennobling influence spurns forever after the meretricious, the vulgar, and the

false, and will not be patient with the common-
place. It excites a thirst for the truest and best.
Wherever Theodore Thomas and his orchestra
go they will sow seeds that will bring forth good
fruit. They will inspire a love for a high order
of music. They will promote local organizations.
The remembrance of these delicious concerts will
have a generous and invigorating effect, and will
powerfully impress on the people the incalculable
delight and the sovereign luxury of such enjoy-
ments. They will begin to know that art is
worthy of all honor, and that what has been said
and sung in its praise is but the fitting confes-
sion of the intellect and heart to the purifying and
strengthening influence of the beautiful. All
honor then to the accomplished gentleman and his
admirable assistants for what they have done, and
for the golden promise of what they will yet do in
building up true musical taste in America."

It has often been said that the press of America
was unjust or antagonistic to Thomas, but this
is a mistaken idea, as may be seen by the foregoing quotations, which are only fair samples
of the manner in which the musical critics generally reviewed his work. Like all men of strong
personality Thomas occasionally made enemies,
some of whom were connected with the press and
used their official positions to revenge their personal grievances. But this did not happen very
often, and the general tone of press comment on
his work throughout his whole career was friendly
and just. He once said in this connection: " I do

not expect all newspaper critics to like me or my work, or that they will never find anything to be blamed. Every man has a right to his own opinions, and I am always ready to learn if a critic can tell me something I do not know already. But I do think that public criticism of an artist's work should be made, at least, in a kindly spirit; then it would not be so discouraging and have such a paralyzing effect on the mind."

Thomas was perfectly sincere in saying that he was willing to learn from anyone. He was not only willing, but eager, and I have often been surprised at the patience with which he would listen to the suggestions of people who knew little or nothing about music, and the care with which he would weigh their advice, and adopt anything which seemed valuable or helpful. He was, however, all his life, keenly sensitive to unfriendly or even unintelligent press criticism, and to read an antagonistic or indifferent notice of one of his concerts, would depress his spirits for twenty-four hours afterwards. So he early gave up reading press notices about himself or his work, except such as appeared in his daily paper, or happened to be sent to him by some friend. By this he avoided much that might have been irritating to his sensitive nature, but he also lost much that would have strengthened and encouraged him at times when encouragement was sorely needed.

The newspaper critics of the period of which we are writing were equal in knowledge and judgment to any America has ever had, and had the success of the Thomas propaganda depended on them it would all have been plain sailing for him. But the general public, except in Boston, Cincinnati, and New York, was almost wholly ignorant of symphonic music, and not only so, but the people had not the slightest interest in being educated to any knowledge of it. To the average concert-goer the word " symphony " was a synonym for " bore," and it repelled rather than attracted an audience. Nevertheless, the people were naturally musical, and subsequent events proved that their indifference was merely the result of unfamiliarity with the higher forms of composition. Little by little, as the years went by, and Thomas familiarized them with one great symphony after another on his oft-repeated visits, the people learned to know and love the master-works of musical literature, and to differentiate between music the art, and music the amusement. But it was the laborious task of a lifetime. For many years the Thomas Orchestra shone, like the evening star, the sole luminary of the musical firmament; at last a sister planet rose above the horizon in Boston, and then orchestral stars, large and small, came out, here, there, and everywhere, until now there is hardly a city in America which does not possess its own excellent symphony organization.

CHAPTER IV

1870-1872

THE fall tour so auspiciously begun in 1869
was continued during the greater part of the winter, and when spring came Thomas brought the
orchestra home again, and on May 9, 1870, opened
the Summer Night season at the Central Park
Garden, where he gave 134 consecutive concerts.
Although the programmes of these concerts were
popular in character, and the standard of technic
was supposed to be a trifle lower than that of the
winter, nevertheless this long series of daily performances, without even Sundays on which to
rest, was a severe strain on the conductor. As a
matter of fact, Thomas never lowered his musical
standard, no matter when or where he conducted,
but the daily concert was so much of a tax on the
strength of his men that he could not add daily
rehearsals also to their work. He, therefore, held
only two rehearsals a week, and in the short time

they afforded, he was, of course, only able to run
through the more difficult passages of the new
music. All the rest was *read at sight* by himself
and the orchestra, in concert, without rehearsal.
It can be imagined, then, how tense was the concentration of mind necessary, when virtuosity had,
for the time being, to take the place of training,
and when he was obliged to depend on his personal
magnetism to carry the orchestra with him, unre-
hearsed, through the infinite gradations of light
and shade, accent, rhythm, climax and pianissimo,
whereby his conception of the music was passed
through the medium of his musicians to the listening public. That he himself felt this strain and
lightened it when possible, is easily seen by a
study of these programmes, for whenever he placed
a new number on one of them, it was enshrined
amidst familiar pieces in which the orchestra was
already " letter perfect," and would be repeated
in subsequent concerts as soon and as often as
possible, until it too, in turn, had been mastered
and perfected. Thomas could never have endured
the tremendous nervous strain of these long summer engagements, and the still greater fatigues of
winter travel, if he had not had a will of iron, and
a magnificent physique, reënforced by his simple
and healthful mode of life. The Summer Night
series of 1870 was very successful financially, and
Thomas also ventured on quite an artistic advance
in making its programmes. His little pocket note-
book for this year contains the following entry,
"*At last* the summer programmes show a respect-

able character, and we are rid of the cornet! Occasionally a whole symphony is given." The series finally ended on September 24, after which he gave the orchestra a few days' vacation while he prepared for the opening of the approaching winter season.

Thomas did not allow his men to be idle long, and early in October he started on a tour over the "highway," which began with a two-weeks' engagement in Boston. The year 1870 was the centennial anniversary of the birth of Beethoven, and Thomas determined to commemorate the event by giving a Beethoven programme in each of the larger cities visited. It was the first time that programmes composed of Beethoven's works exclusively had been given in most, if not all of them, and this made the tours of this season memorable in an historic sense. Another interesting feature of the spring and fall tours was the American début of Miss Anna Mehlig, the first really eminent woman pianist who came to this country. Her name is now hardly even a memory in America, nevertheless she was one of the best artists ever heard in our concert halls.

At this time the most cultivated audience to which Thomas gave concerts was that of Boston. A few programmes selected from the Boston series of October, 1870, will therefore serve to show the highest musical standard of the most advanced American community of that period. They were called "Symphony Concerts" then, but now we should class most of them under the head of "popular." Even the two Beethoven programmes of the series were less severe than those of later years.

BOSTON, OCTOBER 4, 1870

Programme

Overture, "Euryanthe".......................Weber
Concerto, A minor, op. 54.....................Schumann
Miss Mehlig
Vorspiel, "Lohengrin".......................Wagner
Overture, "Egmont," op. 48....................Beethoven
Schlummerlied............................ Buergel
Waltz, "Koenigslieder".......................Strauss
Concerto for trombone........................David
Mr. F. Letsch
Polka, "Pizzicato".........................Strauss
Overture, "Mignon"................Ambrose Thomas

OCTOBER 5

Programme

Symphony No. 6, in F, op. 68................Beethoven
Concerto No. 2, in A..........................Listz
Miss Mehlig
Eine Faust Overture.......................Wagner
March of the Pilgrims, from Symphony "Harold
  in Italy"................................Berlioz
Kamarinskaja .... Glinka
Overture, "Genoveva," op. 81..............Schumann

OCTOBER 7

Beethoven Programme

Symphony No. 3, in E♭, op. 55, "Eroica"
Concerto No. 4 in G, op. 58
Miss Mehlig

Overture, " Coriolanus," op. 62
Septet, op. 20
Fantasia, op. 80, for piano, chorus, and orchestra
    Miss Mehlig, Chorus, and Orchestra

OCTOBER 14

Overture, " The Flying Dutchman "............Wagner
Concertstueck.................................. Weber
    Miss Mehlig
" Gretchen," from the Faust Symphony...........Liszt
Overture, " Ruy Blas ".................Mendelssohn
Andante and Variations, op. 18.............Beethoven
Waltz, " Buergersinn ".......................Strauss
Polka, " Pizzicato ".........................Strauss
Reiter March................................Schubert

OCTOBER 15

Beethoven Matinée

Symphony No. 8, in F, op. 93
Concerto No. 5 in E♭, op. 73
    Miss Mehlig
Overture, " King Stephen," op. 117
Sonata, op. 47, for piano and violin
    Miss Mehlig and Mr. Theodore Thomas,
Overture, " Leonore," No. 3, op. 72

Miss Mehlig's part in this series of concerts deserves more than a passing mention, for, during the two weeks of its progress, she played no less than eight concertos, namely: Schumann, A minor; Liszt, Nos. 1 and 2; Henselt, F minor; Beethoven, Nos. 4 and 5; Hiller, F minor, and Mozart, D minor. In addition to all these concertos, she played the " Concertstueck " of Weber, and the piano parts of the Beethoven Fantasia and of the sonata in which Thomas himself played the violin. And this astonishing list of works was played with such technical perfection and interpretive skill as has rarely been equaled since in America.

The winter of 1870-71 was devoted to traveling, and again Thomas gave no concerts in New York until the Summer Night season opened. As we have seen, Thomas made it a principle, from the very start of his career, to play all the new music that was worthy of a place on his programmes, as fast as it was composed and he could arrange for its performance. It was a matter of pride with him to be the first to play, in America, every important work, and sometimes he was able even to antedate Europe in the matter. He used to say:

" The people cannot read new scores for themselves, as they read new books, it is therefore one of the missions of a symphony orchestra to perform for them the current musical literature. Some of it they will not care for, and those works will be forgotten. But others will be found to have a permanent interest and will become a valued part of the repertoire. As for the American composers, the only way in which to develop composition in our own country is to play the works by American writers side by side with those of other nationalities, and let them stand or fall on their own merits. I do not believe in playing inferior works merely because they are American, nor rejecting good ones because they are not foreign.

Let our composers realize that there is a standard to be reached before they can be recognized, but that if they do reach it, they will be certain of equal recognition with writers of other nations. They will then have an incentive to produce the best that is in them, and will produce it."

It was also a principle of Thomas to include an important work by an American writer on the programmes of all the great festival occasions of a national character which he conducted. For these works he always selected a writer of known ability, and gave him a commission to write in a certain form—generally a festival work of large dimensions for grand orchestra, chorus, and soloists. At other times he would arrange that a prize should be offered for the best composition submitted by any composer of American birth. These competitions were open to anyone, and he took infinite pains to have the works sent in passed upon by the best judges, and would afterwards perform, not only the prize-winner, but also any others which were up to his required standard.

During the season of 1870-71 he gave a number of the works of Liszt, who was then at the zenith of his marvelous career. And in the spring he received the following pleasant letter of appreciation from this master. It was the first of a long series of similar letters from the great composers and executive artists of every nationality who were contemporary with Thomas, and from which hardly a name of importance is missing:

PEST, *May 27*, 1871.

Honored Herr Director:

I have often heard of the famous performances of the orchestra under your direction, and our mutual friend, Julius Schuberth, delighted me especially by telling me of the unusual care which you have given to the performance of my works. They need—even more than other, better compositions—the sympathetic and intelligent care of the conductor, on account of the many changes of tempo and tone color. The unfortunately too frequent reading-at-sight performances are not sufficient for them. Mediocre music-making is a sin against art; we demand something totally different, namely, the uplift and inspiration of the soul, and cry " *Sursum corda!* "

Accept, honored sir, my earnest thanks for your goodness, and be so kind as to give my friendly greetings to the members of your orchestra.*

With the highest respect,

Yours truly,

F. LISZT.

The Summer Night Concert season of 1871 opened at the Central Park Garden on May 15. The programmes of this series of concerts show but little artistic advance over those of previous summers, but during the latter half of the engagement entire symphonies were occasionally played, and amongst the novelties we find the first performances in America of Wagner's " Kaiser March," and " Huldigungs March," on June 22 and September 8, respectively. An exquisite description of the opening night of this season of concerts has been left us by the poet, Sidney Lanier—himself

* Translated from the German.

an orchestra player—who happened to be in the
audience, and wrote his impressions of the performance after his return home the same evening,
as follows:

"This was the opening night of Theodore Thomas'
orchestra at Central Park Garden, and I could not resist
the temptation to go and bathe in the sweet amber seas
of this fine orchestra. So I went and tugged me through
a vast crowd, and after standing some while, found a seat,
and the baton tapped and waved, and I plunged into
the sea and lay and floated. Ah! the dear flutes, and oboes,
and horns drifted me hither and thither, and the great
violins and the small violins swayed me upon waves, and
overflowed me with strong lavations, and sprinkled glisten-
ing foam in my face, and in among the clarinetti, as among
waving water-lilies with flexible stems, I pushed my easy
way, and so, ever lying in the music-waters, I floated and
flowed, my soul utterly bent and prostrate."

The first eight months of the year 1871 had
passed very prosperously for Thomas, and when
fall came he felt happy and hopeful. His summer
concerts had now been successfully carried on for
so many seasons that they seemed to have become a permanent institution for that part of
the year, while the cities of his musical "highway" offered him as many engagements as he
could fill during the winter. All these remunerative engagements enabled him to employ artists
of the first rank for his orchestra, and the daily
rehearsing and playing together under his baton

advanced its technical standard to the highest
point. Furthermore, he had now traveled enough
to have created a demand in the cities often visited,
for the best music, and a little entry in his note-
book for this year says, " Whole symphonies are
included now in the programmes given all over
the country." His professional work was, therefore, not only remunerative financially, but also
satisfactory artistically, and he felt that at last
he was making rapid progress in his self-appointed
task of national education, and that the future
was bright with promise.

At the close of the summer season, Thomas and
the orchestra started westward on their customary
fall tour over the " highway." The Chicago engagement on this trip was to have been an unusually long and important one, for the Crosby
Opera House there had been handsomely reno-
vated and Thomas was to open it with a two
weeks' series of orchestral concerts.

As the train, bearing the orchestra, neared the
city on the morning of October 9, 1871, Thomas
was paralyzed by the announcement that Chicago
was burning, and the Opera House already in
ashes! In short, they had arrived just in time to
witness the terrible conflagration which so nearly
wiped Chicago off the map altogether, and, of
course, the concerts which Thomas had expected
to give there for two years to come, were canceled.
A less scrupulous man than Thomas would have
come out of this catastrophe without such ruinous
results as it brought to him, because in the travel-

ing contracts of concert and operatic troupes, there is a clause which releases the management from financial responsibility in case of extraordinary accidents, such as fire, floods, and the like, and he could have claimed the remission of all salaries and other expenses for the two weeks of enforced idleness on this ground. Nor could anyone have blamed him for so doing, in consideration of his own personal lack of financial resources. But he was unwilling to take advantage of this legal technicality, and would not ask his company to bear their share of loss with him, but assumed the whole burden of the salaries and expenses of orchestra, soloists, managers, and all the other functionaries connected with his large concert organization, just the same as if the concerts had been given. But to make good this large sum out of his private earnings meant financial ruin for him, and it was many years before he was able to recover from the disaster.

When he had ascertained that the Chicago concerts could not be given, and that there was even no place in which the orchestra could be housed in the burning city, Thomas ordered the train to be taken to Joliet, and here he and the orchestra stayed until it was time for the next engagement in St. Louis. While they were waiting he utilized the time for daily rehearsals, and amongst the compositions studied was the *Finale* of " *Tristan and Isolde.*" He had already produced the *Vorspiel* of this opera in one of his Symphony Soirées in New York, in the year 1865, and he now linked it with the *Finale* and prepared it for performance in his next series of Boston concerts.

The return trip of this eventful journey brought him to Cincinnati for the second time. This city, like Boston, had already made genuine musical progress, and possessed its own orchestra and several good choral societies, and was ready for a high standard of art. During this visit Thomas made the acquaintance of Mrs. Maria Longworth Nichols (afterwards Mrs. Bellamy Storer), who laid before him a plan which she had originated for a Musical Festival to be held in Cincinnati in May, 1873, and asked him to be its conductor.

Mrs. Nichols was the daughter of Nicholas Longworth, one of the wealthiest and most prominent men in Cincinnati. She was young, handsome, and brilliantly gifted in many ways. It was she who made with her own hands and baked in her own little kiln the first pieces of the Rookwood pottery, and later founded the institution which has made the name of her country place (Rookwood) famous the world over as that of a great branch of ceramic art. Her new plan for the musical art of her city was not less comprehensive, and when she explained it to Thomas, she found him ready to co-operate with her. He went to her house, and together they sketched the programmes for the festival. This was the beginning of his local work in Cincinnati—a work with which he continued to be identified as long as he lived and which was one of the most important of his life; for the Cincinnati Festivals became a permanent institution, and are still maintained on the lines he laid down, and continue to set the highest standard in America for this class of performance.

Thomas and the orchestra returned from this tour only to set forth on another, and, indeed, most of his life was spent in wearisome journeying over the length and breadth of the land. Someone once mentioned the town of Duluth in his hearing, and he laughingly remarked, " Duluth does not exist, if it did I should have given a concert there." A little later, however, Duluth must have been born, for it, too, began to figure on his concert tour lists. The month of December found Thomas again in Boston for a series of concerts, and the list of compositions which he gave as " novelties " to that city during this engagement is an interesting one, for nearly all of them have long since passed into the regular concert repertoire of every American symphony orchestra. It is as follows:

Symphony, " Im Walde ".........................Raff
Symphony, " Ocean," Adagio and Scherzo....Rubinstein
Symphony in C, op. 30.........................Bargiel
Scherzo, aus " Wallenstein's Lager "......Rheinberger
Symphonic Poem, " Mazeppa ".................Liszt
Symphonic Poem, " Fest-Klaenge "............Liszt
Humoreske, " Gaudeamus Igitur ".............Liszt
Serenade in F, op. 63, for string orchestra......Volkmann
Pastorale from the Christmas Oratorio...........Bach
Prelude from the 6th Violin Concerto............Bach
Lohengrin, Introduction, Chorus, and March,
    Act III.....................................Wagner

Mrs. Bellamy Storer (Formerly Maria Longworth Nichols),
Founder of the Cincinnati Musical Festivals and
Originator of the Rookwood Pottery

Tristan and Isolde, Introduction and Finale.....Wagner
Kaiser Marsch...............................Wagner
Huldigungs Marsch.........................Wagner
Rakoczy March...............................Liszt
Quartette, D minor, Theme and Variations.....Schubert
Maerchen, Ouverture, " Alladin ".............Horneman
Overture, " Dimitri Donskoi ".............Rubinstein
Saltarello................................ Gounod
German Dances..............................Schubert
Hungarian March....................Schubert-Liszt
Fantasia on Hungarian Airs, for piano and or-
    chestra.................................. Liszt
Concerto, E♭, for piano ....Weber
Concerto No. 4, D minor, for piano..........Rubinstein
Concerto, D minor, for piano...............Brahms
Also the latest Dances of Strauss

Again Thomas gave no winter concerts in New York, but confined his performances in that city to the Summer Night series. The remainder of the season of 1871-72 was devoted to traveling engagements, but contained no features of special interest.

CHAPTER V

1872-1873

THE Summer Night season of 1872 opened on May 8, and continued until September 23 as usual. Thomas had now given these concerts for seven consecutive summers and one would naturally expect, knowing the educational design which lay behind them, that he would, by this time, have felt free to advance the standard of his programmes in accordance with it. But no, the programmes for the season of 1872 were even lighter than those of the previous years. During the whole series only three symphonies were given entire, and the single important novelty produced was the *"Walkuerenritt"* of Wagner. Thomas had received the score of this number while traveling, and when the orchestra tried the music over in rehearsal for the first time, they complained that it was so difficult that the violin parts actually *could not be played* in the tempo indicated by the score. In this dilemma he had resource to a characteristically ingenious expedient, and said: "Let

76

each of you begin and end the phrase on the beat, and play as many of the intermediate notes as he can. You will not all drop the same notes, and what one misses will be played by another and the effect of the *ensemble* will be all right." The orchestra followed these instructions and the result was what he had expected. When it was finally played in concert on September 17, it made such an impression that the people jumped on their chairs, shouting and waving hats and hand-kerchiefs until he was obliged to give it a second time.

This piece of music always had a peculiarly exciting effect on the audience, for Thomas played it like the wind, and with such furious reckless-ness that one seemed actually to see the warrior maidens on their winged steeds, hurtling through clouds and tempest to their trysting-place on the mountain-top. An encore was always demanded, but it was such a strain on the wrists of the violin players that it could not be repeated unless it came at the end of a part, so that the men could have time to rest after it before beginning the next number on the programme. The public, not knowing this, could not understand why Thomas would sometimes encore the " *Walkuerenritt,*" and at others, refuse to do so, and it was the cause of many a rousing battle between him and his audiences, and not a little sharp criticism of his " arbitrary and dictatorial ways " afterwards.

The programme on which this favorite number was introduced to the American public was memorable, also, because it was the first exclusively Wagner programme Thomas gave. The selections performed were as follows:

CENTRAL PARK GARDEN

September 17, 1872

Wagner Programme

Kaiser Marsch
Vorspiel to " Lohengrin "
Eine Faust Overture

Intermission

Vorspiel to the " Meistersinger von Nuernberg "
Vorspiel and Finale, " Tristan and Isolde "
Ritt der Walkueren, (First time)

Intermission

Overture, " Tannhaeuser "
Ballet from " Rienzi," (First time)
Huldigungs Marsch

While selecting its numbers, during the previous summer, Thomas was inspired with a great desire to produce the recently-composed *" Bacchanale "* from *" Tannhaeuser,"* and some other excerpts from Wagner's operas, which were not obtainable through the music dealers. In this emergency it occurred to him to write to von Buelow, thinking that perhaps he might own some of the desired manuscripts and would lend them to him. In reply, he received the following letter:

MUNICH, *Aug.* 11, 1872.

Honored Herr Director:
I reply to your valued letter immediately, as I am leaving town to-morrow, and after that it will not be

possible to write in detail, nor, I am sorry to say, in accordance with your wishes. The principal theme of your letter is the longing for certain works of Richard Wagner, which you mention. Neither I, nor any of my friends possess copies of them, or I would, of course, cheerfully put them at your disposal. Furthermore, as you will readily understand, I have no personal relations with the Master, direct or indirect, so that I cannot impart to him your wishes. *You* must go to him yourself— to Baireuth—I believe he would not refuse you. The fame of your wonderful ability and activity, and above all, your special efforts in propagating the Wagner music in the new world, assure you a better reception from the Master, than he is in the habit of giving to similar requests. He absolutely refuses to all German Conductors the permission to perform portions of his later works, (among which he includes the " *Bacchanale* ") and in this he is right, for what is written for the stage, and in Germany is performed there, the composer does not wish to have find its way into the concert hall. I wish you luck in your attempt, and regret with all my heart that I cannot aid you in the matter.

Excuse these hurried lines and accept the assurance of my respectful admiration.

Yours devotedly,
Hans von Buelow.

After reading the foregoing, Thomas did not care to try his luck with the Baireuth Master, but preferred to get the coveted scores through other channels. How he managed to do this will always be a mystery, but when it was a question of a desired score, it had to be well hidden, indeed, to escape his clutches! He had many friends in

Europe who were always ready to help him in securing any music he wanted to produce, for there was not a composer of any nationality who was not under more or less obligation to him for bringing out his works, and nearly all the great executive artists had played or sung in his concerts. As for the music publishers, he was too good and regular a customer not to be favored by them whenever he wanted something out of the common. It is needless to say, therefore, that the *" Bacchanale "* made its appearance on his programmes in due course of time, as well as all the other Wagner selections that he wanted. Indeed, he played the Wagner music so constantly, in all parts of America, that when the operas were given in their entirety they were as familiar as household words to the people, and created a furor wherever they were performed. In this country, there was never any appreciable opposition to the so-called " music of the future," and even the first Wagner programme Thomas gave made a strong impression in New York. After this memorable concert a supper was given to Thomas and the orchestra, by some prominent citizens, and at the supper the New York *" Wagner Verein "* was formally organized, and Thomas elected as its President. The object of this society was, like that of similar societies in Europe, " to aid in furthering the purpose of Wagner in giving his first grand musico-dramatic festival at Baireuth in the summer, of 1874." Thomas was the first American musician to make a specialty of performing Wagner's music; it was therefore natural that he should have been the man to organize such an auxiliary in this country. He had also another object in view which he never lost an opportunity of promoting, and this was to bring the musical world of America into direct association with that of Europe, on an equal footing. During all his life, whenever any project was started in European art centers to which general contributions were asked—such as a statue to some great composer, the preservation of Beethoven's birthplace, a Wagner festival, or the like—Thomas invariably saw to it that America took the same part in assisting that other nations did. He was determined that this country should stand abreast of the world musically, or perhaps even ahead.

The *Wagner Verein* of New York worked to such good purpose for the divinity of Baireuth that Thomas was able to send Wagner $10,000 as its contribution toward his festival performances, in acknowledgment of which he received the following letter:*

BAIREUTH, *October* 15, 1872.

MR. THEODORE THOMAS,

Most Honored Sir:

I announce to you the receipt of your valued letter, for the contents and sympathy of which I am heartily indebted to you. I immediately transmitted your wishes to the committee of my undertaking to attend to, and I beg

* Translated from the original German.

you to express to the honorable gentlemen who have shown
such an encouraging interest in me, my sincere and great
happiness about it.

With the greatest respect,

Yours truly,

RICHARD WAGNER.

New York had now been without any series
of symphony concerts from the Thomas Orchestra
for three winters, owing to its constant traveling
at that season. In August of 1872, however,
Thomas received the following letter:

NEW YORK, *August*, 1872.

THEODORE THOMAS, ESQ.,

Dear Sir:

The undersigned, remembering with pleasure the admirable Symphony Concerts with which you favored us in
former years, take the liberty of requesting of you, if not
inconsistent with your plans, a series of similar concerts
during the coming season. They feel deeply how excellent
an influence such performances exercise in informing and
elevating the public taste for music, and sincerely hope
that nothing will prevent you from giving us the desired
repetition of them.

JULIUS HALLGARTEN,	J. R. G. HASSARD,
CHARLES C. DODGE,	FREDERIC DE BILLIER,
J. R. MOULD,	HENRY DE COPPET,
J. W. SELIGMAN,	WHITELAW REID, and others.

This spontaneous request for symphony concerts from a group of eminent New York men

was very encouraging to Thomas, and he gladly sent the following reply:

NEW YORK, *September* 18, 1872.

MESSRS. JULIUS HALLGARTEN, CHARLES C. DODGE,

    AND OTHERS.

Gentlemen:

Your letter containing a request for a repetition of my former Symphony Concerts has been received. It is a satisfaction to me to know that the remembrance of these concerts is still fresh after the lapse of three years,—in a country where the past is so soon forgotten. This fact speaks for the influence they have had, and prompts me to comply with your request. The interest manifested in your communication, together with the improved taste in the musical community within the last years, gives me the assurance that these concerts cannot fail to be successful.

      Respectfully yours,

            THEODORE THOMAS.

It was not an easy matter for Thomas to arrange his winter tours in such a way that he could bring the orchestra back to New York once a month for a concert, but he kept his word, nevertheless, and hereafter New York, once more, became his most important field of action in the winter, as well as in the summer season. With the exception of the monthly return to New York the winter of 1872-73 was devoted to an almost continuous concert tour, and some idea of the comprehensive manner in which Thomas carried out his plans for musical " University Extension," as it might be called, can be obtained by glancing at the itinerary of the various tours of this season, which followed each other in quick succession from September until March:

Albany.........Sept. 26
Syracuse........Sept. 27
Rochester.......Sept. 28
Buffalo.........Sept. 29
Cleveland....Oct. 1 and 2
Toledo............Oct. 3
Detroit......Oct. 4 and 5
CHICAGO.....Oct. 7 to 12
St. Louis....Oct. 14 to 17
Louisville....Oct. 18 to 19
CINCINNATI..Oct. 20 to 23
Dayton...........Oct. 24
Columbus.....,.,.Oct. 25
Zanesville........Oct. 26
Pittsburg..Oct. 28 and 29
Allentown........Oct. 30
Brooklyn.........Oct. 31
NEW YORK......Nov. 9
Baltimore...Nov. 11 to 14
Washington.....Nov. 15
Baltimore........Nov. 16
Washington......Nov. 18
Philadelphia.Nov. 19 & 20
Lancaster.........Nov. 21
Philadelphia.Nov. 22 & 23
NEW YORK......Nov. 25
New Haven......Nov. 26
Hartford........Nov. 27
Springfield.......Nov. 28

BOSTON..........Nov. 29
Chelsea..........Nov. 30
BOSTON......Dec. 2 and 3
Providence........Dec. 4
BOSTON......Dec. 5 and 6
Worcester.........Dec. 7
Lowell...........Dec. 10
Haverhill........Dec. 11
Portland.........Dec. 12
Bangor..........Dec. 13
Augusta.........Dec. 14
Lawrence........Dec. 15
Salem............Dec. 17
Taunton..........Dec. 18
New Bedford.....Dec. 19
BOSTON....Dec. 20 and 21
NEW YORK.....Dec. 28
NEW YORK and Brooklyn
  (daily).....Jan. 1 to 9
Williamsburg.....Jan. 10
NEW YORK.......Jan. 11
Hartford.........Jan. 13
NEW YORK.......Jan. 15
Baltimore...Jan. 16 to 18
Washington.Jan. 20 to 22
Philadelphia.Jan. 23 to 25
Springfield.Jan. 27 and 28
Bridgeport.......Jan. 29
Brooklyn.........Jan. 30

NEW YORK.....Jan. 31   Madison.........Feb. 28
NEW YORK........Feb. 1   Milwaukee (Wagner)
Poughkeepsie.......Feb. 3   Feb. 29
Troy.............Feb. 4   Bloomington......Mar. 3
Albany...........Feb. 5   Peoria.............Mar. 4
Utica.............Feb. 6   Jacksonville.......Mar. 5
Syracuse..........Feb. 7   Springfield.........Mar. 6
Auburn...........Feb. 8   Quincy............Mar. 7
Rochester.........Feb. 9   St. Louis....Mar. 8 and 9
Lockport.........Feb. 10   Terre Haute.....Mar. 12
Buffalo..........Feb. 11   Indianapolis......Mar. 13
Erie.............Feb. 13   Lafayette..Mar. 14 and 15
Cleveland..Feb. 14 and 15   * CHICAGO..Mar. 17-18-19
Akron............Feb. 16   * CINCINNATI...........
CHICAGO....Feb. 17 to 20   ....Mar. 20-22-23
Milwaukee..Feb. 21 and 22   * Columbus......Mar. 24
Kalamazoo.......Feb. 24   * Pittsburg.Mar. 25-26-27
Grand Rapids.....Feb. 25   * NEW YORK.........
Jackson..........Feb. 26   ....Mar. 28-29-30
CHICAGO (Wagner) Feb. 27

For the last two weeks of March he made a
combination with Anton Rubinstein and H.
Wieniawski, who happened to be in America at
that time. These great artists were the leading
exponents of their respective instruments (piano
and violin), in the world, and with such an extraordinary combination as this, Thomas knew that
the houses would be sold out wherever they played.
Consequently, he was able to make the programmes without any consideration for the box
office, and he was not slow to take advantage of it,

---

* Thomas, Rubinstein, and Wieniawski.

as the following example, given in Chicago, demonstrates:

CHICAGO, MARCH 18, 1873

Programme

Overture, " The Watercarrier ". . . . . .Cherubini

Concerto, No. 5, E flat. . . . . .Beethoven

Mr. Anton Rubinstein

Symphony, " Romeo and Juliet ". . . . . .Berlioz

Concerto, No. 2. . . . . .Wieniawski

Mr. H. Wieniawski

Carnival. . . . . Schumann

Mr. Rubinstein

Huldigungs Marsch. . . . . .Wagner

It was the first time in his life that Thomas had permitted himself to make a series of programmes exactly in accordance with his artistic standards—for even in Boston some concessions still had to be made to popular taste—and this two weeks of great performances, in association with two of the most renowned executant musicians who ever came to America, was an inspiration to him such as he had never before enjoyed. Wieniawski and Rubinstein, on their part, felt the same, and after their return to New York the latter, in a communication to William Steinway, thus described his experience: " I shall take away with me from America one unexpected reminiscence. Little did I dream to find here the greatest and finest orchestra in the wide world. I have been in Munich, Brussels, Amsterdam, London, Paris, Vienna, Berlin, and all the great

European art centers, but never in my life have I found an orchestra and a conductor so in sympathy with one another, or who followed me as the most gifted accompanist can follow a singer on the piano. There exists but one orchestra of sixty or eighty men which plays so perfectly, and which is known as the Imperial Orchestra of Paris, and was created by a decree of the French Senate in the days of the first Napoleon in 1808. Only trained musicians are its members, and they are engaged for life. They may have twenty or more rehearsals for one performance, to insure absolute perfection, and they play as perfectly as the Thomas Orchestra, but, unfortunately, they have no Theodore Thomas to conduct them." *

During this important season, Thomas may be said to have reached, at last, the full stature of artistic maturity. He was now thirty-seven years old, and in age, experience, and knowledge, ripe for larger schemes than any he had as yet attempted. It was, therefore, natural that he should have closed the winter season in New York with a festival of what was then thought to be large dimensions. This festival was given in Steinway Hall, during the last week in April, 1873. The hall was not a large one, but to make room for his musical forces Thomas reduced its size still further by building the stage out over the first nine rows of seats. There was no chorus which suited him then in New York, so he sent to Bos-

* See Mr. Steinway's Speech, as reported in the *Musical Courier*, April 29, 1891.

ton for the Händel and Haydn Society, including
its director, Carl Zerrahn, who directed the choral
works, and its organist, B. J. Lang. The best
soloists were engaged and the orchestra enlarged
to eighty men. In short, the affair was planned
without regard to expense, and although the audiences filled the hall and the critics were loud in
praise of the performances, Thomas probably had
some deficit to make good afterwards. At all
events he never gave a festival again, anywhere,
on his own responsibility. This first festival bore
no subsequent fruit in New York and was, therefore, of no greater importance than any other
fine series of concerts. It is chiefly interesting,
because it was Thomas' first effort in a branch of
art which afterwards became his greatest specialty.

The first Cincinnati Festival followed a few days
after that of New York was over, and marked
the beginning of one of the most important labors
of Thomas' life—important not only to himself,
but to the musical history of America. These
festivals were intended, from the start, to be of
the highest standard. The matter of expense never
entered into the calculation of the Board of Directors to any appreciable extent in planning their
details, as the whole idea was to give a series of
performances which should conform to the standards of similar festivals in Europe. In the end
the Cincinnati Musical Festival standards far surpassed those of Europe, and they became the most
perfect concerts of their class in the world. But they
did not, of course, reach this pre-eminence at first,

either in programmes or performance, but achieved it only after many a long year of hard work, and sincere, unselfish devotion to the highest ideals on the part of everyone who had anything to do with them. The record of these festivals is a very remarkable one, and their influence on the musical development of the western part of America was similar to that of the Händel and Haydn Society of Boston in the East.

The first president of the "Cincinnati Musical Festival Association," as it was called, was Mr. George Ward Nichols, the husband of the brilliant woman who had originated the scheme. Its conductor was Theodore Thomas and its chorus director Otto Singer. The festival of 1873 consisted of seven concerts, three matinées, and four evening performances, with the following programmes:

FIRST CINCINNATI MUSICAL FESTIVAL

May 6, 1873

Programme

Dettingen Te Deum.........................Haendel
    Mrs. Smith, Miss Annie Louise Cary, Mr. Varley, Mr.
      Myron B. Whitney, Chorus, and Orchestra
Symphony No. 5, C minor, op. 67...........Beethoven
Aria, " Misero O Sogno ".....................Mozart
          Mr. Nelson Varley
Chorus, " The Heavens Are Telling," from " The
    Creation".................................. Haydn

May 7

Matinée Programme

Overture, " Jubilee ".........................Weber
Aria, " Rolling in Foaming Billows," from " The
    Creation,"............................... Haydn
Mr. Whitney
Allegretto, Eighth Symphony, op. 93.........Beethoven
Aria from " L'Étoile du Nord ".............Meyerbeer
Mrs. H. M. Smith
Chorus, " Ave Verum "......................Mozart
Scherzo and March, " Midsummer Night's Dream "
    .... Mendelssohn
Overture, " Fra Diavolo ".....................Auber
Trio, " I Naviganti ".....................Randegger
Mrs. Smith, Mr. Varley, and Mr. Rudolphsen
Waltz, " On the Beautiful Blue Danube ".......Strauss
Aria, " Sound an Alarm," from " Judas Macca-
    bæus ".............................. Haendel
Mr. Varley
Traumerei .... Schumann
March and Chorus from " Tannhaeuser ".......Wagner

May 7

Evening Programme

Suite No. 3, in D...............................Bach
Scenes from " Orpheus ".......................Gluck
Miss Cary, Chorus, and Orchestra
Overture, " Coriolanus," op. 62..............Beethoven
Symphony No. 2, in C, op. 61...............Schumann
Aria, " With Verdure Clad," from " The Creation " Haydn
Mrs. Dexter
Chorus, " See, the Conquering Hero Comes!"..Haendel

Theodore Thomas at 40 (1875)

May 8

Matinée Programme

Overture, " Euryanthe ".......................Weber
(a) Morning Hymn..........................Mehul
(b) " See, the Conquering Hero Comes!".......Haendel
Chorus

Aria, " In Native Worth ".....................Haydn
Mr. Varley

(a) " Lift Thine Eyes ".................Mendelssohn
(b) " To Our Immortal Leader ".............Mozart
Chorus

Waltz, " Life Let Us Cherish "...............Strauss
" Shadow Song " from " Dinorah ".............Meyerbeer
Mrs. Dexter

" Welcome, Mighty King," from " Saul ".......Haendel
Chorus

Overture, " The Merry Wives of Windsor ".......Nicolai
Song, " O Ruddier than the Cherry ".........Haendel
Mr. Whitney

(a) Venetian Boatman's Song
(b) Vesper Hymn
(c) " The Cold Frost Came "
(d) " Land of Our Fathers "
Chorus

Polka Schnell...............................Strauss
" Ye Gay and Painted Fair," from " The Seasons " Haydn
Mrs. Dexter and Mrs. Varley

(a) " Sound the Timbrel "
(b) " America "
(c) " The Star-spangled Banner "
Chorus of Public School Children

May 8

Evening Programme

(a) Overture, from " The Magic Flute "........Mozart
(b) Aria and Chorus, " O Isis and Osiris," from
" The Magic Flute ".......................Mozart
(c) Chorus of Priests, from " The Magic Flute ". Mozart
Mr. Whitney and Male Chorus
Chorus, " Gypsy Life," op. 29..............Schumann
Eine Faust Overture.........................Wagner
Symphony No. 9, in D minor, op. 125........Beethoven

May 9

Matinée Programme

Overture to " Leonore," No. 3, op. 72.........Beethoven
Aria, " O God, Have Mercy," from " St. Paul "
Mendelssohn
Mr. J. F. Rudolphsen
Andante and Scherzo from Symphony in C.....Schubert
Chorus, " Gypsy Life," op. 29..............Schumann
" Kaiser Marsch ".........................Wagner
Overture, " William Tell "..................Rossini
Aria, " No, No, No," from " The Huguenots " Meyerbeer
Miss Cary
Waltz, " Wine, Woman, and Song "...........Strauss
Duet, " Flow Gently, Deva ".................Parry
Mr. Varley and Mr. Whitney
Chorus, " To Thee, Cherubim and Seraphim "..Haendel

May 9

Evening Programme

Vorspiel to " Die Meistersinger ".............Wagner
Twenty-third Psalm.......................Schubert
Chorus of Women's Voices

Scena and Aria, " Ah! perfido!" op. 65......Beethoven
    Mrs. Dexter
Symphonic poem, " Tasso "....................Liszt
The First Walpurgis Night, op. 60........Mendelssohn
The " Hallelujah Chorus," from " The Messiah ".Haendel

A few years later in his career, Thomas would
not have used the name " Festival " to designate a
series of programmes of such a popular and miscellaneous character as the foregoing, in any of
the chief musical centers of America; but in 1873
he did not as yet dare to make even his festival
programmes in New York and Cincinnati, or
his symphony programmes in Boston, without the
sugar-coating of a Strauss waltz to make the
public swallow the symphonic pill. Nothing, perhaps, illustrates better than this fact the musical
standards of America in those days; for it was a
fundamental principle of Thomas, throughout his
life, to make his programmes always as much in
advance of the popular taste as the people would
stand. In doing this, however, he had to feel
his way very carefully, because, as he had no
private resources to fall back upon, it was essential for him to make programmes which, in man-
agerial parlance, would " draw." At that time
symphonies repelled, rather than drew, the concert-
going public, and could only be played, little by
little, as the people learned to know and love
them. Thomas would not play trashy music of any
kind, but he saw the necessity of playing much
that was light and tuneful, and no music served

this purpose so well as the Strauss dance music. It was intrinsically good of its kind, and at the same time, very popular. Truly Johann and Josef Strauss did yeoman service in the musical education of America.

The first Cincinnati Festival passed off so successfully that the Board of Directors decided to give a second two years later.

CHAPTER VI

1873-1876

A FEW nights after his return from Cincinnati,
Thomas began his regular series of summer concerts at the Central Park Garden. The two festivals which he had just conducted had given him
a new and progressive impetus in his art, and the
programmes of this season show a great advance
over those of any previous summer. They were
still miscellaneous and light in general character,
but were composed of the very gems of that class
of literature. On Thursday evenings the second
part of the programme always contained a symphony, and on other nights it usually contained
at least one symphonic movement, or some work
written in the sonata form; while the first and

95

third parts were rich with pearls from the works of the masters, skillfully set amongst lighter or more modern numbers. The Strauss waltzes were retained, but they were no longer the chief feature of the evening, but were used like the foam on champagne, to make the programme sparkle.

Thomas was still deeply in debt, as the result of the Chicago fire, but the future, nevertheless, looked hopeful to him once more, because a project was started by some business men to build a hall in New York for the use of his orchestra, and he knew that with the possession of such a building, not only would the financial problems of his organization disappear, but its artistic efficiency would be increased a hundredfold. The proposed hall was intended for use in both winter and summer, and with this idea in view, Thomas sketched the following plan for its construction, and for the Art Institution which he intended to develop within its walls.

PLANS FOR THE CONSTRUCTION AND USES OF AN ORCHESTRAL BUILDING

BY THEODORE THOMAS

New York, as the metropolis of America, ought to establish a permanent orchestra as an art factor, and also as an educational medium. The following scheme for such institution is both desirable and practical, and its first essential is the possession of a building which shall contain all the necessary facilities for its work, and, in particular, a hall suitable for both winter and summer concerts.

This hall shall have a seating capacity of about 2,500,

and shall be so arranged that, by removing partitions so as to include the foyers and corridors, in the summer season, it can accommodate about 5,000.

The height of the hall at the stage end shall be not more than fifty or sixty feet. The floor shall rise towards the rear. The finish of walls and ceiling shall be entirely of wood. Such removable partitions as are under galleries may be of iron.

The hall shall have two galleries, one of which shall extend around three sides of the auditorium, and the other, above, across the rear end only.

For the Summer Night Concerts, small tables may be placed at the extreme rear of the hall, at which wine or beer may be served, and smoking allowed during the intermissions. But no refreshments may be served, or waiters allowed to move about during the music.

The regular orchestra of the institution shall be engaged by the year and consist of 70 men, enlarged to 100 for symphony concerts.

In winter the season shall consist of six months, with four concerts a week, classified as follows:

I.   Symphony Concerts—Twelve Matinées, given fortnightly; Twelve Evenings, given fortnightly.

II.   Sunday Concerts—Twenty-four Evenings, given weekly.

III.   Young People's Concerts—Twenty-four Matinées, given weekly.

IV.   Out-of-Town Concerts—Given fortnightly.

In summer the season shall consist of five months, with concerts given every evening and on Saturday afternoons.

Between the summer and winter seasons, a vacation of two weeks will be given to rest the men, and give time to change and prepare the hall.

It will be the aim of the institution, to form as soon as

practicable, a choral society for the purpose of presenting such works as the Ninth Symphony, in which a highly-trained chorus is needed.   Also a school for the higher instruction of musicians, where all orchestral instruments will be taught, as well as harmony, counterpoint, and composition.   In this school, an orchestra and chorus of the pupils will be formed, and an opportunity given to pupils to conduct and hear their own compositions.

For the school extension a small hall will be needed for chamber concerts, recitals, and for the practice of the school orchestra and chorus.

Had the proposed building been put up in accordance with this simple and practical plan then, when land, building materials, and labor were comparatively cheap, it could have been done for a moderate sum.   And what a magnificent art institution would by this time have been permanently established in New York!   Thomas was then a young man and could have given to its development the best years of his life.   An earnest of what he might have done in New York under favorable circumstances was shown a few years later, in what he accomplished in the Cincinnati College of Music under the most unfavorable possible circumstances in eighteen months.

Cheered by the hope of this longed-for building, Thomas announced the traveling season of 1873-74 as the last.   Alas!   It was much nearer to the beginning than the end of this arduous class of engagement, and the building so essential to the permanency and full development of the institution he was working for, was still thirty years in the

future.   And so the wearisome life of incessant
traveling with the orchestra was resumed, with
periodical returns to New York for the symphony
concerts there and in Brooklyn, and the long
Central Park Garden series in summer.

Except for the little flurry of hope about the
orchestra building, and its subsequent disappointment, nothing unusual marked the flight of time
for Thomas, until the second Cincinnati Festival
in May, 1875.   The evening programmes of this
festival were made in accordance with what he
considered a festival standard.   But those for the
matinées, although the Strauss waltzes were dis-
carded, were still of a somewhat popular character.
At the second concert Mendelssohn's "Elijah"
was given and during the performance an impressive and characteristic incident happened.
There had been a long drought and the country
was suffering very much for rain.   All day the
longed-for clouds had been gathering and just
as Thomas gave the signal for the famous chorus,
"Thanks be to God," the rain descended in torrents.   Nothing inspired Thomas so quickly as a
display of the forces of nature, and, entering instantly into sympathy with the storm, and the
feeling of public thankfulness for the coming of
the rain, he gathered all his forces—chorus, orchestra, and organ—in one sublime outburst,
harmonizing with and rising above the tumult of
the elements without, as they sang that great song
of thanksgiving: "Thanks be to God, He laveth
the thirsty land! The waters gather together, they

rush along, they are lifting their voices! The
stormy billows are high, their fury is mighty,
but the LORD is above them and he is AL-
MIGHTY!" So tremendous and overpowering
was the effect, that to this day, the old members
of the chorus of that memorable evening—now
thirty-six years in the past—cannot speak of it
without tears in their eyes. The festival was so
successful that a third was decided upon, which
was to be given in May, 1878.

Meantime the work of the last ten years in
New York, especially that of the summer season,
began to show its legitimate results, and an audience had been formed which could enjoy the best
music. The programmes of the summer concerts,
the standard of which had been raised so slowly
during their first years, now became of almost
equal importance with the symphony concerts
of the winter season. But the concerts had been
so uniformly successful in a financial way that they
began to attract the attention of the purveyors of
popular amusements, and cheap imitations of them
sprung up in various parts of the city, which took
off just enough of the patronage of the Thomas
concerts to absorb the profits they had formerly
yielded. The summer of 1875 was therefore the
last in which Thomas gave concerts at the Central
Park Garden, and in losing this long home engagement, he lost the only remunerative concerts that
New York afforded, for his symphony concerts
in that city were never profitable.

Perhaps it was because he knew that this last

season would not pay anyway, that Thomas grew reckless as to the box office, and made its programmes only with reference to the taste of the initiated. At all events they were marvels of art. On Thursday evenings, Symphony programmes of the highest standard were given throughout the season, and, after the first of August, Composers' programmes were added on Tuesdays and often even on Saturdays, which included symphonies. This series of Composers' programmes is so remarkable that it is given here entire. Nothing can better illustrate the advance of musical culture in New York during the nine years which had elapsed since Thomas began his Summer Night Concerts there, than a comparison of these programmes with those given at Terrace Garden in 1866. One of the latter—a fair sample of the rest—is also appended by way of contrast.

TERRACE GARDEN, JUNE 11, 1866

Programme

Overture, " Semiramide " . . . . .Rossini
Waltz, " Wiener Kinder " .Strauss
Selections from " Il Ballo in Maschera " . . . . .Verdi
Galop, " Postillon d'Amour " . . . . .Hermann
Intermission
Overture, " Oberon " . . . . .Weber
" S'Hoamweh," Steyer . . . . .Lanner
Fantasia, " Quodlibet, the Musical Confectioner " . .Hamm
Overture, " The Marriage of Figaro " . . . . .Mozart
Intermission
Quadrille, " Bijouterie " . . . . .Strauss

Romanze from " Robert le Diable "..........Meyerbeer
" Potpourri "............................... Gungl

CENTRAL PARK GARDEN, NEW YORK

SUMMER NIGHT CONCERTS

AUGUST 3, 1875

Beethoven Programme

Selections from Ballet Music, " Prometheus," op. 43
  Overture. Adagio. March
Septette, op. 20. Theme and Variations. Scherzo. Finale
Overture, " Coriolan," op. 62
      Intermission
Symphony No. 5, C minor, op. 67
  Allegro con brio
    Andante con moto
      Scherzo
        Finale
       Intermission
Overture, " Leonore " No. 3, op. 72
Romanze in G, op. 40
Turkish March, " Ruins of Athens," op. 113

AUGUST 10, 1875

Schubert Programme

Overture, " Fier-à-Bras "
Octette. (First time)
  Introduction—Allegro
    Andante
      Scherzo
        Andante molto—Allegro
       Intermission

Symphony No. 9 in C
>   Introduction—Allegro ma non troppo
>>   Andante con moto
>>>   Scherzo
>>>>   Finale
>>>>   Intermission

Entr'acte, " Rosamunde "
Theme and Variations, Quartette in D minor. (For string
>   Orchestra)
Overture, " Alfonso and Estrella "

AUGUST 17, 1875

Mozart Programme

Introduction and Fugue, for String Orchestra
Masonic Funeral Music
Concertone, for two Solo Violins, Oboe, Violoncello, and
>   Orchestra
>>   Allegro spiritoso
>>>   Andantino grazioso
>>>>   Tempo di Minuetto
Overture, " Magic Flute "
>   Intermission
Symphony in C (Jupiter)
>   Allegro vivace
>>   Andante cantabile
>>>   Minuetto
>>>>   Finale—Allegro molto
>>>>   Intermission
Overture, " Marriage of Figaro "
Concerto for Flute and Harp
>   Allegro
>>   Andantino
>>>   Rondo—Allegro
Rondo de Chasse

AUGUST 24, 1875

Beethoven Programme

Overture, " Leonore " No. 1
Overture, " Leonore " No. 2
Overture, " Leonore " No. 3
Overture, " Fidelio "
Intermission
Symphony No. 7, in A, op. 92
Poco sostenuto—Vivace. Allegretto—Presto. Allegro
con brio
Intermission
Septette, op. 20
Theme and Variations. Scherzo. Finale
Overture, " Egmont "

SEPTEMBER 4, 1875

Mendelssohn Programme

Overture, " Athalia "
Symphony No. 3 in A minor (Scotch)
Andante con moto—Allegro. Vivace. Adagio. Allegro
Intermission
Concerto in G minor, for Piano and Orchestra
Molto allegro. Andante. Presto.
Molto allegro—Vivace
Intermission
Music to the " Midsummer Night's Dream "
Overture. Scherzo. Intermezzo. Nocturne. Wedding
March

SEPTEMBER 9, 1875

Berlioz-Liszt-Wagner Programme

BERLIOZ

Overture, " Carnaval Romain "

Symphony, " Harold in Italy," op. 16
> Harold in the Mountains
>> March and Evening Prayer of the Pilgrims
>>> Serenade of a Mountaineer of the Abruzzi
>>> Orgy of the Brigands

Intermission

LISZT

Symphonic Poem, " Les Préludes "
Song, " Die Loreley "
> Mr. H. A. Bishoff

Mephisto Waltz, after Lenau's " Faust "

Intermission

WAGNER

Introduction and Finale, " Tristan and Isolde "
Siegmund's Love Song, from " Die Walkuere "
> Mr. H. A. Bishoff

Kaiser Marsch

SEPTEMBER 11, 1875

Schumann Programme

Symphony No. 2, in C
Introduction—Allegro ma non troppo. Scherzo. Adagio
> expressivo. Allegro molto vivace

Intermission

Concerto in A minor for Piano and Orchestra
> Allegro affetuoso.   Intermezzo.   Allegro vivace
>> Mr. S. B. Mills

Intermission

Selections from the music to Byron's " Manfred "
> Overture. Interlude. Invocation to the Alpen Fay

Overture, " Genoveva "

SEPTEMBER 14, 1875

Wagner Programme

" Tannhaeuser "
>   Overture
>   >   Romanze. (Wolfram), Act III
>   >   >   Bacchanale. (Written for the Paris Grand
>   >   >   Opera in 1861)

" Lohengrin "
>   Vorspiel

Intermission

" Die Walkuere "
>   Introduction. (First time)
>   >   Siegmund's Love Song, Act I
>   >   >   Ritt der Walkueren
>   >   >   >   Wotan's Farewell to Brünnhilde
>   >   >   >   The Magic Fire Scene
>   >   >   Intermission

" Die Meistersinger von Nuernberg "
>   Introduction and Prize Song, Act III
>   >   Overture
>   >   Soloists, Mr. H. A. Bishoff and Mr. F. Remertz

SEPTEMBER 16, 1875

Last Central Park Garden Programme

Suite No. 3, in D............................Bach
>   Overture. Air. Gavotte. Bourrée. Gigue

Symphony in G, (B. & H. No. 13)...........Haydn
>   Introduction—Allegro. Largo. Minuetto. Finale.

Intermission

Overture, " Magic Flute ".................Mozart

Masonic Funeral Music.....................Mozart

Concerto for Flute and Harp, First Movement....Mozart

Intermission

Sonata, "Appassionata," for Piano..........Beethoven
Mr. S. Liebling
Symphony No. 5, C minor...................Beethoven
Allegro con brio. Andante con moto. Allegro—
Allegretto

Thus ended the famous Central Park Garden concerts, and hereafter Thomas was obliged to travel in summer as well as in winter, to keep his orchestra together—for he did not even yet give up the hope that it would be made permanent when the time should at last be ripe for it.

It was during this summer that Thomas received the following letter from Sir Arthur Sullivan, the English composer, which is of interest to American readers because his charming light operas have endeared his name to the American public in a greater degree than that of any other writer of similar music. But although he is known here chiefly by his operas, he was also a composer of other classes of music, and Thomas of course had played those of his works which were suitable for orchestral concerts. In acknowledgment of this, Sullivan wrote as follows:

LONDON, *July* 1, 1875.
My dear Mr. Thomas:
May I beg your acceptance of the accompanying two pieces for the orchestra, (of which I send you the score and parts,) as an acknowledgment of your kind endeavors to make some of my orchestral music known to the American public?

They are the orchestral introduction to the first and

second parts of my " The Light of the World," and are
styled, respectively, " Bethlehem," and " Jerusalem." The
two are frequently played together in English concerts,
and I thought they might be useful to you in making up
your numerous programmes. I will send, by the next
post, a few analytical remarks which are generally printed
on the programmes here, in case you might find them useful for the same purpose.

I have only one favor to ask in return, *viz.*: if you go
to Philadelphia, will you play them there, as it would give
much pleasure to a very dear friend of mine there, who
has heard them in England?

I am, my dear sir, with best compliments,

Yours truly,

ARTHUR SULLIVAN.

At the close of the summer season, Thomas
started on his customary winter tours, which
followed each other with but little intermission
until the spring of 1876. But in spite of his hard
work he had been unable to make any financial
headway. He was now nearly twenty thousand
dollars in debt, and there seemed to be no way
by which he could meet this large obligation.
Under these circumstances he was glad to accept
an engagement in Philadelphia for the summer
of 1876, which promised large returns, and so
confident was he that he would make enough
money to pay his debts, that he arranged to have
the profits of his venture paid, not to himself,
but to a trustee, who was to turn them over to
his creditors.

The year 1876 was that of the Philadelphia

Centennial Exposition, and its directors had offered Thomas the musical directorship of the opening ceremonies. A supplementary engagement to give Summer Night Concerts during the six months of the Exposition, was suggested by the Women's Committees of the Board of Directors, at the head of which was Mrs. E. D. Gillespie. These ladies, who represented the wealth and culture of Philadelphia, had acquired, through the gift of a generous fellow citizen, the use of the mansion and grounds formerly owned by Edwin Forrest. A hall seating 4,000 persons was added, and the house itself was fitted up as a restaurant. The use of this apparently ideal place was tendered to Thomas for summer concerts, and, as the Exposition closed at sunset every day, it seemed inevitable that the thousands of strangers in the city would gladly avail themselves of such a delightful way of spending their otherwise unoccupied evenings as these concerts would afford. The Women's Committees did not guarantee the concerts in any way, nor did Thomas consider it necessary, but they promised to promote their success by every means in their power, and under such favorable auspices Thomas felt confident that the season would be a very profitable one.

The president of the Women's Committees, Mrs. Gillespie, was a descendant of Benjamin Franklin, and as public-spirited in her generation as her famous ancestor had been in his. Brilliant, witty, fascinating, courageous, and strong of mind,

as she was warm of heart, this remarkable woman
stands out as one of the first and best of her
country and century. Her whole life was given
to promoting the educational and philanthropic
advancement of her city, and her work as the
president of the Woman's Department of the
Centennial Exposition of 1876 set the model for
all similar expositions since. She was a connoisseur of music as of many other things, and
when Thomas accepted the directorship of the
opening ceremonies of the Exposition, she wrote
him that her committees would be responsible for
all the expenses of a chorus for the occasion, and
also that they would pay an honorarium for the
composing of an inaugural march, if he would
arrange with some famous European composer
to undertake the work.

Thomas agreed to do this and at once opened
negotiations with Wagner on the subject. The
correspondence was carried on partly by Thomas
in person, and partly by Mr. Federlein, who
wrote on his behalf, and the following letters *
from the great composer were in answer to one
or the other of them. Wagner accepted the
commission, and the very large honorarium—
which he took good care should be in the hands
of his banker before Thomas had a chance to examine his score,—but the rest of his part of the
transaction was anything but creditable to a man of
his pre-eminence in the world of art. For he not
only demanded a disproportionately large price for

* Translated from the original German.

Mrs. E. D. Gillespie of Philadelphia

his work, but broke his promise in regard to with-holding its publication in Europe until six months after its publication in America, and, without Thomas's knowledge or consent, actually had a European edition of Rubinstein's arrangement of it printed and shipped to America before the *score itself* was transmitted to Thomas. But, worst of all, when the score did finally arrive, the composition proved to be so poor that it was practically worthless.

I.

BAYREUTH, *Dec. 22*, 1875.

Dear Mr. Federlein:

Please express to Herr Musik-Director Thomas my best thanks for his kind efforts in America in behalf of myself and my enterprises over here. As regards his latest re-quest to me, I will say that it is quite possible that for the opening of the American national festival, something may occur to me—perhaps in broad March form—that I can make use of, although I have not written a note of music for a long time, and have quite got out of the way of so-called composing, which you will easily understand.

Well—if I send you the thing, I shall expect, in return, that the Americans will behave well towards me, especially as regards the furtherance of my festival plays, which I have postponed with special reference to them, to the sec-ond half of August, at the cost of considerable trouble in regard to the singers to be engaged. I hope soon to be assured of the American visitors.

Yours truly,

RICHARD WAGNER.

II

BAYREUTH, *Feb.* 8, 1876.

MR. THEODORE THOMAS,
   Dear Sir:

I seize this opportunity to express to you my hearty thanks for your labors in America, so helpful in promoting the spirit of German music, and which have been also of use in my undertaking.

In respect to the affair, hitherto conducted through Mr. Federlein, I must first express my regret that our correspondence—rendered difficult by the great distance, and recently also by your absence from New York—has been so protracted. I wish, therefore, that this thing may be concluded, and declare myself ready to execute a composition for grand orchestra, of the caliber and character of my Kaiser March, for the celebration of the 100th anniversary of American Independence. To deliver it for shipping March 15, to a banking house in Germany, designated by you, against the payment of five thousand dollars for the receipt of the manuscript. For this sum, demanded by me, I confer upon you the entire ownership of the work in question for America, not, however, for Europe, for which I am bound by contract to B. Schott and Sons. I pledge myself, however, not to allow the German publication to be issued till six months after the American.

I do not know whether it will seem wise to you to pay the sum mentioned for the unrestricted ownership (and naturally also performances) of my composition, but for the largeness of my demand recent experiences determined me. I have already been offered $2,250 for a similar composition, by a Berlin publisher, which, by the way, would have been unconnected with a national celebration. Mr. Verdi has received from his publisher, Recordia, $100,000 for the absolute copyright and performances of his Requiem. Therefore it may be allowed me to draw the conclusion of the value of the composition of an author already celebrated. In this respect also, I have to pay great attention to the value of works until now given away for nothing, because, until now, I have not been able to save from the receipts of the same a penny.

I beg you to communicate to me, therefore, by a telegram, your acceptance of my conditions, and I authorize you to deduct the cost of the telegram from my honorarium. Or, if I do not receive the telegram at the right time, I will take it for granted that you cannot conform to my demand. In either case I will always remain,

Your very humble and obliged servant,

RICHARD WAGNER.

III

BAYREUTH, *Feb.*, 1876.

MR. FEDERLEIN,

Dear Sir:

All that you write me makes me very sorry, and I regret very much the disappointment of Mr. Thomas. I thought little of the intention of the Ladies' Society to make money out of my March, because, in buying it for this society, Mr. Thomas wrote me that no American publisher had wanted to undertake it, because the composition of a foreign composer has no international copyright, therefore no compensating profit could be drawn from the work from Europe. The purchase of my work seemed, therefore, an affair of honor on the part of the Ladies' Society, which presented the work, so to speak, to the Centennial Celebration.

I communicated the letter of Mr. Thomas to my publishers, B. Schott Sons, who, having then no hesitation on account of contract rights, which, (according to that let-

ter), did not at all exist, undertook the immediate publication of my work. According to your letter received
to-day there is something else said again. By this it
appears that there is an American publisher, who will
undertake to publish the March for an honorarium. I
heartily grant this honorarium to Mr. Thomas, or whoever it may be, and I immediately telegraphed to Schott
to keep back their transmissions to America, but they
answered me that the Rubinstein arrangement had already
gone.

I regret this without being able to blame myself, and
only hope that Mr. Thomas will, through the exclusive
right, which the enclosed document secures to him, find
in the course of time a remuneration for his pains. The
score will, for the present, not be sent to America.

Very truly yours,

RICHARD WAGNER.

IV

BERLIN, March, 1876.

MR. FEDERLEIN,

Honored Sir:

I have not Mr. Thomas' address at hand, and will therefore ask you to send him the following information:

The Festival March was sent to Paris to-day, according to my instructions, to be forwarded by Banker Feustal
to America. I could have finished the score a fortnight
ago, had it not been for the very exhausting concert work
in Berlin and Vienna, to which I was pledged at this time,
and which made it almost impossible to finish the score.
I hope, however, that it will arrive in time for them to
copy the parts, and make the necessary corrections of
same, for I am sure that by the first days of April, the
score will be in the possession of Mr. Thomas—who, how-

ever, might have let me know his intentions in regard to the whole matter a little earlier.

The correct tempo is indicated by a little mark over the triad, ========= The always ponderous and heavy accentuation ========= of the same 𝅘𝅥𝅮𝅘𝅥𝅮𝅘𝅥 should, on the other hand, not lead to a certain ˃ ˃ ˃ dragging of the tempo. I indicated on pages 23 and 24, two grand pauses, the impressiveness of which could, especially in the first performance, be increased by the discharge of cannon, as well as muskets, at a place not too near Festival Hall. Perhaps at later performances, the very solemn effect of the artillery could be imitated by the bass drum and so-called rattles, such as Beethoven used in his " Battle of Vittoria." This, of course, should also sound from a distance, and might be placed in a room adjoining the hall.

I presume that part of the honorarium was contributed by the Directors of the Exposition, at least I would find this quite natural, Mr. Thomas has, moreover, the exclusive right of performance for the United States. At any rate, I would like to have a definite declaration as to when the score can be issued by my German publishers here. I believe that the publication should be made in Europe at the same time as in America, as this would be in keeping with the usual custom in regard to international copyright. And this should be done not only in Germany and America, but also in England.

And now I give you my best wishes. The March is very much liked by my friends, and I firmly believe, at least I hope, that it will be liked as well in America.

With best greetings, sincerely yours,

RICHARD WAGNER.

V

BERLIN, *March 25,* 1876.

THEODORE THOMAS, ESQR.

Honored Sir:

I am delighted to receive, at last, a few lines from you personally. As I write, I suppose the score has already completed the first half of its voyage to you. I sincerely hope that it will reach you in time, and I have already written to our mutual friend, Federlein, and told him my wishes in regard to its performance.

In regard to the copyright and royalties for America, I would like to confess that I am not in full sympathy any more with the arrangements previously made, but I promise you to live up to the said agreements. Kindly let me know, in a written document, whatever formalities have to be carried out concerning the copyright, and I will sign and return it to you at my earliest convenience.

I cannot thank you enough for the great trouble you have taken in completing this transaction. I hope that the success of the work will bring you joy. It has cost me much hardship to complete the score in time, as I am almost worn out by the excessive demands upon me of a number of concerts in Berlin and Vienna.

By the motto that I have placed above the title, you will see that I have taken this matter quite seriously. A few soft and tender passages in the March are meant to depict the beautiful and talented women of North America, as they take part in the cortège. I am glad to say that it was my intention to have these noble-hearted women take the first place in the procession, rather than the men, because they were the chief promoters and most energetic workers for my composition. Will you also kindly translate the dedication into English:

Dedicated
To the
Women's Centennial Committees
By
Richard Wagner

With best wishes and greetings, I remain,
Yours very sincerely,
RICHARD WAGNER.

It is needless to say that Wagner's generosity
in granting to the Women's Committees (through
Thomas) the "exclusive American rights" to a
composition of which he had already stocked the
New York music stores with a foreign arrangement was not taken advantage of. However, it
was perhaps fortunate for them that they were
thus handicapped in the matter of publishing the
work, for it was a total failure, and they would
probably have lost whatever they spent in that
way. Even Thomas, the first and most persistent
worker for the Wagner propaganda in America,
rarely performed the March, and I have never
heard of its being played in Europe at all. Wagner himself is said to have remarked, in regard to
it, "The best thing about that composition was
the money I got for it," * and he certainly told the
truth that time.

In addition to the Wagner March, Thomas
arranged that two American composers, John K.
Paine and Dudley Buck should be commissioned
to write choral works for the opening ceremonies
of the Philadelphia Exposition. And, in order

* See "Wagner and His Works," by H. T. Finck. Vol. II, p. 509.

that their works should have a still more distinctively national character, the words used for them were by the American poets John Greenleaf Whittier and Sidney Lanier. The programme, as is customary on such occasions, consisted of alternate musical numbers and speeches. There were four of the former, and Thomas gave the place of honor, in the middle, to the American writers, a custom he always observed afterwards on programmes of this character. The musical part of the programme, in full, was as follows, and it is a good example of the Thomas method of planning the selections for celebrations of a national character:

PHILADELPHIA CENTENNIAL EXPOSITION
Inaugural Ceremonies
May 10, 1876

Grand Centennial Inaugural March. . . . . Wagner
Centennial Hymn (Words by Whittier). . . . . . . J. K. Paine
Centennial Meditation of Columbia (Words by
    Sidney Lanier). . . . . Dudley Buck
The Hallelujah Chorus. . . . . Haendel

The day after the Inaugural Ceremonies, Thomas began the Summer Night season at the Woman's Centennial Music Hall and Garden, as it was called. Mrs. Gillespie and her Women's Committees worked hard and faithfully to " boom " the concerts, but, to the surprise and disappointment of all concerned, their efforts were fruitless. The visiting crowds preferred to stay in their hotels and boarding houses and rest in the evening, rather than go out and listen to music—or perhaps they did not realize that music was going on then, and the concerts were so poorly attended that, after struggling for a short time against adversity, they had to be given up. In the meantime this unexpected calamity had increased the indebtedness of Thomas so much that now the waves of financial ruin closed over his head.

The only valuable possessions he had were his large and costly library and musical appurtenances, on which he had spent many thousands of dollars, and which were as necessary to his work as machinery is to a manufacturer. These precious possessions were now seized by the Sheriff at Philadelphia and publicly sold at auction, and were described by the advertisement as " The entire musical library of Theodore Thomas, consisting of full orchestral scores, operatic and symphonic, instrumental and vocal compositions, as set forth in the complete catalogue belonging thereto, and to accompany this sale. Also one pair of kettledrums, one pair of cymbals, one bass drum, triangle, conductor's stand and platform, writing desk, inkstand, books, etc., etc."

It is a melancholy commentary on the valuelessness of music except to the user, that this large library, which had cost its owner many thousands of dollars (and included, by the way, the $5,000 Wagner March, which the ladies had given him), only brought, under the hammer, the paltry sum of $1,400. Fortunately for Thomas his devoted friend, Dr. Franz Zinzer, of New York, heard of the proposed sale, and, hastening to Philadelphia, bought in everything—music, instruments, and all—and then proposed that Thomas should rent it from him at the nominal sum of one hundred dollars a year. Meantime it was all left in the possession of Thomas, and two years later Mrs. Thomas received, from this generous friend, the following letter:

NEW YORK, *Oct.* 1, 1878.

Dear Mrs. Thomas:

You remember that I am the owner of that old musical library, which I bought at the Sheriff's sale two years ago in Philadelphia. In your present situation in Cincinnati you might be able to render your husband considerable service if you were the owner of it, and I therefore beg you to allow me to make it over to you, as the enclosed paper shows. If you lend him one of the works, tell him to take good care of it.

Very truly yours,

F. ZINZER.

The helping hand thus opportunely held out to Thomas by Dr. Zinzer was the only bright spot in that dark time. As for the rest, his orchestra was disbanded, and himself stranded, a financial wreck, so weighed down by debt that all hope of clearing it away had vanished. Under these circumstances, his advisers urged him to go into bankruptcy, as the only course open to him.

Many years later he told the story of this bitter period, in the following letter:

" . . . When I began my longer tours in the sixties, I had no other purpose than the wish to give the people an opportunity to hear good music. I had all kinds of misfortunes, the Chicago fire not being the least of them, and soon I became so involved financially that I had to keep on traveling. I wanted to stop several times, but my best friends were against it, and yet nobody gave me any help. Everyone saw how the cause of good music prospered, but saw also how I was being sacrificed. The help of a single person was not enough, and a combination was always impossible. To be brief, fires, inundations, snow storms—the people stayed away from the concerts or I could not reach the places. In short, I received no money, but I had to pay salaries. Finally, in Philadelphia, in '79, I got into the hands of the Sheriff, and for twelve long years I could not free myself of him. Of course I would not have got to such a pass as that had I not also been betrayed. Once I decided to become a bankrupt, I could not stand the strain any longer. For a moment I held back and then I threw down the pen and refused to sign. I said to myself, that for the sake of my family and my profession I would not make a bankrupt of myself voluntarily, although I did not see any possibility of ever making enough money to buy up all the claims against me. However, eventually I succeeded and the papers of satisfaction are all safely stored. But twelve years' experience with sheriffs and scoundrels have made their impression on the nerves, and I cannot hear the door bell to-day, yet, without being startled."

CHAPTER VII

1876-1878

FIRST SEASON OF CHICAGO SUMMER NIGHT CONCERTS—THE
EXPOSITION BUILDING—THE THOMAS SOUNDING BOARD
—REQUEST PROGRAMMES—SOME "NATIONAL PRO-
GRAMMES"—THOMAS BECOMES THE CONDUCTOR OF THE
NEW YORK PHILHARMONIC SOCIETY, 1877.

THE Philadelphia disaster prevented Thomas
from giving concerts elsewhere during the summer
of 1876, but when the fall came, Mrs. Gillespie
again interested the Women's Committees of the
Centennial Exposition to promote a series of ten
Festival Concerts under his direction, to be given
at the Academy of Music, between September
20 and November 4. This series of concerts had
the important result for Thomas of calling his disbanded orchestra together again, and giving him
a new point of departure, after which the old life
of incessant travel East, West, North, and South,
was resumed once more, with periodical returns
to New York for concerts there and in Brooklyn.

The winter season of 1876-77 was only an un-
eventful repetition of former years, but when
summer came, and the doors of the Central Park
Garden were no longer open to him, Thomas decided to try his luck in Chicago, and accepted a
long engagement there.

The hall in which the Chicago Summer Night
Concerts were given during this, and many succeeding years, was not built for music, but was
the old Exposition Building on the Lake Front
of Michigan Avenue, opposite Adams Street.
The interior was an immense hall extending over
more than two blocks. It was neither finished
nor decorated within, and yet it had a certain
beauty of its own, for the walls and roof were supported by great arched steel girders, which lent
much grace of outline, and, as the north end of
the hall was not used or lighted, these supporting
arches, one behind the other, vanishing into the
darkness, gave the effect of limitless space. The
end where the concerts were given was made
cheerful by lights and potted plants, and many
evergreen trees in tubs formed a little grove in the
rear, where groups of friends sat at small tables,
where the men could smoke or, in the intermissions, enjoy a glass of beer. There were no fixed
or even reserved seats in any part of the building,
and people sat where they pleased, or moved the
chairs into little groups to suit themselves. But
there were two prices of admission. Twenty-five
cents admitted you to the rear section where the
tables were, but fifty cents carried you past a
certain little iron railing and enabled you to sit
amongst the gods in front.

At either side of the auditorium were broad
arcades, large enough for many thousands of
people to promenade in without crowding, and, in
order to allow them to continue, without inter-

ruption, around the hall, the orchestra stage was built some distance out from the end of the building. In such an enormous place the small orchestra at the command of Thomas would have been nearly inaudible had he not used the device of an

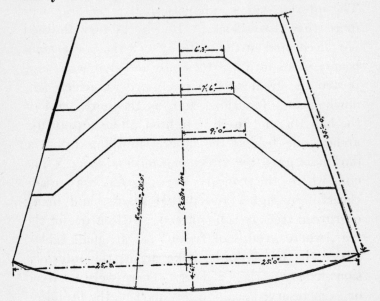

Chicago Summer Night Concerts.—Diagram of Stage, 1883

immense sounding-board of peculiar construction, to reflect the tone. It took him much experiment to get this important adjunct of these concerts just right in size, shape, thickness, and especially in its angle of inclination. In speaking of it afterwards, he said: " The acoustics of the Exposition Building of Chicago were very satisfactory, in spite of its great size and the smallness of the orchestra employed, because of the sounding-board of thin wood which I used. It has been copied several times by others, but never successfully *because my angle was not observed.*

" It should be noted, also, that there is an opening behind the orchestra at the lower edge of the

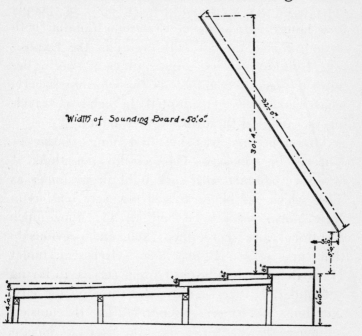

Summer Night Concerts, 1883.—Diagram of Sounding Board

sounding-board. . . . The sounding-board is only useful in the open air, in very large buildings, or, when an orchestra has to play on the enclosed stage of a theater, its purpose being to throw the tone directly toward the auditorium." *

Taken for all in all, the Chicago Summer Night Concerts were amongst the most delightful Thomas ever gave. Nowadays the same audience, which was even then genuinely musical, has

* See article on Sounding Boards, " Dictionary of Architecture," Russell Sturgis, ed.

become so cultured by many years of symphony concerts, that it would probably care but little for concerts of the old Summer Night caliber. But in those days orchestral music was all comparatively new to the Western metropolis, and the people were hungry for a chance to become familiar with it, and, during the hot July evenings, the Exposition Building, always airy and cool, was a delightful place of rendezvous for Chicago society, which had not as yet adopted the habit of traveling or going to the country in summer.

Although this was his first long season of concerts in Chicago, Thomas did not think it necessary to start with such light programmes as those which had characterized his early seasons in New York, because he had already done much desultory work there since 1869, and previous to that time a local Philharmonic Orchestra, under Hans Belatka, had been of great service in laying a foundation for the musical future of the city. Nor must we forget, in enumerating the musical influences that helped to form the taste of Chicago, two large and excellent choral societies,—the Beethoven and Apollo Clubs—which, under their respective directors, Carl Wolfsohn and W. L. Tomlins, gave important choral performances every year. Chicago had, therefore, already made a good musical start, and the programmes of the first Summer Night season show a correspondingly good artistic standard, although they were for the most part light. Each week Composers' and Symphony programmes were given and, towards the end of the season, National programmes were also added. But, from time to time, Thomas measured the real musical standard of his Chicago public by giving " Request Programmes." The idea of asking the people to send in requests for the numbers of a given programme originated with Mr. Geo. B. Carpenter, the Chicago manager of the Thomas orchestra. Thomas thought the suggestion a good one, and used it in his Chicago concerts for many subsequent years, as a means of gauging the musical progress of the city.

The making of a " Request Programme " was not by any means the simple thing it appeared, for, in the preliminary announcement Thomas agreed to play those compositions which should receive the largest number of requests—stipulating only that the requests should be sent in by a given date, and that they should be selected from the programmes previously performed that summer—and the result was that often the numbers he had to put together were very incongruous and difficult to combine. His method of making these programmes was as follows. The letters containing the requests were kept unopened until the day stated by the announcement, and then they were all opened and an alphabetical list made of the compositions asked for. This was no light task, for there were often from six hundred to a thousand requests for a single programme, and before each piece the number of times it was asked for had to be carefully noted. When the list was

ready, Thomas would look it over, and first draw
his pencil through all the pieces which could not
be played because their requesters had not con-
formed to the stipulation that they must be selected from the repertoire of the season. From
the remainder he would select those having the
largest number of votes, and make his programme
from them. He *never* put on a number which
had not really been requested, though once in a
while it would happen that a large number of
requests would come in for two Liszt Rhapsodies,
or two symphonies. In such a case he would have
to substitute, for the one having the smaller number of votes, the next in favor on the list. I have
often seen him spend hours arranging and re-
arranging the numbers asked for, in a vain endeavor to fit them together into harmonious sequence, and finally give up, with a patient sigh,
the hopeless task of making an artistic programme
from such miscellaneous material.

Thomas disliked " Request Programmes " for
this reason; but he was too conscientious to allow
himself to suppress any of the pieces which had a
large number of votes in favor of less popular,
but more suitable selections. Some people found
this out, and used the knowledge to get the pieces
they wanted, by asking a large number of their
acquaintances—sometimes people who did not
even attend the concerts—to sign petitions asking
for certain compositions. I well remember one
" Request Programme " which was nearly wrecked
by a few devotees of Brueckner's music, who

collected three hundred signatures to a request
for a very long and unpopular symphony by
that composer. Fortunately the Brueckner admirers asked for a symphony which was not in
the repertoire of the summer, so Thomas was able
to disregard the request by putting an explana-
tory note on the programme. But for this he
would have been obliged to play it, with the result that hundreds of dollars would have been
lost to the box office, and the very people whom
the " Request Programmes " were made to attract
would have been kept away. After this experience, he added another stipulation to the preliminary announcements of the " Request Programmes," namely, that each request should have
but one signature, and, finally, he had to make the
rule that only one number could be requested at
a time. This last condition was made necessary
by thoughtless people who would send in long lists
of the compositions they wanted, thus complicating
enormously the sorting and classifying of the
requests. There was one man, in particular, who
had the habit of sending in several whole programmes of his own concocting, at once, on
which every number of all three parts was a
movement of a different symphony, and which
were always accompanied by a letter exhorting
Thomas to " peek around at the audience " as he
played it, and see how much more the people
would enjoy this sort of programme than what
they ordinarily got. Another assured him that no
one wanted to listen to symphonies at all, and

asked that he would play only dance music, while the people of the different nationalities— French, Russian, Bohemian, etc.—each clamored for the music of their own country, and those who had attended the last " Request Programme," were a solid phalanx in their desire to hear all of its numbers right over again. In short, there were many snags to be avoided in giving this popular variety of programme. The following is the first one which Thomas gave, and it illustrates very well the musical standard of Chicago at that time. We shall see how rapidly this city advanced in the knowledge and love of good music, until, a few years later, it stood second to none in America, or perhaps even in the world, in sustaining music of the highest standard:

CHICAGO, JULY 16, 1877

First Request Programme

Overture, " Tannhaeuser ".................Wagner

Allegretto, Eighth Symphony..............Beethoven

Largo.....................................Haendel

Rhapsodie Hongroise, No. 2...............Liszt

Intermission

Overture, " William Tell "................Rossini

Traumerei................................Schumann

Fantaisie Caprice........................Vieuxtemps

Carnival of Venice, (Burlesque)

Intermission

Funeral March of a Marionette............Gounod

Waltz, " Wiener Bonbons ".................Strauss

Amaryllis................................Gyhs

Overture, " Zampa "......................Herold

Reading between the lines of this programme Thomas was encouraged, in spite of its very light quality, because there was nothing on it which was not intrinsically good, and on the night following he did not hesitate to offer to his " baby public,"—as someone has called it—as fine a Mozart programme as a Summer Night Concert would permit him to perform. It was a principle with him to advance his standard as fast as the public could follow, for he believed that the only way to hold the popular interest in music, after it had been once aroused, was to lead it along the lines of intellectual and artistic progress.

The first Chicago season of summer concerts was not very successful financially, owing to the great railroad strike and riots in August of that year, and as it drew to a close, Thomas received the following letter from a number of well-known Chicago men:

CHICAGO, *July 27, 1877.*

MR. THEODORE THOMAS,
Dear Sir:
We believe it to be the universal sentiment of our citizens that in the way of pleasure and musical instruction there has been nothing in Chicago comparable to your summer garden concerts. We regret that unlooked for business occurrences have, in some degree, broken the attendance.

While your efforts in every way deserved success, we had hoped that the result of this season would justify your return next summer. In this expectation we trust we may not be disappointed.

Permit us to request you to name an evening for a concert when our citizens may, by their presence, confer a compliment personal to yourself.

Very respectfully,

WIRT DEXTER,	J. M. WALKER,
HENRY W. KING,	C. E. DUNCAN,
MARSHALL FIELD,	E. B. McCAGG,
ROBERT TODD LINCOLN,	JOHN G. SHORTALL,
A. A. MUNGER,	H. W. BISHOP,
EDWARD S. ISHAM,	N. K. FAIRBANK,
J. D. HARVEY,	CHARLES D. HAMILL,
J. S. HAMILTON,	AND OTHERS.

Thomas always disliked anything in the way of so-called "benefit" concerts; he was, nevertheless, sincerely grateful to the men who thus sought to assist his work in the only way then open to them, and accepted their courteously tendered offer in the following letter:

CHICAGO, *July 28*, 1877.

MESSRS. WIRT DEXTER, EDWARD ISHAM, AND OTHERS.

Gentlemen:

In accepting the compliment extended to me in your letter of the 27th, permit me to say that the cordial welcome I have met with in public and private during my stay this summer has greatly attached me to your city.

When, eleven years ago, I inaugurated nightly summer concerts in New York, I did it with a view of elevating my profession and the public taste for music. In a few years these concerts have become a recognized institution of the country. However, as my repertoire extended, my orchestra had to be increased to meet the enlarged demands of modern composers. In order to sustain so large an organization I was obliged to travel a large portion of the year, and it was this necessity which first introduced me to the West. New York, Boston, and Philadelphia enjoyed the fruits of all this labor in the shape of Symphony Concerts which could never have reached the high standard attained, had not the whole country contributed to the support of the organization.

After eleven consecutive years of summer concerts I have been obliged to leave New York for lack of a suitable hall in which to give them. What New York offered I refused, and what I wanted I could not have. That metropolis not having supplied my needs, I was induced to try the West, and I gladly confess I do not regret the experiment. I find the people here open-hearted, generous, and enthusiastic, and in thanking them, through you, for their kind appreciation of the labor my colleagues and myself have done here during the last few months, let me say it would give me pleasure, circumstances permitting, to return here next summer.

The support we have received justifies me in saying that Chicago is the only city on the continent, except New York, where there is sufficient musical culture to enable me to give a series of fifty successive concerts.

Thanking you again for your kindness, I will, with your permission, name August 1st, as the evening most convenient for the complimentary concert, and will combine it with a request programme.

Very respectfully yours,
THEODORE THOMAS.

The proposed concert took place as planned, and a few days later the first Chicago Summer Night Concert season " belonged to history." The season had brought forth a number of inter-

esting developments, as we have seen, but none
of its programmes were more worthy of preservation than the little series of three " National "
programmes, which follow, and which are good
examples of Thomas' work of this kind:

CHICAGO SUMMER NIGHT CONCERTS
JULY 3, 1877
Scandinavian Programme

J. Svendsen (1840)
> Coronation March
> Symphonic Introduction to " Sigurd."

Asgar Hamerik (1843).
> Love Scene, " Evening in the Woods."
> First Norse Suite

Niels W. Gade (1817).
> Symphony No. 1, in C minor

Intermission

C. F. E. Horneman
> Overture, " Aladdin "

A. Soedermann
> Wedding March from " The Wedding of Nefasa "

H. C. Lumby
> " Visions in a Dream," a Fantasia
> Champagne Galop

JULY 20, 1877
French Programme

Étienne Henri Méhul (1763-1817)
> Overture, " Horatius Cocles "

Jean Philippe Rameau (1683-1764)
> (a) Rigodon de Dardanus.   (Transcribed for or-
> chestra by F. A. Gevart)

(b) Air de Danse du XVIème Siècle. (Arranged
for orchestra by Wakerlin)
Daniel François Auber (1784-1871)
Transcription, " Masaniella "
Intermission
Hector Berlioz (1803-1869)
(a) Overture, " Franc Judges "
(b) Scherzo, " La Reine Mab," from Symphony
" Roméo et Juliet "
Charles François Gounod (1818)
(a) Entr'acte, " Colombe "
(b) Danse des Bacchantes, " Philémon et Baucis "
(c) Marche et Cortège, " Reine de Saba "
French National Hymn, " La Marseillaise " (1792)
Intermission
Camille Saint Saens (1835)
Poème Symphonique, " Danse Macabre "
Jules Massenet (1842)
(a) Variations, op. 13
(b) Carnaval

JULY 27, 1877

Italian Programme

Cherubini (1760-1842).
(a) Overture, " Abenceragen "
(b) Introduction to Act III, " Medea "
Boccherini (1740-1805)
(a) Sicilian, String Orchestra
(b) Minuet, String Orchestra
Spontini (1778-1851)
Overture, " Vestalin "

Rossini (1792-1869)
    (a) Cavatina, "Othello."
               Miss Busk
               Intermission
    (b) Overture, "William Tell."
    (c) Aria, "William Tell"
               Mr. A. H. Bishoff
Verdi (1815)
    (a) Andantino
    (b) Scherzo Fuga (String orchestra)
Bellini (1802-1835)
    Rondo
               Miss Busk
               Intermission
Donizetti (1797-1848)
    Selections, "Lucia."
Mercadante (1798-1870)
Aria, "Il Bravo"
               Mr. H. A. Bishoff
Bazzini (1818)
    Gavotte (String orchestra)
Verdi
    Overture, "Nabucco"

After leaving Chicago Thomas took the orchestra to St. Louis and Cincinnati for short supplementary engagements, and then returned to New York, where a new and important field of labor now awaited him.

Thomas had been the conductor of the Brooklyn Philharmonic Society continuously since the fall of 1866. The New York Philharmonic had also approached him with offers of the leadership of their orchestra for several years, but he had not been able to accept the latter because of the conditions attached. Until the formation of the Thomas Orchestra, the Philharmonic Society had been the standard orchestra of America. Founded in the year 1842, by an American violinist named U. C. Hill, and avowedly devoted to the cause of the best music, this society had already an established reputation when Thomas, then a youth of sixteen, became one of its violinists. It is true that the standard of its performances was very inferior, like that of all those early orchestras, and its programmes presented a singular hodge-podge of compositions in which symphonies and all kinds of incongruous material were thrown together apparently at random. For a long time it had no responsible musical director, but sometimes one, sometimes another conductor, directed a concert. Its early programmes often show two or three conductors to have divided the honors of a single concert between them. Nor were its rehearsals any more systematic than its conducting. Any man could absent himself as often as he liked from rehearsals, and the consequence was that the orchestra was never complete in rehearsals, and no very high standard of performance was possible. But in spite of these drawbacks, the Philharmonic Society, nevertheless, stood for art; its aim was the highest, and under the conductorship of Carl Bergmann, who, as we have seen, was a musician of real talent, it became the chief orchestral organization of New York.

After the formation of the Thomas Orchestra,

the Philharmonic suffered much from the competition of its young and far more perfect rival, and at last it became evident that the pioneer society would be permanently disabled unless it could make a combination with the new conductor, and turn his growing prestige towards, instead of away from Philharmonic interests. The leadership of the society was, therefore, offered to Thomas for two successive years, but coupled with the condition that he should give up his own Symphony Concerts in New York. Thomas, however, was not willing to do this, for not only was symphonic work his specialty, but, in fact, the whole object for which he had formed his orchestra. Furthermore, the six Philharmonic concerts could not fill the place of his many Symphony Concerts during the winter, even in New York, nor could he substitute for his own orchestra, always under his own absolute control, a co-operative organization in which every detail of the work must be submitted to, and passed upon, by a Board of Directors. Hence the negotiations with the Philharmonic Society had hitherto always come to naught.

The spring of 1877, however, found the veteran society at the lowest ebb of its fortunes. Its yearly dividend had sunk to only eighteen dollars a share, and its standard of performance was very inferior owing to lack of discipline and training. In this emergency the conductorship was finally offered to Thomas without any conditions, and consequently accepted.

His acceptance of the position removed a dangerous rival from the Philharmonic Society, but it had the singular result for Thomas of creating an equally dangerous and far more powerful one for himself. Hereafter he was his own most successful rival in New York, but he cared not a whit for that, but deliberately made the Philharmonic series his most important concerts, and gave the second place to his own as long as he lived in that city.

The New York and Brooklyn Philharmonic Concerts were given once a month, and the Thomas Symphony Concerts came still oftener. It was, therefore, necessary for Thomas to be in New York the greater part of the time during the winter of 1877-78. But all these engagements, many though they were, did not suffice to support his orchestra without traveling, and yet the short intervals between the home engagements did not allow time enough for concert tours. Thus the same old problem was still ever before him, and he saw no way whereby he could keep together what he had built up during so many years of sacrifice and hard labor.

CHAPTER VIII

1878-1879

THE Cincinnati Festival of 1878 was an especially memorable occasion because it marked the
year when these festivals ceased to be mere spo-
radic sets of concerts, and became an organized art
institution,—the greatest of its kind in America.

Amongst the wealthy men who had become interested in the work of the festival of 1872 was Mr.
Reuben R. Springer, and it was due to his munifi-
cence that, during the three years which elapsed
between the second and third festivals, a centrally-
located lot of land was secured, and a very large
and thoroughly equipped building erected on it
for festival purposes. There is, perhaps, no other
hall in America so admirably adapted for musical
festivals as this, not only because of its large
auditorium, its ample foyers and many other com-
forts and conveniences for the public, but because of its equally roomy accommodations be-

hind the stage, where any number of musicians, and any quantity of musical paraphernalia can be provided for, without crowding. The possession of this building meant perpetuity for the Cincinnati Musical Festival Association, and, as far as I know, there has never been a Cincinnati Festival which ended with a financial deficit—a halcyon state of affairs which could not have been achieved had the Association been dependent on an ordinary hall.

This important building was dedicated on the opening night of the festival of 1878, with the following programme:

CINCINNATI MAY FESTIVAL
Tuesday Evening, May 14, 1878
Music Hall Dedication Ceremonies
Programme
Scenes from "Alceste"........................Gluck
Ceremonies Dedicating the Music Hall
Festival Ode............................Otto Singer
Symphony No. 3, "Eroica," op. 55........Beethoven

On this occasion the place of honor on the programme was given to the composition of an American musician, Otto Singer, who was at that time the Cincinnati Chorus Director, and had been commissioned to compose a work for chorus and orchestra suitable to the event. It is needless to say that a festival around which so many interests gathered was successful beyond any of its predecessors. Artistically its standard was higher, and one of its programmes was made memorable by the first performance Thomas gave of Berlioz' "Romeo and Juliet" Symphony entire. He had often given movements from this difficult work, but had never before given it complete. A few months later he was asked to give his opinion on Berlioz as a composer, and his answer was as follows:

CINCINNATI, *Dec.* 22, 1878.

Dear Madame:

You ask for my opinion in regard to the standing of Berlioz as a composer, and the increasing interest shown in his works. I will give it to you—take it for what it is worth.

Berlioz had not enough creative power, and was not productive enough to be called a genius. But he was very highly gifted and deserves admiration and recognition for his ability and truthful aim. Like Liszt, he is a branch of the tree of which Bach and Beethoven form the trunk. His works are over-rated by some as well as under-rated by others, through ignorance. His scores are sealed books to all but a few, and the musicians who can hear his complicated scores in their minds, with the aid of eyes alone, are not many. To produce his works satisfactorily requires a band of virtuosi, and a conductor who is also a virtuoso on that greatest and most wonderful of all modern instruments, the orchestra. The first it is possible to procure with money, the second is nearly as rare an appearance as was Berlioz himself.

The greatest masters made their deepest impressions with simple means, and even inferior orchestral material; but Berlioz needs and demands masses and virtuosi in order to be effective. If I am right in this you will understand why Berlioz can never be a popular composer.

"Romeo and Juliet" is not a symphony in the sense of the masters, nor is it a development of the form we received from Haydn and Mozart, as is the case with Beethoven, from his third to his ninth symphony. A better designation for the "symphonies" of Berlioz would be "Music for the concert hall, written to scenes from 'Romeo and Juliet,' 'Childe Harold,' etc." His Cantata of "Faust" is likewise nothing but scenes or pictures, strung together, and is inferior to the two first named works.

With Berlioz it was a matter of ambition to write music. He wrote with effort and required a subject for inspiration. To the great masters, Haydn, Mozart, Beethoven, and the rest, it was a necessity to compose, and they needed no outward influence. Music was simply a language to them in which they could express that which they could not say in any other way. They were born musicians. Berlioz will occasionally receive a revival, orchestra permitting, for the sake of novelty and variety in our concert programmes, but a few repetitions of a work do not signify "popularity."

Very truly yours,
THEODORE THOMAS.

After the close of the festival, Thomas returned to New York, and again gave a long season of Summer Night Concerts, this time in Gilmore's Garden. The programmes of this season do not compare in artistic worth to those of the last Central Park Garden season of two years previous. The old summer night audience had apparently evaporated, and a new and less cultivated one had taken its place. It must have been terribly tedious to Thomas to come back from the triumph and exaltation of a series of great festival performances, and go to work grinding out "popular programmes" every night for the masses, and it is no wonder that he often alluded contemptuously to this class of performances, as "shop concerts." Nevertheless he did not allow himself to slight the performance of even the musical trifles of which they were so largely composed, but gave infinite care to the preparation of every number that he played, and would not permit the least slovenliness in their execution. He was especially particular in regard to the Strauss waltzes, which he gave with inimitable grace and a wonderful swaying rhythm. Someone once asked him how he managed to impart such vitality and lightness to these dances, and he replied: "Have you never noticed that I always beat the first stroke of the rhythm up instead of down? You cannot put the life and continuous motion of the dance into a piece of music, if you knock the poor tune down at the beginning of every measure."

And now a great and unexpected change came into the life of Thomas. The president of the Cincinnati Festival Association was Colonel George Ward Nichols, and toward the end of July Thomas received the following letters from him, which explain themselves:

CINCINNATI, *July 22, 1878.*

Dear Mr. Thomas:

For a long time I have thought over a scheme for the establishment of a College of Music in this city with you as its Musical Director. If an arrangement at not too great cost can be made with you, I believe we can have a school of music which will not be inferior to those so celebrated in Europe. We have Otto Singer and can have Whiting and other professors who will give it distinction.

My plan would be to lay out a practical and not too costly scheme, and at once obtain a sound financial backing and go ahead. I would begin next fall as early as practicable. I think we could have the Music Hall with eight or ten rooms.

Are you not tired of carrying the weight of that orchestra? Will you not accept the opportunity of firmly fixing yourself for life in a position which you can if you choose make distinguished and successful?

I wish you to give this subject serious thought and answer me as soon as you can.

Yours truly,
GEORGE WARD NICHOLS.

CINCINNATI, July 29, 1878.

Dear Mr. Thomas:

I wrote you last week asking you to take the Directorship of a musical college which I propose to establish in this city, yet I write again because I have within a few days thought and done a great deal about the matter. It is impossible in a letter to say what I hope and believe may be done here. Of course we can build up a school as complete and efficient as any in Europe. We are geographically well placed. Living is very cheap here. We shall have the Music Hall building for the college. All we require is a staff of first rate professors, a director like yourself, and a good business management. I hope you can widen the school so as to make it a school for orchestra as well as for other branches of musical instruction. With the number of good musicians here you would have an orchestra you would not be ashamed of. Just how much of your Eastern life and work you could keep is a matter for consideration. You are strongly wedded to New York and your reputation is more or less identified with it, but you may be sure that in Cincinnati we shall contend for musical supremacy. We will make this the musical center of the United States, you can wield as strong an influence here. . . . I want you to come here and work with me to organize *a complete and brilliant musical university*. If you can't come I will go to Germany for Raff, Joachim, or some other big fish whose name and experience will give us the prestige which assists success. But I know you can and ought to come. Your life as a conductor of daily concerts is at best a precarious one. . . . This sort of life is killing you. You ought not to be subject any longer to that daily grind. You ought to place yourself in a permanent position where you can have a fixed salary and an honorable station. . . . I have talked this thing over with Shillito, Longworth, and other strong men, and they will back me up financially.

Yours truly,
GEORGE WARD NICHOLS.

CINCINNATI, *Aug.* 2, 1878.

Dear Mr. Thomas:

Your letter of the 29th came to-day. It is very near what I expected you would say. I feel the force of your objections to leaving New York from the artistic point of view . . . but you would be a more influential and useful man at the head of a great college of music than simply as a leader of an orchestra in New York. And if this scheme becomes what I hope, you can have a great orchestra and take it where you please, provided you are not gone *too* long. In saying this I leave out the operatic part of your hopes and desires, and also that part which includes a career in Europe. In my judgment both of these involve too much time and risk to be practicable. In asking you to come to Cincinnati I am not acting upon a hasty impulse, but upon a long thought of and well matured scheme. If the scope of this scheme was not large, important, imposing, I would not undertake it. The conservatories of Europe have men of eminence at their head. We could make this the best and most celebrated in the world. . . . All this I am saying from the artistic point of view, now for the practical. You would not be expected to play in quartette or give singing lessons. You would be the Director of a College of Music with a faculty of six or ten persons, with assistants and teachers celebrated in their several specialties. You would have a fixed income of say from $8,000 to $10,000 a year guaranteed to you for five or more years. . . .

Now there are several questions which remain in doubt. Probably for the above amount we should expect you to lead the orchestra. If it became an orchestra such as you could travel with, how much time would be allowed you outside of Cincinnati? Would it be well for you to calculate on holding on to any of your New York interests? If you did what difference would it make in your salary?

Write me in reply at once as I shall go East in about two weeks and I wish to complete the financial basis before I go away.

Yours truly,
GEORGE WARD NICHOLS.

These informal letters of Colonel Nichols were followed a few days later by an official invitation of the same nature, signed by twenty-two eminent Cincinnati men. It read as follows:

CINCINNATI, *August* 16, 1878.

MR. THEODORE THOMAS.

Dear Sir:

The undersigned citizens of Cincinnati, on the part of the College of Music, cordially invite you, at the earliest possible date, to make your residence in this city and accept the Musical Directorship of the College. It is proposed to establish an institution for musical education upon the scale of the most important of those of a similar character in Europe: to employ the highest class of professors, to organize a full orchestra with a school for orchestra and chorus, and to give concerts.

This city has superior advantages for the success of this project. We have the new Music Hall where the College will be held, and the great organ offers special attractions. Our community is cultivated in music, living is cheap and comfortable here.

In this invitation we recognize your special fitness for a trust so important, and believe that if you accept you will be taking another step forward in the noble work of musical education to which your life has been so successfully devoted.

Signed:

REUBEN R. SPRINGER,
G. K. SCHOENBERGER,
W. H. ANDREWS,
JOSEPH LONGWORTH,
ROBERT MITCHELL,
RUFUS KING,
JOHN SHILLITO,
DAVID SINTON,
WILLIAM RESOR, JR.,
C. H. GOULD,
JOSEPH KINSEY,

GORDON SHILLITO,
R. F. LEAMAN,
J. B. RESOR,
A. HOWARD HINKLE,
JULIUS DEXTER,
M. E. INGALLS,
GEO. WARD NICHOLS,
PETER RUDOLPH NEFF,
LAWRENCE MAXWELL, JR.,
JACOB BURNET, JR.,
CHARLES SHORT.

To this letter Thomas immediately sent an affirmative reply, without having consulted any of his friends, or, in reality, given the matter the careful consideration himself that so important a step should have received. But he was worn out with his long struggle against adversity; and the thought of being free from financial responsibility in the maintenance of his orchestra, and of having a chance to make the money to clear himself of debt and to carry out his long-cherished educational schemes, was so alluring that he accepted, without hesitation, by the return mail, in the following letter:

NEW YORK, *Aug.* 20, 1878.

MESSRS. REUBEN R. SPRINGER, JOSEPH LONGWORTH, AND
    OTHERS.

Gentlemen:

I acknowledge with satisfaction the receipt of your note of the 16th instant, inviting me to make my home in Cincinnati and accept the musical direction of the College of Music. I accept your invitation with a full sense of the importance of the trust.

This is a step in the right direction and Cincinnati is the right place to begin. We want a concentration of professional talent and methodical training, such as we have in other branches of education, and a musical atmosphere. The formation of a college such as you propose realizes one of my fondest hopes, and I shall work hard to make it superior in all branches of musical education.

The faculty must consist of professors eminent in their departments of instruction. With the assistance of a complete orchestra we shall have the professional talent which can teach the use of all orchestral instruments. I am ready to begin all this work at once, and advise that the college be opened during the coming autumn.

Within a few days I shall forward to the Board of Directors a preliminary plan of the course of instruction to be adopted.

With much respect, yours,

THEODORE THOMAS.

Two days after the sending of this letter, Colonel Nichols arrived in New York with a five-year contract for Thomas to sign, drawn up by the new Board of Directors, Messrs. Nichols, Neff, Burnet, Shillito, and Springer. It was as follows:

MEMORANDUM OF AGREEMENT, made this second day of August 1878, by and between the Cincinnati College of Music, a corporation created by and existing under the laws of Ohio, of the first part, and Theodore Thomas, at present of the city of New York, of the second part, witnesseth:

I. The said College engages the services of the said Thomas as its Musical Director for the period beginning with the seventh day of October 1878, and ending with the thirtieth day of September 1883.

II. During the said period the said Thomas shall make his residence in, or in the immediate vicinity of Cincinnati, and shall be in the city and ready to enter upon the performance of his duties by the said seventh day of October next.

III. During the said period the said Thomas shall be Musical Director of the College. The several professors and instructors that shall or may be engaged by the College shall be appointed only upon his nomination. He shall organize and conduct such orchestra as shall or may be established under the direction of the College. He shall act as conductor at all concerts or performances that shall or may be given under the direction of the College. Whatever use shall be made during the said period of the musical library heretofore used by him shall be without charge.

IV. During the said period the said Thomas shall give his entire professional services solely to the said College. He shall, however, be entitled to an annual vacation of at least six weeks, to be taken at such period or periods as shall accord with the College vacation.

V. With the consent of the College, evidenced in writing, signed by one of its executive officers, the said Thomas may engage to act as conductor of an orchestra that may perform, or as Director of musical performances that may be given, not under the direction of the College; but in every such instance he shall account to and pay over to the said College *twenty per cent.* of the compensation that shall be received by him therefor.

VI. During the said period in consideration of the services hereinbefore mentioned, the said College shall pay to the said Thomas the annual compensation of ten thousand dollars, payable on the first day of each and every month in equal monthly instalments.

(Signed)

GEORGE WARD NICHOLS, *President.*
THEODORE THOMAS.

This contract was drawn up by business men on the simple business principle of getting the maximum of service at the minimum of compensation. No doubt the Directors of the new institution meant well and planned to do something fine, but subsequent events showed that they had, from the start, only the vaguest conception of what a musical institution of the caliber they were negotiating with Thomas to organize, really was, or what it would require in either money, ability, or regulations. They probably did not realize, also, what a hard bargain their contract drove with Thomas. Divested of its legal phraseology it bound him to organize a great institution of learning, to select its instructors, plan all the details of its courses of study, and conduct all the ensemble concerts of its students. In addition to these duties, which were sufficient in themselves to have absorbed the entire time of the Musical Director, the contract bound him to assemble and train a symphony orchestra, outside of the College, and conduct all of its concerts. He was also to furnish all of its music at his own expense, as well as to pay one-fifth of his private earnings into the College treasury. Thomas, however, did not worry over the terms of his contract, for he knew that as soon as he had had time to perfect his Cincinnati orchestra he would be able to fill all his vacations with lucrative concert tours, and counted on these, and other engagements, to bring him in enough money to pay his debts, which was what he was chiefly concerned about at that time.

The preliminaries of the Cincinnati engagement having been thus satisfactorily settled, it only remained for Thomas and his family to pack their *lares* and *penates,* and start for their new home in the Western city. Arrived there, a pleasant house was rented in the suburb of Walnut Hills, and Thomas immediately entered with enthusiasm into the new work he had undertaken.

In order to understand subsequent events, it is necessary that the reader should first have a clear idea of what Thomas meant by the term " Musical University," of his designs for such an institution, and the reasons why he considered its creation of vital importance to the musical life of America. He has left two little manuscripts behind him, written at different times, which embody briefly his ideas on these points, and which can be appropriately inserted here:

ON THE NEED OF A MUSICAL UNIVERSITY IN AMERICA

BY THEODORE THOMAS

Music as an art is very little understood in America, comparatively little attention is paid to it by the intellectual classes of the people, and others are attracted to it merely for its emotional or social qualities. And yet a great deal of money is spent in this country for music every year. Costly performances are given, many people are professionally engaged in it and many of our young people are sent to foreign lands to study—often at the greatest sacrifice, not only pecuniarily, but morally. American teachers know well the dangers of sending young people, especially women, to Europe to study music, but no other course is open to them. Not because one cannot learn to play an instrument, or master the science of music in America, but because the atmosphere of an educational institution free from the "make-it-pay" influence is lacking. An institution where the student will meet others of ability superior to his own, join classes where it will require his utmost effort to excel and where he will be guided by superior minds. Where, in short, he may receive some intellectual training, and be given mental food prepared by persons of experience who know what he and the world want.

All of this he can find only in Europe. Nevertheless how unsatisfactory is the result, for, nine times out of ten, he returns from Europe unfit for any practical work at home, because he has stayed away long enough to be out of sympathy with his own country, but not long enough to have gone much beyond the rudiments of his art. The result is disappointment and failure, not because of lack of talent or perseverance on his part, but because the conditions and demands of the two continents differ, and the American public does not esteem art as he has learned to esteem it, is not in touch with him and does not allow him to practice it in accordance with his true ideals.

That, in spite of the many good concerts given every year in America, the musical standards here are undeniably low, can be seen by the class of music used in the churches and theaters, as well as by the tone of much of our press criticism. In the churches, surely, one would expect that nothing of an inferior nature would be tolerated, especially when one considers how much good music has been composed for church purposes. But the standard ordinarily reached in the music of our churches does not go much beyond sentimentality, and is generally out of place and without anything elevated in its character. Perhaps the church music committees imagine, like the ancient Egyptians, that music descends from heaven—only they should look for it somewhere else than in the

works of third and fourth rate composers, and find some
better way of performing it than through the medium
of the customary ill-blended quartette of mixed voices,
or the average choir of badly-trained boys.   I can see
no difference between this and the ordinary third-rate
concert given with the sole object of amusing the listener
and taking in as much money as possible at the door.   In
the churches it is certainly not right to cater to the en-
tertainment of the congregation, and if the object of
church music is to please the ear rather than to elevate the
soul, then no one should wonder at the waning influence
of the church to-day.

As for the theater orchestras, their quality is an insult
to any cultivated mind.

Again, we may estimate our musical standard in
America by our critics.   Before a man is competent to
criticise art he must first be an expert in some branch of
that art, and have had enough experience in his specialty
to transpose—so to speak—his point of view to all the
rest.   Secondly, he must have a broad education to enable
him to be just, and finally he must have unbounded love
for and faith in his art, in order to remain honest.
Theory alone is one thing, but practice quite another,
and it is safe to say that with but a few exceptions our
newspaper critics have not learned their technic or been
properly prepared for this field.   I do not mean to say
that no sincere musical work is done in America, on the
contrary, we have many earnest musicians, and a number
of able critics; but I speak now of the general average,
the rank and file, of which the standard is deplorably low.
Nor can it be otherwise so long as we have not a single
endowed musical institution which can be regarded as
on the same plane with our great universities, nor any
well furnished public library of music and works on music

for reference. Every European country has found it necessary to have such musical colleges, in order, first, to shape the taste of the people, and afterwards to emancipate them from foreign influences and develop national characteristics. America has, as yet, been too young to see the pressing need of such an institution, but it will come in time.

A PLAN FOR A MUSICAL UNIVERSITY

This institution, which I have called a "University" for lack of a better term, should not be a school for beginners, for there are many excellent schools and conservatories already established which are well equipped for the training of amateurs. It should be a school for the training of professionals in the higher branches of music, and should have an endowment sufficient to enable its Board of Directors to conduct it without relying upon the income received from tuition fees for its financial support, and to offer to its students every facility for the broadest training in all departments of art. It should take only such students as are able to pass its examinations, and agree to remain for a sufficient number of years to take its full course.

Executive musicians could here be trained for solo or orchestral work, composers could learn every necessary detail of the art of expressing their musical creations, and teachers could acquire the most approved methods of imparting instruction. Nor would the work in the classroom be the only advantage offered to the students, but they would also receive a constant training in public performance. Those who were training for an orchestral career would be united into a students' orchestra, and those training for solo work would fill the rôles of soloists. The two together would perform in frequent exhibition concerts, on the programmes of which the works of those who were studying composition would find a place. In like manner solo and chorus singers would be trained.

This constant exhibition before invited audiences would stimulate in the highest degree the exertions of the students, and help them to attain, while still in the class-room, the individuality, self-control, and concert style which must now all be learned after the young artist is formally before the public and under the lash of criticism.

In connection with the institution, a permanent symphony orchestra should be maintained, but under a separate endowment. The musicians constituting this orchestra should be the best obtainable in the world; and should not only belong to the orchestra, but should be the instructors of their several instruments in the university. The double engagement thus offered would solve the most serious of the problems connected with the maintenance of both institutions. One business management and one building would serve for both, and thereby the university would be saved the expenses of business management, while the orchestra would be saved the rent of halls and offices. The additional income and prolonged engagement of the orchestra musicians as instructors in the university, would obviate the necessity of sending the orchestra out of town on concert tours, or taking inferior engagements during the summer season. For this reason the very finest talent could be secured—for the most difficult problem in the life of the orchestral musician is to find artistic employment during the summer—and the standard of instruction and executive work in the two institutions would be of the very highest.

Under ordinary circumstances a university must provide for its professors a sufficient salary to pay for their whole time; but by taking them from the orchestra it would be responsible only in proportion to the actual amount of service required of them, which would result in a very great saving on the salaries of many of its faculty.

In short the two institutions would work together and supplement each other in many ways, and create, in combination, an art institution of the highest order, which would exert an incalculable influence in the promotion of musical culture throughout America.

It was with these plans and ideals in his mind that Thomas started his work in the Cincinnati College of Music. But it was not very long before he discovered that they were not, by any means, the plans and ideals of Mr. Nichols and the Board, who, on their part, saw the institution from a very different point of view. In their negotiations with Thomas they had, throughout, spoken of the proposed college as a " Musical University," of the standard of the best European institutions of the kind. But when it came to working it out practically, what they really had in mind was only a good conservatory, such as Tourgée had already founded in Boston. They had raised no endowment sufficient for the maintenance of a scheme of such magnitude as a university, a chorus, and a symphony orchestra, and when Thomas began the work of creating the art institution he had been engaged to organize, he found the means at his command absurdly inadequate for the purpose, and that the Directors even expected it to pay its own way—something no " university," musical or otherwise, ever did, or could do.

It must have been a keen disappointment to him when he realized this, but he did not allow himself to be discouraged, but simply changed his plans, and instead of springing his musical university upon the world full-fledged, as he had intended, decided to begin with a good school and develop it gradually into the higher class of institution, believing that the money would be forthcoming when the public-spirited men of Cincinnati should see what the scope and importance of the college might become under favorable auspices.

The labors of Thomas during his first season in Cincinnati (1878-79) might well be called herculean, for he not only faithfully fulfilled the terms of his contract, but also taught certain classes, organized and held frequent rehearsals with a college chorus and trained a string quartette, in which he himself played the first violin, and which gave a series of twelve concerts during the winter. Outside of the college he gave, with its professional orchestra, a series of twenty-four Symphony Concerts, and also attended to the regular work of the May Festival Association, such as rehearsing with its chorus at frequent intervals, supervising its work in general, and making all the other preliminary arrangements for the festival of 1880. Once a month he spent a week in New York, rehearsing for, and conducting, the concerts of the Brooklyn Philharmonic Society, but this was the only out-of-town engagement which he was able to fill during this busy year. When the summer came, instead of resting in his vacation time, he conducted a long series of Summer Night Concerts at the Highland House.

But, arduous though these labors were, they were nevertheless easy in comparison with the life of incessant traveling which had hitherto been his lot, and the work he was now engaged in was very interesting to him. Thomas had an essentially creative mind, and he was never so happy as when he was planning and executing some colossal musical undertaking. In Cincinnati he hoped to build up a truly great institution of art, as well as a perfect chorus and symphony orchestra, and to make the city the musical Mecca of America. With such a vast scheme as this for his ultimate goal he simply gloried in the work involved in its achievement.

CHAPTER IX

1878-1880

OUTLINE OF THOMAS' METHODS OF WORK IN THE CINCINNATI COLLEGE OF MUSIC—TROUBLE DEVELOPS BETWEEN THOMAS AND THE PRESIDENT OF THE COLLEGE—THOMAS RESIGNS FROM THE COLLEGE—THE MAY FESTIVAL OF 1880

HAVING thus seen what Thomas had in mind as the final development of the Cincinnati College of Music, let us examine his work there in detail, and see in how far he was able to carry out his work there in detail, and see in how far he was able to carry out his plans, and what was actually accomplished under his brief régime of eighteen months.

It might have been expected that, as Thomas was himself an instrumentalist and conductor of orchestra, he would have begun the work of the College on instrumental, rather than on vocal lines. But this was not the case, and, on the contrary, his first months were devoted chiefly to organizing the various vocal departments in the most thorough manner. It was his theory that the voice, being easier than an instrument for a beginner to use, should be substituted for an instrument in teaching beginners to acquire an elementary knowledge of certain important points which are fundamental to all music, whether vocal or instrumental. With this idea in mind he organized chorus classes, which all the students of the College were obliged to attend, irrespective of their specialties, and in these classes they were instructed in pitch, tone quality, time, accent, rhythm, musical expression, etc.; also to read at sight, to sound a given tone without the help of an instrument, to give proper light and shade, and to understand the elements of harmony. In short, all necessary theoretical knowledge was imparted here, in order that the pupils might give their whole time and attention to the technical part when with a teacher for special study.

After the chorus classes, which all the students were obliged to attend, came the vocalization classes, for the singers only. These classes were open, not only to all the vocal students of the College, but also to such outside singers as had the necessary qualifications for admission. Here the work began with simple exercises for placing the voice, after which the students were carried forward gradually to the more difficult feats of vocalization, flexibility, and velocity, and were carefully drilled in pitch, intonation, time, light and shade, etc. These classes were designed to prepare the voices for work of a still more special character.

The third vocal department was the College Choir, which was a small, but very highly-trained chorus for concert purposes. This Choir was open to singers both within and without the College;

it was organized early in January, 1879, and as soon as its membership had been selected, Thomas sent the following circular letter to each of the singers:

CINCINNATI, *Jan.*, 1879.

To THE MEMBERS OF THE COLLEGE CHOIR,

Ladies and Gentlemen:

I desire to address the members of the Choir, and to impress upon their attention and their memories several important considerations. The object of the organization of this Choir is to cultivate chorus singing with a view to instruct the singer in the science of music, develop the voice, and thus produce, in a more perfect way, choral works.

The conditions required to reach this object are: ability in the singers to sing equally well, as far as possible, a harmonious balance of the parts, and the aim of a high standard. All of this can be acquired only by thorough study and cultivation.

The Choir must necessarily be in the beginning crude and misshapen, and the first step is to model it; by careful, painstaking work to obtain from each member the best he can do, and then equalize the whole. To do this effectively I propose to begin with elementary instruction in music. This exercise may with many be a recapitulation of their former studies, but even with them it is necessary.

The exercises will be as follows: 1. Interval exercises. 2. Knowledge of Chords. 3. Harmonic changes. 4. Modulation. 5. Rules and exercises for pronunciation. 6. Exercises for flexibility and velocity of the voice, combined with vocal coloring and pronunciation of vowels.

In order to make satisfactory progress we may, at the start, require more than one session a week for vocal exercises. It may be desirable for the women's voices to be practiced separately during the day, and the men's voices separately at night, and then, at the united session, after some general elementary musical instruction, to study a four-part choral work.

There is another subject about which I must speak very plainly. We invite to this Choir only those who are in earnest, who wish to become skilled singers, and who will meet our effort to teach with corresponding effort to learn, and will attend the appointed hours for study and the concerts. A private student in the College who loses a lesson is the chief sufferer, but the neglect of a member of the Choir injures that symmetry which is made by the perfect balance of the parts. Furthermore it is not desirable that singers should join the Choir for a brief period only. The plan of instruction embraces a term of two or three years.

THEODORE THOMAS, *Musical Director.*

It was Thomas' principle that a chorus should be trained to exactly the same thorough musicianship, and with the same attention to detail, as an orchestra. It was for this reason, therefore, that he was so careful that its members should be prepared for their work in the foregoing manner. He was willing to give infinite time and trouble to these preliminary studies in their own proper classes, but when he conducted a concert rehearsal it was another matter. There, he expected every singer to know his technic and to take his part with the same accuracy and perfection as that shown by the orchestra, and he was very severe to any shortcomings in the matter.

A characteristic story is told of one of the first rehearsals of the College Choir, at which Thomas had reprimanded some of the sopranos sharply for inattention. " He treats us as if we were members of his orchestra!" exclaimed an indignant singer to her next neighbor. Thomas overheard the remark and let it pass for the moment, but at the close of the rehearsal, as the performers were leaving the stage, he passed the lady in question and, turning to her, said very quietly, but with that biting sarcasm which those who knew him did not care to excite: " Madame, you will have to sing a great deal better than you do now before I shall treat you as I treat the members of my orchestra!"

In addition to the foregoing classes for ensemble singing, there was, of course, private instruction for those pupils who wished to study solo singing only. Later also, classes were organized for the training of boy choir singers, and others for the instruction of adult church singers. In short, the vocal department of the Cincinnati College of Music was organized in the most thorough and comprehensive manner.

The second department of the College was the orchestra, and for this the various classes were planned on a similar system. Beginners had to join the chorus classes for their elementary theoretical studies, and then were specialized for technical training on their several instruments. Later they were given a thorough course of instruction in harmony, counterpoint, instrumentation, and, in some instances, composition. As soon as they were theoretically and technically ready for ensemble work they were united into orchestral classes, which were described as follows in the College prospectus of the second year:

ORCHESTRA CLASSES. These classes will be carefully organized with the view of teaching those who are studying orchestral instruments how to play in concerted music, and give them that technical and practical instruction which will enable them to enter the orchestra as a profession. It is part of the plan of the College to give every season a series of orchestra and chamber concerts, and this is the first opportunity ever offered in this country to study in an orchestra class, be graduated and then actually to enter the orchestra. In these classes the students will be trained in playing trios, quartettes, and other chamber music. They will also be taught to play the music of symphonies and other works for the full orchestra. These classes will be under the immediate direction of Mr. Thomas.

The remaining departments of the College were such as are to be found in all good music schools, and consisted of Theory, Piano, Organ, History of Music, Lectures on Musical Subjects, Score Playing and Conducting, Languages, Elocution, Concert-room Deportment, Dramatic Expression, etc.

From the foregoing brief outline it will be seen that, although the College of Music could not, as yet, be considered a " University " in any sense of the word, it was nevertheless rapidly being developed on university lines, and it is reasonable to suppose that the man who could achieve such important results in the short period of eighteen months, would eventually have carried it to its logical conclusion, had time, money, and authority been given him. Unfortunately none of these essentials were at his command in the Cincinnati College of Music. But, in spite of the handicap under which he worked, the close of the first season of the College found it a thoroughly organized school, possessing, in addition to the customary departments of such institutions, a chorus of three hundred thoroughly trained voices, a fine string quartette for chamber music, and a symphony orchestra. In short, with these advantages, and the biennial May Festivals, already established, Cincinnati had only to go on as it had begun and it would soon have become, in very truth, the leading musical center of America and one of the foremost in the world.

This inspiring dream was, however, not destined to be realized, and before the first twelve months were over, friction began to develop between Thomas and the President of the College. Thomas had certain personal peculiarities to which everyone who worked in association with him had to get accustomed, before they could cooperate harmoniously together. Knowing himself to be an expert in his art, he took it for granted that when he was engaged to supervise any artistic enterprise it was because its promoters wanted a man of recognized ability to guide them in matters which they did not understand for themselves. Hence he expected that his suggestions would, in the main, be adopted. He was very willing to lay everything before the Board of Directors and modify or alter his designs in any reasonable way which they desired, if it did not affect the artistic standard of the enterprise in hand. But after they had mutually decided upon a course of action and it had been made public, he insisted that it should be carried out to the letter, nor would any persuasion induce him to change even the smallest detail, for he considered it a breach of faith with the public to do so.

The men who were in sympathy with his ideals worked in perfect harmony with him for many years, and found him amenable, reasonable, and easy to deal with. But there were others, like the President and Board of the College, who did not understand him or his methods, and, after putting him nominally in charge of an undertaking, would either not accept his plans, or, what was worse, would accept and advertise them, and then fail to carry them out as agreed. To these he showed himself an ugly customer. President Nichols also often angered him by small interferences, which, as the president and founder of the College, he no doubt thought he had a right to, and which he perhaps considered too unimportant to consult Thomas about. But to Thomas no smallest detail of his work was unimportant. Everything, even to the punctuation marks on his programmes, was thought out and planned with infinite care and accuracy, and to have any change made after it left his hand aroused his bitter resentment. He used to say of himself, " I can be led by a silk thread, but I cannot be hauled by a ship's cable. In all matters but one—art—I am willing to give up my way, but there I am a tyrant."

In his troubles with Mr. Nichols no doubt there were two sides to the controversy, as there generally are, for Mr. Nichols was not working for any selfish aim, but, on the contrary, was trying to found a noble institution in accordance with his lights. But the two men looked at the matter from such widely separated points of view, that it was impossible, in the nature of things, that they should long continue to work together. The idea of Mr. Nichols and the Board of Directors was that the College should be made a self-supporting institution, and be maintained by its tuition fees, on the principle of a private school. To do this it was, of course, necessary to have a very large number of students, and this, in turn, necessitated accepting every student who applied, and for any period for which he wished to come. The idea of Thomas was that the institution should be supported by an endowment, independent of its tuition fees, and that no students should be accepted who could not show themselves to possess real musical talent, or who were unwilling to remain for a full course of study. These were the chief points of difference between Thomas and the Board, but there were many other

less important matters in which Thomas found
that the promises of the prospectus were not being
fulfilled.   Under these circumstances it was characteristic of him to decide, that unless the Board
would make a complete change in the policy of
the College, he would leave, although he had now
arranged his private affairs so satisfactorily that
his combined income from the College, the May
Festival Association, the New York and Brooklyn Philharmonic Societies, and his vacation concert engagements, was large enough to promise
the speedy payment of his burden of debt, and
that, on the other hand, if he left Cincinnati, he
would be in just the same hopeless financial situation as before he came.   This consideration did not
weigh with him for a moment, however, in comparison with what he considered his artistic integrity, and in February, 1880, matters came to
a climax between him and President Nichols, and
he sent the following letter to the chairman of the
Board:

CINCINNATI, *Feb.* 27, 1880.

MR. A. T. GOSHORN, CHAIRMAN OF THE BOARD OF
    DIRECTORS.

Dear Sir:

I am in receipt of your communication of the 25th, en-
closing the report of your committee for my examination.
There are some minor matters of detail concerning the
curriculum and prospectus which will require further consideration.   But there are two matters of fundamental importance, as to one of which my suggestion is disregarded,
and as to the other the report is ambiguous.

In regard to the first instance I am clear that the

school year cannot be divided into more than two terms.

According to regulation No. 2, of your report, the Musical Director is to be charged with and held responsible for the musical conducting of the College.   I am willing to assume this responsibility but I must insist upon being intrusted with the *exclusive* direction of the school in all its departments, reserving to the Board, of course, all questions involving the expenditure of money.   In other words I insist upon occupying that relation to the school which is ordinarily involved in the office of a President of a college, and I expect the Board of Directors and its officers to sustain the relation ordinarily sustained by the Trustees of a college.

Under these conditions, with a curriculum established, and discipline maintained, I have confidence in the prospect of building up a great musical college.   Under any other conditions I consider further effort in that behalf futile, and I therefore desire to know at the earliest day convenient whether my suggestions are acceptable.   If they are, I think it important that the changes which they involve in the office of the College should be made at once. I shall be glad to receive your answer by, say, next Tuesday.

Yours truly,

THEODORE THOMAS.

This letter was no doubt considered rather autocratic in tone, and the Board did not like it very much.   But they were patient with their restive Director and their reply was a request for a fuller explanation of Thomas' understanding of the relations of the president of a university to its Board of Trustees.   This Thomas sent, concluding his letter with the words:

" I assure you that it is my earnest desire to adhere to my contract with the College, in the success of which, under proper organization, I lack no confidence. But you must appreciate that my professional reputation is at stake, and that I cannot in justice to myself consent to continue longer responsible for a school, the direction of which is not confided to me, and am therefore entitled to know, without delay, what will be done. I simply insist on being in fact what I am now only in name, viz., *Director of Music of this College*. That office I am entitled to under my contract, and I decline to act any longer as assistant or associate Director."

Reading between the lines of these letters, the Directors, of course, knew that Thomas had given them a choice between himself and President Nichols, and this placed them in a very embarrassing position. They could not very well ask for the resignation of the man who had founded, and done most of the work of carrying on the business of the College. On the other hand the controversy between Thomas and the College had been blown far and wide over the country, and, even in Cincinnati itself, the chorus of the Musical Festival Association, and most of its directors, had raised such a strong partisanship in behalf of Thomas that there was sure to be a storm of indignation and protest if the Board should take any action which might be construed into an affront to Thomas.

In this dilemma the Board temporized, and sent him a long, rambling epistle, chiefly devoted to a justification of their course in the past, and giving him no definite answer at all on the points at issue. This evasive reply made Thomas very angry, and he cut the matter short without more ado, by sending his resignation to the Board in the following letter:

CINCINNATI, *March* 4, 1880.

To THE BOARD OF DIRECTORS OF THE CINCINNATI
    COLLEGE OF MUSIC.

Gentlemen:

I am in receipt of the letter of your Committee, dated the 2d instant. I regard it as a misrepresentation of my position, and an evasion of the real issue. That position and issue you certainly cannot misunderstand, in view of the communications, written and verbal, which I have had with your Committee and the President of your Board.

I therefore deem all further negotiations useless, and respectfully request you to relieve me from my duties on October 1st, or as soon thereafter as will enable you to secure my successor.

Yours truly,

THEODORE THOMAS.

No doubt the Board were much pleased to have the Gordian knot thus conveniently cut for them; at all events they accepted the resignation of Thomas on the day following its receipt, and not only so, but added that it would be agreeable to them if he take his departure immediately, and without waiting to complete the last six months of his official year. By this time Thomas was as anxious to sever his connection with the College as the Board were to get rid of him, and five weeks later found him a free man once more, and the College of Music happily relieved of the "white elephant" it had unwittingly captured.

However welcome the resignation of Thomas was to the Board of Directors, it came like a bolt out of the blue to the students of the College, and many expressions of affection and regret came to him from them, of which the following is a touching example:

CINCINNATI, *March 5*, 1880.

Dear Mr. Thomas:

Pardon me for addressing you, but I feel that you should know how sad the students of the College feel at the idea of losing you. I think it will be the greatest loss our city has ever met with if you leave us, and the College, in a musical sense, will be no more. . . . It is the students who will feel and know your loss, for everyone thinks kindly of you, and one single word of advice or praise from you is worth more than a volume from anyone else. All I have had to work for has been your praise and commendation, and if that is taken away then everything is gone. There are hundreds in the school who feel just as I do. . . . Please think of us. Who will we have to work for when you are gone? Your resignation has cast a gloom over the heart of everyone who knows you.

X——.

Meantime, while all this trouble had been fulminating and exploding at the College, the May Festival of 1880 had been steadily progressing towards splendid achievement. The chorus, like every body of musicians that ever came under the magnetic baton of Thomas, were his devoted

Mr. Lawrence Maxwell of Cincinnati

partisans, as were also most of the Festival Board
of Directors. When, therefore, the College turned
its back upon him, the festival promoters of all
classes were a solid phalanx in his defense, and
lost no time in testifying their loyalty by accepting the resignation of Mr. Nichols as President of
the Festival Board, and electing Mr. Edmond H.
Pendleton in his place.

From this time till the close of his life, Thomas
never had any unpleasant experiences in Cincinnati. The men with whom he was henceforth associated there were in sympathy with his art ideals
and worked in harmony with him for twenty-five
consecutive years, and together they achieved the
permanent establishment of one of the greatest
art institutions of its kind in the world. Alas!
that of all the great musical projects he started
in Cincinnati, it alone should have been perfected
as he had designed. In speaking of the men
who had carried on the festival work, many years
later, Thomas said, " So long as a community
has men like these to foster and promote its
interests, it need have no concern about the
future."

Amongst the many sincere workers for the
Festival Association were two who deserve more
than a passing mention: W. N. Hobart and Lawrence Maxwell. Mr. Hobart was its president
for many years and never did a president give
more time, thought, or devoted service to an
organization than he. Mr. Maxwell generally
worked in a less conspicuous office, but almost

from the very inception of the Association he was connected with it in one capacity or another, and brought the whole energy of his powerful personality to bear upon its success, guarding its interests with the tenacity of a bull-dog, and guiding its way through storm or calm, with unerring judgment and discretion. Thomas placed unbounded confidence in, not only the business sagacity, but the musical discrimination of this famous lawyer, and rarely rejected his advice in festival matters—perhaps never. Subsequent events showed that this confidence was well founded, for after the death of Thomas, Mr. Maxwell took up the work where he left it, and as president of the association, has continued it to the present writing, without the slightest lowering of the splendid standard which has always been its fundamental characteristic.

Photograph by Mr. John Closs, taken in 1894

A Festival at Cincinnati

CHAPTER X

1880

THOMAS LEAVES CINCINNATI—EUROPEAN TRIP—RETURN TO NEW YORK—IDENTIFIES HIMSELF WITH THE NEW YORK PHILHARMONIC SOCIETY—FORMS NEW YORK AND BROOKLYN CHORAL SOCIETIES—INCEPTION OF NEW YORK AND CHICAGO MUSICAL FESTIVALS OF 1882—HONORARY DEGREE OF DOCTOR OF MUSIC CONFERRED BY YALE UNIVERSITY

THE May Festival of 1880 realized all that its most ardent promoters had hoped for it, and, both in programmes and performance, surpassed anything as yet heard in Cincinnati. Like its predecessors it was also financially successful.

And now Thomas bade adieu to Cincinnati and returned to New York with his family. No doubt they were all very happy to be back in their old home once more—for what New Yorker is ever contented elsewhere?—but there was, nevertheless, an element of sadness and discouragement in their return, for all the high hopes with which Thomas had gone West, and the arduous labors of the last two years had brought him nothing but failure and disappointment, and he returned as poor as he had gone away, with the old load of debt still unpaid and bankruptcy still staring him in the face, and must once more begin life at the bottom of the financial ladder.

Under these circumstances one would have expected him to start at once on the labor of mending his shattered fortunes, but he did nothing of the kind. Instead, he settled his family pleasantly at the seashore, arranged a "nest egg" for his future income, with the New York and Brooklyn Philharmonic Societies, and also for an orchestra with which to give concerts during the coming winter season, and, putting all cares and anxieties out of his mind, went gayly off to Europe for a little rest and refreshment before starting anew on his struggle with the problems of existence.

It was a fortunate trait of Thomas' character that he was always able to command his thoughts and moods at will. He used to say, " I live in the future and hardly know what has gone before." In one sense this was true, for although he had the most retentive memory imaginable, he did not allow himself to dwell upon the past. It seemed as if he kept all past memories locked in some secret safety deposit from which they were only taken when needed for special reference, as occasion required. In the same way he was able to banish from his thoughts, at will, all the people who had offended or injured him, and to cut them off from his life and consciousness as completely as if he had never known them. This was the only form of retaliation he ever indulged in. No matter how great an injury was done him, or how malevolent the enmity of those who hated him, he never retaliated by word or deed beyond the simple ultimatum, " He must not speak to me or come near me again." This was all, and yet, strange to say, the people who were thus banished and ignored seemed to feel it more bitterly than if he had taken some active form of revenge, and could never forget or forgive it.

The short European trip of 1880, like that of fourteen years previous, was devoted entirely to hearing musical performances and meeting musicians. On his first visit to Europe Thomas had gone as a student, to learn from the masters of his art and measure himself by their standards. Now, on the contrary, he went for rest and relaxation, and, a master himself, he measured them in turn by his standards, and, it must be confessed, often found them lacking. As in 1867, he again kept a little diary in which he noted briefly his impressions of men and music, and from it the following extracts are quoted:

London, June 4, 1880. I arrived here this afternoon, and in the evening heard "Lohengrin" in Her Majesty's Theater, Hans Richter conducting. Candidus (Lohengrin) was good for a small theater. Wilson, a milk-and-water gruel. Treneille (Ortrude), good. Richter is a very able conductor, but like all other European conductors, he does not drill his orchestra. The intonation was poor, tone color, precision, and phrasing mediocre, and the whole orchestra, but especially the wind choir, seemed to have no idea of *sostenuto*. The chorus was miserable. And this is the best material in London!

London, June 7. Orchestral concert, Richter conducting. Overture, "Carnaval Roman"; *tempi* the same as mine. Schubert's Unfinished Symphony; *tempi* faster than mine. Saint Saens, Concerto No. 4; the composer at the piano, he is a remarkable artist. " Tristan and Isolde "; go ahead and don't drag! Seventh Symphony, Beethoven; the introduction up to the sixteenth figure was good, after that everything was hurried. The first movement, *Allegretto*, was taken *Vivace*, the second movement began well, but after the first statement it was hurried and was a very mediocre performance in every respect. The last movement was taken faster than I play it, later it was simply hurried to pieces. Richter resembles our Bergmann. He has the same talent and education, but Bergmann had the more refined conception.

London, June 8. " Faust," with Patti as Marguerite. She sings like a bird, enunciation wonderful. The voice is deeper and perhaps fuller than when I last heard it.

London, June 11. Piano Recital by Charles Halle. He is a very good pianist of the old school (Hummel). Madame Norman Neruda, violinist, played with a beautiful, very pure, and good intonation and is absolutely musical. In the evening a Richter concert again. " Faust Symphony," Liszt; *tempi* stiff. The cymbal player was not there, the programme having been changed at the last moment. His part was played by a substitute. He came in seldom and when he did it was wrong! Siegfried Idyl, Wagner; good. I see that I have taken it too slow. Act III " Meistersinger "; very good. When Richter conducts Wagner the performance is a hundred per cent. better. Overture, " Leonore " No. 3; very fast *tempi*, the close very effective.

London, June 17. Sembrich, a young singer, in " Lucia," a light soprano voice, quality and execution both good. On the 14th I heard the ninth and last of the Richter concerts, which ended with the Ninth Symphony of Beethoven. In the first movement he took the *tempi*

the same as mine, execution mediocre. The second movement was very fast, Trio, *alla breve*. Third movement,
tempi the same as mine, execution very bad. Last movement, recitative presto, without tone or expression, the
end of the phrases always very slow, "*Freude schoene
Goetter Funkeln,*" *alla breve*. The rest of the *tempi*
like mine, but always with an inclination to hurry. Richter does not seem to me to stand on his own feet, in spite
of his undoubted ability. What he has learned with
Wagner is fine, but the rest is not much beyond mediocrity.
It appears to me as if he himself had never played any
stringed instrument, for the string choir of his orchestra
played as it would without attracting his attention. No
two of the violinists bowed alike, but each man bowed
as he pleased.

London, June 18. Attended the rehearsal of the Haendel Festival. Very good. The tone was what I have
always expected it would be from a great mass chorus—
immense. Male voices exquisite, especially the basses.
The women's voices were too weak for a good balance,
and the altos were hardly audible. All the *tempi* and
general execution were satisfying to a great extent, in
spite of some shortcomings. It all flowed so quietly and
naturally, especially the chorus and organ, that it was
highly impressive. The double choruses from " Israel in
Egypt," were splendid. At last I have learned the proper
way to perform Haendel. One must come to England to
understand him. It would, I think, be desirable to have a
Haendel cult in all countries. There is nothing in the
world which cannot be criticised, and many things here
also need improvement. Nevertheless, the performance
was generally good enough that one lost sight of all
shortcomings. Costa was the conductor—the best man
for the place.

Here, at last, I find a tradition which realizes my own ideals. Come here, ye modern composers, and learn with what simple means pure music can be made! I am coming to a different conception of things, and believe that music, healthy for the soul, ended with Beethoven. What good does it do to double intervals to such an extent that the original character is lost? And the modern harmonies and harmonic resolutions, which begin with the chord of the Ninth, and end with the chord of the Twenty-fifth, but always without foundation! What is the worth of a building, however richly ornamented, without a foundation? Is not one fresh, healthy kernel worth a long unwholesome *menu*?

Received word from Saint Saens, asking when he could call upon me. In the evening I again saw "Faust," from a big comfortable box, sent me by Mapleson. It was a mish-mash. The soprano I always detested, and the tenor sang as if he had a hot potato in his mouth, but he had a good voice. Arditi conducted. He tried to make a great many holes in the air. I looked at it as one would look at a Punch and Judy show. Impossible for me to stay through the performance.

London, June 19. Attended the concert of Mans, at the Crystal Palace. Thalberg soloist. Orchestra composed of good material.

London, June 21. Received two season tickets for the Haendel Festival with the compliments of the Directors. Attended the performance of the "Messiah," but was much disappointed, after what I had heard at the rehearsal. The chorus was better balanced—probably they were not all present at the rehearsal—the women's voices were stronger, and the altos were supported by a hundred high tenors, which gave the part force and power, but at the expense of tone-quality. The performance as a whole was slipshod. The chorus did not mind the conductor, and he in turn took no notice of them. But they all know their parts so well that they could not get out, even when, as often happened, they were a quarter of a beat apart! All the principal choruses were accompanied by the bass drum and cymbals.

London, June 22. A memorable day for me. During breakfast a Mr. Campbell, whom I once met in Boston, called on me with a direct offer from the London Philharmonic Society. He wished to know if I would be willing to come to London and take the conductorship of the Philharmonic orchestra. I have made an appointment for to-morrow to lunch with some of the directors, and also some of the musicians. Campbell tells me that London needs a man to take charge of musical affairs in general, and that if I will take the position it is mine. It seems that he went several times, in Boston and New York, two years ago, to hear my conducting of such works as the " Faust Symphony " of Liszt.

London, June 23. I dined with Mr. Campbell as arranged, and met several of the Philharmonic Directors and others. A very pleasant occasion, and we talked a good deal about the Philharmonic offer. It certainly looks like a good opening for me.

Weimar, June 29. I arrived here at seven this evening, went at once to the Hotel Erdprinzen, and afterwards sent my card to Liszt. To-morrow Zinzer will join me and we will go to Leipsig together.

So this is Weimar! Here I think one must have to die of good health! It is very nice, but a little *too* quiet for me, and does not come up to my expectations. Now I am really in Germany—but, oh, how far I am from home! Yes, here one can compose. If I lived here, I believe I should compose also.

Weimar, June 30. A memorable day. Liszt received me in his private room, and alone. At first I instinctively looked *up* to meet his eye, and could hardly believe my own when I found myself as tall as he—perhaps a half an inch difference! His geniality was beyond all expression, and this meeting with him was, in itself, worth the journey from New York.

I meant to have taken my leave after a short call, but Liszt persuaded me to stay, and urgently requested me to remain during the evening and meet the Grand Duke of Weimar, and a party of about twelve others. But I did not accept the invitation, although Liszt was good enough to include also my friend Zinzer. No, there is no use to stay here and listen to the piano-klinking of pupils, for probably Liszt would not play himself. Besides, I do not want to have the impression he made on me this morning spoiled. He was too courteous for me to feel that I could ask him to play if he did not offer to do so, for I think he would have played without my asking him if he had been in the mood.

After my call, he accompanied me not only downstairs but even through the garden by a private way, to my hotel. I smoked a light German cigar which he gave me, remarking, " Beckstein always sends me cigars; I do not smoke Havana cigars because they are too expensive." As we walked to the hotel it began to rain and I expected to see Liszt turn back, but he continued to walk with me, unconscious of the storm. " You do not seem to mind the weather," I exclaimed. Liszt laughed and replied, " I never take notice of that which takes no notice of me! "

Now I am very glad to have seen the giant, for the world looks so much the smaller to me.

Leipsig, July 1. This morning a pleasant visit with

Raff, who was very courteous to me, and cordial. He introduced me to his wife and they are to dine with me to-night.

Berlin, July 4. This morning, at the invitation of Joachim, I went to his house to hear his famous String Quartette in Chamber music, and had a very interesting experience. They played for me three of the Schumann Quartettes, and Joachim showed me the original manuscripts. Many changes had been made in them by Schumann himself—very interesting.

The Trio from the Scherzo of the First Quartette has to be played much faster than the metronome indicates, and at the same time faster than the Scherzo proper. This passage,

must be played staccato, in one bow, by all the instruments. The second Quartette starts with a stringendo. The introduction to the first Quartette,

has to be played, according to Schumann's own directions, with a separate bow for each note. The same rule refers to the variations. The *tempi* in general are fast. The third Quartette, Joachim took in the same *tempi* as mine, except, perhaps, the last movement, which he took a little faster. I think the movement loses thereby a little of its effectiveness. In the first and second Quartettes his *tempi* were the same as mine, except in the last movements, which here were a little slower. Joachim plays everything with a very supple bow.

Berlin, July 11. Visited the Conservatory, where I heard an examination which took place at eleven o'clock in the Odeon Hall. Later Levi invited me to luncheon. In the evening I heard " Tristan and Isolde "—disappointed—I do not believe this music will ever be popular.

Berlin, July 15. Heard Mozart's " Magic Flute." The scenery was extra fine, orchestra mediocre, and the singers bad. I do not believe that opera with German singers would be a possibility in New York. The only chance of success for good operatic performances in America would be opera with American singers, it seems to me.

Berlin, July 23. I have heard, since the last entry, the " Nibelungen," " Meistersinger," and " Tannhaeuser." Splendid scenery and poor performances as usual. Also " Aida " ; in the last named the orchestra was good again. I have engaged my passage for home on the 31st.

As may be gathered from the foregoing extracts from his journal, Thomas had many pleasant experiences during this short European sojourn. And although he criticised sharply the inferior technical standards of European orchestral and operatic performances, he was, nevertheless, always keenly on the watch for any hints or suggestions which seemed authoritative enough to either correct or confirm his own interpretations. In America his professional life was such an isolated one that it was a rare treat for him to come into close personal touch with the masterminds of his art, especially Liszt, Joachim, Saint-Saëns, and others. Wagner he was to have met in Weimar, but something interfered, and before Thomas made another visit to Europe Wagner died. Perhaps, however, it was just as well that they did not meet personally, for Thomas never quite forgave Wagner for his action in regard to the Centennial March, and did not feel very cordially towards him, though he recognized him as the greatest musical genius of his day, and for many years rarely gave a concert without playing some of his music on the programme.

The offer of the London Philharmonic Society, coming as it did at the moment when Thomas had been so little appreciated or understood in the Cincinnati College of Music, was dazzling. Writing about it to his friend, Lawrence Maxwell, he said:

" This morning the conductorship of the London Philharmonic Society was offered to me. I have a meeting with the Directors to-morrow, and also with others regarding choral work. In plain words, the most influential musicians of London offer me everything—Philharmonic concerts and Costa's work besides, for they tell me he is too old, and must give up. It seems curious that this should come to me just now, but there are a few men here who know me from my Boston work, and this thing seems to have been decided upon ever since I left New York for Cincinnati. What will come of it I do not know yet; it is too new to me. I do not want to leave America—at the same time, if you could see how grateful the British people are for good music, and how enthusiastic, you would certainly think it worth my consideration."

In the end Thomas refused this brilliant offer, although it must have cost him a hard sacrifice to do so. But two strong influences drew him back

to America. The first was patriotism towards the
land of his adoption, and the desire to complete the
work he had been identified with there for so
many years. The second, his unalterable determination to pay his heavy burden of debt, for in
those days European conductors did not make the
large incomes they now command, and this he
could only hope to accomplish by remaining in this
country. So he renounced the temptation and
turned his face resolutely toward America once
more, and, in spite of the fact that his outlook
was so uncertain, both artistically and financially,
he was apparently as cheerful and as confident of
success as if he had never known the meaning of
the word failure in his life!

His many old friends in New York gave him a
royal welcome on his arrival, and offers of
concert engagements poured in upon him from
all sides. Hardly had he landed from the steamer
when he was called upon by the usual host of
newspaper reporters, and amongst them one from
the *Herald,* who found him in such a genial
mood and reported what he said so admirably,
that I cannot give a better sketch of the Thomas
of that day, of his plans for the future, and his
critical estimates of musical matters in Europe
and America than by quoting from his article as
follows:

" And so, Mr. Thomas, you are back in New York," the
interview began. " Are you going to make your home
here again? "

"Yes," he replied earnestly, and in a very cheery, pleasant tone. "Yes, I intend to make New York my home after this. I have been about the world somewhat, with varying experiences, pleasant and otherwise. New York was long my home and I believe that there is no place like home after all. The place, the people, the associations are all congenial, and here I desire to stay. For years I have labored here in the cause of musical art—many, many years—and have seen growing under my hands, and those of others interested in the like work, the result of our patient toil. Ah! very few can realize what the struggle of twenty years ago was. Then the people here knew little about classic music, and the presentation of programmes of the best class met with little or no recognition. It was disheartening work to play again and again before small, unappreciative audiences, who seemed to care nothing for the end we had in view, and who little knew the privations we were subjected to in order to keep together the band of musicians we had gathered here. But the awakening came at last, if slowly, and to-day, from small beginnings, the musical public of New York has grown to grand proportions, and its sense of critical judgment has become so keen that this city stands now prominently, if not first, among the musical cities of the world. There is a great future here in art."

"There is a report here, Mr. Thomas, that you have been engaged to give concerts at Barnum's Museum, in its new building; is this so?" said the reporter.

"Oh, dear, no!" replied the musician. "I did not conclude any business arrangements of any kind while I was in Europe, although it is true that Mr. Barnum's representative did write to me in regard to such an engagement. What did I think of it? Well, leaving myself out of the question, and looking at the matter as a mere musical and business proposition, I do not think it is a bad one. It would depend altogether upon how much music and how much museum were to be combined. I understand that there is to be on the top floor of the new building an immense tropical garden under a glass roof, with a horticultural display of great beauty and elegance. In such surroundings I can well understand the success of a series of concerts of a high standard. But on the ground floor of the building there are to be giants, dwarfs, Circassian beauties, and roaring lions. Here a programme of classic music would be decidedly out of place. The serious question is how near to the tropical garden, and how far from the roaring lions, would the band be? And would we be classed as a cage of wild animals or a flower show? Seriously, however, as I have said, the scheme might be practical if the concerts were kept entirely distinct from the show, and only the highest class of performances given."

"While you were in Europe, Mr. Thomas, you no doubt heard a number of the famous artists and musical organizations of the day," continued the reporter. "Will you tell me how you think our season and our musical culture compares with that of London?"

"I was amazed to find, after my long absence from Europe," replied Thomas, "that now we are really a long way ahead of London in the matter of critical judgment, as well as in performance. Our programmes are better, our musicians play better, and our people—I speak of New York and Boston especially—listen more intelligently. The enthusiasm of the English audience carries away its judgment completely. I have seen an audience applaud wildly a crude performance of a familiar selection as though its rendering had been perfection. . . .

As for novelties, they are equally far behind, and I have
seen advertised as 'novelties' there compositions which
were actually hackneyed here. It is extraordinary that
so great a metropolis should be so far behind the times.
. . . In Paris I saw 'Aida,' at the Grand Opera House,
with the most sumptuous mounting, and was delighted
with the superb orchestra, the playing of which was mar-
velously good. In Munich I attended various performances of opera. I can best characterize the artistic standard there by saying that the stage-setting seemed to be
considered first, then the orchestra, and last the singers.
. . . Of the great artists I heard, I was most impressed
by Joachim and Saint Saens—the latter is a giant amongst
pianists. But the most delightful hours of all my days,
on this pleasant trip, were those I spent with Liszt. I
stopped for a day in Weimar, and sent my card to Liszt,
who at once sent me, in return, a kindly message of welcome, and begged me to come to him that afternoon. I
did so and was most cordially received by the great master, who at once put me at my ease, and, laying aside
all formality, spoke as though we were old friends rather
than new acquaintances. Two things struck me about
Liszt—his exceeding modesty in referring to himself when
our conversation turned on his place on our American programmes, and his assertion that he was growing old, and
that the world would receive no further compositions from
his pen. These struck me forcibly because one would
have excused even egotism from a man so surrounded all
his life with devoted admirers as Liszt, and, in regard to
the second remark, because the vigorous old man seemed to
be in his mental prime. I do not remember his exact
words, but he spoke very quietly to this effect: 'You are
all very kind to me in America, you place me too often
on your programmes,—I do not look so old, but I feel

very, very old, I shall write no more. My pen is tired and I have done.' "

The only definite engagements which Thomas had in prospect for the winter season of 1880-81, when he started for Europe, were those with the New York and Brooklyn Philharmonic Societies. He had been elected the conductor of the former in May, and in view of his contemplated return to New York, he had decided to identify himself wholly with the Society, believing that the cause of music would be better served if the chief authority were vested in an association of the reputation and influence of the Philharmonic, than in himself alone. Upon receiving notification of his re-election as conductor of the society, therefore, he had sent the Directors the following letter:

NEW YORK, *May* 8, 1880.

TO THE BOARD OF DIRECTORS OF THE PHILHARMONIC
    SOCIETY.

Gentlemen:

It is my intention to identify myself with the Philharmonic Society altogether. I am also willing to say to the Board that I do not mean to give a series of Symphony Concerts myself in New York this year. I am not ready to make this statement to the society at large for the reason that I do not wish to have my plans for the coming year known and discussed as yet. I shall give lighter concerts with a symphony, perhaps, but not a regular series of Symphony Concerts which could have any influence on the Philharmonic series.

Now then, I must live, and the basis of my income must

be the New York and Brooklyn Philharmonic concerts. I
repeat that I am willing to identify myself with the New
York Philharmonic Society, and as I shall have to live in
New York again, I can accept the position of conductor
without any guarantee, but I do not think that twenty
shares are too much to ask for my services under the
circumstances.

Yours very truly,

THEODORE THOMAS.

Hitherto Thomas had received as his remuneration from the New York Philharmonic Society
ten shares of stock, and a sufficient additional sum
to bring his salary up to fifteen hundred dollars.
But he now felt that his services were worth a
larger sum, and decided that the two Philharmonic
Societies could each afford to give him twenty-
five hundred dollars a year. In Brooklyn this
salary was paid as such, but the New York Philharmonic was differently organized, and in asking
for twenty shares, Thomas named the number
which he calculated would yield him about that
amount in dividends, but in doing so he released
the society from any obligation to make good any
deficit in the amount should it fall short of the
expected sum.

The Directors readily agreed to this, but neither
they nor Thomas realized how valuable his work
for the Society was to become, financially, as well
as artistically. During the first two years of his
leadership the dividends went up from eighteen
to one hundred and twenty-three dollars a share.
After that they often reached, and even passed the

two hundred dollar mark. But, although his
twenty shares thus yielded him a far larger sum
than he had expected, he accepted only the
twenty-five hundred dollars, which his contract
had been originally intended to provide, and, year
after year, returned into the treasury of the society, whatever surplus his shares paid him over
and above that amount, as long as he continued
to be its conductor.

Artistically the Philharmonic benefited by its
association with Thomas even more than financially. He not only made its concerts the chief
musical events of the New York season, but he
drew from its ranks his private orchestra, hence
the greater part of its members were assured of
constant engagements at the largest current
salaries, and as it thus came under the exclusive
leadership of Thomas all the year around, it soon
became the most perfect orchestra America had
ever had. In short, he carried out his promise of
identifying himself with the society so thoroughly
that it was hard to say whether the Philharmonic
had annexed him, or he had annexed the Philharmonic. At all events they worked together,
and for the most part harmoniously, as long as
Thomas continued to live in New York, and had
this distinguished band of musicians had as much
money as they had artistic ability, he would never
again have had to leave his home. On his side
Thomas thoroughly appreciated the loyal friendship its members extended to him. He was affectionately known amongst them as " The Old

Man," long before he had even begun to grow old, and if his autocratic ways occasionally aroused some protest from objecting members, they always ended by letting him do as he pleased, and they never had any serious differences of opinion.

Having thus satisfactorily provided an orchestra for future use, Thomas' next step was to organize a chorus. It is probable that he planned to organize in New York regular biennial musical festivals, similar to those of Cincinnati, for he had already started a chorus in Brooklyn, and now he did the same in New York. Each chorus numbered about two hundred singers, and was trained to the very highest point of efficiency. It was his intention to utilize the two choruses separately in orchestral concerts in their own cities, for such works as Beethoven's Ninth Symphony, Brahms' Requiem, etc., and to combine them occasionally in very large choral concerts. With a body of four hundred highly trained singers as a nucleus, a festival chorus of any dimensions could, he knew, be created almost without effort, by simply inviting the co-operation of the requisite number of outside singing societies on any given occasion.

When asked what were the difficulties of training a chorus, and what compensation he made his singers for all their time and trouble, he replied:

" I think there is no difficulty in training a chorus if the leader is careful to develop the intelligence of the singers. It has been an old custom to treat a chorus of singers like a body of children, telling them simply to do so and so, or repeat a phrase as directed, as if they were so many bullfinches to whom a tune was whistled. What can you expect from that kind of training? Treat them like bullfinches and they will be little more than a body of those imitators of airs. But if you appeal to their intelligence, force them to read their music and to think it out; directing, not dragging them in the right direction; promptly correcting, but intelligently explaining their errors, you will have, at last, a thoughtful, accomplished body of singers, who comprehend what they undertake and succeed in its accomplishment. Treat them like musicians and they will become musicians. Music should be to the vocalist what painting is to the artist, the score should be his brush and pigments. Let these vocal painters once understand that you expect them to think out their musical pictures and they will astonish you with the breadth and truth of their imagination.

"As for the matter of compensation, they receive only that of all such volunteer work in the cause of art. Bach, Beethoven, and other masters whose music we study, have given their whole souls to these compositions. To the chorus-worker the earnest study of these grand creations opens a new world of musical thought; their whole musical outlook is made interesting by a fuller knowledge and more complete comprehension of the beauties existing in these oft-repeated works of the old masters. To the intellectually active man or woman this work affords recreation, and even the humblest member of the chorus takes a profound pleasure in the grand result in which he was an assistant, and feels that he has been fully compensated by the higher cultivation of his musical intelligence and the development of his vocal talents."

Thomas was not without substantial reasons for hoping to establish a Festival Association in New York, for a number of prominent New York men had attended the Cincinnati Festival of 1880, and on their return had entered into negotiations with him to conduct a Festival of similar character, but even larger dimensions, in May, 1882. By the time he had returned from Europe, this association was thoroughly organized. It consisted of one hundred and sixty-three men, most of them wealthy, and all lovers of music. The officers were as follows:

GEORGE WILLIAM CURTIS, *President*.
CYRUS W. FIELD, *First Vice-President*.
HENRY G. MARQUAND, *Second Vice-President*.
DANIEL LORD, JR., *Secretary*.
JOSEPH W. DREXEL, *Treasurer*.

As the preparations for this and the Cincinnati Festival advanced, the people of Chicago also became interested, and formed an association to give one in their city, under Thomas' direction, during the same month as the other two. The three festivals were to follow each other, and were to consist of seven concerts each. The same orchestra and soloists were to be engaged for all, but as no two of the twenty-one programmes were duplicates, the detail work of preparing them was enormous, especially as Thomas had to visit and personally rehearse with the choruses of Chicago and Cincinnati from time to time, as well as with those at home.

In addition to the work already enumerated, for the Philharmonic, Choral, and May Festival Associations, Thomas gave a long series of nightly popular concerts in Metropolitan Hall, from October 13 to December 7, and all this kept him so busy that he found no time to travel over his old "Highway" during this winter.

In closing the record of this eventful year I must not omit to mention an honor conferred upon him by Yale University, and which was officially announced to him in the following letter:

YALE UNIVERSITY, NEW HAVEN, CONN.,
September 27, 1880.

THEODORE THOMAS, ESQ.
   Dear Sir:
   It is my duty to inform you officially of the action of the President and Fellows of Yale College at the recent Commencement, in conferring upon you the honorary degree of Doctor of Music, by way of recognition of the substantial service which you have rendered to musical culture in the United States.

The diploma certifying to this degree is sent by mail herewith and I must apologize for the long delay in forwarding it, owing to my ignorance of the fact that you had returned from Europe.

I have the honor to be
   Very respectfully your obedient servant,
      FRANKLIN B. DEXTER, *Secretary.*

Of the many honors of which he was the recipient during his long career, none were more acceptable to Thomas than the degrees conferred upon him by several universities, and yet, strange to say, he never used his Doctor's title, for he considered it out of keeping for a plain American citizen to ape the customs of the old world by prefixing a title of any kind to his name.

CHAPTER XI

1881

THE year 1881 was a very busy one for Thomas, and every moment was occupied with the training of the New York and Brooklyn choruses; with the Philharmonic concerts, the Symphony Concerts in Orange, Boston, and other cities, and, finally, with the preparatory work of the three great musical festivals to be given in New York, Cincinnati, and Chicago, in May, 1882.

The new chorus societies of New York and Brooklyn made their début at the Philharmonic concert of February 14, and the following vivid description of the performance is quoted from a long article about it which appeared in the New York *Tribune* the next day:

" An audience, such as crowded the Academy of Music last night, on the occasion of the fourth Philharmonic Concert, has not been seen there for many a long day. . . . Certainly the concert was worthy of it, for it was one of those performances of which one hears but two or three in a lifetime, and the memory of which stays long to brighten and cheer amidst all the dull mass of mediocrity to which one is so often condemned. . . . The programme consisted of only two numbers, Bach's Cantata, 'A Stronghold Sure,' adapted for performance by Theodore Thomas, and Beethoven's Ninth Symphony. In the form in which the Cantata has come down to us from Bach, the accompaniments are very incomplete. Three of the numbers have only a figured bass to indicate what they should be, and in no case are anything like the full parts for even the small orchestra which Bach employed to be found. The work which Mr. Thomas had to do to fit the composition for performance in the modern concert room, included not only the entire reconstruction of Bach's score, as nearly as possible in its original form, but the still further task of adapting this score to the requirements of the greatly increased resources of the modern orchestra, while at the same time religiously preserving the spirit of the original. It was a task requiring the utmost tact and delicacy, and demanding thorough musicianship and the completest and most intimate knowledge of the character and powers of the orchestra. Some of the instruments for which Bach wrote are now obsolete. The part for the organ, which was either not indicated at all, or only in the most meager way, and which Bach was accustomed to supply himself, *ad libitum,* had to be supplied and transferred to the orchestra. Finally, the increased band and a host of new instruments had to be utilised, without sacrificing in any way the spirit of Bach's music, to fit the work for performance by a large body of singers and instrumentalists. This difficult and delicate task Mr. Thomas has accomplished with signal success. Great as are the changes which he was obliged

to make, there is not in the entire work a single effect
which is not indicated in the original score, a single phrase
which is not wholly characteristic of Bach, or a single
passage in which the pure flavor of the original is not
preserved with the utmost fidelity. It is a triumph of
technical skill, pure taste, and entire sympathy with the
spirit of the composer.

" As for the performance, both of the Cantata and the
Ninth Symphony, it is difficult to speak coolly, or convey
any adequate sense of its marvelous perfection and beauty
without employing expressions which, while they would
be strictly within the truth, would sound like exaggerated
and extravagant praise. . . . The new chorus, which Mr.
Thomas has been training for the last four months, proved
a veritable revelation, and gave startling testimony to
what judgment and training can accomplish in a very
short time, with green singers. They sang with a firmness, precision, and confidence in themselves and their
conductor which were absolutely amazing, and which appeared incredible in a chorus which had never before sung
in public. The promptness of the attack, the delicacy
of shading, the smoothness with which the most difficult
roulades and the most involved passages were executed,
and the clear, fresh resonant quality of the voices, together with their excellent balance, were absolutely satisfying and delightful. No severer test could be applied
to a chorus than the intricate numbers of the Bach Cantata and the difficult Finale of the Ninth Symphony; and
no chorus could have come out more triumphantly from
such a trying ordeal than did the 480 singers who were
under Mr. Thomas' baton last night. And, admirable as
the work of the chorus was, that of the orchestra was
still more remarkable. . . . Every man in the Philharmonic orchestra seemed under the influence of a sort of

exaltation, and the result was what it always is when this band and its incomparable leader are at their best. The splendid accompaniments which Mr. Thomas has supplied to the Cantata, were given with magnificent sonority and the utmost completeness and delicacy of finish, and the Symphony received a performance which was rich, glowing, sympathetic, and inspired far beyond anything we have ever known here before." *

From the foregoing description of Thomas as a choral conductor, it will be seen that he had not forgotten his own musical education while he was engaged in furthering that of others at the Cincinnati College of Music. For there he had, for the first time, an opportunity which he was not slow to take advantage of, to try out and formulate all his theories about chorus singing, and to study in detail all the points relating to voice-building, tone-quality, breathing, and balancing the parts, as well as to experiment as to the best methods of imparting real musicianship to the singers. In Cincinnati, in short, he had given his chief attention to the voice, and had mastered every detail of the singers' art so thoroughly that from that time he understood the voice as well as the violin, and his chorus was as perfect as his orchestra, when it came under his personal supervision all the time. In other cases, as, for instance, when a chorus was prepared for him by a chorus director in some other city, for a festival performance of which he was to be the conductor, he did not attempt to get the same results,

* New York *Tribune,* Feb. 15, 1880.

which were possible only under his exclusive training, but would, instead, endeavor to secure a good performance through the inspiration of the moment.

In February, Thomas went to Chicago to conduct some choral concerts of the Apollo Club, the leading choral society of that city, and a short subsequent season of orchestral performances. The week happened to be a very stormy one, and one night such a blizzard raged that the street cars were unable to run. When the hour for beginning the concert arrived there were hardly a dozen people in the audience. Seeing this, the manager came to Thomas to ask if the concert would still be given. " Of course," was his prompt reply. "It will not only be given, but I shall try to make it an especially good performance, for the people who have braved such a storm as this to hear us, must surely be true music-lovers, and deserve the best we can give them."

As the winter progressed and the New York and Brooklyn choruses became more thoroughly trained, Thomas was able to utilize them in the manner he had planned, and the following programmes, given in these cities, show the kind of music which it is possible to perform with a chorus of this class, and which can be adequately given only when the conductor has at his command a choral body of the very highest efficiency. These programmes, as will readily be seen, are not choral programmes in the ordinary sense, but symphony programmes, pure and simple, in which the chorus is used as an extension of the orchestra in the same way that special instruments are introduced occasionally by composers to produce certain extraordinary effects. Even when Thomas used the chorus in selections purely choral, such as the Utrecht "Jubilate," it did not form a special feature of the programme, but was merely an integral part of the whole scheme, subordinated to the symphony, around which, as the dominating number, all the others were grouped:

I

The New York Philharmonic Society
Programme
Cantata, " A Stronghold Sure "................Bach
Intermission
Symphony No. 9, D minor, op. 125..........Beethoven

II

Brooklyn Philharmonic Society
Programme
Symphony No. 3, op. 97 (Rhenish)...........Schumann
Scenes from " Alceste "........................Gluck
Soloists, Chorus, and Orchestra

Intermission
Overture
Aria from the " Flying Dutchman "...........Wagner
Minuet and Fugue from Quartette No. 9 in C, for
    String Orchestra ....Beethoven
Duo Nocturne, " Beatrice and Benedict ".......Berlioz
Festival March and Chorus, " Queen of Sheba," Goldmark

III
Brooklyn Philharmonic Society
Programme

Symphony, E flat..Mozart

Cavatine, " Euryanthe "............................Weber

Mrs. Osgood

Music to " Œdipus Tyrannus," op. 35 .... John K. Paine

Mr. Georg Henschel, Chorus, and Orchestra

Intermission

(a) Overture ⎫

(b) First Scene ⎬ " Genoveva," op. 81......Schumann

Mr. Georg Henschel, Chorus, and Orchestra

Sanctus, from Missa Solennis, op. 123.........Beethoven

Violin Obbligato, Mr. Brandt

Mrs. Osgood, Miss Winant, Mr. Toedt, Mr. Henschel

Chorus and Orchestra

Gloria, Utrecht " Jubilate ".....................Haendel

Chorus and Orchestra

The work of rehearsing with the festival chorus of Chicago was begun during the winter of 1881, and the following extract from a letter written by a member of this chorus illustrates Thomas' methods of conducting when leading a body of singers who came under his direction only occasionally:

" Last night we had for the first time a grand mass rehearsal of our festival chorus under Thomas, who had come to Chicago for that purpose. It was great fun and I wish we might have him oftener. He conducts with exquisite grace of gesture, and yet so steadily and definitely that there is no chance of mistaking anything. One knows instinctively exactly what every gesture is intended to indicate, and the whole body of singers is kept together perfectly. I cannot describe the volume of sound produced by a thousand people singing the 'Hallelujah Chorus' from Haendel's 'Messiah,' accompanied by the full power of a large organ, in a hall not more than large enough to contain them. When Thomas announced this chorus, he gave a little upward hitch to his sleeves, and, motioning to us all to rise, said, with a challenge in his tone that keyed up every singer to his best effort: 'Now then! We shall hear something!' And verily we did! When that first, great, triumphant 'Hallelujah!' burst forth from a thousand voices, the effect was so overpowering that I had all I could do to keep from tears, and I was so excited that I could not get my breath to sing for a full half-page. As for Thomas, he let himself go full swing. His arms swayed wildly in the air, and he kept shouting, first to one part and then to another, like a charioteer in a race urging on his horses, until he worked the singers up to a perfect frenzy of excitement. I was lost in astonishment, for he is always so quiet in concert, and every movement is the quintessence of grace and dignity when he is before the public. Not that there was any lack of either grace or dignity in the rehearsal—with Thomas those attributes seem to be 'bred in the bone,'— but I was unprepared for all this animation. The insight he gave us as to the meaning of the music was a revelation, and he stamped his conception on our minds with such clarity and definition that I do not think it would be possible for any of us ever to think of it or sing it in any other way again."

It was a fundamental principle with Thomas, in rehearsal, to keep his musicians so absorbingly interested in their work that their attention was riveted on his every gesture. He permitted no talking or moving about during a rehearsal, and if he saw the attention of even the remotest singer of the back row begin to waver, he would recall the delinquent to his duty with such a sharp rebuke that not only the offender, but everyone else on the stage would " come to time " in a hurry, each fearful lest the searching eye of the conductor might pick him out for the next rapier thrust. But if the reproofs of Thomas were severe, they were, on the other hand, never insulting, and were framed to spur the inattentive to duty, not to humiliate their pride. If he had anything of the latter kind to say to one of his performers, it was said in private, never before the rest, unless the case was such a serious one that he felt it necessary to make an example of the offender, which very rarely happened, and nothing made him so indignantly angry as when his orchestra was treated with discourtesy by any other conductor. So particular was he about this that sometimes, when an inexperienced or ill-mannered conductor was rehearsing with them, I have known him to sit on the stage himself throughout the rehearsal, in order to make sure that nothing of the sort should happen. His orchestral rehearsals were apt to be long as well as strenuous; he was careful, however, not to fatigue his musicians unduly, in order to keep their work fresh and vital. As long as the music itself was sufficient to hold their attention, he would keep them closely at work. But when he saw that they were beginning to flag, he

would brighten the atmosphere with all sorts of
fun and nonsense, or by a little recess for relaxation, and he rarely held more than one rehearsal in a day with the same body of musicians,
or rehearsed on the day of a concert. When
things went particularly well, he would say, with
a contented little smile, " It sounds very good—
very good," and sometimes, in an orchestra rehearsal, he would say, " Well, *Kinder,* you have
played so well to-day that to-morrow you may
have a holiday and I will omit the rehearsal."
In short, he had a thousand ways of keeping his
musicians fresh, and their performances vital, and
he was equally careful not to allow his own work
to become perfunctory, but studied each composition anew, *every time* he put it on a programme,
no matter how often he had performed it before,
or how simple or unimportant it might be. Another matter about which he was very careful was
the cultivation of an *esprit de corps* in the orchestra. He could not afford, nor did he think it wise
to pay salaries which were larger than those paid
by other organizations similar to his own, but he
had other ways of making membership in his orchestra desirable to musicians of the first rank.
Not only did they learn much in their art from
him, but he would use every opportunity to advance them professionally, by giving all who were
equal to it solo appearances in his concerts from
time to time; by printing their names on the programmes whenever they played obbligatos, or by
helping them to gain reputation or extra money

in any other way that came to hand. If one was taken ill Thomas was the first to head an orchestra subscription to help out the sufferer financially, and he would hold the man's place open for him for months at a time—sometimes even years— awaiting his recovery, rather than have a faithful member of the orchestra lose his position through misfortune. And even in the stormiest periods of his career, when he himself was financially ruined, he always managed that the orchestra did not suffer at all. He was also scrupulously just to all alike, and no matter how much he might personally dislike a member of the orchestra, as long as the man did his duty he could be as certain of retaining his position and of having the same consideration shown him as anyone else. In addition to guarding their interests so carefully, Thomas attached his men to him by his warm and genial nature, and whenever one of them was in any sort of trouble or perplexity, he would bring it to Thomas, certain of finding from him both sympathy and help. Under these circumstances, it is not surprising that the *personnel* of the Thomas Orchestra was composed of the finest musicians Europe and America could produce, and that its membership changed but little from year to year. The men did not often leave unless they were discharged, and Thomas did not discharge anyone who did his duty, was competent for his work, and respected by his colleagues. But woe betide the man who was found lacking in any of these essentials. He got no mercy from his

chief.   The implacable message, " Tell him not
to speak to me again," would come to such an
one, and he knew it was final.   This happened
so seldom, however, that most of the musicians
held their positions in the orchestra for many
years, and even at the present time there are still
a few of the " old guard " playing at the same
stands where they have sat for more than a quarter
of a century—and not only so, but playing as well
as ever.   " The training we had from the ' Old
Man ' went into our bones," they will tell you,
" we can never forget it as long as we live."

During the summer of 1881 Thomas again conducted a long season of summer night concerts in
Chicago, in the same old Exposition Building of
happy memory that he played in in 1876.   At its
close he gave a short series of similar performances in Milwaukee and Cincinnati, and then, at
last, allowed himself to go home and take a little
rest.

The fall season of 1881 opened at Boston, with
two concerts on October 14 and 15, and these concerts closed his regular connection with the musical life of that city.   Ever since the year 1869
Thomas had been the chief purveyor of orchestra
music to Boston, and had given more symphony
concerts there every season than in any other
city.   Now his twelve years of service bore their
legitimate fruit.   It had long been a city of
musical culture.   Thomas did not have to create
a taste for good music there, for it existed already before he came.   But what he did do for

the music of Boston was to create a higher standard of performance and of programme-making than any that had previously existed. As soon as he began going there regularly, its local orchestra died a natural death, because it was too inferior to stand a comparison with that of Thomas. But now the Boston public began to want an orchestra of its own again, and in response to this desire, Mr. Henry L. Higginson, a wealthy and public-spirited citizen, came forward, and at his own private expense founded the now justly celebrated Boston Symphony Orchestra, which gave its first concert on October 22, 1881, under the conductorship of Georg Henschel.

The establishment of this orchestra, which was soon developed by its founder to the same standard of size and perfection as that of Thomas, naturally resulted in the loss of Boston as a regular musical field to the latter. This was a serious matter to Thomas, both financially and artistically, for it had hitherto been the most profitable city of his "Highway," and its advanced musical culture had afforded him the artistic satisfaction of giving there the highest class of music, with the certainty that it would receive instant recognition from audience and critics alike. Later, as the Boston orchestra became larger and more excellent in its work, it was inevitable that it too should travel over the "Highway," for it is hardly possible to maintain an orchestra in this country without taking it on occasional concert tours, and this cut into the engagements of Thomas everywhere, especially as the Boston orchestra, being a subsidized organization, could afford to play for less than his, which was entirely dependent on its earnings for its maintenance. Thomas of course understood and expected this, and the two orchestras were always on the most friendly terms, and their respective managements were careful to interfere with each other as little as possible. It was also the ultimate object of his mission to stimulate the local art of every city in which he gave concerts, in order that when the time should come when he no longer traveled with the orchestra himself, the standard he had raised all over the country might be maintained. But as one orchestra after another sprang up in his wake in the cities of the " Highway," it naturally made the problem of maintaining his own increasingly difficult of solution as the years went on, and forced him to travel further and further West for his musical field. This was a benefit to the country at large, but in his later years it was a real hardship to him to have to continue to devote himself to pioneer work in remote places, which he felt might be done as well by others, and to be denied all opportunity to do the great musical work in the art centers of the world for which his training and experience had fitted him, and which others could not do. But so Fate ordered it to the last.

CHAPTER XII

JANUARY TO OCTOBER, 1882

THE LEADERSHIP OF THE BOSTON PHILHARMONIC SOCIETY
CONCERTS IS OFFERED TO THOMAS—A TRIAD OF GREAT
FESTIVALS IN NEW YORK, CINCINNATI, AND CHICAGO,
IN MAY, 1882

In the early days after the founding of the
Boston orchestra, and before it had reached the
high development of its later years, the music-
loving public of that city continued to want their
customary Thomas concerts, and as Thomas had
decided not to give any there on his own account,
the Boston Philharmonic Society sent him the following invitation through its president, John K.
Paine:

BOSTON, *Jan.* 18, 1882.

Dear Mr. Thomas:

In behalf of the Philharmonic Society of Boston, I wish
to inquire if you would look favorably on the proposition
of giving a series of six, eight, or ten concerts in Boston
next winter (1882-3) with your own orchestra of fifty
to sixty men, under the auspices of this society, provided
a sufficient inducement were held out to you? For the
past two seasons the concerts have been well supported
by a large number of subscribers, filling the Music Hall,
and I am sure we can make them permanent if you assume

214

the direction, as we have everything that relates to the business of the concerts in good order.

Yours very truly,
JOHN K. PAINE.

Thomas did not accept this pleasant offer, much as he would have liked to do so, for he did not care to come into rivalry with the new orchestra, but regretfully crossed Boston off the list of his " Highway " cities, and with it, nearly all the rest of his New England territory, and left a clear field to Mr. Higginson and his men.

At the time when Thomas and the New York Philharmonic orchestra had combined their interests in 1880, he had laid before the society a plan which had been in his mind for some time, to lower the concert pitch of the orchestra about $\frac{9}{16}$ of a tone, and asked them to give him their co-operation in carrying it into effect two years later. They agreed, and during the season of 1881-82 this important and far-reaching change was made, in spite of the enormous difficulties it involved. To the uninitiated it may seem a simple thing to lower the pitch of the little group of eighty or ninety musicians who comprised the Thomas Orchestra, but no other single act of his life illustrates so well how intimately Thomas was associated with the musical life of the whole country as this, for no sooner had he lowered the pitch of his orchestra than every orchestra player and solo instrumentalist in America bought a new instrument, or adapted his old one to it. Consequently all the manufacturers

of pianos, organs, harps, and wind instruments
had to conform to the popular demand and make
their instruments in accordance with it.   The
reason of this general following of Thomas' lead
in the matter is not far to seek.   In America, at
that time, it was essential to the standing of a
musician that he should have played under the
direction of Thomas, either in the orchestra or as
soloist, and no musician in any part of the country would cut himself off from this possibility by
the lack of an instrument of suitable pitch.
Furthermore Thomas and his orchestra formed
the basis of nearly all the great festival performances in America, consequently, the organs in
the local music halls everywhere had to be tuned
to his pitch, and all the choruses trained in it.
This, in turn, reacted on other bands and musical
organizations so that they too had to adopt the
new standard.   The change was not accomplished
without a good deal of opposition from those whom
it inconvenienced, and some fighting on the part
of Thomas, but that did not stop him for a
minute.   He had fully made up his mind that it
ought to be done, and when that was the case, he
would not be deflected from his course by any
considerations of a personal nature, for either himself or anyone else.

The day after the lowering of the pitch was
formally accomplished, the following notice appeared about it in the New York *Tribune:*

" The Philharmonic Society is to adopt a new musical
pitch—the so-called ' reformed German pitch,' which is

practically the same as the 'normal diapason' adopted
by the French Government Commission twenty-five years
ago, by which the whole orchestra is lowered about a semi-
tone.   It is also identical with the 'classical pitch' of a
century ago and with the 'philosophical pitch' theoretically assumed upon mathematical principles.   Many
of the leading players of the society had supplied themselves with new instruments last fall, and now the entire
new set of wind instruments has been completed, and the
required alterations of the stringed instruments have been
made.   The musicians have for months been occupied in
the work of accommodating themselves to the change and
learning the peculiarities of the new instruments.   The
change of pitch was formally made at a rehearsal on
Tuesday of this week, and was first introduced at a concert under the direction of Theodore Thomas in Orange,
on Thursday.   The result was satisfactory, and the conductor and all the musicians are delighted by its effect.
They say that the tone is softer, fuller, and richer, and
that the quality of the orchestra will hereafter be finer
than it has ever been before.   One immediate effect of the
reform will be the pleasure of hearing classic works performed as they were designed and written.   Another will
be the relief of all solo and chorus singers, who will henceforth avoid the strain under which the human voice has
for some generations painfully striven to match the growing intensity of the modern orchestra."

With the exception of one short Western concert tour in January, Thomas devoted himself
entirely to his New York interests during the
winter of 1881-82, and to the preparations for the
three great musical festivals of the coming May.
That of New York came first, and was the largest,

as well as one of the most artistically perfect musical enterprises Thomas ever undertook. It was given in the Seventh Regiment Armory, on May 2d to 6th, and consisted of the seven following programmes:

I

Musical Festival

New York

May 2, 1882

Programme

Cantata, " A Stronghold Sure "..................Bach
 Miss Annie Louise Cary, Mr. William Candidus, Mr.
M. W. Whitney
Chorus, Orchestra, Organ

Symphony, C major (Koechel, 551)...........Mozart

Recitative and Aria, " Abscheulicher " (Fidelio),
Beethoven
Madame Amelia Friedrich-Materna
Intermission

Jubilate (written for the Peace of Utrecht)....Haendel
 Miss Cary, Mr. Theodore J. Toedt, Mr. Georg
Henschel
Chorus, Orchestra, Organ

II

Classical Programme

Iphigenia in Aulis...........................Gluck
 (a) Overture
 (b) Scene I, " Diane impitoyable "
Signor A. F. Galassi

Symphony in C major, No. 9...............Schubert

Aria, " Der Hoelle Rache " (Magic Flute)......Mozart

Madame Etelka Gerster

Intermission

Overture (Manfred)......................Schumann

Aria, " Der Kriegeslust ergeben " (Jessonda)....Spohr

Mr. Georg Henschel

Recitative and Aria, " Ocean, Thou Mighty Monster,"

Weber

Madame Materna

Overture (Ruy Blas)....................Mendelssohn

III

Beethoven Programme

Symphony C major No. 5, op. 67

Intermission

Missa Solennis, D major, op. 123

IV

Wagner Programme

Soloists—Mme. Materna, Misses Schell, Wurmb, and
Henne ; Messrs. Campanini, Galassi, Candidus, Toedt,
Remmertz, and Steins

Das Rheingold

(a) The theft of the gold. (b) Wotan's Apostrophe
to Walhalla. (c) Loge's tidings. (d) Grand
closing scene

Die Walkuere

(a) Introduction to Act I. (b) Siegmund's Love-
song. (c) The Ride of the Walkyries. (d)
Wotan's farewell and the magic fire scene

Intermission

Siegfried

The forging of the sword

Die Goetterdaemmerung
 (a) Siegfried's Death. (b) Finale, Brünnhilde's
   Immolation.

V

Haendel Programme

Israel in Egypt

VI

Italian Programme

Sonata in D (String orchestra),
       Arcangelo Corelli (1653-1713)
Aria, " Se i miei sospiri,"
      Alessandro Stradella (1645-1678)
Miss Emily Winant

Minuetto (String orchestra),
       Luigi Boccherini (1740-1805)
Aria, " Pria che spunti " (Il matrimonio segreto),
      Domenico Cimarosa (1754-1801)
Signor Italo Campanini

Les deux Journées.........Luigi Cherubini (1760-1842)
 (a) Overture. (b) Sestetto Finale, " O Ciel!", Act I
La Vestale............Gasparo Spontini (1784-1851)
 (a) Overture. (b) Scene " Del tuo gran Ministero,"
  Act II

Intermission

Guglielmo Tell.................Rossini (1792-1868)
 (a) Overture. (b) Terzetto, Act II
Duo, " Ah Leonora il guardo " (La Favorita),
       Donizetti (1797-1848)
Miss Cary, Signor Galassi

Aria, " Ah non giunge " (Sonnambula),
        Bellini (1802-1835)
Madame Gerster

Romanza, " Eri tu " (Un Ballo in Maschera),
        Verdi (1814)

Signor Galassi
Overture (Re Lear)..................... Bazzini (1818)

VII

Programme

Symphony to Dante's "Divina Commedia ".......Liszt
Orchestra, Chorus of Women's Voices, Organ
Scene "Der Daemon," Act I.................Rubinstein
Madame Gerster
Intermission
"The Fall of Troy," Act II................... Berlioz
Soloists, Chorus, and Orchestra
Chorus, "Die Meistersinger," Act III.........Wagner

The musical forces which were to render this remarkable series of programmes consisted of an orchestra of three hundred players, a chorus of three thousand singers, and the world renowned solo artists, Madame Amalia Friedrich-Materna (who created the great soprano Wagner rôles at Baireuth), Madame Etelka Gerster, Miss Annie Louise Cary, and Messrs. Campanini, Galassi, Georg Henschel, Remmertz, Myron W. Whitney, and others. The basis of the great mass-chorus was Thomas' own New York-Brooklyn chorus of twelve hundred singers, which was reinforced by the Haendel and Haydn Society of Boston, the Cecilian Society of Philadelphia, the Musical Association Chorus of Worcester, the Oratorio Association of Baltimore, and the Choral Society of Reading. The orchestra was composed wholly of musicians who had at some time belonged to the Thomas Orchestra. It was a great reunion—the only reunion that Thomas ever enjoyed with his

former "Boys"—and there was no end to the
fun and jollity that went on amongst them in
spite of the hard work. In speaking of the manner
in which he placed this great orchestra on the
stage, Thomas said, " I arranged them so that they
formed a triple orchestra, similar to the three
manuals of an organ, which I could play on singly
or in combination at my pleasure. Of course the
orchestra parts were all marked, and had been rehearsed accordingly, but in such an immense hall
as that in which the festival was given, the difference in the acoustics when it was empty or when it
was full of people was so great that I had to be
prepared for any emergency. In the concerts I
made good use of my combinations and accomplished some unusual shading by manipulating
my triple orchestra, even in such works as the
Jupiter Symphony of Mozart. Some of the works
were given with overpowering effect, but others
again, for instance the Beethoven Mass, disappointed me. The greatest and most enduring
effect was made by the Wagner programme. This
performance created the greatest excitement I
ever witnessed in a concert. Considered from every
point of view this festival was one of those
unusual occasions which rarely come twice in a
lifetime." *

Some idea of the detail work of the rehearsals
alone of such a festival, given as Thomas was
accustomed to give them, may be had from the
following list of the final week of orchestra rehearsals:

* See " Theodore Thomas, a Musical Autobiography," Vol. I, p. 90.

DAY	MONTH	DATE	PLACE	TIME			ORCHESTRA
				Morning	Afternoon	Evening	
SUNDAY..	April	16	Steinway Hall	10.00 A.M.	......	......	{ Wind, Percussion and Harps
"	"	"	"	......	3.00 P.M.	......	Strings
MONDAY..	"	17	7th Regt. Armory	10.30 A.M.	......	......	Full Orchestra
THURSDAY	"	27	"	......	4.00 P.M.	......	"
FRIDAY...	"	28	"	9.30 A.M.	......	......	"
"	"	"	"	......	2.30 P.M.	......	"
SATURDAY.	"	29	"	9.30 A.M.	......	......	"
"	"	"	"	......	......	8.00 P.M.	"
SUNDAY..	"	30	"	9.30 A.M.	......	......	"
"	"	"	"	......	2.30 P.M.	......	{ Orchestra for Solo Accompaniments
MONDAY..	May	1	"	9.30 A.M.	......	......	Full Orchestra
"	"	"	"	......	2.30 P.M.	......	"

From this list (a copy of which was furnished to each member of the orchestra), it will be seen that during this week Thomas often rehearsed with them five or six hours a day. In the evenings he probably rehearsed with the chorus, using a piano accompaniment, for this was his custom at all festivals. Thomas' conception of a musical festival was somewhat different from the generally accepted idea of the public. To most people a festival simply means size, and denotes a series of concerts in which an unusual number of performers, vocal and instrument, give a series of concerts in a place of great magnitude, before an audience of vast dimensions. Thomas also included the foregoing essentials in his scheme of a festival, but added to them others which were in his estimation of far more importance. First, the programmes must include great works which could not be adequately given without a large body of performers, and were for that reason rarely heard in concert. Second, the standard of performance of both the orchestra and chorus must be the very highest possible. The solo artists must be the greatest obtainable. He would not conduct a series of concerts under the name "Festival," unless these conditions could be reasonably fulfilled, nor would he give a festival without two years of preparation for the same.

When the month of May finally arrived, all was ready for the event, which proved to be the greatest single achievement of its kind in the life of Thomas, for he was never able again to combine the two antagonistic elements of quality and quantity to the extent that he combined them in this remarkable series of performances.

As the programmes of the various concerts required different musical forces, and a different arrangement of the chorus, Thomas had diagrams prepared of the seating for each of the concerts, for the directors in charge of the different societies which made up the chorus. Each society had its own color, represented here by a number, so that its director could tell at a glance, by consulting the diagrams, just where his sopranos, altos, etc., were to sit at each performance. Thus all confusion was avoided in spite of the nightly changes in the seating of the vast body of singers.

When the doors of the Armory were thrown open to admit the expectant throngs, they saw a very handsome hall, with a seating capacity of more than seven thousand. At the Fourth Avenue end rose the immense parterre of three thousand chorus seats, and at its base spread the great stage for the orchestra with its platforms of graded heights and its three hundred chairs. The chorus part of the stage was draped on either side with heavy folds of dark maroon stuff, and the balustrade, which railed its lower edge, was beautifully festooned with greens and flowers. The balcony just above its upper row, back of which extended the big sounding board, was trimmed with greens and pine branches, and at its two extremes were banked palms and potted shrubs, forming a dark rich background for the bright colored dresses of the singers grouped in front. All along the front of the stage were rows of geraniums and other blossoming plants, which

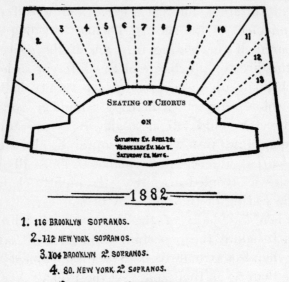

SEATING OF CHORUS

ON

Saturday Ev. April 29.
Wednesday Ev. May 3.
Saturday Ev. May 6.

1882

1. 116 BROOKLYN SOPRANOS.

2. 112 NEW YORK SOPRANOS.

3. 104 BROOKLYN 2º SOPRANOS.

4. 80. NEW YORK 2º SOPRANOS.

5. 47. BROOKLYN 2º TENORS.

6. 46. NEW YORK 2º TENORS.

7. 35 BROOKLYN, 26 NEW YORK TENORS.

8. 42 BROOKLYN, 58 NEW YORK BASSOS. (2º).

9. 69. BROOKLYN, 66 NEW YORK BASSOS. (1º).

10. 76 BROOKLYN 1ST. ALTOS.

11. 62 NEW YORK 1ST ALTOS.

12. 53. NEW YORK 2² ALTOS.

13. 40. BROOKLYN 2² ALTOS.

completed the floral frame to the picture, and the platform for the conductor and his stand, as the central point of the whole, showed also its appropriate decorations.

It is needless to say that after so much careful preparation, the performances were as nearly per-

fect as they could be made.   Unfortunately
Thomas rarely read or preserved press notices
about his work, and the only material of this kind
which is at the command of his biographer is that

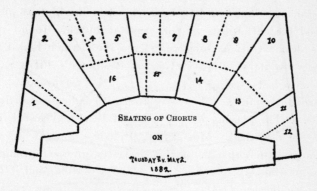

SEATING OF CHORUS

ON

TUESDAY Ev. MAY 2.
1882.

1. BROOKLYN SOPRANOS.
2. NEW YORK SOPRANOS.
3. READING TENORS
4. NEW YORK TENORS.
5. BROOKLYN TENORS.
6. WORCESTER TENORS.
7. BROOKLYN BASSOS.
8 READING BASSOS.
9 WORCESTER BASSOS.
10. NEW YORK BASSOS.
11 READING ALTOS.
12 WORCESTER ALTOS.
13. NEW YORK ALTOS.
14. BROOKLYN ALTOS.
15. READING SOPRANOS.
16. WORCESTER SOPRANOS.

which could be gleaned from the scrapbooks of
his friends.   In this instance only three short
clippings from the musical notices of this festival
are at hand, but perhaps they will serve as well as
if they were longer, to describe the general

character of the work accomplished and the impression it produced on the listeners. They are as follows:

" Public interest in this concert (the Wagner Programme) seemed to have been raised to the highest pitch, and the enthusiasm of the crowded audience found vent in demonstrations surpassing even those which hailed the extraordinary interpretation of Beethoven's Fifth Symphony last evening. To say that the performance was brilliantly successful is very feebly to indicate its effect. . . . The playing of the ' Ride of the Valkyries ' is not to be described. Most of us probably thought we had gauged the capacity of this orchestra pretty thoroughly on Wednesday, but here was a new sensation, and it left us wondering whether Thomas has any more surprises in store for us, and just how much he can do with his band. . . . At the end, and this is not a figure of speech but a literal statement of fact, the people fairly jumped from their seats. . . ."

Of this performance Madame Materna said, " I can give no better idea of my opinion of this concert than by saying that when I was listening to it I was wishing that Wagner himself were here to hear his music rendered so perfectly. It was magnificent, grand, and so far as the orchestra was concerned, nothing could be finer. . . . That here, in America, Thomas so faithfully reproduced the same effects which I myself have heard Wagner studiously teach his musicians, amazes me. . . ."

Another notice describes the performances of the Haendel programme as follows:

THE MUSIC FESTIVAL

HANDEL NIGHT

It might have been thought that after the extraordinary performance of the Wagner music on Thursday—the grandest performance, we presume, that the music of " The Ring of the Nibelung " ever received—nothing could be done to sustain the remainder of the Festival on the exalted level then reached. But last night the sensation was increased. It would be difficult indeed to dwarf " Israel in Egypt." Its effects are in the strongest possible contrast to those of the modern school, but they never have been surpassed; and if the demonstrations last evening were less exciting than those of the day before, the impression was at least as deep, and the satisfaction certainly as general. In the Wagner programme the orchestra earned its chief triumph. In Handel the chorus mustered its fullest force and scored its most startling success. The opening of the work is a strange one, but last night it was singularly effective. There is no instrumental prelude. The oratorio begins with a tenor recitative, beautifully delivered by Mr. Candidus; then, after a brief passage for alto solo, the double chorus enters. And here, when the three thousand singers broke out, with their stupendous tone and their miraculous attack, the audience experienced the first of an evening of sensations. The splendid work accomplished in the " Jubilate " on Tuesday, ought to have prepared us for this, but in the " Israel " the chorus was about twice as large as in the smaller composition, and its excellence seems almost to have increased with its size. The effect was so grand that the surprised and delighted audience seemed disposed to encore everything. " He spake the word " was repeated; so was the " Hailstone " chorus; after which Mr. Thomas announced that owing to the great length of the oratorio it would be impossible to repeat anything else, a determination which, however, later in the evening, he was induced to break. The vigor and persistency of the applause were all the more significant because this is one of the least diversified of all oratorios, most of it being a succession of massive choruses, seldom relieved either by an interval of solo or even by a relaxation of the stupendous dignity assumed in the very first choral number. If the execution had been anything less than stupendous, the excitement of the listeners would infallibly have died away before the end.

What we said of the chorus after the first night may be repeated now with added emphasis. This is a body of singers possessing all the good qualities of a chorus in a very high degree. Their volume of tone is overpowering. Their purity of tone surpasses everything within our experience. Their precision is irreproachable. They are never at a loss, never uncertain, never confused, never afraid of their music. They sing with an elegance of expression which would do credit to a glee-club, and a finish of style which artists might envy. What justness of sentiment, what poetical sensibility, they showed in the contrasts of their manners last night, the sturdy magnificence of " The Lord Shall Reign," for instance, the refinement of " He Led Them Forth Like Sheep," and the solemnity of passages like " The Depths Have Covered Them," where the organ asserts itself so gloriously. The whole of the series of five choruses and double choruses beginning with the last mentioned number may be cited as the final expression of good singing. Of course a great deal of the majesty of last evening's performance was due to the visiting organizations, the famous Handel and Haydn of Boston, always so sure and so well trained, and the admirable societies from Philadelphia and Baltimore. But the basis of it all was our own force (New York and

Brooklyn), and the whole body took their beautiful style
and their animation from Thomas.   It did not need this

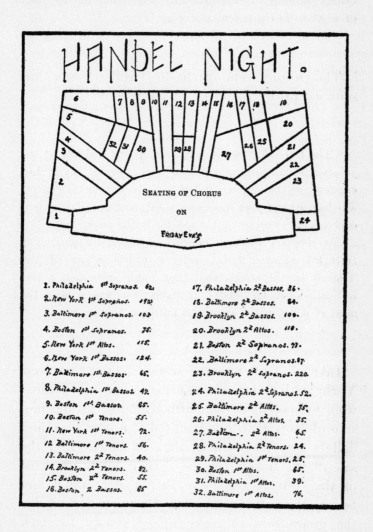

festival to prove that he is not less great as a leader of
choruses than as a master of the orchestra, but the fact

is now brought home to thousands who have been slow to realize it.   To the best of our belief there has never been chorus singing in New York to approach the splendor of what he has given us this week.

The closing scene of the final concert was thus summed up by the critic of the *Tribune:*

" The festival closed in a blaze of glory and amidst the jubilant shouts of thousands of music lovers. . . . The capacity of the hall was tested to the full, and the concert was listened to by no less than 8,500 persons. Every incident of the evening quickened the enthusiasm, and when at the close the audience refused to leave their places for fully five minutes, and thundered for the return of Mr. Thomas to the stage, that they might give him a last testimonial of his labors, the spectacle was among the most striking in the annals of music in this country."

Like most of Thomas' schemes, the great New York festival was an expensive luxury to those who promoted it, for although the astonishing sum of more than one hundred and nine thousand dollars was taken in at the box office from the sale of the tickets for its seven concerts, the cost of the festival was more than one hundred and twenty-three thousand, thus leaving a deficit for the guarantors to make up of nearly fourteen thousand dollars. Its financial report was as follows:

RECEIPTS

Guarantee Fund called...................	$ 29,560.00
Subscription Certificates................	53,325.00
Single Tickets.........................	48,044.00
Auction Premiums......................	8,081.50
Interest...............................	455.40
	$139,465.90

DISBURSEMENTS

Rent and Fittings of Halls and Armory...	$ 29,875.07
Soloists...............................	26,654.62
Orchestra..............................	19,205.20
Transportation and Board of Choruses, and Chorus Expenses......................	17,083.95
Advertising and Printing, etc............	11,637.68
Conductor and his Assistants............	9,984.91
Music and Organ.......................	5,485.39
Business Manager......................	2,500.00
Cable Telegrams, Messenger service, and labor...............................	1,143.08
	$123,569.90
Amount returned to Guarantors..........	15,896.00
	$139,465.90

JOSEPH W. DREXEL, *Treasurer.*

As, however, the guarantors had been prepared for a deficit of fifty thousand dollars they did not complain, but paid the money cheerfully and considered it well spent. At the same time they presented Thomas with a beautiful ivory baton, around the golden mounting of which was inscribed the opening theme of the Fifth Symphony

—a work which, to those who knew and loved him, seemed peculiarly descriptive of his own life and character. Accompanying the baton was the following letter, illuminated on vellum and bound in crimson velvet:

NEW YORK, *May*, 1882.

THEODORE THOMAS, ESQ.

Dear Sir:

We, the Advisory Council of the Music Festival of 1882, desire heartily to congratulate you upon its memorable result. We have known the untiring energy, patience, skill, and devotion with which you have discharged the immense duties which have devolved upon you in organization and preparation; we were witness of the signal triumph which was achieved by your direction of the friendly host of vocal and instrumental forces drawn from widely separated communities, but all inspired by the spirit of their leader. Gratefully recalling your long and faithful service in educating the musical taste of the country, by the noblest choral and orchestral interpretation of the greatest works of the greatest masters, a service of which the late festival was a worthy illustration and monument, we have desired to offer you some simple and fitting token of so striking an event in the musical history of America, a token which should derive all its value from friendly sympathy and regard. We beg, therefore, respectfully to ask your acceptance of a conductor's baton, which in itself is of no worth, but which we hope may serve to remind you of our friendship and gratitude, and of our unalloyed pleasure in the associations of the festival. Surely, if he be justly happy whose unselfish public career has surrounded him with love, honor, and troops of friends, we can wish for you no greater blessing than the continuance of your present happiness.

We are, dear Sir, with the highest regard

Very truly yours,

GEORGE WILLIAM CURTIS, *President.*

HENRY G. MARQUAND, *First Vice-President.*

CYRUS W. FIELD, *Second Vice-President.*

DANIEL LORD, JR., *Secretary.*

JOSEPH W. DREXEL, *Treasurer.*

JAMES W. ALEXANDER	JOSEPH LYMAN
WILLIAM WALDORF ASTOR	HENRY C. WHITNEY
WM. R. BUNKER	HERBERT SEYMOUR
SETH LOW	JOHN D. ELWELL
RICHARD IRWIN, JR.	HENRY SELIGMAN
J. C. RODRIGUES	WM. A. WHITE
CHARLES A. PEABODY	FREDERICK D. BLAKE
ARPAD G. GERSTER	EDWARD L. OWEN
FREDERIC CROMWELL	D. A. LINDLEY
B. T. FROTHINGHAM	CHARLES F. TRETBAR
LOUIS C. LEWIS	SAMUEL S. SANFORD

In all Thomas' long career—a career which was devoted to a succession of great enterprises— hardly any of them paid their own expenses. And it is surely the strongest proof of the genuine love of art inherent in the American people that year after year there were always to be found public-spirited men to finance these costly musical enterprises. Thomas was not an extravagant man, either in his private expenditures or those of his profession, and his long experience and wide professional connections enabled him to get artistic results with a smaller outlay than most people could, but he despised from his very soul anything that savored of meanness, nor would he for one minute allow the art standard of anything he was responsible for to be lowered for financial considerations, and many a time he paid from his own pocket losses for which he was in no way responsible rather than have the artistic quality of his work suffer.

Immediately on the close of the New York festival, Thomas and his musicians, orchestra and soloists, went to Cincinnati, and again plunged into a week of double and triple daily rehearsals and all the high-pressure labor incident to the final preparations of a festival, and again he passed through the anxieties of seven colossal performances and tasted the glory of triumphant success. One of the leading critics of Cincinnati thus summed up the impressions created by the performances of this festival in his notice of the final concert:

" The May Festival of 1882 is at an end. Last night witnessed its close with an audience which packed the house to its utmost. From the beginning to the end there was a continuous flutter of excitement. At times the vast sea of humanity gave vent to wildest applause. Men yelled and ladies clapped their hands and waved their handkerchiefs. It was a marvelous termination to a remarkable week of music . . . and if the cause of high art in music has made rapid progress in this city during the past two years, if our people have been educated to a still better appreciation of classic music well performed, the first acknowledgment of thanks is due to Theodore

Thomas. . . . He has been the moving and leading spirit through which it has been made possible to provide for our people every two years a pure musical feast—the consummate conductor,—the calculating, far-seeing organizer who supervised the work."

No sooner was the Cincinnati festival ended than Thomas went to Chicago to prepare for the third time a set of festival performances. Here, however, his work was far more difficult than in either of the two preceding festivals, for he had a chorus which had neither the organization nor the training of those in the other cities. With only a week in which to tune it up to concert pitch, it may be imagined that he called for rehearsals morning, noon, and night. Each part of the chorus was rehearsed separately during the day, and in the evenings mass rehearsals of all the singers were held. Finally the orchestra was added. The result was a fine series of performances, the standard of which was not much below that of the two preceding festivals. Amongst the choral numbers of this festival must be mentioned one which was remarkable, even in such a series of great performances as these. The credit of this number was not, however, due to Thomas, but to the chorus director, W. T. Tomlins. This was a chorus for women's voices from one of Bach's Cantatas. The number was not written for a chorus, but for two solo voices, but Tomlins had a fancy to have it sung by the full soprano and alto choirs of the chorus. When, however,

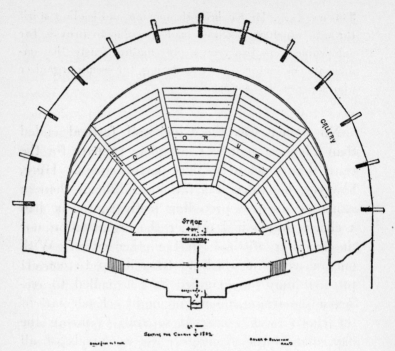

Seating for Chorus of Chicago Festival, 1882

he began to rehearse it he found it far more difficult for the singers than he had imagined. Rehearsal after rehearsal passed during two years, and still the choirs always became hopelessly involved in its polyphonic mysteries and could never sing it through without a breakdown. Tomlins at last began to despair of being able to carry out this little piece of virtuosity, and was on the point of giving it up; but one day, when the chorus had muddled it even worse than usual, he exclaimed, " Shut your books and sing from memory." The chorus did as they were bid, and lo, to everyone's amazement the thing went perfectly!

The explanation was simple. The music was so difficult, and the singers so anxious to do it well, that as long as they had it before them they kept their eyes glued to their notes and would not look at the conductor. But as soon as the notes were taken from them they were entirely dependent upon watching his beat and were, of course, guided correctly. After that the notes were never used for this number, and when Thomas conducted it in the festival it was without either notes or orchestral accompaniment, and it was so wonderfully sung that even he laid down his baton, as it ended, and joined the audience in demanding an encore—an extraordinary proceeding for him, for at festivals he made and enforced the strictest rules against encores.

Like its predecessors, the Chicago festival was a great artistic achievement, and its final concerts were summed up in the following clipping taken from the notice telegraphed to the New York *Herald,* at its close:

" Chicago, May 26, 1882. This, the last day of the Chicago festival, has been significantly the day of days of the series. At the matinée a great Wagner programme was given. It was simply perfection and aroused the greatest enthusiasm in an audience which numbered fully seven thousand people. At the evening concert, notwithstanding the fact that the rain poured down in torrents, the hall was crowded to its utmost capacity. There were present in the building over ten thousand persons, of whom twenty-five hundred stood throughout the entire performance."

The cost of the festival, in spite of the large attendance, nevertheless exceeded its receipts by $6,000, but it was not only cheerfully paid, but its promoters immediately set about planning for another, to be given two years later.

At the close of the Chicago festival, we may conclude that even Thomas needed a recess, and took it, for there are no records of concerts given by him for three weeks. But after that we find him taking the orchestra to the West again, and giving nightly concerts of the Summer Night class in Chicago, Milwaukee, Cleveland, and Cincinnati from June 19, to August 26, as a coda to the arduous season of 1881-82, and then, at last, he allowed himself a taste of pleasure in the quiet enjoyment of his home and family at the seashore, for a few weeks.

CHAPTER XIII

OCTOBER, 1882—OCTOBER, 1885

THOMAS ELECTED CONDUCTOR OF THE NEW YORK LIEDER-
KRANZ SOCIETY—PRODUCES GOUNOD'S " REDEMPTION "
—FIRST TRANS-CONTINENTAL TOUR IN 1883—CHIL-
DREN'S CONCERTS—LETTERS FROM RICHARD STRAUSS—
A CONCERT FOR WORKINGMEN—WAGNER FESTIVAL TOUR
—PROGRAMMES OF BOSTON WAGNER FESTIVAL—PRO-
POSAL OF MAYOR GRACE AND THREE THOUSAND OTHERS
—SECOND TRANS-CONTINENTAL TOUR IN 1885

EARLY in October we again find Thomas back
in New York, and busier than ever, for he now
added to his other choral work the leadership of
the New York Liederkranz Society. Indeed it is
almost impossible to believe that one man could
accomplish such a mountain of work as that with
which Thomas loaded himself down during the
season of 1882-83. Some idea of it may be
gained from the following leaf copied from his
memoranda of concerts and rehearsals during the
last week of November:

Nov. 20—Chorus rehearsal...Brooklyn
  " 21—Chorus rehearsal...Liederkranz
  " 22— { Chorus rehearsal.New York
          { Orch. rehearsal..Brooklyn Philharmonic
  " 23—Orch. rehearsal.....Jersey City
  " 24— { Concert ....Brooklyn Phil. (matinée)
          { Chorus rehearsal.Liederkranz

Nov. 25—Concert ....Brooklyn Phil. (Evening)
" 26— { Concert ....Liederkranz
       { Orch. rehearsal..New York
" 27— { Chorus rehearsal. Brooklyn
       { Orch. rehearsal..For Reading Concert
" 28— { Chorus rehearsal. Liederkranz
       { Orch. rehearsal..For Philadelphia

From the foregoing it will be seen that during the eight days recorded, Thomas held eleven rehearsals and gave three concerts. This was at the beginning of the season before things were really well started. Later were added the rehearsals and concerts of the New York and Brooklyn Philharmonic Societies, and preparations for a great spring concert tour, which kept him working at high pressure literally every moment of his waking hours.

The most important musical event of the fall season was his production of Gounod's recently composed work, "The Redemption," of which Thomas had secured the concert rights for America. No doubt when he made the arrangement with Gounod's publishers he thought it would be an easy matter to carry it out, but in this he found himself much mistaken. There was a tremendous interest in the work, and as chorus copies with the piano score were easy to get, more than one choral society learned it, trusting to luck to get the orchestra score and parts when the time should come for performance. Thomas had agreed to pay the publishers a royalty of two hundred dollars every time the work was performed from the genuine score, of which he, of course, had the only copy in America. He, therefore, had to charge the same rental for its use, plus the expenses of transporting it. These expenses were very large because he could not trust so valuable a work to the careless handling of all sorts of people, and had to send his own librarian with it whenever it was performed. Of course there were many complaints and all sorts of trouble in connection with handling the work, including even one lawsuit, so that it resulted in a loss of both time and money to himself, and the only satisfaction he got out of it was the pleasure of being the first to produce, in America, a great choral work, fresh from the hand of the most renowned of the French composers of the day. This was, however, no small satisfaction to him, for he took infinite pains all his life to be the first to perform the music of all nationalities, and when he got a chance to bring out a really important work of any kind, it was an event of which he was very proud. He was forever on the lookout for musical novelties, and nothing pleased him more than to find—as often happened—some work included in the list of novelties in Berlin or Paris, which he had already played a year or two previously in America.

One of the novelties of the fall of 1882 was the Scandinavian Symphony of the English composer, Frederic Cowen, who, on hearing of its production sent to Thomas the following pleasant letter of acknowledgment:

LONDON, *Nov.* 26, 1882.

My dear Mr. Thomas:

I have just heard of the performance of my Scandinavian symphony under your direction in New York, and I hasten to send you these few lines to thank you sincerely for your kindness in making the work known to the American public. That you should have taken up the symphony spontaneously is to me sufficient proof that you think well of it, and that is, I assure you, much more gratifying to me than all the applause of the public. I had the pleasure of hearing some of your concerts when I was in the States in '78 (when I was introduced to you by Mr. Hassard), and I feel quite sure that the work received an interpretation at the hands of your orchestra under your guidance which perhaps could not have been excelled by any other orchestra in the world, not even excepting the Vienna Philharmonic.

Once more pray accept my heartiest thanks, and, in the hope that you may some day feel disposed favorably towards some of my other works (perhaps my sacred cantata, " St. Ursula," written for the Munich Festival last year), believe me, dear sir,

Yours very truly,

FREDERIC H. COWEN.

The winter and early spring of 1883 were devoted to preparing and giving nine sets of concerts in New York and vicinity, which were as follows:

New York Philharmonic
Brooklyn Philharmonic
Steinway Hall Popular
Raphael Joseffy Concerts
Orange Symphony
Philadelphia Symphony
Liederkranz (Choral)

New York and Brooklyn Chorus Societies (Choral)
Jersey City Symphony

In addition to these regular series of concerts, he conducted a large number of single performances, one of which was given in January for the sufferers by inundations in Germany. Thomas was always expected to give a concert for the benefit of sufferers from the calamities of all nations, or when any special fund was being raised for a public purpose, and in this way he donated, in the course of his life, many, many thousands of dollars to every imaginable kind of philanthropic or artistic object. In this connection I am reminded of one other musician whose heart is always ready to respond to such appeals—the great-souled Paderewski, who has never come to America without leaving a large public benefaction to art or philanthropy behind him.

For the spring and early summer Thomas planned a very long and important concert tour, which was to end in a Summer Night season in Chicago. In announcing this tour the Chicago *Tribune* commented as follows:

" The most extensive and extraordinary concert tour ever made in this country by a symphony orchestra will be begun by Theodore Thomas on April 26. His circuit includes thirty cities and seventy-four concerts, and reaches from Baltimore to San Francisco. On the route, festivals will be held in Baltimore, Pittsburg, Louisville, Memphis, St. Louis, Kansas City, St. Paul, Minneapolis, San Francisco, Salt Lake City, Denver, and Omaha. For

every one of these twelve festivals, a chorus has been organized and rehearsed, the smallest comprising 380 voices,
at Minneapolis, and the largest, the great Mormon Choir
at Salt Lake City, of three thousand. Besides these twelve
festivals, there will be concerts in many intermediate cities.
The final concert of this extraordinary tour, which
stretches from ocean to ocean, will be at Burlington, Iowa,
on July 7. . . . It is a remarkable fact that every one
of these seventy-four concerts has been guaranteed and
the money raised without the slightest difficulty. This
shows a remarkable interest in music in these distant
cities. Out of all this enthusiasm and zeal will result a
decided, healthy impulse for music in this country. Having heard this splendid body of musicians under so great
a leader, the people will not be so contented as heretofore
with trash. They will demand a higher standard in their
home performances, and in every direction music will advance to a higher and more dignified plane. There is only
one cause for apprehension. The route is one of extraordinary length and duration. For three months Mr.
Thomas cannot take a single day of rest. He will be traveling or conducting almost without an hour's intermission,
from April 26 to July 9. His health has not been of the
best of late, and this trip will require herculean powers
of endurance. It would be appalling to almost any other
musician. In what trim, therefore, will he be at the close
of this march from sea to sea? "

No one who has not personally followed the
work of preparing for a musical festival can have
any idea of the amount of detail in which it
involves the conductor. First he must select the
programmes and map out the work of the chorus
and its local director. For this, editions of the

works to be performed must be studied and compared with the score, translations revised, cuts made, mistakes corrected and, if possible, personal rehearsals conducted from time to time. Often no good edition of a choral work selected is obtainable, especially if it is an excerpt from a long composition, such as an opera or oratorio. In this case the music has to be arranged, a translation of the words made, and an edition especially printed for the occasion. After the chorus work is arranged for, comes the still more difficult task of apportioning the work of the soloists. The solo artists are the popular "drawing card" of a festival, and are depended on, not only to complete the artistic unity of its programmes, but also to attract the general public, and thus dispose of the surplus seats not sold in the season ticket sale. For this reason it is necessary that each programme shall have its own star attraction in the matter of soloists, but that no soloist shall sing in two consecutive concerts. Also, as great singers are human, and liable to the ills that flesh is heir to, there must be an "understudy" for every number of every singer, ready to take his or her part at a moment's notice, in case of sickness or accident. Finally, the orchestra must be prepared, scores corrected, bowing marked, extra parts copied, and diagrams made of platforms for both chorus and orchestra, and the seating arrangements required for the various concerts. There are also programmes to be printed, and proofs corrected, traveling arrangements to be made, and schedules of the time of the arrival and departure of trains, and the hotels where the troupe is to stay in each city, as well as the dates and hours of the concerts and the halls where they are to take place. In short there seems to be no end to the multitude of details incident to this class of musical performance, and Thomas required that every one of them should be passed under his critical eye, whether attended to by himself or by one of his numerous subordinate officers.

For the twelve festivals of the spring of 1883, nearly every programme was different, and only in a few instances was a programme given in one city repeated without change in another. Nothing illustrates Thomas' powers of organization better than this tour across the continent, planned and arranged for, in all its hundreds of details, at the time when he was carrying on nine distinct series of concerts in New York and vicinity, and conducting three chorus societies as well as his own orchestra. And so thoroughly was the work done that when the concerts actually took place, one after the other, not a detail was lacking, but in every city each performance moved along with the perfect smoothness and certainty which characterized his work at home.

One secret of his achievements in this respect, was his habit of keeping a little memorandum book always in his pocket, in which he jotted down every detail which had to be remembered. As soon as an item was attended to, it was immediately crossed off. These little books tell the

story of his life day by day, and the following
is a page copied at random from one which he
carried at about this time:

As this long and important tour neared its close, and Thomas and his orchestra approached Chicago, he began to bethink him of a place to live in during the five weeks of summer concerts in that city, for the hotels were very inferior there at that time, and he was all worn out with the strain and fatigue of the trip, and longed for the peace and quiet of a home. Some years previously he had made the acquaintance of my sister Amy Fay and myself, at one of his Eastern Symphony Concerts in which she had made her American *début,* as pianist, under his leadership. The acquaintance thus professionally begun had been continued from time to time, as he visited Chicago, and gradually included other members of the family, for we were all ardently devoted to music, and more or less connected with the musical interests of the city. It was therefore natural that in his search for a boarding place in a private house, he should have turned to us, and towards the end of June I received from him the following letter:

DENVER, COLO., *June 23, 1883.*

My dear Miss Fay:

I am going to ask you to do something for me. I dislike the hotels in Chicago so much that I dread to go there at all. I have written to some friends to try to secure rooms for me elsewhere if possible, but they never succeeded before in finding anything suitable, and probably will not this time. Then it occurred to my mind that your sister, Mrs. Peirce, told me last year that she could have made it possible to have accommodated me in her house.

Will you kindly find out if this is possible this year and let me know?

I will tell you what I need. Two rooms, connecting, one as a sitting-room, the other to sleep in. I would like a bathroom, but would be satisfied with a " *Sitzbad* " in my bedroom. I must have strong coffee (poison) for my breakfast, and plenty of meat for my dinner. Also a little cold luncheon, consisting of bread and meat, after the concert, if possible in my room. My wine I, of course, provide for myself. I receive no calls.

There may be one drawback, that the dinner hour is too near the concert for me. In that case perhaps I could have a substantial luncheon in the middle of the day, and a bite with a cup of tea at the late dinner hour. If another room is to be had anywhere, I would like it for my secretary, or for my orchestra manager, Mr. Sachleben. In return for giving you all this trouble I will help you with the winter programmes of your Amateur Musical Club, or with anything else in which I can be of service. Our stay in Chicago will be five weeks, and I inclose the list of our last week of the tour that you may know where to address the answer.

Very truly yours,
THEODORE THOMAS.

The reply to this letter was in the affirmative, and the appointed day saw Thomas and his companion arrive at Mrs. Peirce's house with his accustomed punctuality. He was extremely tired, but nevertheless cheerful and happy, and apparently none the worse for his long and hard trip, and a few days in the quiet comfort of a well-ordered home put him into his normal state of physical well-being. After this sojourn in my sister's house, all formality between Thomas and the Fay family naturally vanished, and, as the years went on, the tie then formed drew ever closer and closer until, at last, it became the dominating influence of the closing period of his career.

Another friendship which had an important influence on all of Thomas' Western life, and which began to mature into a closer relation than that of mere acquaintanceship at about this period, was with George P. Upton. He had long known Mr. Upton in a formal way, as a gifted and able writer, and a learned, discriminating critic of music and musicians. Now, as he came to know him more intimately, he found him to be, not only a sincere and earnest man, but one who, although the musical autocrat of one of the most powerful American newspapers, was as unassuming as he was influential, and used his commanding position on the press, not for his own advantage, but for the furtherance of art in its highest sense. Chicago music to-day owes a debt of gratitude to George P. Upton which should never be forgotten, and which, owing to his own self-effacing modesty, is but imperfectly realized by the present generation which is reaping the harvest he helped to sow.

The Chicago Summer Night Concert season was a mere bagatelle to Thomas, after the labors of the preceding year, and partook of the nature of almost a rest. At its close he went to Milwaukee for a short series of concerts, and the

following letter, announcing his arrival, well expresses the effervescing joyousness of his mood
as the time drew near in which he could throw
off his heavy professional cares and enjoy a vacation with his family:

MILWAUKEE, *August* 14, 1883.

Dear Miss Fay:

Milwaukee again! The weather is very cold here, and
everybody is wearing winter clothes—at least all those
who have any, I suppose, for I saw a cadet having on a
linen duster, who evidently possessed a warm imagination!
The sudden cold weather affects the pitch of the orchestra,
and the light was very poor at the concert last night, so
I was thoroughly MAD by the time we got to the second
piece on the programme. The third piece was the
Allegretto from the Seventh Beethoven Symphony, which
of course suffered under the circumstances, but the fourth
and close of the first part was the Liszt Rhapsody, which
gained under the influence of temper and angry feeling.
(A conundrum, which is the best piece of music? Ask
your friend Mr. Jones.) The public became very enthusiastic and made a noise in turn, but I did not thank for
their noise, so they got mad and I became tranquil, after
which the playing improved.

I did not sit so long at breakfast this morning as at
Mrs. Peirce's, but the meal was good even after her table,
but not so refined. My coffee, a pot strong and good,
was brought for me without asking, the people remembering from former years how I like it, a waiter of old, and a
table reserved for a " particular private boarder," with
extra and particular care arrayed, plates, and silverware.
You will say " he is getting spoiled there as everywhere
else."

If you want me to come to breakfast on my way through Chicago next Sunday morning, you will have to send me an invitation signed by the whole family, for I was treated at times rather plainly by Fräulein Lili, not to call it by any other name. Think of it! however, I am forgiving. Give my warmest regards to S. and F., not forgetting Mr. X., who always looked at me like a dog, growling and waiting for a chance to get a piece out of my calf! Well, I forgive them also, and perhaps they forgive me since I am gone—that old Thomas.

Sincerely,
THEODORE THOMAS.

The delicate health of Mrs. Thomas, and his desire to give his children the advantages of some European study and travel, had decided Thomas to send his entire family to Europe for a couple of years, immediately after the New York festival. As soon, therefore, as the Milwaukee season was over he sailed for Europe and spent his vacation with them there. Thomas led so busy a life that he had very little time to devote to intercourse with his family. But in his rare moments of leisure, or during his summer vacations, he gave himself up to the pleasures of home life unreservedly, and was so gay, joyous, and full of fun that he was more like an older brother than a father to his children. His idea of a good time was to collect all his family around him, exclude the world, and have some sort of a feast, with all kinds of fun and nonsense, and ceremonies, many and various, which he had carefully planned beforehand, to give zest to the occasion. At such times he would exert all his charm of personality to make the hours pass delightfully, and only then did he permit himself to cast aside the mantle of reserve in which he habitually wrapped his inner thoughts and feelings before the world.

His stay in Europe was very brief, and by early fall he had again returned to New York, and plunged into a season of which the concerts followed each other with hardly a day of intermission until July, and included a Wagner Festival tour of the largest dimensions at its close. All thought of pleasure was now banished from his mind and he was again the stern, intensely serious artist, concentrating all his powers on his work. During the late fall he made a short tour in the South, and the following letter, written on that trip, gives a glimpse of his busy life:

ATLANTA, GA., *December 2, 1883.*

Dear Miss Fay:

Yours of November 24 received yesterday. I certainly meant to have written you long ago, but you cannot understand the amount of work I am loaded with this year. I had determined to free myself from certain engagements, such as chorus societies in New York, and some other matters not belonging to my specialty. But in every case personal influences were brought to bear that I felt I must yield to, or at least I did, at the risk of ruining my health. It is a serious question that I am at present not able to solve. I have a secretary who assists me much, and other helpers who keep every-day matters off of me, nevertheless I have not had a moment to myself since I returned from Europe.

In Europe I did not find the expected rest on account of the many discomforts of traveling. I hate the Continent, and that is much for me to say, and I would never go over again but for my family. This country is good enough for me. Here in the sunny South, however, I have been sick for the last two days from overwork and poor food.

To me the future does not look dark, but only like an idle dream. I have not had the good fortune of a Christian education to sweeten my life. Believe me always

Truly yours,

THEODORE THOMAS.

While in Europe, the previous summer, Thomas had, as usual, been on the lookout for musical novelties for coming programmes. He had met, in Munich, a young and almost unknown composer, one Richard Strauss, who had recently finnished writing a symphony. Thomas secured the first movement of the work, and was so much impressed with it that he requested young Strauss to let him have the other movements, promising to bring out the whole work in a concert of the Philharmonic Society. In answer to his request, he received the following interesting letter:

MUNICH, *Sept.* 20, 1883.

MR. THEODORE THOMAS.

Highly honored sir:

As I was unfortunately unable to welcome you here this summer—having only learned of your presence in Munich from Mr. Lockwood on the eve of your departure—I must not neglect to express to you in writing my heartiest and warmest thanks for your kind intention to give my second symphony the great honor of a New York performance. My father also wishes to be remembered to you, and joins me in thanking you in advance.

According to your request, I have had the score of the three movements not already known to you written out, and also single parts of the string quartette, and have already corrected them. I must ask you to kindly paste the two inclosed changes in the *Scherzo* into your score. I have made these changes for harmonic reasons, in order to avoid the too strong predominance of the C minor key in the Ab major *Scherzo*. The number of measures is indicated on the back of the slip. In the parts the changes have already been made.

Thanking you again most sincerely, and begging you to remember me to your family, I remain, with the highest esteem,

Your ever grateful

RICHARD STRAUSS.

The symphony was received too late for Thomas to perform it during the season of 1883-84, but on December 13 of the following winter, he fulfilled his promise, and gave it its first American performance, as we shall see later.

The early months of 1884 were only a continuation of the regular routine, but two new features were added. These were a series of concerts especially designed for young people, planned by a number of New York women, and a series for workingmen inaugurated by a society named "The People's Concert Society," an organization founded for the philanthropic purpose of giving the best class of music to working people, free of charge.

Thomas was, at first, interested in both of these projects, and even in after years he was always willing to lend his aid to such work, but a little experience taught him that neither children nor what are called " wage-workers " were sufficiently advanced intellectually to be able to appreciate the class of music which was his specialty. " Symphonic music," he once said, in speaking of these concerts, " is the highest flower of art. Only the most cultivated persons are able to understand it. How, then, can we expect the ignorant or the immature mind to grasp its subtleties? The kind of music suitable for them is that which has very clearly-defined melody and well-marked rhythms, such, for instance, as is played by the best bands. The orchestra, with its unlimited palette, whereby the modern composer paints in every shade and gradation of tone color, as well as the complexities of symphonic form, are far beyond the grasp of beginners. There should be, it is true, concerts for these classes, which would prepare them for the higher grade of musical performances. But it is waste of time for a great symphony orchestra to do this work, which could be equally well accomplished by smaller and less costly organizations. In my judgment an orchestra, such as mine, can be of more service to the community by selling a certain number of twenty-five-cent tickets to all its concerts, for the benefit of students and other music-lovers of small means, than by giving an occasional free concert to people who can only enjoy it in a limited degree." Thomas was, nevertheless, very willing to try the experiment, and he must have found that some good resulted from the series for young people, at least, for he continued them, off and on, all the rest of his life. A programme is given from each class as an example of the music which he thought suitable for audiences of these kinds:

YOUNG PEOPLE'S CONCERT

Steinway Hall, February 2, 1884

Programme

Overture, " Jubilee ".........................Weber
Andante from the " Surprise " Symphony.......Haydn
Aria, " Batti, batti," Don Giovanni..............Mozart
Miss Emma Juch
Symphonic Poem, " Rouet d'Omphale ".....Saint Saens
(a) Humoreske............................Grieg
(b) Minuet..............................Moskowsky
Miss Mary Garlichs
Cavatina, " Bel ragio," Semiramis..............Rossini
Miss Juch
Minuet ....Boccherini
Overture, " The Merry Wives of Windsor ".......Nicolai

WORKINGMEN'S CONCERT

Steinway Hall, February 24, 1884

Programme

Prelude, Choral and Fugue (arranged for orchestra by Abert)...........................Bach

Song, " Am Meer " (for orchestra by Theo. Thomas),

Schubert

Mr. Franz Remmertz

Symphony No. 5........................Beethoven

Overture, " Midsummer Night's Dream "......Mendelssohn

Song, " The Two Grenadiers ".............Schubert

Mr. Remmertz

Invitation to the Dance (orchestration by Berlioz),

Weber

Overture, Rienzi..........................Wagner

Until the middle of April, Thomas was kept busy by his many home engagements, and by the preparations for the great spring Wagner Festival Tour, already alluded to, which was to begin at Boston, on April 22, and end in Montreal on June 28. All things considered, this was, artistically, the most important concert tour he ever made, as well as one of the longest. It consisted of about seventy consecutive concerts, nearly all of which were festival performances, and, as usual, very few of the programmes were repeated literally, though Wagner's music was the chief ingredient of which most of them were composed. As in the tour of the previous spring, choruses had been trained in every city in which these performances were to be given, and their expenses guaranteed. The soloists were Wagner's three most important Baireuth artists—Emil Scaria, bass; Hermann Winkelmann, tenor, and Amalia Materna, soprano—as well as Christine Nilsson, Emma Juch, Max Heinrich, Franz Remmertz, and others. The preparatory work of this tour was almost too much for even Thomas, and the following note, scratched off so hurriedly that it is hardly legible, was the only word we had from him during the entire winter:

New York, *March* 31, 1884.

Dear Miss Fay:

Your letter I have duly received. All I can do at present is to acknowledge it, when the time comes that I can breathe again I will write. At present I am not only occupied day and night, but have constantly about me six men, sitting in different rooms in my house correcting and copying orchestral parts for the spring tour. The orchestral rehearsals and piano rehearsals have begun, and I do not hesitate to say that every twenty-four hours I have enough work to do to kill the average man. The singers are on the ocean, and to-day week the first concert belongs to history.

Yours hastily,

THEODORE THOMAS.

A still more eloquent witness to the labors of this season is the book in which he habitually entered with his own hand, and with the most absolute accuracy of detail, every programme he conducted, in chronological order. During this season the programmes are written in another hand, and are so full of errors that no reliance can be placed upon them, showing that Thomas did not even have time to read over and correct them. This was something unheard of for him, for he kept the book for reference, and was so particular to have it accurate that he never even

omitted or abbreviated the words " Programme,"
or " Intermission," or failed to write out in full
all the movements of symphonies, suites, etc., as
well as the names and initials of the soloists, the
opus numbers, and every other smallest detail.

The most important festivals of this tour were
those of Boston, New York, Cincinnati, and Chicago. The concerts of the first named were given
in the Mechanics' Hall, and were on the largest
scale. The chorus was the Haendel and Haydn
Society, reinforced by the New York and Brooklyn
choruses, and the programmes are given in full,
as they are typical of, not only the Wagner
" Festival Programmes," which Thomas gave in
the above-named cities during this season, but of
similar programmes given throughout his life in
all parts of the country:

WAGNER FESTIVAL CONCERTS
Mechanics' Hall, April 22, 1884

BOSTON

Programme I

TANNHAEUSER
  (a) Overture, Bacchanale, Chorus of Sirens, Act I
  (b) Scenes I, II, III, Act II
  (c) March and Chorus
     Frau Materna, Herren Winkelmann, Remmertz,
               Scaria, and Chorus
               Intermission
DIE WALKUERE
  (a) Ride of the Walkyries

(b) Wotan's Farewell, Act III
(c) Magic Fire Scene
Herr Scaria

SIEGFRIED
   Finale, Act III—Siegfried's Wooing
Frau Materna, Herr Winkelmann

Programme II

CENTENNIAL EXHIBITION MARCH
TRISTAN AND ISOLDE
   (a) Vorspiel, Act I
   (b) Love-duo and Finale, Act II
Frau Materna, Miss Juch, Herren Winkelmann
and Scaria

Intermission

DIE MEISTERSINGER.   ACT III
   (a) Prelude
   (b) Sachs' Monologue
   (c) Quintet
   (d) Chorus of Cobblers, Tailors, and Bakers
   (e) Dance of Apprentices
   (f) Procession of Mastersingers
   (g) Chorus, " Awake! "
   (h) Prize Song and Finale
Misses Juch and Winant, Herren Winkelmann,
Toedt, Scaria, Remmertz, and Chorus

Programme III

THE FLYING DUTCHMAN
   (a) Overture
   (b) Introduction, Spinning Song and Ballade, Act II
Misses Juch, Winant, and Chorus

DIE MEISTERSINGER
  (a) Vorspiel, Act I
  (b) Pogner's Address
                Herr Scaria
GOETTERDAEMMERUNG.   ACT III.   (*Complete*)
      Frau Materna, Herren Winkelmann, Remmertz,
        Toedt, Mrs. Hartdegen, Misses Juch and
        Winant
                Programme IV

HULDIGUNG'S MARSCH
LOHENGRIN
  (a) Prelude, Act I
  (b) Grand Duo, Elsa and Ortrude $\Big\}$ Act II
  (c) Bridal Procession, and Chorus
  (d) Introduction
  (e) Chorus, " Faithful and True " $\Bigg\}$ Act III
  (f) Grand Duo, Lohengrin and Elsa
  (g) March
      Madame Nilsson, Frau Materna, Herr Winkel-
                mann, and Chorus
PARSIFAL
  (a) Vorspiel, Act I
  (b) Flower-girl Scene, Kundry's Solicitations, Act II
  (c) Good Friday Spell, Funeral Procession, Finale,
        Act III
      Frau Materna, Herren Winkelmann, Remmertz,
        Scaria, Mrs. Hartdegen, Mrs. Denniston,
        Misses Sims, Earle, Zelie de Lussan, and
        Hirsch; New York Chorus Society and
        Brooklyn Philharmonic Chorus

                Programme V
RHEINGOLD
  (a) Alberich and the Rhine-Maidens
  (b) Wotan beholds Walhalla

(c) Loge's Narrative

(d) The Rainbow Bridge and Maidens' Lament
   Misses Juch and Winant, Mrs. Hartdegen, Her-
      ren Remmertz, Scaria, and Toedt

DIE WALKUERE

(a) Introduction

(b) Siegmund and Sieglinde, Love-song and } Act I
   Duo

(c) Ride of the Walkyries

(d) Bruennhilde's Supplication } Act III

(e) Wotan's Farewell and Magic Fire Scene
   Frau Materna, Herren Winkelmann and Scaria

The tour thus brilliantly inaugurated in Boston was continued, without any untoward happenings, to its close in Montreal on June 28. While in this city he received the following letter from the eminent English composer, Alexander Mackenzie, a number of whose works he had produced from time to time:

FLORENCE, ITALY, *June* 17, 1884.

My dear Mr. Thomas:

I think it is hardly needful for me to introduce myself to you, since one of the objects of this letter is to thank you for introducing me to a great many people! It has been my intention to write to you for a long time, but during my recent stay in London my time was so much occupied that I preferred to postpone doing so until I returned to my home in Italy. I arrived here only two days ago, and am already making up for much lost time, and am again in the midst of the pleasant agonies of composition!

First let me thank you most cordially for the trouble you have given yourself with some of my works, and for the great service you have already rendered me by your performances in America. I am fully sensible of the benefit you have done me, and I hope the result justified your choice. I confess I am very ambitious to be heard in America, and these performances make me the more anxious to produce better work in the future.

At present I shall remain here until the first of October, when I return to London for a short time to bring out my "Rose of Sharon." As I passed through Paris last week I rehearsed with Miss Nevada, who is cast for the principal soprano part. I should say that her innocent, almost childlike voice will be quite adapted to the character of the Sulamite, and I am hatching hopes of a success.

I heard with great pleasure that the oratorio had been already accepted by you, and that an early performance was already decided upon. There is a great deal for the soprano and a great lot of chorus work; in fact, the chorus, although I think there are no difficulties, have their work cut out for them as far as quantity is concerned. The book is, it is agreed by all who have seen it, a very fine one, and has the merit of being something new in oratorio.

I am now occupying myself with a violin concerto, for the Birmingham Festival, and a new opera for Carl Rosa, after that—well, the easel is full, but luckily I have been able to make more liberal terms as to time than hitherto, and for me I hope there will be no more hurry, and writing against time, which is the bane of our present musical system in England.

Pardon me for having chattered so much about myself in this, my introduction to you—it is not my usual wont. I follow your concerts and musical doings by means of

the various musical papers, and delight in reading your
programmes, which are amazing in every respect. . . .
I trust that at no distant period I may have the pleasure
of meeting you in person, and in the meantime permit me
to thank you once more.

Believe me, my dear Sir,

Most faithfully yours,

ALEXANDER C. MACKENZIE.

As soon as this concert tour was ended,
Thomas joined his family for a long summer of
rest and enjoyment in Europe, and when he returned in the fall, he brought them back with him
to the house in East Seventeenth Street, which had
been their home since their return from Cincinnati.

Thomas was soon in harness again, and giving
a concert or two nearly every day. But he seems
to have felt the need of a mental rest after the
severe labors of the two preceding years, for, during the winter season of 1884-85, he gave no festival
performances, and embarked upon no musical
schemes of great magnitude, but contented himself with his regular work at home, as conductor
of the New York and Brooklyn Philharmonic
Societies, the three Choral Societies, and his many
concerts in the immediate vicinity of New York.
The most interesting event of the winter, though
it did not appear to have any unusual significance
at the time, was his production, in December, of
the Strauss symphony, already alluded to. If I
am not mistaken, Thomas was the first to play
it either in America or Europe. It scored an immediate success, and was given many times by

the leading conductors of Europe, within a short time afterwards. The young composer was very anxious in regard to this first performance of a work so important to him. Thomas did not immediately find the time to write him the good news about it, but one of those delightful " friends," whose sweet privilege it is to repeat disagreeable things to one, immediately sent poor Strauss a very *bad* notice, clipped from one of the New York papers. This distressed Strauss so much that he wrote the following letter to Thomas:

MUNICH, *Jan.* 2, 1884.

Highly Honored Mr. Thomas:

To-day, for the first time, I got some sign of life from the performance of my symphony in New York, in, it must be confessed, a very bad criticism of my work from I do not know what paper. This, combined with your absolute silence in regard to the performance, points to the certainty that my work has made a fiasco in New York. This, however, will not prevent me from expressing to you, much honored sir, my fullest, deepest, and most hearty thanks that you had the extraordinary goodness to present my symphony to the New York public. It is principally on your account that I deplore the nonsuccess of the work, and regret that your remarkable kindness was not rewarded by the applause of the critics. I console myself for the failure of my symphony with the critics and public, with the thought that the judgment of the musicians was favorable to me (which I care most for) and especially that you, most honored sir, considered my work worthy of production in your concerts. It would be very friendly if you would write me

a few lines giving me your own judgment of the performance, and your exact opinion of my work, adding, perhaps, a few criticisms of it. At the same time, I beg of
you to express my sincere thanks to your orchestra, and
believe me always gratefully

Your devoted

RICHARD STRAUSS.

The next letter was in a different strain, and
shows that the young giant had, in the meantime,
already taken some strides towards the Olympus
he reached in later life:

MUNICH, *April* 12, 1885.

Honored Mr. Thomas:

The joy your delightful letter gave to me and mine you
can scarcely conceive; it was one of the most beautiful
and happiest surprises that I could possibly have had!
Receive therefore, once more, my warmest thanks for
bringing out my work in New York, as well as for so
kindly sending me the good news of its success. Your own
extremely flattering opinion of it increased my pleasure,
if that were possible. The criticisms I had received of
it were not of a nature to allow me to indulge in the hope
of success, taken as the only ones. With one exception
they were all so ordinary and superficial that they pointed
to failure rather than success. That the latter was the
case, rejoices my heart, especially on your account, as it
was a dreadful thought to me that my work might have
brought discredit on you.

As you have perhaps heard, Dr. Wuellner brought out
the work a month later in Cologne, and there it had an
extraordinary success, with both critics and public. I myself heard the work there for the first time. Here in
Munich it will be given next winter, without doubt.

Your kind offer to conduct my next orchestral work in New York I accept with the most cordial thanks, and will surely avail myself of it. In the way of new things I have lately worked at a Suite in four movements (Prelude, Romanze, Gavotte, Introduction, and Fugue) for the thirteen wind instruments, and a piano quartette. Just at present I am busy with a chorus work, Werther's "Trauerlied," by Goethe, for six-part chorus and grand orchestra.

My father begs to be remembered to you, with thanks, and I remain

Your most respectful and grateful

RICHARD STRAUSS.

The gratitude of this great composer for the recognition given him by Thomas was a striking contrast to the egotism and greed of Wagner, for whose art Thomas had done so infinitely greater a service. Strauss never forgot the helping hand thus held out to him when he was young and unknown, or lost an opportunity, as long as Thomas lived, to express his appreciation.

In January of this year Thomas received a letter signed by the Mayor of New York, and 3,000 citizens, which seemed to promise, at last, the fulfillment of his long-deferred hopes for a permanently endowed orchestra. It was as follows:

NEW YORK, *January* 1, 1885.

MR. THEODORE THOMAS.

Dear Sir:

For the promotion of musical culture in this country, the undersigned are desirous of having a series of weekly

concerts and matinées similar to those which are so successfully given in the great cities of Europe—London,
Paris, and Berlin—and recognizing your eminent services
in the cause of music in the past, may we beg that you
will undertake the same, and communicate to us at your
earliest convenience your decision, and at the same time
favor us with your views as to the character and scope of
the concerts, as we have ample assurance of financial
success in case of your acceptance.

We are, dear sir,
                    Yours etc.,
                         WILLIAM R. GRACE,
                              Mayor of the City of New York,
                                   and 3,000 others.

To this letter Thomas sent the following answer:

                              NEW YORK, *January 3*, 1885.

The Hon. William R. Grace, Mayor of the City of
New York, and 3,000 Others:

Your proposal of two weekly concerts in this city during the winter months makes possible the realization of a
long cherished hope—the establishment of a permanent
orchestra in the city of New York. By a permanent orchestra I mean one which plays under the same conductor
all the year around. This means daily employment, and
your proposition, in connection with my other engagements, will enable me to give that to the members of the
orchestra.

I have already engagements for next winter which insure four concerts a week. The Philharmonic Society of
Brooklyn, under whose intelligent and liberal management
the musical taste of the public of that city has developed

so rapidly that additional concerts have been given each year to meet the increased demand, propose next year to extend their already large list, by adding to the number of popular concerts. Then, beside the New York Chorus and Popular concerts, we have had for several years a regular series of Symphony concerts in Philadelphia, Orange, Jersey City, and this year New Haven has joined the list. These with two New York weekly concerts would give the orchestra six performances a week for six months. For the other six months there are traveling engagements for spring and fall, and the regular series of Summer Night concerts in Chicago during July and August. This fills out the year.

The benefits of a permanent orchestra and frequent performances are of great value. We shall thus be enabled to give, in a finished manner, a class of musical works which have now little opportunity to be heard. The Philharmonic Society, with its high standard, and few concerts, can only give standard works of the highest character. It cannot give experimental music. My idea of the concerts which you propose, would be to give the lighter symphonies and all the best novelties. The second part of the programme would always be devoted to lighter music, or music of a popular character. The concerts would be, in fact, educational, leading the public taste up to the Philharmonic standard. In short, the programmes would be similar to those given years ago in the Central Park Garden Concerts. For the matinées it might be well to have the programmes of the alternate concerts especially arranged for young people, like the present series of that name.

The assurance of support given me by the three thousand signatures appended to your letter, including, as they do, so many of our leading citizens, seems to guarantee

Theodore Thomas as He Appeared in Concert

the entire success of the project, and if my views of the character of the concerts meet your approbation, I shall be glad to undertake the work.

Faithfully yours,

THEODORE THOMAS.

" There is a tide in the affairs of men,"—saith the poet,—" which, taken at the flood, leads on to fortune." This was the flood-tide of Thomas' career. If he had only known it, and taken advantage of its splendid opportunity, all the rest of his life would have been plain sailing over a calm sea. But Thomas was not born for peace and a quiet life, and we shall presently see how altered musical conditions in New York, on the one hand, and his own errors in judgment, on the other, involved him in storms and tempests which wellnigh wrecked his life beyond all hope of rescue.

During the winter of 1884-85 he did not travel, but towards the end of April he made another trans-continental tour which began at Portland, Me., and extended to San Francisco, and return. This was not, however, a festival tour, although some of the performances were choral, and he took with him some celebrated solo singers for the rendering of certain Wagner selections—Frau Materna, Madame Fursch-Madi, Miss Emma Juch, and others—so the preparatory work of it had been comparatively light. Nor were the performances themselves so taxing, except in a few instances, as those of the two previous spring tours had been.

It was while on this trip that an amusing incident occurred in connection with a troop of old-time Western " Cowboys." The train had halted at a small way-station on the prairies of the Far West, and as there was to be a half hour to spare before it started again, Thomas strolled off for a short walk. As he returned he saw some commotion going on around the train, and that it was surrounded by a band of rough-looking men, armed to the teeth, who were talking excitedly to some of the orchestra.

" What is the matter? " he inquired, as soon as he came within speaking distance of the first man he met.

" They want some music," was the unexpected answer. " What shall we do? "

" Better give it to them," said Thomas calmly. " Let somebody play something for them." But no one seemed anxious to be the soloist of this particular concert; meantime the cowboys began to get impatient.

" Well then, give me a fiddle and I'll play myself," said he, and taking a violin from the case he tuned it and began. The cowboys listened uninterestedly and then announced that that was not what they wanted. By this time Thomas began to lose patience, and, turning to the spokesman, remarked, " You don't know what you want." This angered the cowboy and he promptly replied, with more force than courtesy:

" We know pretty —— —— well what we want. We want some *singing*." Thomas glanced at the revolvers, and the fierce faces of the men, and concluded that this was one of those occasions when prudence was the better part of valor. So he called to his European songbirds, but they had all locked themselves securely in their state-rooms, and declined to come out. The situation was finally saved by the plucky little American, Emma Juch, who stood on the rear platform of the car and sang "Home, Sweet Home," her fair hair blowing in the wind and her clear voice ringing out over the desolate prairie. The cow-boys were enchanted, and as she sang the train moved off, leaving her enthusiastic audience firing off guns and pistols, and yelling vociferous applause!

At the close of this tour Thomas gave his customary season of Summer Night concerts in Chicago, but as Mrs. Peirce had given up her house there, he was once more driven back to a hotel for his living place, and during this summer his whole time was so engrossed in planning a new and very extensive musical project, that we rarely saw him away from the concert hall.

CHAPTER XIV

OCTOBER, 1885, TO OCTOBER, 1887

THE GERMAN, AMERICAN, AND NATIONAL OPERA COM-
PANIES, AND THEIR OUTCOME—PURCHASE OF A COUN-
TRY PLACE AT FAIRHAVEN, MASS.

IN order to understand the events of the following chapter it is necessary to go back a little
and quote from a letter from Thomas to his friend,
Lawrence Maxwell, written in February, 1883.
In this letter, he said:

". . . Abbey, the New York impresario, wants to
engage me for next year as the musical director of the
proposed new 'German Opera Company.' He would expect me to give up everything except the Philharmonic
concerts, and promises that I need not travel with the
troupe. I would have an assistant for the Italian operas.
Yes, I understand that, but who would conduct the German operas in Boston, Chicago, or Cincinnati? When
the time came I should have to go just the same. Besides, my income is so large and permanent from my own
specialty, my only trouble is that I cannot accept half of
the engagements offered me. And as for opera in this
country—no wardrobe, no library, new opera house, and
everything new—it may be all over again after one season,
or deteriorate into a second-class concern."

This offer Thomas at first refused, but he finally
accepted on the condition that he should be allowed

a year in which to go to Europe and study the methods of European opera companies and conductors, in order that the German operas should be given in the very best and most up-to-date manner. This was agreed to, and he engaged the three great Wagner singers—Materna, Winkelmann, and Scaria—to interpret the *rôles* they had created under the instruction of Wagner himself, at Baireuth, and which were to be the chief feature of the new company, as, up to that time, Wagner's operas had most of them only been heard in the concert hall in America.

Meantime, the furor over Wagner's music, created by the many performances of it Thomas had given in New York, especially at the festival of 1882, had suggested to others also, that Wagner, or " German " opera, as it was called, might be profitable, and a company was formed to antedate the scheme of Thomas, and put into immediate execution a plan similar to that which he was expecting to bring to maturity the following year. Engagements were offered to the famous Wagner singers by the management of the new opera company, and although Winkelmann and Scaria kept their faith with Thomas and refused to come, Materna broke hers, and accepted. Of course, with another company in the field, and in possession of his chief *prima donna,* it was useless to attempt to carry out his plan of reproducing the Baireuth performances, and it was consequently abandoned.

To give up the German opera scheme did not

cost Thomas much sacrifice, for he had not had much faith in the enterprise, nor was he wholly in sympathy with the way in which it was to be carried out, which was what is called the " star system," a system by which everything about the performance is made subservient to the artists who sing the principal *rôles*. His ideal opera was one in which all the concomitant parts—soloists, chorus, orchestra, and scenery—should be equally balanced and excellent. He also wanted the text sung in English, and as many of the parts as possible sung by Americans. Thomas felt no interest in art as a commercial enterprise, and when he undertook anything he always had in mind the object of advancing the music of the country, in one form or another. He wanted to establish a high standard of operatic performance, in all parts of America, in the same sense that he had already established a high standard of orchestra performance. But he cared not at all for opera considered as a fashionable social function.

It would have been fortunate for him had no other operatic offer come to him, for in that case probably the intention of the Mayor and the 3,000 music-lovers to make his orchestra permanent, would have been carried out, and he would never have been tempted to return to the treacherous domain of operatic enterprise. But hardly had he given up the German opera scheme when an offer came to him which was so exactly in accordance with his desires that he accepted it, despite the warnings and advice of friends, who had his best interests at heart and saw more clearly than he the weak points of the new project, and the difficulties in the way of its success.

It is needless to say that the scheme which had now enlisted the coöperation of Thomas was a very extensive one, and was essentially educational in character. It was planned and, in the main, executed by a cultivated and wealthy New York woman, Mrs. B. F. Thurber, although a number of wealthy men lent it the prestige of their names as members of the board of directors, officers, incorporators, etc. It was the presence of these powerful names which assured Thomas of a strong financial backing to the scheme, in spite of its apparently small capital, for how could he dream that an institution incorporated and officered by men, many of whom were the most able financiers of the country, would be left to go to wreck under the sole guidance of one inexperienced woman and her salaried manager?

Mrs. Thurber's plan was splendidly conceived, and one would have thought it would have commended itself at once to every public-spirited man who cared for the art and the education of his country. Her idea was to found a great national conservatory, having its headquarters in New York. This conservatory was to start as a school for opera, and gradually add other branches, in accordance with the plan Thomas had long had in mind. In affiliation with the " American School of Opera," as it was called, an American Opera Company was to be maintained, the members of which were to be, as far as possible, native or naturalized Americans, and the operas performed *were to be sung in English*. Thomas was offered the musical directorship at a salary of twenty thousand dollars. Such an organization as this, of course, provided for the maintenance of his orchestra, and therefore the plan of Mayor Grace and the 3,000 was no longer needed, as Thomas could give the proposed weekly symphony concerts as part of the work of the school, as he had done in Cincinnati.

In calling into being the American School of Opera and Opera Company, Mrs. Thurber simply endeavored to found an institution for which there was urgent need in this country. Her plans were of the broadest and most far-reaching character, and as long as the money lasted, they were carried out to the letter. The weak part of her scheme was that which at the first glance appeared to be its strength, namely, its " national " character. It was her plan that the institution should not be a New York concern, but should be owned and managed by a combination of affiliated societies in all the large cities of America, merely having its headquarters in New York, because that was the largest and most convenient place for the transaction of its affairs. The school, of course, had to have a permanent home there, but the opera company was expected to go to each of the affiliated cities in turn, taking its complete paraphernalia of scenery and costumes, as well as the full personnel of its soloists, chorus, ballet, and orchestra, and to give in each one a season, which should be in every particular an exact replica of that given in New York. This plan looked very attractive on paper, and seemed practical enough in view of the festival associations everywhere, with which Thomas had so often worked in a somewhat similar way. But when it came to be tried out, it was discovered that the millionaires of other cities had not the least interest in financing an institution located in New York; while the millionaires of New York had no interest in financing an institution which was supposed to belong equally to other cities. Hence the capital actually subscribed was—as had been the case in Cincinnati—far too small to finance a scheme of such magnitude, and it should never have been attempted, especially under the inexperienced management to which its affairs were confided. When the enterprise came to the inevitable catastrophe to which it was foredoomed, Mrs. Thurber was very harshly criticised, but she, at least, " stood by the ship " to the end, while of the many other officers, directors, incorporators, etc., whose names had made the prospectus so brilliant, only Thomas, its heaviest loser, remained faithfully at his post, and gave his utmost effort, his time, and his money to palliate the situation for all concerned. But for him its hundreds of chorus singers, dancers, orchestra players, and employees of all kinds, would have been left stranded, penniless, and friendless, on the Pacific coast, with the continent between them and their homes.

No premonition of the disastrous future, now so near at hand, warned Thomas of his danger, and the season of 1885-86 was a very happy one for him. The return of his wife, with health seemingly restored, and of his children, now rapidly growing to maturity, once more surrounded him with the home atmosphere he loved. His many engagements provided him with a large and steady income, and his whole life seemed so prosperous, successful, and well-established, that it was impossible to imagine that anything could happen which could seriously injure it.

The year was spent in the usual duties of his profession, to which he now added the preparatory work of the new enterprise, in which he was interested heart and soul, and he was never so well satisfied as when planning or executing some new and extensive scheme. He gave so many concerts every year that he was always fearful of becoming *routiné* through the constant repetition of the repertoire, and had many devices whereby he kept himself and the orchestra fresh. For instance, he would not play the same selection of compositions during two consecutive seasons, nor, as we have seen, repeat the same programmes. Each time a number was performed—it made no difference whether it was a symphony or a waltz— he studied it afresh before it was rehearsed, and made little changes of interpretation or execution, here and there, to give it a new interest. In the case of the master-works of classic literature, which he knew so well that he once offered a bet to a friend, that he could write the Fifth Symphony *backwards* from memory, without a mistake (a bet, by the way, which the friend refused to take), he not only studied them afresh each time they were to be performed, but studied everything that others wrote about them in either German or English, or in translations from other languages; trying all the new effects suggested, and adopting or discarding them afterwards, as they proved to be better or not so good as his own. It was not surprising, therefore, that he was happy in his new musical departure, and enjoyed the work of preparing all its multitudinous details, especially as he had done so much operatic conducting in his early years that he was thoroughly conversant with all its branches and understood exactly what was needed in each of its departments.

The prospectus of the new company was substantially as follows, only a few unimportant paragraphs having been omitted:

THE AMERICAN OPERA COMPANY

PROSPECTUS

The management of the American Opera Company feel confident that this enterprise will meet with encouragement not only from American citizens, but from those who, though not born upon our soil, have made America their home, and must share in all that redounds to the honor and advancement of the land of their adoption. . . .

The music-loving people of American cities have long been desirous of hearing grand opera sung in their national tongue. The management will strive to realize this expectation. The artists engaged are in the front rank of American singers, and are supported by an *ensemble* which has never been equaled in this country. The American Opera Company represents an honest endeavor on the part of its incorporators to prove that there is no lack of American singers who require only encouragement and opportunity to do honor to the musical reputation of their native land. Its object is to present ensemble opera, giving no single feature undue prominence to the disadvantage of others, and distinctly discouraging the pernicious star system. Its distinctive features may be enumerated as follows:

    I. Grand opera sung in English by the most competent artists.

    II. The musical guidance of Theodore Thomas.

    III. The unrivaled Thomas Orchestra.

    IV. The largest chorus ever employed in grand opera in America, and composed entirely of fresh young voices.

    V. The largest ballet corps ever employed by grand opera in America.

    VI. Four thousand new costumes, for which no expense has been spared.

    VII. The armor, properties, and paraphernalia made from models by the best designers.

    VIII. The scenery designed by the Associated Artists of New York, and painted by the most eminent scenic artists of America.

It should be borne in mind that the American Opera Company is not a local, but a national enterprise, and all musical circles of the nation should be interested in its success. Among its leading artists are natives of twenty American cities, while the chorus represents twenty-six different states of the Union.

Incorporators

Levi P. Morton
Parke Godwin
August Belmont
Andrew Carnegie
John McGinnis, Jr.
Henry Seligman
Theodore Thomas
George C. Cooper
Caroline S. Belmont
Jeannette M. Thurber
E. Frank Coe
H. L. Horton
Arabella S. Huntington
A. B. Blodgett
F. B. Thurber
John H. Beach
N. K. Fairbank
George M. Pullman
W. B. Bininger
Horace Porter

Brayton Ives
Henry Hilton
Russell H. Hoadley
W. B. Dinsmore
A. B. Darling
F. W. Peck
H. J. Jewett
Charles Crocker
Robert Harris
Chauncey M. Depew
Edward Winslow
W. E. D. Stokes
W. D. Washburn
S. L. M. Barlow
John W. Mackay
C. O. Brice
S. V. White
C. E. Locke
S. B. Eaton

President
Andrew Carnegie

Vice-Presidents
Mrs. August Belmont, Mrs. William T. Blodgett,
Mrs. Levi P. Morton

Secretary and Treasurer
Mrs. F. B. Thurber

No operatic venture in this country ever started with a seemingly brighter promise of success than when the curtain rose on the opening night of the American Opera Company, January 4, 1886, in the old Academy of Music, which had been beautifully remodeled for its use. Every one of the glittering promises of its prospectus was more than fulfilled, and, as the season progressed, and the company was trained into ever increasing proficiency, its work was thus summarized by a musical writer in the *Century Magazine* for May:

" The incomparable orchestra, the fresh young chorus, always correct, sure, and in tune, and the whole assembly of stars and satellites respond to the command of Theodore Thomas, and respond together, exactly as the well-trained band answers him as if by one impulse, in Beethoven's 'Eroica.' . . . There we saw great conducting. There we had an earnest of the high artistic purpose with which the new enterprise has taken up its work. An American Opera Company which begins its career with such an achievement takes rank at once as a very important institution."

For a more detailed description of the company and its chief characteristics, I cannot do better than to quote from a letter from Amy Fay to one of the Chicago musical journals,* of which she was at that time the New York correspondent.

" . . . The inception of this enterprise was particularly difficult for the reason that the motive of its being lay, not in any necessity to supply a demand made by the public, but in the endeavor to supply a need long and bitterly felt by American artists for some field higher

* The *Indicator.*

than comic opera, in which they might make name and
fame for themselves in their own country. The scheme
was not a money-making one for anybody, but simply an
earnest, honest endeavor on the part of a number of the
leading capitalists of the country to establish an institution which would be of permanent value in helping to
develop the national art of America. . . . The incorporators of the organization are men and women who are
amply able to sustain it against any amount of opposition, and such names as Vanderbilt, Marquand, Belmont,
Carnegie, and Thurber, of New York; Fairbank, Pullman, and Peck, of Chicago; Higginson of Boston, Hop-
kins and Mackay of San Francisco, and many others
equally well known, are a sufficient guarantee for the
solidity of the foundation upon which it stands. The
building in which the company has its home is the old
Academy of Music. This has been charmingly decorated
in crimson, white and gold, the ceiling is frescoed, and
the old-fashioned proscenium boxes are retained, handsomely draped with crimson satin. One gallery only is
devoted to boxes, of which there are three rows, one
behind the other, and the partitions which separate them
are no higher than those between the pews in old-fashioned
churches, and do not interfere in any way with the sight
or hearing of any one. As a whole the building, though
not so gorgeous, is pleasanter than the Metropolitan as
far as the auditorium is concerned, but the stage is not
nearly as large, which is of course somewhat of a disadvantage. But though this is an inconvenience in New
York, it will be a convenience to the company in traveling,
as the scenery used at the Academy can be used without
alteration at all the theaters engaged for the performance in the West, and the representations can therefore
be made much more artistic and complete.

" The company numbers twenty-nine solo artists, of whom more than twenty are Americans. Of these, the artists who have made the most marked success of the season are Madame Hastreiter of Louisville, Madame L'Allemand of Syracuse, Miss Juch, and Myron Whitney, the splendid basso-profundo of Boston. Madame Hastreiter in particular is rapidly developing into a truly great artist under the tuition of Theodore Thomas, combined with the immense stimulus of singing constantly to such distinguished and appreciative audiences as nightly throng the Academy, and she has already received magnificent offers of operatic engagements in Europe. Madame L'Allemand is not a novice in operatic singing, having sung with success in Europe before her American engagement. But she is none the less a delightful musician, and has made an excellent reputation for herself already as a genuine and conscientious artist, whose impersonations are remarkable both for their dramatic power and musical excellence. Miss Juch and Mr. Whitney are both too well known to need comment. But it is not upon the greatness of its solo performers that the American company relies as yet for its success, but upon its artistic completeness as a whole. Of course, the organization is still too young to be in all respects *perfect;* it would be absurd to expect that with only eight months of existence the greatest results could be achieved, no matter how great the labor expended to bring them about. Perfection is only to be attained by the mellowing influence of time and experience upon human effort, and the managers of the American company, though satisfied and encouraged at the success it has already attained, regard its achievements this winter as but the beginning of what they hope ultimately to make it.

" I have spoken elsewhere of the leading characteristic of

the German company as its brilliancy. The leading characteristic of the American company may be said to be its
refinement. The operas selected for its performances are
much lighter than the music-dramas of the German company, its singers are much younger and prettier, and have
graceful, girlish figures, which makes them look more
delicate, and better suited to the youthful parts which
generally form the leading rôles. The chorus is composed of fresh young voices and sings with confidence and
precision, almost never falling from the pitch or lagging
in the attack. The orchestra of course is perfection, and
all these component parts are welded into a harmonious
whole under the guiding baton of its distinguished conductor, who, while giving to each soloist full latitude in
which to exercise his or her individual conception, yet
keeps everything moving smoothly along without hitches
or roughness in any part. Nor is the stage-setting in any
way inferior to the performance. The scenery and costumes are all of American manufacture, and were made
under the direction of the celebrated 'Associated
Artists' of New York, and some of the scenes are exquisitely beautiful, particularly in the arrangement of
light. In the 'Merry Wives of Windsor,' for instance,
we have a moonlight scene which is particularly charming.
The curtain rises revealing the interior of a grove, with
a dimly seen landscape between the tree trunks. Presently the moon slowly rises, big and red—a real July
moon. Gradually, as it ascends, it grows yellow, and then
white and clear, in very artistic style, and instead of stopping, as theatrical moons ordinarily do, at the height of
ten feet above the horizon, it keeps on rising and rising,
gleaming behind branches, and through the interstices
of the foliage, till it passes out of sight overhead, and
a flood of light from above, shining through the trees and

gradually shifting as the scene progresses, marks the continued moving of the now invisible moon, and adds the finishing touch to a lovely stage picture. Another exquisite scene is that of the last act of 'Lakmé,' which represents the interior of a forest in India, and has in it a wonderful cascade at the back of the stage which pours over the rocks, waving and gleaming in a manner which defies the inquiring powers of even an opera glass as to its *modus operandi*. I have said nothing about the ballet of this company, though it is large and well trained, because it has nothing distinctive to the company about it, but is like any other good opera ballet.

" Those who go to the performances of the American company expecting to hear vocal pyrotechnics, or to see anything startling or sensational, will be disappointed. But those who take pleasure in a good thing thoroughly well done cannot fail to enjoy each and all of the operas, and to rejoice that at last a company has been formed where we can hear our own charming artists in a language we can all understand, and that the day is near at hand when it will no longer be necessary for American musicians to hide their nationality under foreign names before they can get recognition from their own countrymen.

" If Mrs. Thurber and her coadjutors can accomplish this they will earn the gratitude of American singers for all time, and lay sure foundations for the American music of the future.   AMY FAY."

From the foregoing details, it will be seen that Thomas aimed to give opera in the same way that he gave all his other musical performances. Every detail was accurate, perfect, and harmonious, and nothing was too small to escape his attention if it could contribute to the artistic effect of the whole.

For instance, when Lohengrin entered for the first time, drawn by the swan, he wished to express the excitement which such an event would naturally create in a crowd of witnesses. Instead of trying to make his chorus do all the necessary action, as is customary, he had them drawn up at the back, with instructions to attend strictly to their music. In the foreground he utilized the members of the ballet, to give all the action, and the result was a climax of the most tremendous power and effect. In explaining his reason for this, he said: " The music is very difficult for the chorus and requires all their attention in order to do it well; if they try to combine acting with singing here, both are a failure." Still smaller details than this were carefully prepared, such as the fizzing of the satanic wine into the glass of Mephistopheles, which is represented by a little orchestral figure. As Thomas played it, one could hear that fizz to the life. Or, the clanking of the chains as the anchor of the phantom ship in the " Flying Dutchman " is dropped. This is also produced by an orchestral figure, and not by a real chain, and Thomas rehearsed it over and over again with infinite patience until it, too, was perfected.

The repertoire of the American Opera Company was quite different from that of any opera company this country had ever had, and contained a number of operas which have rarely been given by other organizations. It was selected to include both classic and modern works, and contained operas by German, French, Italian, and Russian composers, as well as a number of little musical pantomimes for ballet and orchestra. The operas given during the two years of its existence were all sung in English, with the delightful result that the listeners could understand what the singers were trying to express, instead of having to guess what was going on by watching their pantomime. They were as follows:

Orpheus and Eurydice.........................Gluck
The Merry Wives of Windsor...............Nicolai
Lohengrin ....Wagner
The Flying Dutchman.......................Wagner
Faust ....Gounod
The Taming of the Shrew...................Goetz
Lakmé ....Delibes
The Magic Flute.............................Mozart
The Huguenots...............................Meyerbeer
Aïda ....Verdi
Martha ....Flotow
Nero ....Rubinstein

But, perfect and artistic though its performances were, the company lacked one thing which the American public has always held to be essential to grand opera, and that was the very thing it sought to avoid—great " star " singers of the first rank. The singers of the American Opera Company were all fine artists, and Thomas was so experienced that he cast them in *rôles* which they were fitted to interpret as well, or even better than more famous artists would have done, but the public, nevertheless, missed in its performances the great emotional climaxes of a Materna or a Lehmann, the marvelous C *in alt* of a Campanini, or the rich voluminous bass of a Scaria. And the more perfect the orchestra, chorus, scenery, and supporting artists became, the more apparent became the need of great dramatic singers to fill the leading *rôles*. Had the American Opera Company become the permanent institution Thomas supposed it would be, when he undertook its direction, he might, perhaps, have added them when the time seemed ripe for it, but the life of the institution was too brief for him to do more than lay the foundation for future development. The audiences which thronged its performances were large and enthusiastic, and the press was a unit in admitting their superior artistic standard, but there was nevertheless much antagonism to the company in New York. There had gradually developed in the musical world of that city a strong faction of people whose interests were opposed to those of Thomas. As long as he kept to his own specialty of symphonic or choral work, he was master of the situation, for there no one could compete with him. But when he entered the operatic field, his opponents were financially stronger than he, and had, in reality, the solid financial backing which, he discovered too late, belonged to the American company only in name. No operatic organization can live on its box office receipts alone, and therefore, in spite of the large audiences that greeted its performances everywhere, the close of its first season found the company already somewhat behind in its expenses.

The spring tour of the company, over the old familiar Thomas " Highway," was a very successful one, and a volume might be filled with the press encomiums over its performances, but a few quotations from some of the most important will suffice to show the general impression created throughout the country in regard to its work:

In the case of the American opera season, musical Boston's highest anticipations have been more than realized. If there ever was any doubt felt as to the possibility of producing the lyrical dramas of the great masters with a company drawn almost exclusively from the ranks of our native singers, and under purely American direction and management, that doubt is certainly dispelled by the superb performances of this week at the Boston Theater.— *Boston Globe.*

There was probably no one in all that great throng at the Boston Theater last night who, observing and appreciating the thoroughness of the presentation of Wagner's most popular opera, did not admit that the enterprise deserved all of the success that its projectors asked for it. Such a performance of " Lohengrin " had not been heard here before. Let us stretch a point and say at once that no such performance of any opera had been heard here before. . . .—*Boston Transcript.*

The performance of " Lohengrin " last evening at the Boston Theater sets finally at rest any vague doubt which there might have been in regard to the scale and standard set up by the managers, or to their ability to carry into full execution their plans and promises. It is not too much to say that no person in the crowded and distinguished auditory had ever seen in this country any representation by any other organization nearly commensurate with this.—*Boston Daily Advertiser.*

There was but one sentiment and one regret. The sentiment agreed in praise of the royal manner in which the American Opera Company redeemed, and more than redeemed, all the promises made. The regret was that the season was ended before it had fairly blossomed.—*Philadelphia Press.*

Nothing could have better shown the undeniable strength of the American Opera Company than the operas chosen for performance yesterday (" Lakmé " and " The Flying Dutchman "). That these operas, so widely contrasted in style, each received a faultless and characteristic representation, showed at once the wonderful resources of this organization.—*National Republican (Washington).*

The inauguration of the American Opera Company's season of four performances at the Academy of Music proved an event in the musical history of Baltimore. It is safe to say that no such company ever visited the city before. It consists of almost an army of artists in all the lines of musical and dramatic expression. The soloists are of the highest order. The chorus numbers over a hundred young, fresh, well-trained voices. The orchestra, that of Theodore Thomas, is far superior to any that ever took part in an opera performance in this city. The ballet is a revelation of perfection in drill and costumes, as well as in forms and numbers.—*Baltimore Sun.*

It is no exaggeration to say that " Lohengrin " as presented last evening by the American Opera Company at McVicker's would have found favor in Berlin or Munich. Gluck's " Orpheus " as presented by the American Opera

Company is the smoothest and most consistently finished operatic performance ever given in this city. To the story the American Opera Company has joined a pageant of almost unequaled wealth.—*Chicago Tribune.*

Mrs. Thurber went with the company on the tour, and worked hard in every city to organize the auxiliary societies which were such an essential part of her plan. But she could not accomplish anything of sufficient importance in this line to make up for the lack of capital in New York. Nor, in spite of the artistic laurels with which the company returned to its home city, was she able to raise any large additional sum of money for it there. Under these untoward circumstances the only practical course to pursue was to disband the company and close up its affairs. But after it had made such a brilliant artistic success, Mrs. Thurber was naturally loath to give up the enterprise until she had tried every possible expedient for its continuance, and it was finally decided by its management to reorganize the company in the state of New Jersey under the name of the National Opera Company, and to try and recuperate its fortunes by selling the capital stock of the new concern.

Meantime Thomas had not by any means given up his concert work, but gave, during the winter of 1885-86, ten distinct series of concerts: 12 New York Philharmonic Concerts; 24 New York Young People's Matinées; 24 New York Popular Concerts; 2 Liederkranz Concerts; 16 Brooklyn

Philharmonic Concerts; 8 Brooklyn Popular Matinées; 6 Philadelphia Symphony Concerts, and three or four concerts each in Jersey City, Newark, New Haven, and Orange, as well as single performances in neighboring cities. This extraordinary season finally ended with the regular biennial musical festival of Cincinnati, and a subsequent five weeks of Summer Night Concerts in Chicago.

But such labors as these were too much for even a man of the iron will and strong physique of Thomas, and when the time came for making his engagements for the next season, he decided that he could no longer give such a large number of concerts and conduct opera also, and that he must give up one or the other. It may be thought incredible that a man of Thomas' age and experience should have given up his extensive and remunerative concert work for the sake of an opera company which was in such questionable shape financially as the National Opera Company, but Thomas was not much of a business man, he knew very little about stock companies or corporations of any kind, and he believed implicitly everything that was told him by those with whom he was associated. When asked why he allowed himself to be deceived in business matters so often through life, his answer was: " I cannot work with those I do not trust, and I had rather be deceived, even though it costs me dear, than suspect the honesty of those with whom I am associated, so long as we are working together." In the case of the National Opera Company he supposed that the reorganization was done merely to keep off the creditors of the "American Company" until the sale of the capital stock of the new concern should bring in enough money to pay their claims in full. This seemed reasonable, and so he did not hesitate to sign a contract with the management as its musical director, for the season of 1886-87, and even allowed himself to be made its president, and to hold a few shares of its stock. Consequently, when the final catastrophe came, he found himself so involved in its affairs, that, although he was not held to be financially responsible for its debts by the court, he nevertheless had to fight the lawsuits brought against him by its creditors for years afterwards.

During its second season the performances of the ill-fated company were even more finished and perfect than before. Its home was transferred to the Metropolitan Opera House, the large size of the stage there offering unlimited opportunities for magnificent stage settings. The last weeks of its New York season were devoted to the production of Rubinstein's "Nero" in the most sumptuous manner, and the following description of its opening night appeared in the New York *World* the next day:

"The opera of 'Nero' was produced by the 'National Opera Company' last night. Placed upon the stage on a scale of splendor never before given to opera in this country, with scenes, pictures, and groupings of extraordinary magnificence, culminating with the burning of Rome; and sung with enthusiasm, intelligence, and ar-

tistic devotion, it made an overwhelming success. The
production, marking, as it does, an epoch in grand
opera in English, in this country, the names of the singers
deserve to be recorded. Nearly every member of the company was in the cast:

Nero Claudius, Imperator...........William Candidus
Julius Vindex, Prince of Aquitania.....William Ludwig
Tigellinus, Prefect of the Pretorians....Alonzo Stoddard
Balbillus, an astrologer...............Myron Whitney
Saccus, a poet.....................William Fessenden
Servirus, high priest of Evander's Temple ⎫
A Centurion   ⎬ Wm. Hamilton
                                         ⎭
Terpander, a Citharist, Agrippina's freedman..W.H. Lee
Poppæa Sabina, Otho's wife, afterwards married to
    Nero. ....Bertha Pierson
Epicharis, a freedwoman.........Cornelia Van Zanten
Chrysa, her daughter...................Emma Juch
Agrippina, widow of the Emperor Claudius and
    mother of Nero....................Agnes Stirling
Lupus, a Roman gamin............Pauline L'Allemand
Piso   ⎫   ⎧ ....Joseph Silvers
Rufus   ⎪   ⎪ ....Frank Hadley
          ⎬ Plotters⎨
Sporus   ⎪   ⎪ ....James Dubois
Messala   ⎭   ⎩ ....H. S. Dale
Thrasaes, a Senator.....................John Alton
Delia, Poppæa's slave..............Lauretta Creede
An aged Christian....................H. Heinemann
The leader of a band of jugglers.........Frank Perry
A public crier.....................John McGrayne
A street vender.......................Jacob Mermer
Salvius Otho......................... _____

"It is difficult to say which part of the opera produced
the greatest effect. Scenically the eye was fairly wearied
last night, watching the gorgeous settings, the superb

pictures, and the wonderful spectacular effects. From eight o'clock until midnight, the Rome of the Cæsars was presented in costume, scenery, characters, and dramatic action in a way that fairly surprised and bewildered the audience. Rubinstein has charged his score also with many lovely musical numbers. His choruses, ballet music, and processional are superlatively grand, and he has furnished some duets for 'Vindex' and 'Chrysa,' of surpassing beauty and which must be declared to be amongst the loveliest in modern opera. The brilliant manner in which the work was produced was the result of weeks and weeks of rehearsal under Theodore Thomas."

Early in April the company was sent on a tour which extended to San Francisco and ended on its return, at Buffalo. The details of its experiences after it reached the Pacific coast are better imagined than described, and the return trip resembled the retreat of Napoleon's army from Moscow! Like the famous French general, Thomas stayed with his company until they were back in their home state, and but for his presence they would never have got there. Sometimes he even paid for their food himself, rather than see them go hungry. Finally, at St. Louis, he could contain his indignation no longer, and in answer to a request from the New York Board of Directors, asking for a statement of the condition of affairs, he sent the following telegram:

St. Louis, Mo., *June* 7, 1887.
Troupe completely wrecked. Workingmen have gone without meals to the shame of the Directory. I have nothing to do with the business management, but I did not

dare to leave the troupe in San Francisco, and only stay now until everyone can reach New York. We have been deserted and sold by everybody, and if you will get us home after the Louisville engagement you will save money.

THEODORE THOMAS.

The company was not, however, disbanded at Louisville, but filled another engagement in Buffalo, where Thomas conducted it for the last time. On the back of the programme of this performance he wrote, " The most dreadful experience of my life." Having now got the unfortunate members of the troupe back to within a short distance of home, he deemed that his duty was done, and saw no reason why he should continue to give any more gratuitous service to its Board. He therefore left, and, stopping in New York only long enough to place his claims against the company in the hands of his lawyer, he joined his family at the seashore.

Had Thomas not been so weighed down in spirit by the disappointment and humiliation of the experiences he had just been through; by his own heavy financial losses, and by the doubtful outlook of the future, his home-coming this year would have been peculiarly happy, for, during his absence in the West, his wife had found and purchased a pleasant and commodious country-place in the beautiful little seaside village of Fairhaven, Mass., and for the first time in his life he came to his own home and fireside, and not to temporary quarters rented from someone else.

Thomas lived so incessantly before the public, and had so little time for intercourse with his family, that the few days which he was able to devote to them in summer were like a sort of idyl to him, which he dreamed of and longed for all the rest of the year. Perhaps for this reason his feeling about his home was unusually deep, and he had long had a great desire for a real home, in which he could feel a sense of possession and permanency. The Fairhaven house was quite in accordance with his generous ideas of what a home should be, for it was very large and a fine specimen of the " Old Colonial " style of architecture. The rooms were lofty, and the wood-work carved in low relief, and painted white, after the manner of this style. Mrs. Thomas, who was a connoisseur of architecture, had had the necessary repairs and alterations made to harmonize with the rest, and had furnished it throughout with the old mahogany furniture belonging to the period when it was built. Everything about the house was genuine, and this pleased Thomas. The things that looked old *were* old, and those that were modern were not imitations, but only selected so as to be in keeping with the rest. Each room had a big, generous fireplace for wood, with polished brass andirons and fender, and the house was surrounded outside with large grounds, laid out in lawns and gardens and shaded with fine old trees.

But Thomas was not allowed to remain long in this quiet retreat, for the Chicago Summer Night season was at hand, and this year of all others he could not afford to lose any chance of earning money. He had rented a little furnished flat to live in while in Chicago, and shortly before leaving home he wrote me the following letter:

FAIRHAVEN, MASS., *June 29, 1887.*

Dear Miss Fay:

I shall leave Boston on Saturday afternoon, and arrive in Chicago Sunday evening at half-past nine. Sachleben and the orchestra go by another line, but arrive at the same time.

If that girl of mine—cook—could have some cold meat for us, and perhaps some very cold sliced tomatoes, German rye bread, and a bottle of claret, I should be more than thankful not to have to go out to a restaurant that night for a meal. Will you kindly tell her, and perhaps lay out for us anything that is necessary? I will refund you at once, for although I have not received a penny of salary from the National Opera Company, I am still " flush " enough to pay my expenses. I have given my claim into the hands of my lawyer. My vacation has been much broken up by this business, but I have had some rest anyway.

Thanking you in advance for many kindnesses, believe me   Sincerely yours,

THEODORE THOMAS.

The Chicago season passed uneventfully, and at last the time came when Thomas found himself peacefully installed in his new Fairhaven home for a long rest. As he looked from the windows of his study, and watched the sunset glow fade behind the leafy arches of its graceful elms, he gave the place the name " Sunset," adding, " And may it prove to be a fair haven for us all."

While at Fairhaven Thomas received another letter from Strauss,—now no longer an unknown youth, but a composer of rapidly widening reputation,—in regard to a new orchestral work which he had just published:

MUNICH, *Aug.* 27, 1887.

Highly honored Mr. Thomas:

When you were so kind, two years ago, as to write me in regard to the performance of my F minor symphony, you were good enough to hold out to me the promise that you would bring out in the western world another orchestral work of mine. A second composition of this kind is to be published in October, score and parts; it is a Symphonic Fantasie in four movements:

I. The Campagna (*Lento*).
II. The Ruins of Rome (*Allegro con brio*).
III. On the Strand of Sorrento (*Andante*).
IV. Neapolitan Folks' Life (*Allegro vivace*).

Would you permit me to ask, encouraged by your friendly offer, whether I might venture to hope that the work might be given under your direction in New York?

I myself conducted the first performance of it here in Munich, March 1, and achieved a fine success, although a not altogether uncontested one. The Fantasie offers an especial freedom of form, entirely new and unusual, and it would naturally be viewed with hostility by the old musicians who were brought here to fill positions as functionaries. As to the technical part of the work, it belongs to the most difficult which the modern school of music has produced, and we have very few orchestras here which

The Thomas Home at Fairhaven, Mass.

could cope with it, especially the last movement. Few concert organizations have great orchestras and conductors of genius who can grasp the intellectual contents of a work, such as the New York Philharmonic Society, which, under your leadership, stands in the first rank. It is therefore all the more important for me that the Philharmonic Society should not refuse my Italian Fantasie.

Under these circumstances, honored sir, you will readily understand how cheerfully I recalled your very kind promise of two years ago. Buelow has accepted it for his concerts in Berlin and Hamburg next season, and has expressed himself most strongly in its favor. It is not quite so long as the F minor symphony. With the latter I have had prodigious luck, and it has now been played eleven times. In Hamburg by Buelow, in Cologne by Wuellner, in Berlin twice by Rodecke and Klindworth, in Amsterdam by Verhnlot, in Meiningen, Munich, Frankfort, Dresden, and Wiesbaden—the two last named under my own direction. Next winter I am invited to conduct it in the Leipsic Gewandhaus.

You are already aware that I have been for the last two years conductor at the Hof Theater here. I like the position very much, as it allows me time for my composition. How goes the world with you? Well, I hope. With heartiest greetings, in which my father joins, I remain

Yours with sympathy and respect,

RICHARD STRAUSS.

It is needless to say that Thomas consented to perform the new " Italian Fantasie " with pleasure, and brought it out during the following March.

CHAPTER XV

1887-1888

THOMAS RETURNS TO CONCERT WORK—DISAPPOINTMENT—
THE CINCINNATI FESTIVAL OF 1888—DISBANDING OF
THE THOMAS ORCHESTRA IN CHICAGO—PROGRAMME OF
THE LAST CONCERT—ILLNESS OF MRS. THOMAS—AN UN-
RECORDED SEASON—THE DEATH OF MRS. THOMAS

DURING the second season of American opera,
Thomas, as we have seen, had given up the greater
part of his concert work, in order to devote his
time wholly to the opera, retaining only the New
York and Brooklyn Philharmonic Societies, and a
few other engagements. He had resigned from
the Liederkranz, and disbanded his two chorus
societies. In short his own business was scattered
to the four winds, and must now be built up anew
from the foundation. Unfortunately it is much
easier to scatter a clientèle of any kind, than
it is to gather it together again, and Thomas
was not long in discovering that he had made a
terrible mistake in allowing the splendid audience
he had formed, and which had hitherto been like
a bed-rock foundation for all his musical enterprises, to slip away from symphonic influence for
even a single year. They had followed him unquestioningly from concert to opera, but now they
did not follow him back again from opera to con-

cert, for all New York had become opera-mad, in the meantime, and when the Thomas audience could no longer go to the opera he conducted, they simply transferred over to the Metropolitan Opera Company and remained there. He could not get them back again in anything like the numbers that he had always been able to count on before. Nor was this the only reason why his concert audiences were diminished. The first conductor of the Metropolitan Opera Company, Dr. Damrosch, having died, his place had been filled by Anton Seidl, a musician who had been associated with Wagner very closely, and who was consequently received in New York as the very apostle of modern music. In addition to his musical claims upon the interest of the public, Mr. Seidl possessed a winning personality which soon created for him a strong following, not only in opera but also in concert, and he gave a great many concerts with the large orchestra of the Metropolitan company. The Boston orchestra was also in the field, not only in New York, but, what was much worse for Thomas, it now visited all the cities of the " Highway," thus giving him a formidable competitor which cut off his profits everywhere else. Add to this competition, the newly-passed inter-state transportation laws, which prevented traveling troupes from getting reductions on their railroad expenses, and it is not difficult to understand why, although he gave many concerts during the season of 1887-88, he was unable to make them pay, but steadily lost money throughout the year. Thomas was now some years beyond the half-century mark; hard work and disappointments had left their scars upon his soul, and robbed him of the buoyant confidence of youth and hope with which he had formerly faced the world. The future began to look dark, and anxious forebodings filled his heart. In May, however, the Cincinnati Festival allowed him to forget, for a time, the reverses of fortune and once more enjoy the pleasure of great work successfully accomplished. During the first week of the month he went to Cincinnati for a few preliminary rehearsals, and while there wrote me as follows:

CINCINNATI, *May* 1, 1888.

Dear Miss Fay:

I arrived here yesterday, held a rehearsal last night, and have another to-night. I leave for New York to-morrow morning. I hope to get through my business there in time to go to Fairhaven Friday night, and rest at home four or five days, after which I hold two rehearsals in New York preparing the orchestral works of the Festival and leave Sunday morning, the 13th, again, for Cincinnati, to hold chorus rehearsals there during the rest of the week. By the 18th the orchestra and all soloists are in Cincinnati and the first full rehearsal takes place Friday evening.

Why don't you and your sister, Miss Amy, come to the Festival in time for all these rehearsals, as well as the concerts? The Festival promises to be very enjoyable, and the standard high. For the orchestra I bring every man with me from New York. I am sorry that Miss Amy heard the last Philharmonic rehearsal instead of the concert. The former was very poor this time. The weather was bad—warm and rainy—the men tired out, everybody busy with ending the New York season, and I myself tired out, even fearing I might drop. I was so tired that I even opened the wrong scores at home in the evening. But by Saturday night I was all right again, and the men also, and the result was a memorable performance.

As to the invitation you forwarded in behalf of the Music Teachers' National Association, to write a paper for its next meeting, all I can say is that anyone who expects me to do anything of the kind does not take in my work and has no idea of the amount and quality of it. Please ask Miss Amy to tell the Committee that I am too busy and too tired to do it.

In regard to a flat for the Chicago Summer Night season, I do not intend to rent one. I lost heavily this winter again, and I am too poor to allow myself anything beyond reasonable comfort. I shall take one room in a hotel, be saving during the five weeks in Chicago, and bring home all I can.

I am tired, but what makes me tired is that I have no audience to play to. The public learns, but I also learn and advance more than the public does, and the breach between us grows wider. I am very tired.

Yours sincerely,

THEODORE THOMAS.

It had been the custom of my sister and myself to attend the Cincinnati Festivals as the correspondents of two of the Chicago journals, and we were very glad to have a chance to hear some of the last private rehearsals, as well as the public performances. We reached Cincinnati, therefore, a day or two in advance, and the following quotations are taken from Miss Fay's account of the

Festival which appeared in the *Indicator,* the leading Chicago musical paper of that day:

" The day preceding the opening of the Festival was my birthday," wrote Miss Fay, " and as I had been invited by 'Mr. Thomas to hear the final private rehearsals, I made up my mind that my birthday was going to be celebrated in exactly the way I most enjoy! There is nothing more delightful than to attend the last rehearsals of a great musical festival. Everybody arrives in the best of spirits, and is delighted to meet everybody else. The music is already learned, and all are curious to get the general effect of how it will sound when chorus and orchestra come together. The solo artists have the pleasing expectation of new triumphs, and the conductor has a sense of responsibility and achievement, and arrives armed to the teeth with scores and determined to put his forces through in a manner undreamed of by them. One goes to the music hall in the cool of the morning, and the solitude and emptiness of the great auditorium are refreshing as contrasted with the swarms of human beings who will shortly fill it. Thomas had given us our orders, ' Be at the hall punctually at ten o'clock, for I mean to begin sharp.' We obeyed to the minute—for there is nothing Thomas dislikes so much as unpunctuality—but he had already begun. As we entered the building the divine strains of Tannhaeuser greeted our ears. How deliciously the sirens called to me as I passed up the corridor, preceded by Frau Lilli Lehmann and her husband, Paul Kalisch!

" The Wagner numbers selected by Thomas for the rehearsal were those with Lehmann, Kalisch, and the great English tenor, Edward Lloyd, in the solo parts. Before we left the hotel, we had met Thomas on the stairs and he had expressed himself as feeling very tired, and indeed he looked completely wilted. I was therefore amazed to find him conducting with all the fire and freshness that is pent up in this extraordinary man in an apparently inexhaustible store, ready for him to draw upon whenever he needs them. The moment he grasped his baton—which, by the way, is a delicate little white wand, hardly larger than a pencil—and felt himself the presiding genius of that great orchestra, he seemed to rise to his work with Titanic vigor. . . . The rehearsal closed with the singing of ' Walther's Preislied ' by Lloyd, and we went back to the hotel with our ears fairly ringing with music.

" By evening, however, we were ready for another dose. Punctually at seven Thomas was on the stand again, and we settled down to a purely orchestral rehearsal this time. Space would fail me to describe all the things we heard on that delightful evening, but I must not forget to mention the wonderful effect that Beethoven's Pastoral Symphony made with so large an orchestra. I had never heard it under such circumstances before, and I must say that never did its surpassing beauty shine out so to my mental vision. The storm episode was perfectly thrilling. While it was going on, J. K. Paine, the composer, had slid quietly into the hall and sat down beside me. He had just arrived from Cambridge, having come on to hear the performance of his new Cantata, ' Song of Promise,' which was to be given at the Festival.

" ' What fire Thomas puts into that orchestra, and what wonderfully sensuous colors he gets out of those instruments ! ' he exclaimed.

" ' Yes,' said I, ' but he has some very remarkable artists in the orchestra, you must remember.'

" ' That is true,' said Paine, ' but he does it all the same with any musicians he conducts. Why, I am sure he would make even *me* do it if I went, up on the stage and blew one of those horns, this minute—though it might happen that I would squawk occasionally,' he added prudently.

" I had another great sensation in Chopin's Funeral March, which Thomas has orchestrated in a manner that could not be surpassed by Wagner himself. The effect as he plays it is stupendous. The muted horns and clanging cymbals make it seem like the march of all humanity into the grave. One feels that they are all going down into that pit—millions of lives are to be extinguished in it, and the tramp of feet is bringing it nearer, nearer. It is frightful. And then the middle portion, played by those wailing violins, is like a dirge sung by the universal spirit, and is indescribably mournful and pathetic, and yet heavenly too. Yes, that Funeral March gave me more than a sensation, it was a positive shock, I could scarcely rise from under it. Luckily Thomas ended the rehearsal with Liszt's jolly and exciting Second Rhapsody, and Rubinstein's ' La Russie.' The last is a sort of *potpourri* of folk songs leading up through all the different tribes of Russia to the national hymn. The close is like a regular Fourth-of-July ' hurrah-boys.' The orchestra was by this time fatigued almost to the point of exhaustion; to brighten them up as they neared the close of the last number, Thomas started a ' Hurrah! ' and at once they all began to cheer like mad. This, with the rolling of the organ, the beating of the drums, the clashing of cymbals in general co-operation with all the other instruments, not to speak of horns and trumpets blown full-blast, was a *finale* such as I never experienced, even in Europe!

" After the rehearsal Thomas joined us, and we all walked back to the hotel together, to a pleasant little sup-

per which he gave in honor of my birthday. While we
were at the table the conversation turned upon the storm
in the Pastoral Symphony, and Thomas told us the following interesting incident:

" ' Once in my life I had a great sensation while conducting that movement. We were playing in the Central
Park Garden, which, you know, is built upon a rock.
The night was stormy, and, being warm, all the windows
were open. Exactly at the instant when Beethoven brings
the crash of thunder in the storm episode of this symphony, a real thunderbolt of the most terrific kind rent
the heavens—it came precisely with the fall of my stick!
Ah, that was a moment to live for! Only I ought to have
had an orchestra of a thousand to match such an instrument of percussion! '

". . . The sixth concert of the Festival was a matinée,
and the programme was composed of orchestral and solo
numbers, no chorus work being given. Amongst the solos
was Rossini's ' Cujus Animam,' sung by Lloyd, rather
against his will. I heard him complaining about it the
day before. ' Mr. Thomas has put me down for two
sacred selections for to-morrow. Instead of the number
from the " Stabat Mater," I would rather have sung
something by Gounod, and on the list I sent him I under-
lined twice an aria from " La Reine de Saba " that I was
particularly anxious to sing. It has a fine orchestral
accompaniment, too, and I do not see what Mr. Thomas'
idea was in preferring the other,' said Lloyd, in a tone of
well-bred disapprobation. After this I was very much
interested to see how Lloyd would come out on this number, for I too thought it queer in Thomas. The result,
however, entirely justified the judgment of that sagacious
programme-maker. The ' Cujus Animam ' was familiar
to the public, and as Lloyd sang it magnificently there

was a perfect storm of applause. It was such an ovation, in fact, that it resulted in one of those curious battles that Thomas sometimes has with the public in regard to giving encores. At festivals his rule is that no encores are permitted, so he stood there like a rock, baton in hand, while Lloyd was recalled three times, the expression of his very back growing more obstinate every minute. As the fourth round of applause began, Thomas stepped from his stand and sat down in the orchestra, as much as to say, ' Now clap away till you are tired, and I'll wait here till you get through.' There was a laugh from the crowd, which recommenced applauding frantically. Lloyd came out and made his fourth bow. The audience continued clapping and stamping harder than ever, but this time Lloyd did not appear immediately, and after some minutes Thomas got up and with an air of resolution disappeared down the stairway leading into the green-room. There was a howl of triumph from the audience, who thought he was vanquished, and would bring Lloyd out to sing again, and the applause continued still more furiously. Little did they know the iron Thomas! When he reappeared at last, he brought out, not Lloyd, but Mme. Valda, who was the next on the programme. This was a master-stroke, for the crowd seeing a beautiful woman, dressed in the aërial robes of spring—green tulle trimmed with garlands of roses—was too gallant to object, and felt constrained to continue the applause for her reception. In the evening I went to the final concert of the Festival with some misgivings, fearing that the audience would make some unpleasant demonstration after the contest of the afternoon. Strange to say the public seemed to be in high good-humor. The conductor's stand was trimmed with masses of crimson roses, and it was he who received the ovation this time. It reminded me of a re-

mark he once made to me after a similar battle, in which
nine thousand people had roared and stamped, and even
drowned him out every time he attempted to go on with the
next number, till he shouted for his trumpets, and drowned
them out in turn. ' The public and I have our little fall-
ings-out, but we always meet again ! ' Thomas is always
master of the situation."

The festival over, Thomas went home for a
month, and the first of July saw him in Chicago,
as usual, for the Summer Night season. During
this sojourn he was in a very melancholy frame
of mind, and seemed weighed down by the presentiment of impending disaster. The future offered
him no promise for the reconstruction of his fallen
fortunes. New York was now flooded with the concerts of other organizations, and the only means by
which he might have held his own against all these
competing institutions—the possession of a suitable
building for his orchestra—was beyond his reach.
He saw no possible way by which he could continue to maintain his orchestra and he was not
willing to run into debt again, so there was but
one course open to him—to disband his orchestra
and give up the long, fruitless struggle against
fate.

Thomas did not often place solo numbers on the
programme of his Summer Night concerts, but
during this season he brought out a Concerto of
the American composer, Edward MacDowell, with
Teresa Carreño as its interpreter. Carreño had
been the first teacher of MacDowell, in his child-

hood, and Thomas had been the first to recognize the genius of Carreño in her childhood. So the two were much in sympathy in their desire to give this beautiful American work the best presentation. The next day he received the following letter from his *protégée* of so long ago, who had now become one of the foremost pianists of the time:

CHICAGO, *July* 6, 1888.

Dear Mr. Thomas:

It would have given me the greatest pleasure to come and see you this morning instead of writing, but knowing how pressed for time you are, I deprived myself of this pleasure, thinking that you would feel thankful that I did not come to take away your valuable time from your numerous occupations.

I only wish to thank you from all my heart once more for the kindness and consideration with which you treated me yesterday, and to tell you how proud and happy I feel that once again I have been allowed the pleasure and the privilege of playing under your masterly baton.

Let me also thank you in Edward MacDowell's name, who feels highly honored that his composition should have come under your notice, and that it should have been brought before the public under your leadership.

I sincerely hope that I may have the pleasure of seeing you again, and, if I may, I will come and knock at your door when you are in New York, and hope that you will always look upon me as the same little girl whose tottering footsteps in her profession you, with your powerful hand, were the first to guide and support.

Yours very sincerely,

TERESA CARREÑO.

Another pleasant and very unexpected letter which came to Thomas during this summer was from Italy, and announced, in the customary grandiloquent language used by Europeans in their official communications, the award of a diploma of honor to him by an Italian Musical Society, under the patronage of the Queen of Italy, of which Verdi was the Honorary President. Thomas had often been called "Meister," "Maëstro," "Doctor," and even "Boss," but I think this was the only time in his life when he was addressed as "Your Grace!"

MILANO, *Sept.* 15, 1888.

TO THE MOST ILLUSTRIOUS SIGNOR THEODORE THOMAS,
 Honored Sir:

The President of the *International Society of Mutual Protection of Lyric Artists and Affiliated Masters* has the honor to express the admiration of all its members, by inscribing the record of your artistic achievements upon a grand Diploma of Honor, the brilliant art-work of the illustrious Senator Tullo Massarani, reproduced in *aqua fortis* by the celebrated painter, F. Colombi Borde.

Will your Grace kindly accept this testimonial and accord to the Society your welcome and powerful endorsement.

Il Presidente,
 DOCTOR LODOVICO CORIA.

It had always been the custom of Thomas at the final rehearsal of the Chicago season to inform the members of the orchestra of his plans for the ensuing year. On Thursday, August 2, 1888, there-

fore, he made them the following address at the
close of the rehearsal:

"Gentlemen:—The time has come to communicate to
you what I can offer for next season. This, however, is
more easily said than done, owing to the peculiar circumstances in which affairs in New York have placed me. I
pray you, therefore, listen attentively in order that you
may understand and appreciate them.

"You will remember that last spring, after the close of
our winter season, I told you that our future prospects
were encouraging. What caused me to believe this was,
first, that the building of a large and well-appointed
music hall in New York seemed assured. I was shown
the detailed plans and understood from the architect and
other interested persons that its construction would begin
May 1, and that it would, consequently, be in readiness for
our concerts next winter. But for this I should have
told you then that our prospects were bad and we had
better stop. In the second place, my friends gave me the
assurance that they would raise a guarantee fund which
would guard us against losses and insure our position in
the winter months in New York. Thus encouraged, I
looked at a theater—the Broadway—which was suitable
for matinées, and hoped to get through without serious
loss until the hall was built. In regard to the hall, I only
know that there are no signs that it will be built, so we
are still without one. The guarantee fund is in better
shape, and has been started, but it is accompanied by the
condition that our concerts shall be given in some place
uptown, more favorably located than that to which we
have been accustomed. As we have no hall, all that is left
is the theater, which would confine our concerts to matinées.
Even if we should take the Metropolitan Opera-house,

it is questionable if we could make dates that would be advantageous to us. From a business point of view I have no fears of non-success, but for Popular concerts we should have to have an orchestra of eighty or ninety men, and give our concerts with one rehearsal. Such concerts are not desirable and can lead to no good results.

" To retain a permanent organization there is only one thing we might do, and that is to travel in the West the whole year. You, however, would not be willing to lead such a life, even if I were, for it is wearisome and not conducive to any high standard. So long, therefore, as New York gives us no hold upon success in the shape of a hall where the public can be pleasantly and conveniently accommodated, a permanent orchestra seems to me to be no longer possible.

" It was only last week that I wrote the committee of the guarantee fund that I could not say whether we could give the proposed matinées or not, as that would depend on the orchestra at my disposal. I can however tell you this; I have been requested to give winter concerts in Chicago, and offers have been made to guarantee them. But the number of the concerts would depend on those we could give in other cities. We should have to give one, at least, between here and New York, both going and returning, in order to make it practicable.

" This, even if it could be arranged, would take a long time to accomplish. I hope you understand, therefore, why I cannot say now how much work I can promise you. It would seem that there may be some concerts, but the standard of such desultory work would be doubtful. It is only lately that I have been able to come to a decision, and know just what is best and right to do. It goes without saying that I cannot prevent you from making other engagements, signing other contracts, or

giving lessons. But I shall expect that you will notify
me if you make any engagements that will hinder you from
appearing at any time in concerts in or out of New York,
and meantime I will ascertain as expeditiously as possible
how many concerts will be at my disposal."

The foregoing statement from Thomas came
like a bolt from the blue to both orchestra and
public. But, although many beautiful and appreciative tributes to Thomas and his work appeared
in the press all over the country, and much lamen-
tation was expressed by music-lovers everywhere,
no one came forward to save the organization,
which for nearly a quarter of a century had been
the cornerstone of American music, and had taught
the people, of not only the large cities, but of the
remotest towns, in every part of the land, to know
and love the very highest flower of musical art.
Consequently, the closing concert of the Chicago
Summer Night season was the final performance
that the old Theodore Thomas Orchestra gave as
an organized institution, owned and controlled by
its founder and leader.

Had Thomas been sure that this was to be the
case, no doubt he would have arranged the programme with some reference to the occasion, but
he still hoped that something would happen which
would call his men together again before they
were scattered irreclaimably, and enable him to
reconstruct the orchestra once more on a permanent basis. He, therefore, made no difference in
the programme of this concert, which was similar

in character to any other Saturday night programme, except for the final number, Wagner's
grandiose Kaiser Marsch, which ends with Luther's
inspiring choral,*" Ein' feste Burg ist unser Gott."*
Whether this selection was intentional or not, I
cannot say, but it was certainly fitting that the
passing of an institution which had achieved such
great work for art and humanity should have
been accompanied by the most stately and impressive music. It was also a curious coincidence that
the last official concert of the Thomas Orchestra
should have taken place in Chicago, the city in
which it was subsequently reassembled.

THE LAST PROGRAMME

OF

THE THEODORE THOMAS ORCHESTRA
OF NEW YORK

Chicago, August 4, 1888

Festival Overture.............................Lassen
Wedding Music................................Jensen
Spinning Chorus, and Sailors' Chorus, " Flying
    Dutchman " ....Wagner

Intermission

Gavotte, Sicilienne, Bourrée....................Bach
Fugue, A minor (string orchestra)...............Bach
Bal Costumé, Second Suite................Rubinstein

Intermission

Tarantelle for Flute and Clarinet...........Saint Saens
    Messrs. Otto Oesterle and Joseph Schreurs
Album blatt..................................Wagner
Kaiser Marsch...............................Wagner

Heart-breaking as his professional disasters had been to Thomas, a far deeper and keener anxiety awaited him at home.   His wife, never very strong, had become very ill during his absence, and on his return he found her condition so serious that he thought it important to place her under expert medical care, and the family consequently went back to New York earlier than usual.   In acknowledgment of some pictures of himself which I had ordered at his request from a Chicago photographer, he sent me the following letter just before leaving for the city:

FAIRHAVEN, *September 30, 1888.*

Dear Miss Fay:

I have been packing all day, and trying to sort and answer my letters, but made little headway.   It is late now, but I will write a few lines to-night, yet, for fear that I will not have time when I reach New York.   Thank you for the photographs, which I received safely.   I have written a few lines to Mrs. Stone and sent her the promised picture, so that is attended to.

Mrs. Thomas went to New York a few days ago, very ill.   I am very anxious about her.   Hector and Hermann went with her, but Minna and Marian remained behind with me.   To-morrow we lock up the house and follow, servants and all.   I am sorry to have to leave the country so early.   I have a house, but that is all.   Had I worked in Europe one year, as I have worked here every year, I would have had money to live on besides.   There are two sides to everything, and I do not care much for the funny side, but sometimes a serious matter becomes or appears funny to me.

I did not score your Chopin Polonaise—which, by the way, Rubinstein also wanted me to score, when he was in this country long ago,—because there is another arrangement already, by the same man who scored the Liszt Second Rhapsody. I never played this arrangement because the scoring does not do justice to the composition: at the same time there are so many points in his scoring exactly like the sketch that I made that I thought I could alter his work and make it satisfactory. But I finally came to the conclusion that I would rearrange it altogether. You can understand, however, that all this caused loss of time, and took away my desire to score this Polonaise. But I will score it some time this winter, and start fresh at it. Meantime I have composed an Inaugural, Festival, or Wedding March—we will see what name Providence will give it.—The score is fully as long as that of an overture, and is now in the hands of the copyist.

I had a nice letter from your brother Norman, and I will try to meet him and tell him some things I can hardly write in a letter. Tell Miss Amy that I read her book, "Music Study in Germany," with interest on the cars, and have sent it back to her. I hope she received it.

Sincerely yours,
THEODORE THOMAS.

The winter of 1888-89 was the most terrible year of his life to Thomas. His professional career was wrecked, his orchestra disbanded, his property lost, and his beloved wife lying on her death-bed during all those fearful months. He conducted many concerts, it is true, and this enabled him to keep in touch with the members of his orchestra for the time being, but no high standard was possible in this desultory kind of work, when his men played anywhere and everywhere between times. "My men are all ruined," he said mournfully, "by constant playing at balls and dances, for a living. A nice state of affairs, truly, that after a lifetime of hard work the members of my orchestra must play for *dancing* in order to live." He did not have to conduct for dancing, fortunately, but his contempt for the class of work he was obliged to do, is shown by his programme record-book for this year. Not a single programme was entered in it from August 5, 1888, to July 1, 1889, but the pages where they should have been were left blank. He did not take enough interest in these "shop concerts," as he called them, to record them. Even the Philharmonic programmes were only jotted down in a pocket note-book. He worked as conscientiously as he could, to return good measure for "value received," but it was work, pure and simple, without inspiration or future, simply for a living, and Theodore Thomas could not be satisfied to work in that way. To give what he considered mediocre performances merely for money, was deadly to him, and made him feel actually dishonest. Early in December, he wrote:

NEW YORK, *Dec.* 4, 1888.

Dear Miss Fay:

I returned Sunday from a short concert tour, all broken up. I have received your letter and inclose the Philharmonic programmes you ask for. On the 3d Brooklyn I have placed some Bach numbers which I have transcribed for orchestra during my wife's illness, while waiting on her.

So far I have had the men of my orchestra in New York yet, but Bour leaves for Paris this week, and Schreurs also leaves for Europe a week later. Four weeks more and the Thomas Orchestra will belong to the past, for I think the men have waited long enough now. As for myself, I will not and cannot play in New York any longer, under these conditions. I long for the Philharmonic concerts to come to an end, and only wait for my wife to improve in health so that I can leave in French fashion. Do not expect me to write letters. I am very busy and very nervous. I want the world to let me alone— and also my friends. I know exactly what I want, and my work is laid out. I am not " blue," but the illness of my wife makes me very nervous, and of course I do not like this unsettled state of affairs either.

Very truly,

THEODORE THOMAS.

What plan he had in mind I do not know, for it was never carried out. Mrs. Thomas did not improve in health, but after lingering through the winter months, died on April 4, 1889. Thomas was nearly prostrated by the blow. His iron will enabled him to conduct the few concerts which remained of his spring contracts, but as soon as they were over he retired, in an almost dazed condition, to his Fairhaven home.

CHAPTER XVI

1889-1891

THOMAS IN HIS HOME—A NATIONAL TESTIMONIAL CONCERT
TOUR—A MEMORABLE PERFORMANCE OF THE NINTH
SYMPHONY—THOMAS MARRIES MISS ROSE FAY OF
CHICAGO

WHEN Thomas left New York for his country
home, in the spring of 1889, he was a heart-
broken man. He did not care so much about his
financial losses, for he knew he would be able to
make them good again, but two of the greatest
calamities that could have happened to him—the
death of his wife, and the loss of his orchestra—
had devastated his life. The future was all a
blank, turn which way he would, and seemed to
offer him no rallying-point at which to collect his
scattered forces. Fortunately for him, his children were still under his roof and to be provided
for, and the spur of necessity forced him to renewed effort in spite of himself, and left him little
time for idle repining.

When he reached Fairhaven he was so prostrated mentally, that, for the first time in his
life, he found himself unable to fix his attention
on any kind of work, or to form any plans for the
future. "I have had no sense for music or anything else, since my loss," he wrote, "except to be

with my children. These lines are the first I have
written, or, in fact, the only thing I could bring
myself to do, except the few concerts I had to
conduct, and in which I took no interest. I need
rest and am glad I am at home." After a time,
however, the companionship of his family and the
quiet beauty of his country home began to exercise
a soothing influence on his perturbed spirit, and
he became calmer, and then it seemed to afford him
some relief to write letters—a strange thing for
him, who had never before put pen to paper when
he could avoid it. These letters give a graphic
picture of Thomas in his home life, and of his
gradual return to a more normal and healthy condition of mind; they are, therefore, quoted somewhat at length:

" FAIRHAVEN, *May*, 1889.

" I meant to have written last week, but I have so many
ups and downs that I could not. I have at last begun
to read, and have sent to New York for some material for
work, so I hope to begin to do something again after
this.

" The weather has been particularly favorable for vege-
tation and the country looks more rich and beautiful than
I have ever seen it. At least our grounds and garden do.
We have planted a number of young trees and there is
no end to little improvements. Our life here consists of
three divisions—exercise, good, plain living, and sleep. I
have even gone back to a pipe, but don't be afraid! I
shall not bring my pipe along to Chicago, but here in
the country the boys and I have decided that we will only
invite guests whose constitution can stand a pipe!

" Do you know that I have one of the finest dogs in the

country? He is a mastiff, given me by the secretary of the Mastiff Club,—a fine beast about ten months old. We had a bulldog too, a very funny and good-natured animal, but I was forced to get rid of him, there was too much dog about the place, and really danger for outsiders. The place has a fine reputation in consequence, and people are afraid to come near us, so we are happily left alone."

———

" Yesterday the boys and I went to Boston to do some shopping. I need them to help me with mine, they do not need me to help with theirs. Most of the things I wanted I did not find, and got thoroughly disgusted hunting about all day in the rain. Well, I came home only to appreciate it the more. Two items, however, I did find, and I will tell you about them.

" My study I have furnished very inexpensively. In the first place I sent from my New York house two tall cases, one for books and the other for scores. On one stands a bust of Shakespeare, on the other a bust of Bach, both life-size. Over the fireplace, between them—in which at present is burning a cheerful wood-fire—hangs a large engraving of Mozart at the court of Vienna. On the wall opposite hangs Beethoven, under whom I sit, before a writing table, which I had made twenty-five years ago, and which faces the fire. To the left is a large window, which enables me to look out upon the lawn and trees. On one side of the window hangs Goethe, a picture I bought in Weimar. It represents him as an old man, but strong; I have never seen one like it before or since. Opposite hangs a picture of Schiller's house and garden, as I saw it in Weimar. I do not admire the likenesses of Schiller, but I do admire Schiller's *Geist*, therefore I prefer a picture of his house to a portrait of himself. On the other

side of the window will hang, next week, a picture of
Schubert, and opposite to him one of Schumann. These
I purchased to-day in Boston. Here you have my
'*Glaubens Bekenntniss*.' * To complete the description
of my study, on either side, behind me, is a long window
leading to the front piazza, which is shaded by large
elm trees. To my left, under Schubert, stands an old sofa;
to my right, under Schumann, is an upright Steinway
piano. The rest you must imagine.

"My other purchase was for another room, where I want
a 'Dutch door' leading into the garden. For this I
had to find a man to come and take the measurements.
This room is used by the children in the morning, to study
in. I also bought yesterday for it an engraving of Lincoln, to hang over the fireplace, opposite to one of General Grant, which hangs over an old-fashioned 'highboy.'
On either side are maps—the largest procurable—one of
the United States, and the other of Europe. The room
contains also pictures of the California big trees, which
I brought from the Yosemite Valley. An American room,
is it not? You see I am comfortably placed and my children are all so good that I ought to be happy, but—I
miss my 'home.' "

"We have so much rain that one is confused, and hardly
knows in what climate or season one is living. This morning, at last, it promised to be clear, and my red, Scotch
Peter went to work to cut the rye. Hardly had he finished his murderous work when the heavens began to
frown again, and a first-class storm filled out the rest
of the day. It has rained so constantly that exercise is
hard to obtain and I have been in the house too much and
read more than is good for me. As a little by-play last

* "The articles of my belief."

week I arranged Siegmund's Love Song for orchestra, and yesterday I began on Schubert's ' *Erlkoenig,*' which is already half-finished. I will bring them to Chicago when I come, and play them some time during the summer-night season. To-day I tried to make the first week's programmes for Chicago. Work for a living begins again—Brrrrr!

" A friend of mine asked me if I could tell him why Switzerland is called the paradise of earth. I answered him that nature is so grand there that one forgets the rest of the world, and the hotels and service are so good that the demands of the body are all satisfied, consequently there is a harmony between spirit and body one cannot have anywhere else. Switzerland is the only country I have a desire to visit again."

" At last we have charming weather, and have had visitors staying in the house also. The change to a cool temperature is delightful, though the warm weather brought us an abundance of strawberries and vegetables of all kinds. I have been working on the score of the ' *Erlkoenig* ' again. The scoring itself is so easy for me that the writing down of it is doubly tedious. The score makes some thirty closely written pages, and in the hot, damp weather we have had it is not pleasant work, and is slow besides. But if I do not finish it now so that I can play it in Chicago, the time already spent on it will be thrown away. Amongst our other guests we have had Mrs. Gillespie with us for a few days, so I gave up my time to her while she was here. But I find it very hard to live as other people do in summer—doing nothing. If I cannot do a certain amount of work every day I feel very *mean*, which is the lowest depth I can conceive. But when I can work I am satisfied. I am poor in lucre, but

I am glad to be poor, beyond a homestead and a simple living, and I hope always to have strength enough to provide that as long as my shadow is moving about."

When Thomas spoke of being " poor," he meant in the sense of accumulated property. Before he went into the American Opera scheme, he had saved a sum which was large enough to have provided comfortably for his family and himself in his declining years. Now nothing was left of it but his country place and his library. His income, however, although much reduced, was still ample, for, like all great musicians, his earning power was always very large. His idea of " simple living " was not quite in accordance with the popular meaning of the term, for he was, both by nature and training, a *connoisseur,* not only in art matters, but in everything else that interested him, and he was not satisfied with anything but the best. His " simple life," therefore, included rare wines, fine cigars, clothing of the best material and make, horses and carriages, delicate cooking, large and handsomely furnished city and country houses, books, scores, and expert service of all kinds. His children were given every educational and social advantage, and no reasonable wish of theirs was ever denied that he could gratify. In fact, the only simplicity to be found in his home was in its kindly and unconventional atmosphere, and the absence of all ostentation. He himself, however, knew very little about the actual cost of anything, and really imagined that he only lived in reasonable comfort. He did not wish to have anything to do with money matters, and would not even cash his checks, as they came in, but merely signed them and turned them over to his wife to spend or invest as she thought best. All he wanted was to have two new fifty-dollar bills in his pocket. He would keep them unbroken as long as possible, partly because he enjoyed the feeling of having the two nice big bills in reserve, and partly because he did not like to carry the dirty money he got in exchange. When he handled the latter, he would either put on gloves or carefully wash his hands afterwards! Indeed it would be difficult to find a man of more fastidious tastes and habits than Thomas.

July and August were, as usual, passed in Chicago, for the most part, and after the season there was finished, he returned again to Fairhaven for the interval before the opening of the winter season in New York. He tried to be cheerful, for the sake of those about him, but he could not shake off the gloom and loneliness which enveloped his spirit, and his letters during the fall were weary and sad.

" My box of scores," he wrote in August, " has come from New York, to enable me to complete my various programmes for the fall, winter, and spring concerts. This keeps me busy enough, but I dislike the work. Artistically speaking, I have no satisfaction, and my daily life is at present very tedious. Formerly I delighted in being alone, now I dread it. Artistically there is nothing for me to

do any more in this world. What I am doing now others
can do as well. What I am good for, and my talents and
experience have ripened me for, and others cannot do, I
have no longer any opportunity for. And so I am tired
of everything. I am tired of staying in the country, I am
dreadfully tired of the kind of work before me this winter.
Circumstances force me to prostitute my art and my
talents."

From New York, in September, he wrote in
the same strain:

" I am not exactly sad, but I realize that I am not
normal; I seem to have no memory, and do the most curious things. I am tired—you will get tired also of my
everlasting lamentations. I tried to work this evening,
but it is of no use. I cannot work, I am not myself any
more, I do not know myself. The only explanation I can
give is that this is the terrible reaction of the strain of
the last twenty years of my life. But I ought to have
some common sense left, and do my business, and know
that by and by everything will come into satisfactory
shape again. But what is common sense? I have none.
Try to have a little patience with me, and I hope to get
better after a while—I am sorry for you, that you have
to read all these melancholy letters, but my only pleasure
seems to be in writing to you. The world is so tedious
to me, but I must go on for the sake of my children,
for a few years yet. What you imagine to be gratifying
in the fall concert tour is to me only distasteful. I do
not care to be ' lionized,' as the saying is, when all my work
must be at such a low standard."

The fall tour, alluded to in the last quotation,
was of a peculiar character. It was designed to

be a sort of national testimonial from the people of America, in appreciation of the labors of Thomas for the musical culture of the country. The suggestion was first made in a letter from Minneapolis to the New York *Tribune,* signed "Many Music Lovers." It was the outcome of a conference of several officers and members of the Minneapolis Philharmonic Society. After outlining a plan for a tour of the country, this letter continued:

" Such a tour might be made a grand triumphal march for the great conductor. Understand that no ' benefit ' scheme is contemplated by this suggestion, Mr. Thomas would be the first to turn his back upon such a proposition. Let him simply take his orchestra and give in the various cities a ' *quid pro quo,*' and more, as he always does, for all that he receives; but let the tour be understood to be a distinctive opportunity for the people to testify the high estimate they place upon Mr. Thomas' life-work in behalf of the music of this country. If Mr. Thomas doubts that there is a deep feeling of regard for him amongst the musicians and people of America, and that, whatever may be said of the sharp points of his character, they are ready to testify to it, let him give them an opportunity in the way now suggested. Minneapolis will be glad of the coveted opportunity to testify with other cities throughout the country the high esteem and sincere admiration that is felt by the people everywhere both for the man and his work."

This suggestion found immediate favor in many of the cities of the old Thomas " Highway," and so many invitations were received from those wishing to be included in the testimonial tour that it took a month of traveling to visit all the places. In each city the invitation was signed by the most eminent men of the place, but the most remarkable one of all was that of New York, both in the beauty of its wording, and the personality of its fifty signers, many of whom were men of national fame.

NEW YORK, *June,* 1889.

THEODORE THOMAS, ESQ.

Dear Sir:

Learning that you have been invited to undertake a series of concerts in various parts of the country during the next autumn, we desire to express to you our sincere interest in the enterprise proposed, to assure you of our heartiest good wishes for its complete success, and to ask that New York, which is your home and the scene of your most arduous labors, may be included among the cities which are to share the opportunity of showing their appreciation of your work. In this Centennial year of national pride and joy, not the least pleasant reason of general congratulation is the growth and development of a taste for the higher forms of art, because this taste is one of the powerful forces to which we must look for the necessary chastening of the material and commercial spirit, which has thus far largely dominated American progress. Among these forces none is more popular or more effective than music; and in the education and elevation of musical taste in this country, no individual influence is more universally acknowledged, and none is more distinctive, constant, intelligent, and effective than yours.

Your public service of this kind has been so signal that to call attention to it on the eve of a tour such as is contemplated is but to refresh the grateful memory of lovers and students of music throughout the country, and to secure their cordial co-operation in earnestly promoting the success of the projected series of popular concerts, which will be peculiarly significant among our centennial commemorations as illustrating in themselves the character and degree of the advance of the public taste, knowledge, and skill in music.

With sincere regards, we are, dear sir,

Respectfully yours,

LEVI P. MORTON
CARL SCHURZ
WM. M. EVARTS
HORACE WHITE
THEODORE ROOSEVELT
WM. C. SCHERMERHORN
E. FRANCIS HYDE
J. Q. A. WARD
H. DRISLER
HENRY HOLT
EDMUND C. STEDMAN
R. S. MACARTHUR
THEODORE C. WILLIAMS
C. L. TIFFANY
W. D. HOWELLS
R. W. GILDER
R. M. HUNT
GEORGE WILLIAM CURTIS
CHAUNCEY M. DEPEW
WARNER MILLER
JOSEPH H. CHOATE
B. H. BRISTOW
J. PIERPONT MORGAN
D. B. VAN EMBURGH
D. HUNTINGTON
VINCENZO BOTTA

JOHN BIGELOW
HJALMAR H. BOYESEN
C. VANDERBILT
CYRUS W. FIELD
HENRY VILLARD
R. G. INGERSOLL
JOHN F. PLUMMER
CALVIN S. BRICE
GROVER CLEVELAND
C. A. DANA
W. R. GRACE
PARKE GODWIN
F. R. COUDERT
HOWARD CROSBY
ROBERT COLLYER
AUGUSTUS ST. GAUDENS
S. G. W. BENJAMIN
BRANDER MATTHEWS
MONCURE D. CONWAY
CHAS. S. ROBINSON
C. P. HUNTINGTON
GEO. F. BAKER
ANDREW CARNEGIE
WILLIAM STEINWAY,
and many others.

To these invitations Thomas sent the following reply:

FAIRHAVEN, MASS., *June,* 1889.

To MESSRS. HENRY K. SHELDON AND JOHN D. EL-
WELL, BROOKLYN; LEVI P. MORTON, GEORGE
WILLIAM CURTIS, GROVER CLEVELAND, AND
OTHERS, OF NEW YORK; OLIVER AMES, HENRY
L. HIGGINSON, JOSIAH D. WHITNEY, AND
OTHERS, OF BOSTON; AND TO THE MANY
OTHER FRIENDS THROUGHOUT THE COUNTRY
WHO HAVE SIMILARLY HONORED ME.

Gentlemen:

To one who has endeavored to do his duty, the knowledge that his work is appreciated is peculiarly encouraging. Your invitations, therefore, gratify as well as honor
me, and I cordially and gladly accept them, and will as
soon as possible indicate the dates of the concerts to be
given upon the tour proposed, beginning early in October
of the ensuing autumn.

I will not refuse to believe that this movement represents the popular feeling. It therefore seems appropriate that the people should have a voice in the selection of
the music to be performed. Hence in every city whose
citizens care to indicate a preference, " Request Programmes " will be made as the result of their choice.

Thanking you for the kind consideration which has
inspired this compliment, I am

Very truly yours,

THEODORE THOMAS.

But even this unique tribute, the like of which
had never been offered to any other American
musician, failed to arouse him from his despondency and, instead of anticipating the tour with

pride and pleasure, his only feeling was one of humiliation that he must appear before all these gala audiences with an orchestra which he considered inferior in quality and imperfectly trained, and could only give the people who would gather in his honor, performances the standard of which he despised. That the people themselves would not notice the difference was no consolation to him, for he took that only as evidence that, after a lifetime of labor, the public was still a long way from the musical culture he had striven to inculcate. Of course all this was morbid and hyper-sensitive on his part and the outcome of his melancholy state of mind, but he had had so much adversity that he was discouraged, melancholy, and broken—a dangerous mood for a man of a strong and passionate nature.

In this emergency it was his children who sustained and brought him back to spiritual convalescence again. They were now youths and maidens, old enough to be his companions, and kept him surrounded with an atmosphere of tender affection, and of gay young life without which he might have sunk into hopeless despair. For their sakes he determined to put the past resolutely behind him and begin life anew, though he knew not as yet how or where it was to be done. "I feel," he wrote, "as if the curtain had fallen on one act of my life, and the scenes were being set for another."

Immediately on his return to New York in the fall Thomas began the preparations for the Testimonial Tour, which was to begin in Brooklyn on October 9, and end in New York on November 6. In spite of himself, Thomas found the return to musical life inspiring, and worked hard to get the orchestra at his command into presentable shape.

"I had a rehearsal of three hours this morning," he wrote, "and you know I lose no time. I must laugh at the amount of work I can do without getting tired! I am not old yet, but I will confess I have a great deal of anxiety. I want to give some help to my children for a few years yet, and I am not afraid but that I can carry it through, but it may cost a great deal of fighting and hard work. I am willing to work, as you know, but art and business do not blend, and everything is so uncertain.

"My rehearsal this morning was very pleasant, and I have all the old power, or rather I have more strength than ever. I am growing all the time, and feel my strength, if I could only use it to better purpose. But I trust in God that all will come out right—perhaps not exactly in the same way that others do, but every honest soul in his own way.

"We start for the fall tour in a few days, and are in Albany on October 11. Will you let me have a letter on that day? It is my fifty-fourth birthday."

The first concert of the series took place in Brooklyn, and like all his Brooklyn experiences it was pleasant and successful. Then the traveling began, and the following letters give some of his experiences on the trip in his own words:

" ALBANY, *Oct.* 11.

" As you want me to tell you about the concerts and other events connected with the tour, I must begin with the Poughkeepsie night. The concert went off very well, the people were very enthusiastic, and I gave them all the encores they wanted. Men rushed around to the stage to shake hands, American fashion, and rushed off again, etc., etc. We left after the concert and arrived here (Albany) in time for me to get to bed at a quarter after three. I slept till a quarter past seven, and then some children overhead made too much noise for me to sleep any longer. It was my birthday, and after breakfast I walked to the hall for my letters and telegrams, of which there were a great many. The first telegram I opened was from General Merrill, it read, ' You have my sympathy in your old age, but never mind, one must either grow old or die! ' I shall answer him that I will die, if necessary, but *I will not grow old.* The next was from George William Curtis, who is still at Ashfield. After this a large number of telegrams came pouring in, from very pleasant ones to very boshy ones.—Well, well, it is, after all, pleasant to have the good will of one's friends, that they take all that trouble. Finally came your letter and the volume of Emerson. It was a nice thought to send me that and I think it is just what I want to read.

" After this I made a call on a lady. She is a very wealthy woman and showed me all over her house, where she has an accumulation of relics and treasures only possible to have been brought together by several generations. One thing interested me particularly, and I took it in my hand—Luther's wedding ring. It was quite a nice ring. On my return to the hotel, I found the children above still too lively for me to get any peace in my room, so I again went out and took a walk, which I needed, but

I need sleep still more, and so have declined all invitations for to-night and hope to get to bed by twelve o'clock."

" Cleveland, *Oct.* 18.

" Yesterday was a very hard day, and although I was up before seven, I could not even get time for a walk. Of course a rehearsal took up the extra time. I do not wish to complain, but this traveling business I cannot stand any more. I cannot live like other travelers, and to try to get anything different or according to my individual needs while traveling is almost impossible, and only to be accomplished by a constant fight. I do need a decent glass of wine, and I do need a cup of strong coffee when I work as I must—both are impossible to get. The traveling public drinks beer or whisky, and I am forbidden to drink either. As for the wines, they are so poor and so sweet that they upset me. Last night after the concert I was so tired that I refused to speak. I told Sachleben to come with me, for he does not talk when I do not, and when I know that I cannot be pleasant I am as silent as a clam. I was so hungry that we went to a restaurant, but it was an hour before we could get anything to eat, and when at last I got back to the hotel I was too tired to pack, and therefore had to get up early this morning in order to have my trunk ready for the baggage-man at eight. And so it goes, and will go, I foresee. This kind of life is impossible, and I had found it so before, as you know. I shall continue this year in order not to run behind, but next year if I cannot make twenty thousand dollars, I will have to learn to live on ten, or even less if necessary. Other people do, and so can I, and if I want to help my boys for a few years yet, until they are established in life, I must economize. They deserve all I can do for them, for it is such a blessing to have good sons, when one thinks of what trouble they might cause one.

" Emerson says, ' Nothing can bring you peace but the triumph of principles.' This I have known myself for years, and very clearly from experience. But while I have become clearer in my mind these last years, I have been so unmercifully tossed about on the waves of the ordinary world that I have not been able to anchor anywhere. And still I have blessings which so few men have—I must surely find a haven somewhere to cast my anchor. I found Emerson very interesting reading in the cars yesterday, nevertheless Kant, Goethe, or Schopenhauer—not to mention Shakespeare—will any one of them say in one page as much as Emerson says in forty."

———

" JACKSON, *Oct. 23,* 1889.

" This was a very noisy morning for me. While the soul can live without the body, the body can, nevertheless, make the soul sick. Yesterday afternoon I made up my mind that I must find a decent restaurant where I could get something I could eat. Mahnken went with me, and at last we found one. It was in a basement, an all-night place, and for some minutes we could not make any headway. All at once the atmosphere changed, and what they had not in the house they would get for me if it was in the town! To make the matter short, the place was kept by an old showman who recognized me, and the kindness, civility, and good taste which I experienced there I cannot exaggerate, nor have I ever eaten better food in my life. Everything had to be brought from outside, but no matter, market and butcher were across the street and God was in that place. I have taken all my meals there, and last night I slept as of old, from two o'clock until seven this morning, soundly and undisturbed, and I have felt like a different being to-day in consequence. Of course we were roasted on the cars to-day, but I have taken plenty of luncheon with me, for we will not be able to get a single meal again until we reach Chicago, day after to-morrow, and I have a heavy cold, which I contracted a few days ago."

———

" NEW YORK, *Nov.* 6, 1889.

" At home once more—How quiet and restful it is! You know enough about me by this time to know that my home is very sacred to me. In fact, it is my world, and I do all I can to make it a heaven for my family. It is very seldom that I am cross, because I seldom get so tired that I cannot control myself. Even when I do I always have my brains, and my bad temper does not last but a few minutes, and if no one fights me then I show my gratitude.

" The last ' testimonial ' performance will be here on Saturday, and I have just come from rehearsal. I am sorry I am not in better condition, but I am all broken up by the trip, and have a stiff neck and shoulders. I hope to be better by Saturday. For once every musician has thrown off all personal feeling, and I will have an orchestra the best the country can afford. The whole profession have offered their services, and I could have an orchestra of a thousand! It will be as large as the stage of the Metropolitan Opera House can accommodate. Joseffy has also volunteered his services as soloist. I have just written a letter of thanks to the musicians."

When the concert came off it was very successful, as such things go. There were the customary crowd, ovation, recalls, encores, flowers, laurel wreaths, and complimentary press notices, in-

separable from such occasions. Thomas had been
the hero of similar scenes so many times that it
did not make very much impression upon him.
What he did value about the affair, however, was
the public good-will, of which it was the spontaneous expression, and, in particular, the cordial
and affectionate attitude of the professional musicians. In the course of his long career in New
York its musicians gave him many similar marks
of their sincere friendship and admiration for him,
and he valued them amongst the most precious
tributes of his life, and was never so pleased as
when something of this kind came from his orchestral associates.

After the fall tour was over Thomas settled
down to the musical drudgery of the winter. The
only artistic food he had during this tedious season was the concerts of the New York and
Brooklyn Philharmonic Societies. And even
here, he imagined that his work suffered some
deterioration as compared with previous years,
because the men were not under his leadership all
the time, as they had formerly been, but only rehearsed with him for such concerts as he engaged
them for, taking engagements elsewhere in the
intervals between. The following letter describes
the difficulties of getting artistic results under
these conditions:

"New York, *Dec.* 1, 1889.
"This morning I had a curious rehearsal. It was the
first Philharmonic, and I had a good deal of fighting to
do. I could not get the men to play as I wanted, and

finally threw the score down on the floor and took up
another with the same difficulties. But at last, by talking
and insisting and making stands play alone, I began to
get the effects I wanted, and, behold! it went to the ears
and hearts of the men, and then, of course, all was easy.
They were more delighted than I when they heard the
result and understood what I was after. But it was a
terrible fight—over a hundred men of ability, trying for
something, and one man beating the stand, shouting at
the top of his lungs, scolding, entreating, etc., and finally
taking out his watch to show them that all this had taken
an hour. The trouble is that the men can now play elsewhere as they like, and when they come back to me after
a short interval it always takes half of the first rehearsal
before they realize the proportions and proper conditions
again. I am not dead yet, it seems. But I still have that
cold hanging about me, and have not been well since my
return from the tour."

Ever since Thomas had been the conductor of
the New York Philharmonic Society he had made
its programmes the very highest expression of his
art. The Philharmonic audience was almost
unique in America at that time, and there was
only one other in the entire country like it—
that of the Boston Symphony Concerts. The
whole seating capacity of the Metropolitan
Opera House, in which its concerts were
given, was " sold out " to season ticket holders,
who came regularly, year after year, and had become so cultivated, in consequence, that they were
connoisseurs. Hence Thomas had none of the
so-called " popular " element to cater for in

selecting its programmes, and his only thought was to make them the unquestioned standard of the musical art of America. Each programme was composed of the greatest symphonic works, and the most important novelties, and only first-rank artists appeared in the solo numbers. As for the orchestra, it was the largest and best in America, and always included in its ranks the entire Thomas Orchestra, as well as its own players. The rehearsals were of the most exacting nature, and, in short, every concert of the Philharmonic Society represented the very best that Thomas could produce season by season. The history of his art may be read in these programmes, during the long series of years when he was their conductor. Of course this artistic standard was not raised and maintained for so long without more or less of what he called " fighting." Now and then some member of the Philharmonic orchestra of long standing would become superannuated, and decline to resign in favor of a younger and better man, and much unpleasantness would ensue before the matter could be finally adjusted. Other points were also occasionally raised, for the society was a stock company and had a right to say how its affairs should be carried on. But, on the whole, they did not interfere with Thomas very often, and when they did he simply stood firm until they came around to his point of view, which they were pretty sure to do after a while, for he always had a good practical reason for everything he did, and they had the most absolute confidence in his justice and disinterestedness. Thomas had no more loyal and devoted friends in the world than his colleagues of the New York Philharmonic Society, and none, I think, of whose friendship he was so proud.

But a man who had been accustomed to the enormous mass of important work that Thomas had been doing for the last twenty years, could not be satisfied with a single series of symphony concerts—no matter how fine—when all the rest of his work was what he considered inferior. Again the darker mood clouded his spirit, and he wrote:

" NEW YORK, *Dec.* 29, 1889.

" I would like to write you a nice letter, but I have nothing to say. Musical affairs are so unsatisfactory now that, while I know that decent work is impossible under the present circumstances, it is hard to fight it through, especially as I always did good work. I take it philosophically, but I shall be glad when this season is over, and meantime I must look for some other occupation than orchestra and concert work. Well, I do not care any more, but let things go as they must. But if the people see or can read in my back that I now play for money, let them—I cannot help it, and they deserve nothing better. All I want now is to make enough for us all to live on decently, for I have the feeling that nothing will be done in this country at present where my services will be needed. This we have to thank Wagner for; how long it will last no one can tell. Meantime I will learn to do something else for a living—but it is rather late, and tough for me.

" As you see, I have the blues and all the world looks gray to me. Nothing has happened, but the general condition of affairs gives me no inspiration, and I feel resigned enough to-night to give up all claim to anything and everything in this world."

Of the many concerts Thomas conducted during this tedious season, only two were especially noteworthy. One was given in aid of the Beethoven Society at Bonn, and the other was a performance of the Ninth Symphony, early in the spring. Thomas always approached a performance of this master-work with such seriousness and reverence that it resembled the celebration of some high religious festival by a prelate of the church, rather than the mere giving of an orchestral concert. He not only prepared the music by thorough study, and the orchestra, chorus, and soloists by training and rehearsal, but he carefully prepared himself in both mind and body, by rest, exercise, and sparing diet. On the day of the performance he would receive no calls, and as the concert hour drew near, he did not even come to the family table, because he wished no outside thoughts to distract his mind from the music.

Thomas did not often speak of his work in concert by any higher term than merely " good," but after this concert he wrote as follows:

" New York, *April* 13, 1890.

" Last night's performance was great in every sense of the word, and the ripest and greatest I ever gave at any time and of anything. The audience knew what was going on and stood on their chairs, and waved hats and handkerchiefs when they got me out on the stage again, and the members of the orchestra congratulated not only me but each other! After the concert I had a little supper at my house, which was also pleasant. The guests were friends from out of town who happened to be in New York—Miss Long of Boston, Mrs. Nicholas Longworth and Mrs. Bellamy Storer of Cincinnati, and Mrs. Gillespie of Philadelphia. There were also the Gersters and a few New York friends, altogether a jolly party.

"Replying to your question about the Ninth Symphony, I think, taken for all in all, the first movement of this symphony may be considered the greatest, and nothing about it is more remarkable than its opening sixteen measures. Beethoven apparently wished to produce here the effect of a mysterious foreshadowing of something great and portentous to come. So well has he succeeded that the mode, the key, and the theme are all wrapped in such vagueness that only careful analysis can discern the last two, while the first is not to be determined by any process. In other words, he gives a chord without the middle note, so it is neither major nor minor. This chord he places on the fifth step of the key of D, and thus it can be mistaken for the key of A; while the theme here announced is only begun, and is not given in completion until the seventeenth measure. I therefore consider the first sixteen measures as a prologue. At the seventeenth measure the mystery and presentiment of the prologue end, and the minor mode, the key of D, and the first subject are all blazoned forth with all the power of the whole orchestra in unison. This mighty theme is somber, grandiose, and fraught with a restless energy which knows no peace nor satisfaction."

This concert closed the season of 1889-90, a period which might be called a spiritual convalescence for Thomas after the heartbreaking calamities of the three previous years. Very slowly and with many a relapse into the old discouragement and gloom, a healthier, braver tone began to pervade his mind. Not that he had any hope of reconstructing his artistic future in New York, he realized that that was hopeless, at least for the present, but he had been brought down at last to the renunciation point, and the bitterness of death was past. "This life," he wrote, "is, after all, mostly ' *Entbehren sollst du, du sollst entbehren,*' * and the world is only a combination against any kind of elevation. It combines to pull everyone down to its level, and one must fight daily, and every moment, for a respectable standard in anything. I cannot fight any more, so I have renounced, for I would rather take my fiddle and play on the streets for a living than sell my honor as a man or an artist."

In this determination to renounce his art and his "cause," Thomas was quite serious, and he fully intended to leave the concert stage and seek a livelihood in some private walk of life, such, perhaps, as a musical professorship in some college or school of music.

All his thoughts and interests now centered around his family and, as the time passed, he became, also, more and more dependent on me. One beautiful evening, May 7, 1890, we were married, and a few days later went to Cincinnati for the Festival.

* "Renounce, thou shalt—thou shalt renounce."

The year which followed our marriage was the most artistically barren year in the life of Theodore Thomas. It contained not one single musical event of sufficient interest to record, and was all on one dead level of mediocrity which at times was almost unbearable to him. But his home life was very happy, and his income ample, so he accepted the situation with what philosophy he could. Meantime the dawn began to break again, at last, and by the time spring came, the sun of promise was shining gloriously above the horizon of a new life for him.

CHAPTER XVII

1891-1892

THE reconstruction of Thomas' artistic career
was brought about by my brother, C. Norman
Fay. It was, perhaps, facilitated by our marriage,
which naturally brought the two men intimately
together, but Mr. Fay had been a devoted admirer of Thomas for many years, and long before
we knew him personally had planned to organize
an orchestra in Chicago under his direction, and
was only waiting for the opportunity to put his
plan into execution. The following letter, written
in 1879, was his introduction to Thomas, and gives
some of the details of his original scheme:

THEODORE THOMAS, ESQ. CHICAGO, *Sept. 23, 1879.*

Dear Sir:

You have doubtless heard from Mr. George B. Carpenter (from whom I inclose a letter of introduction)
that some of the gentlemen here have taken an interest
in an attempt to organize a " Philharmonic Society " in
Chicago, with the idea of working under your leadership.
We are aware that some of the local musicians have al-

Matzene Studio, Chicago (1910)

Rose Fay Thomas

ready corresponded with you, and had started to form a society last July, but that society seems to us to have little strength or cohesion, and will probably come to nothing. We have therefore canvassed the matter with some of the wealthy and public-spirited men here, and are now in a position to organize a society and make any series of concerts undertaken by it under your leadership the event of the season, and entirely successful: either taking the organization already existing, or forming an entirely new one, with an active membership of the best people here as well as the professionals.

Mr. Carpenter, who knows more of such things than I do, thinks a difficulty might arise from the jealousy of local leaders, about filling an orchestra without importing fifteen or twenty men. This brings me to the point I wish to ask. What could be done with such an orchestra? Is it worth my while to work up such an organization unless it is going to attain its object? Could you favor me with a frank answer to this?

I do not want to make a great stir about this business if it is only to end in nothing as the first attempt did, and would rather not undertake it at all. Yet, as far as money goes, I can form a strong and satisfactory society, with little delay, and it seems a pity not to do so.

Yours truly,   C. Norman Fay.

This project did not come to anything because Thomas was not able at that time to accept an engagement which involved his training an orchestra in a distant city; and Mr. Fay, on his side, did not care to have any other conductor at the head of the orchestra he wished to found. So the matter was dropped for the time being. The disbanding of his orchestra in 1888, however, left Thomas free to leave New York, and Mr. Fay took advantage of the opportunity to secure his co-operation in putting into effect his long cherished plan for a great symphony orchestra for Chicago. Now, however, the project was revived on a much more extensive scale, and instead of a Philharmonic Society of local talent, with its traditional twelve concerts, it was proposed to form a permanent symphony orchestra of the largest and most perfect kind, and give two performances a week during twenty weeks of the year—to follow, in short, the model which had already been set in Boston.

After his previous experiences with musical institutions of one kind and another, it may be imagined that Thomas did not accept the Chicago proposal without many doubts as to its ultimate success. It meant, also, some very real sacrifices on his part, for he could not leave New York without breaking up his family, and leaving two of his sons behind. Nor could he earn as much in Chicago, by ten thousand dollars a year, as he was making in New York. But to his art-hungry soul all personal considerations were outweighed by the one great advantage offered—the assurance that he could once more have his own orchestra, and an opportunity to do the highest class of musical work. He had a very genuine affection for Chicago, where his experiences had hitherto always been pleasant, and he hoped—and in this he was not disappointed—that a nearer acquaintance with the men whom Mr. Fay was planning to associate together in the orchestral scheme would be productive of good results. He, therefore, consented to be the conductor of the new orchestra. Mr. Fay lost no time in completing the organization, and soon sent Thomas the following letter:

Dear Thomas: CHICAGO, *Oct.* 1, 1890.

I have received your telegram, and the guarantee fund for the orchestra is practically secured. I have changed my original plan a little, and instead of asking for five thousand dollars apiece, per annum, from ten men, I am asking one thousand apiece from fifty. I have now thirty-eight thousand dollars pledged on that basis for three years, and as N. K. Fairbank, Marshall Field, and I are willing to subscribe five thousand dollars each, per annum, the fund may be considered to be complete, although I shall go on filling up the list as far as possible on the thousand-dollar basis, in order to enlist the active support of fifty of our leading men, instead of thirty-eight.

I have had refusals from only two men. Every one else said " Yes " at once. The details are in shape entirely satisfactory to me, and will be to you.

Yours truly,
C. NORMAN FAY.

A little later followed a copy of the prospectus and form of guarantee, with its fifty subscribers, and the contract to be signed with the now incorporated association. This was a clear, concise document, very plain and business-like, but so liberal in tone, and showing such confidence in Thomas as man and artist, that his last doubts vanished as he read it.

Under the head of "The rights, powers, and duties of the Musical Director," was a clause which read as follows:

"II. The Musical Director is to determine the character and standard of all performances given by the Association, and to that end make all programmes, select all soloists, and take the initiative in arranging for choral and festival performances. The intention of the Association being to lodge in the hands of the Director the power and responsibility for the attainment of the highest standard of artistic excellence in all performances given by the Association."

This clause delighted Thomas, and he exclaimed, "I never expected to see the day when I would be told I would be 'held responsible' for maintaining the highest standard of artistic excellence in my musical work. All my life I have been told that my standard was too high, and urged to make it more popular. But now, I am not only to be given every facility to create the highest standard, but am even told that I will be *held responsible* for keeping it so! I have to shake myself to realize it."

The Chicago contract was signed in December, 1890, and the prospect of a return to his old artistic standards of work banished all the gloom and depression of the past, and once more Thomas was himself again—bright, hopeful, boundlessly energetic as of yore, and intensely interested in making the new Western orchestra the best he had ever conducted, and returning measure for meas-

Photograph by Matzene, Chicago (1910)

Charles Norman Fay,
Founder of the Chicago Orchestral Association

ure to the men who had shown such entire confidence in him. The next few months were devoted to perfecting the plans for the Chicago organization, and to trying and selecting the musicians for it, for he was to bring with him sixty men from New York, for the "regular orchestra," as it was called, and to take the remaining thirty "extra" men from the ranks of the resident musicians of Chicago. The best artists of the old Thomas Orchestra were recalled, and those who were not so good were replaced by others, imported from Europe. So many of the former were retained, however, that it might fairly be said that the Chicago Orchestra was, in reality, the original Thomas Orchestra, simply reconstructed, improved, and transported to Chicago, and even to-day (1910) there are still to be found in its ranks a number of those incomparable artists whose faces were as familiar as household words to all the cities of the old "Highway" in the days when its headquarters were in New York.

As soon as it was known that Thomas had decided to go to Chicago, the people of New York woke up. He had a large and really devoted following of cultivated people there who appreciated and understood the value of his work, and who would probably have made his orchestra permanent long ago if there had been some prominent person to take the initiative in such a movement. But the New York people have little public spirit, and are too busy and self-absorbed to give the time

and work necessary for the founding and maintenance of great public institutions—even those
they really care for. When, however, they realized
that Thomas was actually going to leave in good
earnest, three different groups of people came to
him with propositions to raise any guarantee he
would name, if he would only stay. But it was
too late, the contract was already signed, and
all that remained to them was to wish him " God
speed " in his new life.

The last concerts of the season took, of course,
the form of ovations to the departing leader, and
especially impressive was that of the New York
Philharmonic Society, when the vast audience
which filled the Metropolitan Opera House from
floor to ceiling, arose, tier on tier, applauding,
cheering, shouting, waving hats and handkerchiefs, and even weeping as the expression of their
last affectionate farewell. The laurel wreath which
the musicians of the Philharmonic orchestra gave
him on this occasion was taken to Chicago, and
hung on the wall of his library until its leaves
dried and crumbled into dust, and the golden-
lettered white ribbon with which it was tied,
though now yellow and time-worn, is preserved
there still, bound across the arms of his vacant
chair.

Thomas had planned to start for his new Western home at the end of April, and the night before,
a large public dinner was tendered to him in farewell. His ever-loyal friend, George William
Curtis, presided at this dinner, and the following

speech, in which he proposed the health of the guest of the evening, was remarkable, even for such a master of language as he:

" I rise to propose the health of a public benefactor—an artist whose devotion to a beautiful, refining, and ennobling art has greatly distinguished his name and given great distinction to the city in which he lives—the health of the central figure of the musical life of New York for a generation, and your hearts go before my lips in saluting Theodore Thomas. He has made the conductor's baton an imperial scepter, with which he rules not only an orchestra but an ever-widening realm of musical taste and cultivation. In his hand it has been an enchanter's wand, which has transformed our musical ignorance and crudity into ample knowledge and generous appreciation. While it has introduced to us the known and acknowledged masters of the past, it has summoned and revealed those still shadowy figures of music of the future. Musical artists have come and gone. Virtuosos of every kind have appeared, have charmed us, and have vanished. Our private accomplishment has advanced from the ' Battle of Prague ' and the variations of Henri Herz to the fantasies of Schumann, the songs of Rubinstein, the Schubert transcriptions of Liszt, and is still pushing on and on, like Columbus, sailing beyond the horizon into the unknown seas. But through all changes the one figure which has remained, the laureate of the past and the herald of the future, is Theodore Thomas.

" Now, gentlemen, I suppose there are very few guests at these tables of memory so daring as mine, which recalls the coming of Jenny Lind to this country. I remember her always with a certain selfish pleasure, because I heard her, I believe, every evening that she sang in this city, and when on the last evening she sang her farewell to America at Castle Garden, she held in her hand a bouquet that I had sent her, and which still perfumes my recollection of that incomparable singer. A few years before, when Fanny Elssler was here, bewitching the heels rather than the heads or hearts of the golden youth of that time, they unharnessed the horses from her carriage and drew her across the street to her hotel, merely substituting, as an elderly cynic of the time remarked, jackasses for horses! We did not draw Jenny Lind in her carriage, but the youth of her day—of whom my young friend Parke Godwin was one, who paid his tribute in the charming tale of 'Vala'—have borne her in their hearts across a generation, and their hearts still rise at the mention of her name as the *Garde du Roi* sprang cheering to their feet when the Queen appeared. There is one story of Jenny Lind which I always recall with entire confidence in its truth, because it ought to be true. After her return from her American triumph she was in Italy, and went one day from Florence to the convent at Vallombrosa, to which the young Milton went when on his travels. When she came to the chapel the monks, with courteous and deprecating regret, told her that unhappily no woman could enter. She smiled as she said, 'Perhaps if you knew who I am you would let me in.' 'And who might the gracious lady be?' returned the monks. And when she said 'I am Jenny Lind,' every head bowed, and the doors were flung wide open. Then when she seated herself at the organ and sang where Milton had sat and played and sang, I can imagine the heavenly visions that floated before the minds of the monks, and that they crossed themselves reverently as they listened and believed that St. Cecilia had descended.

"That is what I have always thought of her visit to

America. St. Cecilia descended upon these shores, coming to give the right impulse to our musical development. But St. Cecilia would have descended in vain if there had been no continuing personal force in the country of her own spirit in art of a kindred enthusiasm and lofty purpose. Happily, in the orchestra at her concerts there was a youth who played the first violin, and who has continued to play it ever since, everybody else playing second fiddle to him! To the genius, the untiring enthusiasm, the intelligence, the energy, and masterly skill of that youth more than to any other single force we owe the remarkable musical interest and cultivation and the musical preeminence of New York to-day.

" I do not mean, of course, that there have not been other admirable artists and effective influences co-operating to this noble result. Certainly I do not forget Bergmann, nor those upon whom my eyes fall at this moment, nor the Mendelssohn Club, which last evening celebrated its twenty-fifth year of memorable achievement under the superb leadership of Joseph Mosenthal; nor all the other clubs and societies and companies of singers and players that have wrought in the good work. But during all this time the constant dominating personality was that of Theodore Thomas. It was Thomas with Bergmann, Mosenthal, and Mason in the old Dodworth *salon;* it was Thomas in the Central Park Garden, Thomas in the Philharmonic Society, Thomas in the great festival of 1882. It was always Thomas and his orchestra and always Thomas and his baton, like the valiant Henry of Navarre and his white plume waving in the van of victory.

" The great works of the great composers, the mighty music of the masters who have given to their art an equal renown with the kindred arts of literature and painting and sculpture; the music of Bach and Händel, of Mozart

and Haydn, and Beethoven—names that in their kind
shine with equal luster with those of Raphael and Angelo
and Shakespeare—has been played continuously from year
to year under Thomas' direction in a manner not even
surpassed at the Conservatoire or the Gewandhaus in Leipsic; while the music of a later day and of another charm
has been so interpreted by him that after the great Wagner afternoon at the festival of '82, Materna said to me
that Wagner had never heard that work of his own so
magnificently rendered. Thomas' whole career has been
a campaign of education. If he has revealed to us more
fully the Beethoven whom we knew, it is he also who first
showed us that there was a Wagner who might be worth
knowing. He has given to New York a musical distinction, without which no great city is a metropolis, and Chicago has shown the true metropolitan instinct in securing
his musical leadership. It is because of the dignity of his
career, its absolute fidelity to a high ideal, its total freedom from charlatanry of every kind that his service to
this city has been so signal a public benefit and that his
departure is a public misfortune.

" But a great interpreter of music, and such is a great
conductor, wherever he goes carries his own welcome with
him. It is not as a stranger that he goes to Chicago; it
is because he is not a stranger, because Chicago knows
him well, that she asks him to come. And he does not
go alone. He takes with him our gratitude, our admiration, and our affection. He goes wreathed and garlanded
with our cheers and hopes and our perfect confidence in
his return. For New York only lends Theodore Thomas
to Chicago. With metropolitan magnanimity she deco-
rates with one of her own precious jewels her younger
and successful competitor for the prize of the great fair.
But presently she will reclaim it and restore it to her

crown with a fresher luster gained from her sister's coronet. Therefore, on your behalf, on behalf of the great multitude of New Yorkers, lovers of music and of Thomas, who follow him with a pang of farewell but with a hearty godspeed, I say to him, in a language familiar to him before he knew that in which I am speaking, ' *Wir sagen nicht, leb' wohl, wir sagen nur, Gott befohlen, bis auf wiedersehen!* ' *

" Gentlemen, I give you the continued health, the unfailing prosperity, the perfect good fortune, and the speedy return of Theodore Thomas."

The day after this memorable dinner we moved out of the house on Seventeenth Street, leaving every mantelpiece in the large old-fashioned rooms banked high with the farewell flowers that had been sent, and a full-sized conductor's stand and baton made of roses, in the deserted study where Thomas had labored in joy and sorrow for so many years.

During the summer months Thomas returned and gave a season of Summer Night Concerts in the new Madison Square Garden. It was his last series of this class. They had done their work, and from henceforth he was able to devote his life exclusively to that for which he had so long prepared the way—the symphonic form of art. At the close of this—his last long concert engagement in New York—the musical " profession " took its leave of him in two large banquets given in his honor by the Liederkranz and Aschenbroedel So-

* We do not say " farewell." We say only " God keep you till we meet again."

cieties. Of the first of these occasions, he wrote as follows:

"New York, *August* 12, 1891.

"The Liederkranz banquet last night was a big affair. I was called for at the Garden, about half-past nine o'clock, and driven to the clubhouse. The manner in which I was received was very impressive. The President and several other officials met me at the door, and word was sent up, '*Er ist da.*' As we entered the large hall, every man rose and remained standing. Having bowed my acknowledgments at the entrance of the hall—which seemed to have no end—I accompanied the President to the seat of honor, while the building fairly trembled with the shouting of a thousand men, '*Hoch soll er leben! Hoch! Hoch! Hoch!*' This was certainly a very nice thing for the Liederkranz to do, and the highest honor they could bestow on anybody."

The early fall saw Thomas hard at work in his new field of effort in the West. The project looked fair and hopeful on the outside. It was backed financially by fifty wealthy and public-spirited men, and directed by five genuine music lovers, two of whom had been prime movers in every musical scheme of importance in Chicago previous to this, and had been personal friends of Thomas for many years—N. K. Fairbank and Charles D. Hamill. The press was also friendly to the institution and the trustees were all confident in regard to its success. They were, however, quite inexperienced in orchestral matters, and did not know the rocks and snags beneath the surface as Thomas knew them, or the great difficulties they would have to overcome before such an institution as they aimed to create could be permanently established in Chicago. In talking the matter over beforehand, he said:

" In New York I could make an orchestra permanent with a comparatively small guarantee, or, if we had a suitable home for it in a good location, I could carry it on without any guarantee at all, as it would then take care of itself. The reason for this is that New York already has a large number of resident musicians of the first rank, who would be available material from which to form an orchestra, and I would not have to import any men from Europe. The city is also near to many other large cities, and to most of the Eastern summer resorts, so that we could place our surplus concerts out of town, in both winter and summer, with small expense for transportation.

" In Chicago, on the other hand, there is very little resident material of the grade required for my orchestra. Sixty men must be imported, either from New York or Europe, and to induce fine musicians to take their families so far, and exile themselves from their homes, we must offer higher salaries than are paid in the East. Then, Chicago is an almost isolated city, the only place of any size near it is Milwaukee, all the rest are so far off that the expense of transporting the orchestra to them for concerts consumes more than the profits, and results in financial loss. So we cannot count on out-of-town engagements to help with the expenses. In Chicago there is now a fair-sized audience which has become genuinely musical, but it remains to be seen whether it is large enough to support forty symphony concerts a year. That is a great many concerts to give in one city during a season. Moreover we will have a terrible handicap in the immense size of the Auditorium Theater, where our concerts are to be given. It requires an orchestra of the very largest dimensions, and the seating capacity—nearly five thousand—is so great that many people will not buy season tickets, knowing that they can always get seats for single concerts when they want to attend. This will make our audience dependent on the weather, special attractions, the season of the year, or other conditions, and the single ticket sale will be unreliable. Finally, we do not control the Auditorium, and our season will be interrupted whenever some other organization engages the theater, such as the opera, the flower shows, charity balls, and bazaars, etc. Such interruptions always cause a loss, for it takes the public several weeks before they resume regular concert attendance after one of them. In other even more important ways, the Auditorium, in spite of its remarkable acoustics, is not adapted to concert work of our class. It is a theater, and the orchestra must sit on an inclosed stage. In order that the tones of the various choirs—string, wood-wind, brass, and percussion—may be thrown out into the main body of the house, we shall have to use sounding-boards of canvas and wood, above, below, and on either side. In other words, the orchestra will play in a box, having one end only open toward the audience. The effect of this will be that we cannot blend and balance the choirs as we wish, and the heavier instruments, being at the back, and consequently nearer to the sounding boards, will strike sharply through the more delicate wood-wind and string choirs, instead of combining with them, and giving the rich, sonorous quality to the whole that is possible when the orchestra plays on an open stage without sounding boards. In short, the conditions in Chicago are by no means ideal for the success of the enterprise, but the men who are interested in it are not easily discouraged, and they will carry it through successfully if anybody can."

The Chicago Orchestral Association, now thoroughly organized, consisted of the following members:

J. McGregor Adams
Allison V. Armour
George A. Armour
Philip D. Armour
S. E. Barrett
A. C. Bartlett
H. W. Bishop
T. B. Blackstone
Charles Counselman
John M. Clark
R. T. Crane
C. R. Cummings
N. K. Fairbank
C. Norman Fay
Marshall Field
Henry Field
Charles W. Fullerton
Lyman B. Gage
John J. Glessner
T. W. Harvey
H. N. Higginbotham
W. G. Hibbard
Charles L. Hutchinson
R. N. Isham

Albert Keep
S. A. Kent
Henry W. King
W. C. Larned
Victor F. Lawson
L. Z. Leiter
J. Mason Loomis
Franklin MacVeagh
E. B. McCagg
Cyrus H. McCormick
O. W. Meysenburg
Thomas Murdoch
H. H. Porter
O. W. Potter
Eugene S. Pike
George M. Pullman
Norman B. Ream
Martin A. Ryerson
Byron L. Smith
A. A. Sprague
Otho S. A. Sprague
John R. Walsh
C. H. Wacker
Norman Williams

Executive Board
N. K. Fairbank, *President*
C. Norman Fay, *Vice-President*
P. A. McEwan, *Treasurer and Secretary*
Milward Adams, *Manager*

The foregoing list is a remarkable one, because almost every name on it is that of one of the great pioneer " Captains of Industry," who created the Western metropolis of Chicago. Having developed its business resources, and amassed large private fortunes, their next thought was to build up its art and educational institutions. The Western " Captains of Industry " are an extraordinary class of men. Quiet, dignified, unostentatious, and simple in manner and habits, these men combine the keenest insight and the most accurate judgment with a princely generosity and boldness of action which give them the immediate mastery of every situation. They are serious men, with many cares and few pleasures, and when they are not in their offices, superintending their own extensive interests, they are generally to be found at a Directors' meeting of one or another of the philanthropic, educational, or æsthetic enterprises which they have called into being for the uplift of the city, and for which they work with equal fervor.

As soon as the Orchestral Association was fully organized, Mr. Fay quietly dropped into the place allotted to him on the Board, and from henceforth he worked, not alone, but in association with others, as sincere as himself in their love of art and their desire to establish the orchestra as a permanent institution. Amongst these must be especially mentioned Mr. Charles D. Hamill. He had been a warm personal friend of Thomas for many years, and an ardent worker in the cause of music.

He remained an active member of the executive
board of the association as long as he lived, and
no one devoted more time and unselfish effort to
its welfare than he.

Immediately after his appointment as the musical director of the Chicago Orchestra, Thomas
received a similar appointment from the directors
of the World's Columbian Exposition, which was
to be held in Chicago during the summer of 1893.
Before accepting the latter, he made it a condition that the Bureau of Music should be taken out
of the department of liberal arts, of which it was,
at first, a section, and be made an independent
department, controlled by a committee under the
local Board of Directors, and not by the National
Commission of the Fair. He foresaw that an
exhibit of the art of music might conflict with
that of the music trade, and he wished to avoid
the trouble which might result, by separating the
two interests wholly at the start. This was
agreed to by the men in authority, but, unfortunately, in the press of business they did not
realize the importance of going through the necessary formalities at once, and the separation was
not actually accomplished until the opening of the
Fair. We shall see, later, the disastrous results
of this procrastination.

The Chicago Orchestra—as it was called—was
the very finest that money and experience could
bring together. As we have said, it was no crude,
undisciplined set of men, but simply the famous
old Thomas Orchestra of New York, reorganized,

enlarged, and perfected. No finer or better equipped body of musicians could be found in the world than the sixty men who composed the "regular" orchestra, and but little inferior were the thirty "extra" players who were added to its ranks for all Chicago performances. The fact, however, that the latter did not travel with Thomas and were permitted to take engagements under other conductors between times, always made a discrepancy between the standard of the two bodies which it was difficult to adjust, and it generally took him a whole week of rehearsing before they were equalized. On Monday morning he would come home from rehearsal tired and disgusted. "The orchestra sounded like a jewsharp," he would say impatiently. The next day it would go better, and by the Friday matinée all would be in good order. But the next Monday a new programme would be on, and he would have the work all to do over again.

The season of 1891-92 was a regular "oldtimer" for hard work, traveling, and difficulties of all kinds. In order to increase the revenues of the association it was necessary to give concerts in the ratio of four performances to the week throughout the season. But, as this was double the number of concerts which could be supported by Chicago, Thomas planned to distribute them unequally, spending several weeks at home, when only two concerts per week would be given, and then taking the orchestra on a short tour when ten or twelve concerts would be given in as many

The Chicago Orchestra in the Auditorium, Chicago

days. By some mistake, his instructions were misunderstood, and the manager supposed he was to place two extra concerts somewhere every week. Consequently, when Thomas arrived in Chicago, early in September, and needed every possible hour of rehearsal to bring the local contingent of the orchestra up to the standard of the imported section, he was appalled to discover that engagements in other cities—often necessitating long journeys—had been made for Monday, Tuesday, and sometimes even Wednesday of *every week* of the season, so that he could have only one single rehearsal each week in which to prepare two or three programmes, and that he and the men would be kept traveling so constantly that there would not be time enough between the journeys to even get rested and in fit condition for performance.

As the engagements were made, however, there was nothing for it but to " fight it through " as he had so often done before, and do the best he could. Fortunately his old orchestra players were so much in the majority, and so well trained from former years, that they were able to carry the rest along with them, but no very high standard was possible under these conditions, and it was not until its second year that the " Thomas standard " began to be stamped on the performances of the Chicago Orchestra.

Thomas now created a new " Highway " for himself in the Western country. Its boundaries were not quite so well defined as those of the old

" Highway " had been, but in a general way it lay within the region limited by St. Paul, Omaha, Kansas City, St. Louis, Nashville, Cincinnati, Cleveland, Milwaukee, and the intermediate cities, and he began to do the same kind of work for these places that he had already done for the cities of the East, visiting them so frequently that the people learned to know and love the highest class of music, and raising the local standards of art in every way. But Thomas was getting on in years now, and he longed to play to an audience which could understand his best, without any more preparatory effort—an audience like that of Boston, or of the New York Philharmonic Society which he had left behind in the East—and missionary work did not appeal to him as it had in former years. " I long for rest," he said, " and the opportunity to devote myself to my specialty. I ought not to be expected to travel about and do pioneer work any more, and I have not the physical endurance for it now, either; it will be my ruin if I have to keep it up much longer."

During May a short series of festivals were given in Nashville, Kansas City, Omaha, and other places, and while on this tour he wrote as follows:

"NASHVILLE, TENN., *May* 4, 1892.

" To-day matters do not run smoothly with me at all. It is summer heat here and the town overcrowded in consequence of the races. I was not expected at the hotel last night, and had to wait a long time before I could

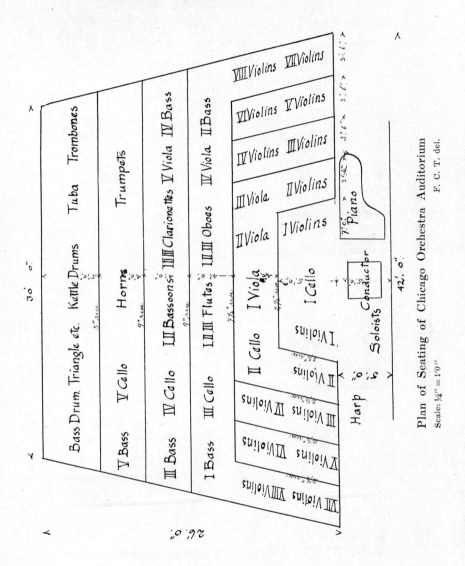

Plan of Seating of Chicago Orchestra Auditorium

Scale: ¼″ = 1′0″

F. C. T. del.

be accommodated with a room, and got one then only with difficulty. I had no sleep, and my trunk was lost and did not turn up until this morning. Finally I have an overwhelming mail, and must write letters instead of studying my scores,—in short, everything seems to go wrong to-day!

"Here I was interrupted, and meantime we have traveled to Kansas City. The heat in Nashville finished me, and I have not been well since, but my stay there was not without its pleasant features also. After the first concert a gentleman came rushing into my room, who I learned afterwards was a recent convert of the evangelist Moody —a nice man, whole-souled and sincere. Seizing my hand he inquired earnestly, 'Mr. Thomas, are you a Christian?' I did not know quite what to reply to this unexpected demand, as his idea of a Christian and mine might not blend. So I took refuge behind you and murmured something to the effect that 'my wife went to church.' This seemed to satisfy him, and he said, 'I just wanted to make sure that the Lord had some of your kind on his side!' and off he went.

"The next day some ladies made up a very pleasant party to drive out to General Jackson's old home, the 'Hermitage.' It was a picnic, and although I generally do not like picnics, it was, after all, a pleasant change and rest for me. The 'Hermitage' is a fine old Southern mansion, thirteen miles out in the country; for our party all barriers were opened, and we had the freedom of the house, and were even allowed to eat our luncheon in the dining-room. My friend of the night before was one of the party, and no sooner were we seated at the table, with baskets and boxes opened for the feast, than he turned to me, as the guest of honor, and said very solemnly, 'Brother Thomas, will you ask the blessing?' I was so taken aback at this unexpected request to officiate in the rôle of priest, that I believe I would have said my ' *Vater unser*,' in German, as the nearest approach to a ' grace ' that I could command, had not a quick-witted woman extricated me from the dilemma by hastily replying for me, ' I think as we have a descendant of General Jackson here with us to-day, it would be more appropriate to ask him.' And so it was arranged ! "

At the end of this tour came the regular Cincinnati biennial festival, which brought this difficult and fatiguing season to a close. Taken for all in all, it had been a great disappointment to Thomas. He did not so much mind the inferior standard of the performances, because he knew that that would be corrected another year, when he should have command of the proper number of rehearsals; but what did disturb him and make him very anxious for the ultimate success of the institution was the forlorn little audiences scattered through the vast empty reaches of the Auditorium all winter, and the mighty deficit of $53,000, which the balance sheet of the Association showed as the financial result of its first year. That was something he had not expected, and it seemed to him to indicate that Chicago was not yet ripe for a symphony orchestra, and that it could not be supported there. To his surprise, however, no one complained. The financial loss was met, and the trustees did not ask him to lower the standard in any way, but, on the contrary, told him to go right on and perfect the institution on the original

lines. One concession only was made to the popular demand. During the first year, ten of the
forty concerts given had " popular " programmes,
—that is, programmes of miscellaneous numbers,
without a symphony,—the rest had symphony
programmes of the regulation type. For the second season it was decided to give a larger proportion of programmes without a symphony, and
work the audience up to the symphonic standard
a little more slowly, though it must be admitted
that the " popular " programmes of Thomas were
now not much lighter than the others, as a matter
of fact, and the unpopular symphony was generally replaced by a long Suite, or Symphonic
Poem of some sort, which differed from the real
article chiefly in being the vehicle of some specified
dramatic action or mood, of which the story was
printed on the programme. The trustees also
decided to add a short series of concerts for
workingmen, similar to those Thomas had previously given to the same class of hearers in New
York. With these exceptions, the orchestra was
to be maintained on the same lines as during its
first season.

CHAPTER XVIII

1892-1893

THOMAS AND THE WORLD'S COLUMBIAN EXPOSITION—LETTERS FROM SAINT SAENS, RICHTER, NIKISCH, TSCHAIKOWSKY, BRAHMS, AND MASSENET

THE second year of Thomas' sojourn in Chicago began with an interesting event—the opening ceremonies of the World's Columbian Exposition. It had been intended to hold this great Fair during the summer of 1892, in commemoration of the four-hundredth anniversary of the discovery of America by Columbus. But, meantime, the plans for buildings and exhibits had become so extensive, that it was impossible to have the Exposition ready so soon. It was therefore decided to postpone it until 1893, but to hold the official inaugural ceremonies during the preceding October.

The architecture of the Fair had been placed in the hands of the well-known Chicago firm of Burnham and Root, and to Mr. John Root belongs the credit of suggesting its original scheme, although it was eventually carried out on much more beautiful and extensive lines than those he had sketched. The death of Mr. Root left the matter entirely in the hands of his partner, Daniel H. Burnham, one of those master-minds who im-

part greatness to everything they touch. Instead
of keeping the work in his own office—which most
men would have done—he conceived the idea of
bringing together all the most eminent architects
of the nation, and creating a city of exhibition
buildings which should surpass, in artistic beauty,
anything the world had ever seen. The architects
readily agreed to this alluring plan, and at their
first consultation it was decided to adopt the classic
style for the architecture of the " White City," as
it was called. Each firm was given *carte blanche*
to design a building in this style, and as the material of which they were to be constructed was
a sort of plaster called " staff," which could be
molded into any kind of ornamental shape, there
was no limit, but artistic taste, to architectural en-
richments in the matter of columns, moldings,
cornices, etc. Next, the sculptors of the country
were called upon to design suitable statues, foun-
tains, and monumental pillars, for buildings,
bridges, and grounds; and the painters were invited to design decorations in color for wall-
surfaces and domes. Finally, Frederick Law Olm-
stead was given the work of planning the water-
ways, islands, and landscape features of the Fair,
and of indicating the sites where the buildings,
bridges, etc., should be erected. In short, the
Chicago World's Fair of 1893 represented the
combined effort of all the architects, sculptors, and
painters of America, working in harmony and
enthusiasm under the inspiring captaincy of Burnham—the greatest and yet the most modest of

them all. The result was a miracle of beauty which those who saw it will never forget, and which is not likely to be repeated in any other city or land during our time.

One of the most interesting features of the Inaugural Ceremonies of the Fair was when all these Master Artists came forward in a body and received the medals presented by the Exposition

Medal Presented at the Inaugural Ceremonies to the Artists who Designed the World's Columbian Exposition

officials. The list, which is given below, includes nearly all the leading architects, sculptors, and painters of America of that day:

CHARLES F. McKIM
WILLIAM R. MEAD
JOHN G. STEARNE
RICHARD MORRIS HUNT
HENRY VAN BRUNT
LOUIS SULLIVAN
W. L. B. JENNEY
SOPHIA G. HAYDEN

ROBERT S. PEABODY
GEORGE B. POST
S. S. BEMAN
FRANK M. HOWE
DANKMAR ADLER
FRANCIS M. WHITEHOUSE
HENRY IVES COBB
CHARLES B. ATWOOD

Daniel H. Burnham,
Architect in Chief of the World's Columbian Exposition

Francis D. Millet	Daniel H. Burnham
W. J. Edbrooke	F. W. Grogan
Frederick Law Olmsted	Martin Roche
William Holabird	Philip Martiny
Carl Bitter	George W. Maynard
Daniel C. French	Theodore Baur
H. T. Schladermundt	John J. Boyle
Carl Rohl-Smith	Miss Enid Yandell
Lorado Taft	Olin N. Warner
Miss Alice Rideout	James A. Blanckingship
Edward Kemeys	Frederick Macmonnies
Henry A. McNeil	Walter McEwen
Miss Mary Cassatt	J. Alden Weir
Gari Melchers	Charles Reinhart
Robert Reid	A. Phimister Proctor
E. H. Blashfield	John Charles Olmsted
Edward C. Potter	Henry Sargent Codman
Mrs. Frederick Macmonnies	J. Carroll Beckwith
Walter Shirlaw	Kenyon Cox
E. E. Simmons	Richard W. Bock
Elmer E. Garnsey	Louis J. Millet
George L. Healy	C. Y. Turner
Maitland Armstrong	Robert Kraus
M. A. Waagen	William L. Dodge
Johannes Gelert	Augustus St. Gaudens
Alexandre Sandier	Frederick Sargent
Edward C. Shankland	William S. MacHarg
Rudolph Ulrich	Ernest R. Graham
John W. Alvord	J. K. Paine
Theodore Thomas	G. W. Chadwick
W. L. Tomlins	Harriet Stone Monroe
Stanford White	

As architecture, sculpture, and painting were to have such a splendid exhibit at the Fair, it was fitting that the sister art of music should be equally well represented, and Thomas, therefore,

made his plans on the most extensive scale. Two
music halls were built for his use on the Exposition grounds; one of moderate size, for symphony
concerts, and the other of very large dimensions,
for festivals and free popular concerts.

Even the largest of these halls, however, was
not large enough to contain a tithe of the people
who were expected to be present at the inaugural
ceremonies, and the building used for them was
that in which the exhibit of the Liberal Arts was
afterwards installed, nor was it any too large
to accommodate the attending multitudes. A letter, written by a member of our party on this
interesting occasion, gives the following detailed
account of the day:

"CHICAGO, *October*, 1892.

"The Inaugural Ceremonies of the Columbian Exposition took place yesterday. The weather was perfect,
and we got up at half-past five o'clock in order to reach
the Exposition grounds in season, for they are a long way
from here, and Mr. Thomas had to hold a rehearsal before
the ceremonies took place. The Exposition management
had provided a small steam launch to transport our party,
and the sail up the lake in the cool, early morning was
charming. We reached the grounds at nine o'clock, and
went at once to the building where the rehearsal and ceremonies were to take place. I wish I could convey any idea
of the size of this mammoth hall. I was told that it is
one mile in circumference, and that if the Capitol at
Washington should be put into it, dome and all, there
would still be plenty of room to spare between its highest
point and the top of the great steel arches which support

the roof. The stage for the musicians, which was built at one end, was as large as the entire Metropolitan Opera House in New York, but it only seemed of ordinary dimensions. The speakers' stage was placed in the middle of the eastern side of the building, and yet was so far from ours that communication had to be carried on between the two by telephone. Regiments of soldiers— cavalry and infantry—marched in at the great doors in double platoons, performed evolutions under the colonnades at the side, and marched out again without being noticed, and the Washington Marine Band, which was stationed at the north end of the building, and played for the entrance of the state dignitaries, could hardly be heard at all from our end.

"By the time the ceremonies began, all this great space was filled with one solid, compact sea of humanity, and when the President of the United States and his train entered, the multitude rose and a deep, portentous roar, like the ocean, resounded through the building. Then every man and woman pulled out a handkerchief, and waved it, and it was as if this strange human sea had suddenly broken into thousands of foaming billows. Our little party sat on the lower step of the conductor's stand, right under Mr. Thomas' hand. On my expressing surprise that he should put us in this conspicuous place, he laughed and said, ' No one will see you in such a crowd, you will be as well hidden as if you were on the floor, and it will be worth your while to be where you can see what is happening yourself.' The event proved that he was correct.

"As everything was on such a vast scale, Mr. Thomas had 5,500 voices in his chorus, two hundred players in the orchestra, two large military bands, and two drum corps, of fifty each. The latter were stationed in a balcony above, on either side of the stage. As he could not speak to this great body of performers, by reason of the distance, and they could not see his baton distinctly, he did not use one, but instead held a handkerchief in his hand, gathering in the ends so that they could not flutter, but leaving enough of it visible to catch the eye of even the remotest singer on the top row. As the time for each of the musical numbers drew near, he gave a signal to the two drum corps, who immediately began a long double roll, which started softly, swelled louder and louder, fell and rose again in obedience to the hand which held the handkerchief, until every performer had found his place, every instrument was in position, every eye fixed on the conductor, and every listener spell-bound in attention, and then, CRASH! the sound was like the last trump, and the attack of these thousands was as sharp and steady as in an ordinary concert. Mr. Thomas was in his element with all these masses to handle, and controlled them without any apparent effort. The full programme of the ceremonies was as follows:

INAUGURAL CEREMONIES

OF

THE WORLD'S COLUMBIAN EXPOSITION

CHICAGO, OCTOBER, 1892

1. Columbus March and Hymn.........John K. Paine
2. Prayer, by Bishop C. H. Fowler of California.
3. Introductory Address, by Director-General G. R. Davis.
4. Address of Welcome, by Mayor Hempstead Washburn.
5. Recitation of Harriet Munroe's Dedicatory Ode, set to music by George W. Chadwick.

6. Presentation of medals to the master artists of the Exposition.

Music, " To the Sons of Art " . . . . Mendelssohn

7. Address, by Mrs. Potter Palmer, President of the Women's Department.

8. Tender of the Buildings, by the President of the World's Columbian Exposition to the World's Columbian Commission.

9. Presentation of the Buildings, by the President of the World's Columbian Commission to the Vice-President of the United States.

10. Dedication of the Buildings, by the Vice-President of the United States.

11. Hallelujah Chorus, from " The Messiah " . . . Haendel

12. Dedicatory Oration, by Hon. Henry Watterson.

13. The Star-Spangled Banner.

14. Columbian Oration, by Hon. Chauncey M. Depew.

15. Prayer, by Cardinal Gibbons of New York.

16. Chorus, " In Praise of God."

17. Benediction, by Rev. C. H. McCook of Philadelphia.

18. National Salute.

" The musical numbers were all received with enthusiasm, and the works of the American composers, Chadwick and Paine, brought out hearty applause. But when Haendel's ' Hallelujah Chorus ' burst forth from the fifty-five hundred voices of the chorus, the crowd cheered mightily, and after those at our end of the building ceased, the audience at the far north end took it up, and sent an answering cheer from the distance. It was a strange and thrilling sound.

" The ceremonies took so long that it was already dark when we left the Fair grounds on the little steam launch for the voyage home, and a slight haze obscured the stars. For a time we steamed along quietly, through the dim atmosphere, when suddenly there appeared athwart the sky a great, snow-white, transparent arc of light, broad and soft as a summer cloud, glowing with white fire, like a moonstone, extending from the shore to the eastern horizon across the lake. It was the new search-light, now used for the first time—the most beautiful, unearthly effect of light imaginable, and impressed me more than the five thousand rockets which I saw exploded simultaneously later."

The second season of the Chicago Orchestra opened auspiciously with two crowded audiences, at its first concerts. This year the orchestra had its full quota of rehearsals, and its standard was correspondingly high. But, to the disappointment of Thomas and the trustees, the audiences, after the first week, were but little larger than those of the previous year, and the traveling, though at less frequent intervals, was harder than ever, and the tours longer. The following letters were written on these trips:

" Toronto, *December 28, 1892.*

" I feel as if I had been away from home a long time; I suppose because I was tired when I started. We did not arrive in London (Canada) until two or three o'clock this morning, and my trunk did not reach me till six. The hotel is an old house, and run down. It was cold, and although I had a fire lighted, the room could not be warmed. I suppose it never was heated before and the walls are chilled through and through. So I did not take off my underclothing or socks from Sunday morning till Monday night. The washing arrangements were also not

inviting enough to make much use of. We finally left
London on an accommodation train at half-past seven
A.M., traveling six or seven hours to the next stop. The
car was overcrowded, and filled with bad odors and crying
children. It is difficult to believe the difference cleanliness
makes, but I felt utterly demoralized by the time we
reached Toronto. Here I have a steam-heated room,
which drives me nearly mad it is so hot. This is also
a second-class hotel, but though cheap it is clean and I
have a bathroom. The weather is clear and cold and I
hope now to get into better condition in a day or two."

" SANDUSKY, *January* 1, 1893.

" This seems to be a curious place. I have never been
here before and am told that it was merely a railroad station until lately, and that it has developed into quite a
town since the Chicago fire, when many people came here
from Chicago. It is certainly very trying to travel when
the thermometer is below zero. The cars are overheated,
and then, in these miserable second- and third-rate hotels
the rooms are rarely heated at all, consequently one is
either freezing with cold or uncomfortably hot. The days
are all taken up with traveling and there is little chance
for letter writing. To-day is Sunday, but many of the
stores are open here and all the theaters. To one of them
the orchestra is invited, and probably every man of it
will go but myself. After the theater I have invited them
all to a glass of beer with me. The spirit of an organized
body, and a natural pride are making themselves felt in
our orchestra, and I like to foster it by an occasional
little social festivity of this kind. Your letter I received
yesterday, and I hope that after this the deaf old furnace
man will behave himself, for I know that a regular life,
good food, and good air are the greatest safeguards

against drunkenness. You need not quote the Bible in justification for giving them to him; I do the same, even without the authority of that much abused book.

" In Toronto, Busoni was the soloist. We played the Liszt concerto, without any rehearsal, even of the orchestra parts, and you know I do not like to do that very often. But it could not have been played better, although I doubt if a dozen of our men had ever seen the music before. I long to be at home again, and am sorry that when I am there I must be so busy and get so tired every day. The World's Fair is very near now, and already I am anticipating the quiet restful atmosphere that I shall enjoy next winter after it is over."

Thomas might well say that he was busy and tired while at home, for during the winter, spring, and summer of 1892-93, he worked from eight o'clock in the morning until one or two o'clock the following morning, day in and day out, and sometimes he would even be called out of bed to interview people on the business of the World's Fair, or receive them while at his meals. But he was so interested in the work that he did not care how much time and effort it cost him.

The Bureau of Music of the Columbian Exposition consisted of three officers: Theodore Thomas, Musical Director; William L. Tomlins, Choral Director, and George H. Wilson, Secretary. In planning its exhibit Thomas grouped his performances around two central ideas. First, to make a complete showing to the world of the musical progress of America, both executive and creative, in all departments. Second, to make a complete showing to America of the music of the world, as exemplified by the most enlightened nations of Europe. In pursuance of this plan, he arranged fourteen different series of concerts as follows:

CONCERT SCHEME

OF

THE WORLD'S COLUMBIAN EXPOSITION

CHICAGO, 1893

- I. Daily free orchestral concerts by the Exposition Orchestra in Festival Hall.
- II. Daily open-air concerts by the Exposition bands.
- III. Symphony concerts by the Exposition Orchestra in the Music Hall.
- IV. Symphony concerts by visiting orchestras, in the Music Hall.
- V. Band concerts by visiting Military Bands.
- VI. Choral concerts by the Exposition Chorus.
- VII. Choral concerts by visiting choral societies.
- VIII. Children's concerts by the Exposition Children's Chorus.
- IX. Concerts in which famous European musicians play or conduct their own works.
- X. Chamber concerts.
- XI. Artists' Recitals.
- XII. Musical Festivals.
- XIII. Concerts by Women in the Women's Building.
- XIV. Concerts by a National Convention of Women's Amateur Musical Clubs from all parts of America.

For the execution of such an extensive scheme as this, it was, of course, necessary to provide large local orchestral and choral forces. First of these was the Exposition Orchestra, which consisted of the Chicago Orchestra, enlarged to 114 men, and two large military bands. Next came the Exposition Chorus of 1,000 voices, and, finally, the Children's World's Fair Chorus of 1,200, the two latter being under the leadership of Choral Director Tomlins.

The visiting organizations which were heard singly, or in combination, in the various concerts, were as follows:

INSTRUMENTAL

Boston Symphony

New York Philharmonic

New York Symphony

The Kneisel Quartette

BANDS

Sousa's

Gilmore's

Cincinnati Military

Elgin

Iowa

Garde République

Marshall Military

Sanford's

Mexican

Hungarian

Neapolitan

The Royal Scottish Pipers

CHORAL SOCIETIES

Chicago Apollo Club

Russian Chorus

St. Paul Choral Association

Minneapolis Choral Association

Cincinnati Festival Chorus

Milwaukee Arion

Brooklyn Arion

German-American Women's Society

New York Liederkranz

Cleveland Vocal

Columbus Arion
Dayton Philharmonic
Louisville Musical
Omaha Apollo
Pittsburg Mozart
Philadelphia *Junger Maen-*
  nerchor
American Union of Swedish
  Singers
The Scottish Assembly
Stoughton Musical Society
Lineff Russian Choir

Choral Societies from Nine
  Kansas cities :
  Topeka
  Emporia
  Abilene
  Newton
  Leavenworth
  Hutchinson
  Modoc
  Lyons
  Stirling

American composers of the first rank were asked to say which of their works they wished to have performed during the Fair, and two of them were commissioned to write special compositions for it. Those of less reputation received the following notice a year in advance of its opening:

" The Musical Director of the World's Columbian Exposition desires to include in the programmes of its concerts, representative choral, orchestral, and chamber compositions by native Americans. All scores received before October 15, 1892, will be submitted to the following committee: Sir Alexander C. Mackenzie, London; Asgar Hamerick, Baltimore; B. J. Lang, Boston; William L. Tomlins and Theodore Thomas, Chicago. The favorable recommendation of this committee will be final and will insure performance."

In response to this invitation twenty-one composers sent in compositions of various kinds, from which the committee selected seven as being worthy of performance. Amongst them was one from the pen of a woman—Miss Margaret Lang. Other women were similarly honored, for Mrs. Ellen Beach, of Boston, was commissioned to compose a Jubilate for chorus and orchestra, and the works of Ingebord von Bronsart, of Weimar, Frances Elliot, of London, and others were also performed.

The list of artists who appeared in one or another of these series of concerts, included nearly every eminent American musician, as well as many of the most celebrated foreigners, such as Dvořák, Paderewski, etc. Of the works of foreign composers which were given, it is only necessary to say that the best examples of every school and nationality were heard in the course of the summer. In short, Thomas followed Burnham's splendid example and endeavored to combine the musical art and artists of America and Europe, as he had combined the architects, sculptors, and painters, and to give an exhibition of every school, period, and nationality, such as had never before been attempted in any country, and perhaps never will be again. His associates in the Bureau of Music, Messrs. Wilson and Tomlins, also worked with untiring zeal to achieve the best results, each in his own department.

About 200 concerts in all were given by the Bureau, during the three and a half months of its existence, 125 of which were conducted by Thomas in person. The scheme was a magnificent one, but the hostile forces which seem always to have been lurking in ambush to destroy the fruit of his labors before he could garner it, were as active in Chicago as they had previously been in Philadelphia, Cincinnati, and New York; and this great enterprise, so carefully planned, and so arduously worked for, was wrecked and ruined ere its completion, like all that had preceded it.

This time the trouble came from the source which Thomas had feared when he made the condition that the Bureau of Music should be entirely independent of the musical trade exhibit. Had this been promptly attended to, all the subsequent difficulty would have been avoided; but the necessary formalities were delayed until the opening of the Fair, and in the meantime Thomas and his Bureau were technically under the authority of the National Commission, a political body which knew little about art, and cared less, but which was thoroughly in sympathy with the interests of the business firms which were exhibiting instruments and other musical paraphernalia. Amongst these, the piano manufacturers have always—because of the sharp competition in their trade—been at war with each other. At the time of the Fair the Steinway firm was in the ascendant, in so far that it had secured the indorsement of most of the great European pianists who visited America, nearly all of whom used its pianos while here. For reasons of its own, the Steinway firm declined to exhibit their pianos at the Fair, and on this, the other firms promptly demanded that the Steinway piano

should be debarred from the concerts of the
Bureau of Music, arguing—not without justice—
that a firm which was not furthering the interests
of the Fair by exhibiting its instruments with the
trade should not be given the best exhibition of
all, by having its instruments played in the music
halls, by the most famous artists. Had the matter
developed earlier, Thomas would have been willing
to make this concession, in the matter of all non-
exhibiting firms, of which there were others as well
as the Steinways, for he felt that the demand of
the exhibiting firms was not unreasonable. But
long before the trouble had come to a head, he
had sent out invitations to a number of great
foreign artists, in the name of the Exposition,
which had been accepted, and, of course, it was
impossible for him to either withdraw these invitations, or to dictate to men of high rank in the
art world, who were honoring the Exposition by
their presence, what instruments they should play
in the concerts. He therefore refused to take
any action which would involve these guests of
honor, although he agreed to make them the only
exceptions in the use of the pianos of the non-
exhibiting firms. As there would be only a few
concerts in which these guests were to appear—
not more, perhaps, than a half a dozen during the
entire six months of the Fair—the non-exhibiting
firms would certainly have gained a very moderate
amount of gratuitous advertising by having their
pianos played in them. But the exhibiting firms
would not make even this small concession, and

when they found that Thomas was obdurate on this point, they next determined to get him removed from his office of Musical Director, and appealed to the National Commission to ask for his resignation, charging that he was accepting a bribe from the firm of Steinway & Sons, to exploit their instruments. On this, the Commission promptly appointed a committee to investigate the charges against Thomas, and summoned him to appear before it and answer the same. If all this had not been so insulting it would have been simply amusing, and Thomas himself thought it of so little consequence that he did not take the trouble to disprove these ridiculous accusations, but simply stated that they were untrue. The Chicago *Tribune,* commenting upon the interview between Thomas and his investigators, printed the following editorial:

THEODORE THOMAS' DEFENSE

" Mr. Theodore Thomas at last has appeared before the committee of the National Commission which is investigating gratuitously and unofficially the musical controversy, and has made his statement, though not bound to do so, as he is not responsible either to that committee or to the commission. His statement was concise, manly, and straightforward as might have been anticipated by anyone who knows his character. As to the piano dispute, Mr. Thomas said:

" ' If you will believe the word of an honest man, I take no more consideration for the firm you mention than I do for Jones or Smith. It is my wish simply to have the best instruments possible in use in my orchestra. It so happens that this firm either manufactures or controls most of the instruments which please me best. It is a question of art, pure and simple.'

"The committee then turned its attention to the letter written by Mr. Thomas' harpist, which it intended should be a bombshell. Before the committeeman could finish reading it, Mr. Thomas quietly set at rest the slanderous accusation that he was responsible by declaring that he had never heard of the letter until he saw it in the papers, and that he never had issued an order forbidding members of his orchestra to play on Lyon and Healy harps. Mr. Thomas went further than this, and settled at once this silly harp business, as will be seen:

"'Now suppose several of your harpists should tell you they preferred the Lyon and Healy harp to the one sold by that New York firm; what would you do about that?'

"'I should immediately instruct them to play any instrument they desired. *That is the right of all artists* and I should certainly insist on its being observed in my orchestra.'

"Upon the subject of his official relations to the Fair, Mr. Thomas frankly and concisely said:

"'When I took charge of the Bureau of Music for the Exposition company, I did so with the distinct understanding that I was to run the affairs of the bureau after my own fashion, without interference from any source. I have been conducting such affairs from the sole standpoint of art and I shall continue so to do.'

"It is not to be expected that the members of this committee, representing Utah, Kansas, Arkansas, Rhode Island, Virginia, and Wyoming, will comprehend or appreciate what Mr. Thomas means by conducting the affairs of his department from the standpoint of art. But those

who do know something of these 'affairs' will sustain
Mr. Thomas in the position he has taken and will protest
against this attempt to humiliate and persecute the man
who has done more than any other for the cause of music
in the United States, who has held his high and honorable
position for forty years without swerving from what he
believes to be the best interests. of his art, and who has
labored patiently and courageously against a wilderness of
obstacles and at great private sacrifice to maintain his high
musical standard. In this long career no mercenary taint
has attached to him. His bitterest enemies cannot point
to any act of his that savors of self-seeking. He may
have made mistakes, that is human, but he always has
had a lofty ideal of his art and little patience with charla-
tans. It is too late in that long and honorable career for
even members of the National Commission from the great
art centers of Wyoming, Virginia, Utah, Kansas, and
Arkansas to injure his fame."

By this time the long deferred arrangements
for separating the Bureau of Music from the Department of Liberal Arts had been completed,
and Thomas was answerable to no one but his
own committee, which consisted of a number of the
most cultivated art lovers in Chicago, all of whom
were his personal friends, and ready to indorse
his actions to the letter. The National Commission was, therefore, powerless to remove him
so long as the Music Committee refused to co-
operate in the matter. But it did not, on that
account, cease its endeavors to do so, and erelong
Thomas received the following letter from Director-General Davis, demanding his resignation:

CHICAGO, *May* 17, 1893.

MR. THEODORE THOMAS, MUSICAL DIRECTOR, DE-
PARTMENT OF LIBERAL ARTS, WORLD'S COLUM-
BIAN EXPOSITION.

Dear Sir:

In compliance with a resolution adopted this day by
the World's Columbian Commission, I have to request your
resignation as Musical Director in the Department of
Liberal Arts.

You will please turn over all property, records, and
documents belonging to and appertaining to your office,
to the Chief of the Department of Liberal Arts.

Respectfully yours,

GEORGE R. DAVIS, *Director-General.*

As, however, Thomas was now no longer in
the Department of Liberal Arts, he did not think
it necessary to make any personal reply to this
entirely gratuitous request, which would appear to
have been sent in the hope of insulting and angering
him into giving up the office on his own initiative,
since it was not backed by any authority. It
would certainly have succeeded in achieving this
result had Thomas had only himself to consider,
for he was by this time so irritated and disgusted
that all his pleasure in the work had been spoiled,
and he would like to have taken " French leave "
of Chicago for ever and a day. But he had engaged 114 men for six months to play in the
Exposition Orchestra, and he did not dare to leave
them without his protecting presence, for fear
that after he was gone the National Commission
would attack the orchestra next, and the musicians
—many of whom were married and depended on

the engagement for the summer maintenance of their families—would be left unprovided for. So he stood firm and took no notice of the besieging army for the present.

When it became publicly known that Thomas had been treated in the foregoing insulting manner, the entire country rose in a perfect geyser of indignation, and the press, from Maine to San Francisco, was almost a unit in its denunciation of the action of the National Commission. There were, however, two of the leading Chicago papers which indorsed it, and they did their best to make up by the violence of their attacks on Thomas for the partisanship of the rest. Every day their columns were filled with malicious accusations, criticisms, ridicule—anything and everything that could be turned, twisted, or invented to cast opprobrium on the old soldier, who paid no more attention to them than if they had been a couple of gad-flies buzzing around his head, but quietly continued his work, *nach wie vor,* and did not even read what was written on either side of the question, unless someone brought him some special clipping which was either unusually good or bad, with a personal request that he would do so. Amongst the former was one from *Freund's Weekly,* one of the leading New York musical journals, which is a fair sample of the popular view of the case, and read as follows:

" Theodore Thomas has been living in a seething volcano for days, yet has maintained his nerve, strength, and determination, and his decriers have been unable to dislodge him from the stand he has taken. Nor will he be driven out, for while snarling and malediction are his portion just now, he is ably supported by the Chicago Directory at the Fair. . . . Those who know him, and have watched his career, will have noticed his possession of three characteristics: absolute honesty, aggressive independence, and determination to serve the highest musical interests of this country. His honesty cannot be impugned or assailed. His independence is sometimes overbearing and occasionally almost brutal in its directness. His aim in life is to render musical composition in the highest manner. . . . The glorious record of Theodore Thomas now spans many years. It is marked by the force, power, and command which come from undisputed and indisputable fitness and ability. A lifetime spent in the cause of music in its highest forms, has culminated in the magnificent position he now occupies. In elevating him to it, Chicago elevated herself. His removal would be her eternal disgrace, and the world of art would demand to know who was responsible for the insanity which could drive her to trying to snatch the crown from her head and fling it foolishly away. Then would the petty rivalries of trade be proved to reign supreme in the councils of an exposition which was intended to be a beacon to the world, a phase of history of which every true American would be justly proud.

" But such a deplorable result will not occur. The name of the great conductor of his times; the honest unswerving administrator; the unimpeachable gentleman and erudite musician will remain at the head of musical art in the Columbian Exposition of 1893. . . . Undisturbed by commercial differences, seeing before him the splendid goal of triumph,—criticised, abused, and at times almost

hounded, he has shaken off the fetters of the ordinary
bonds which encircle a man's career, and in his record at
the Columbian Exposition the American public rests assured that the greatest and truest interests of the noble
art of music are under the guidance of a master mind.
Freund's Weekly, as an independent journal, takes pride
in paying this deserved tribute to him."

The list of concerts to be given by the Bureau
of Music during May, June, and July had been
announced early in April. It included, beside the
daily free orchestral and band concerts, the
following special performances, for which an admission of a dollar was charged, given in the music
hall forming the northern wing of the famous
peristyle of Corinthian columns between the Court
of Honor and the Lake.

MAY 2—INAUGURAL CONCERT, MUSIC HALL

Overture, " Consecration of the House ". . . . . .Beethoven
Concerto for piano. . . . . .Paderewski
I. J. Paderewski

Symphony, B minor, " Unfinished ". . .. . .Schubert
Piano solos—
I. J. Paderewski

Vorspiel, " Die Meistersinger ". . . . . .Wagner

MAY 3—ORCHESTRAL CONCERT, MUSIC HALL

Symphony, " Heroic ". . .. . .Beethoven
Allegro con brio, Marche Funèbre

Concerto for piano. . . . . .Schumann
I. J. Paderewski

Symphonic variations......................Dvořák

Piano solo—   I. J. Paderewski

Overture, " Romeo and Juliet ".............Tschaikowsky

[Note.—By invitation of the Musical Director, Mr. Paderewski has delayed his return to Europe in order to participate in the opening concerts of the Exposition.]

MAY 5—ORCHESTRAL CONCERT—MUSIC HALL
SCHUBERT PROGRAMME

Entr'acte from " Rosamunde."

Song, Cyclus.

Symphony in C major.

MAY 9—ORCHESTRAL CONCERT—MUSIC HALL
BRAHMS PROGRAMME

Serenade, op. 16.

Song, Cyclus.

Symphony No. 4 in E minor.

MAY 12—ORCHESTRAL CONCERT—MUSIC HALL
BEETHOVEN PROGRAMME

Overture, " Egmont "—

Triple Concerto, for piano, violin, and 'cello—

Mrs. Fanny Bloomfield-Zeisler, Max Bendix, and
Bruno Steindl

Symphony No. 5 in C minor.

May 15—Boston Symphony Orchestra, Music Hall.

May 16—Boston Symphony Orchestra, Music Hall.

May 19—New York Symphony Orchestra, Music Hall.

May 20—New York Symphony Orchestra, Music Hall.

May 22—Kneisel String Quartette, Recital Hall.

May 22—Inaugural Concert, Festival Hall, Wagner programme. Selections from " Tannhäuser," " Tristan and Isolde," and " Die Götterdämmerung." Soloist, Mme. Amalia Materna.

Peristyle at the World's Columbian Exposition, Chicago, Showing Symphony Hall at the Left.
D. H. Burnham & Co., Architects

May 23—Kneisel String Quartette, Recital Hall.

May 23—Orchestral concert, Music Hall.

May 24—Kneisel String Quartette, Recital Hall. Mendelssohn's "Elijah," by Chicago Apollo Club, Festival Hall. Soprano, Mme. Lillian Nordica; alto, Mme. Christine Nielson Dreier; bass, Mr. Plunkett Greene; tenor, Mr. Whitney Mockridge.

May 25—Kneisel String Quartette, Recital Hall.

[Note.—The Kneisel String Quartette programmes will include a new "Sonata Tragique," for piano and violin, by E. A. MacDowell, and a quartette for piano and strings by Arthur Foote. Pianists, Mr. MacDowell, Mr. Foote.]

May 25—Haydn's "Creation," by Chicago Apollo Club, Festival Hall. Soprano, Mme. Lillian Nordica; bass, Mr. Plunkett Greene; tenor, Mr. C. A. Knorr.

May 26—Exposition Children's Chorus, 1,400 voices, Festival Hall.

May 26—Orchestral Concert, Music Hall. Raff programme. Programme will include Concerto for Piano.

May 27—Wagner Concert, Festival Hall. Soloist, Mme. Amalia Materna.

May 30—Orchestral Concert, Music Hall.

June 2—Symphony Concert, Music Hall.

June 3—Concert by Children's World's Fair Chorus.

June 5, 6, 7, 8—Concerts by Lineff Russian Choir.

June 9—Schumann Programme, Musical Hall.

June 10, 11, 12, 13—Concerts by Lineff Russian Choir.

June 12—Max Bendix's String Quartette, Recital Hall.

June 13—Max Bendix's String Quartette, Recital Hall.

June 14—Handel's "The Messiah," by Chicago Apollo Club, Festival Hall.

June 15—Bach's "St. Matthew Passion," by Chicago Apollo Club, Festival Hall.

June 20—Concert by St. Paul and Minneapolis Choral Associations; S. A. Baldwin, conductor; Music Hall.

June 21, 22, 23—Festival by first section of representative choral societies of the Western States. Three concerts in Festival Hall; massed chorus of 1,500; orchestra of two hundred; organ and eminent soloists.

June 24—Performance in Music Hall of Brahms' " A German Requiem," by Cincinnati Festival Association Chorus; conductor, Theodore Thomas.

June 21, 22, 23, 24—Session of representative Women's Amateur Musical Clubs of America, Music Hall.

June 26—Children's World's Fair Chorus.

June 27—Concert by Arion Society of Brooklyn, N. Y.; Arthur Claasen, conductor; Music Hall.

June 28—Handel's " The Messiah," by Chicago Apollo Club, Festival Hall.

June 29—Ballad Concert by Edward Lloyd and orchestra.

June 30—The Apollo Club: " Stabat Mater," Rossini; " Hymn of Praise," Mendelssohn.

July 1—German-American Women's Chorus.

July 3—Wagner Programme.

July 6—American Composers' Programme.

July 7—American Composers' Programme.

July 8—Chicago Columbian Chorus.

July 10—Wagner Programme.

July 7, 8, 10—Concerts by New York Liederkranz; conductor, Heinrich Zollner; Music Hall.

July 11—Concert by Cleveland Vocal Society; conductor, Alfred Arthur; Music Hall.

July 12, 13, 14—Festival by second section of representative choral societies of the Western States. Three concerts in Festival Hall; massed chorus of 1,500; orchestra of two hundred; organ and eminent soloists.

July 15—Children's World's Fair Chorus.

July 15—*Junger Maennerchor* (Philadelphia).

July 18—Symphony Concert.

July 20, 21, 22—Festival by American Union of Swedish Societies.

July 25—Symphony Concert.

July 27, 28—Festival by United Scandinavian Societies.

August 1—Symphony Concert.

August 2—National Union Concert.

August 4—Scotland's Day.

August 8—Symphony Concert.

August 12—Bohemian Day, United Bohemian Singers.

This immense list of concerts was performed exactly as advertised with the exception of four of the massed festival performances by visiting choral societies. It was found impracticable to get them to the Fair together; they were, therefore, heard in separate concerts instead of in combination, as had been planned. For the final weeks of the Fair, Thomas had arranged the following performances:

I.   A series of Symphony concerts, to include several Wagner programmes, and the Ninth Symphony, under the conductorship of Hans Richter.

II. A series of concerts under the conductorship of Sir Alexander Mackenzie of London, including a performance of his Oratorio, " Bethlehem," with Lillian Nordica and Ben Davies as soloists.

III. A three weeks' series of concerts under the conductorship of Saint Saens, including his best choral and orchestral works.

The celebrated musicians who were to have taken part in the closing performances of the Bureau of Music had, like those who had appeared in the spring, been offered no financial remuneration besides their expenses. That they should have been willing to undertake the long and fatiguing journey to America was remarkable, and the following letters * show how keenly interested they were in taking part in the work of Thomas, and how anxious to give of their best to the American audiences gathered at Chicago:

S. Germain, *September 25, 1892.*

My dear Colleague:

All that you do is well done, and I put myself entirely in your hands as to my programmes in Chicago. I am enchanted that they will be short, for that will make them so much less fatiguing for me.

If there will not be the means for theatrical representations, I would much prefer not to give fragments of "*Samson et Dalila.*" I only like to give in concert antitheatrical compositions; for, to me, the concert and the theater are two separate worlds, and I deplore the invasion of the concert by operatic excerpts.

I should think that it would be preferable to finish, rather than to begin, the concert with the C-minor Symphony, but you know the customs of the American public better than I, and I leave the matter to your judgment. It is true that if we can finish with the " Hymn to Victor Hugo," the programme will be excellent in commencing with the symphony. Between the two numbers I will play my Concerto in G minor, or the " African Fantasie."

* Translated from the original French and German.

Once more, you are the best judge of everything, and
I will conform entirely to your advice.

I have learned that you have performed my symphony
in America, and for this I send my sincere thanks.

With my most affectionate compliments,

CAMILLE SAINT SAËNS.

———

Honored Sir: BROOKLINE, *Oct. 29, 1892.*

First accept my most cordial thanks for your kind
letter. If I answer it in German it is for the reason that
I am not, as yet, sufficiently master of the English language to give in it expression to my thanks and appreciation
in the most courteous manner, and prefer to use the German, in order that I may not be obliged to confine myself
to conventional phrases.

Permit me then, most honored Sir, to express to you,
both for myself and on behalf of the Boston Symphony
Orchestra, our warmest thanks for your cordial invitation to Chicago, and your kind proffer of all the moral
support which we shall need there. Be assured that the
genuine hospitality with which you have placed all your
artistic resources at our disposal will be appreciated by
us in the most grateful manner. I have sketched the programmes of both concerts on the inclosed sheets, but will
gladly make any alterations you may suggest.

I also take advantage of this opportunity to give expression to my pleasure that at last I can meet you personally in Chicago, and say to you that I well know how
deep a debt musical America owes to you, and how different the musical situation would be in this country but for
your long years of self-sacrificing pioneer art work.

Accept my respectful, colleagial (*kollegialische*) greeting, with which I remain

Faithfully yours,

ARTHUR NIKISCH.

VIENNA, *January* 16, 1893.

Honored Colleague and Friend:

Your letters both came to hand at a time when, because of the sudden death of my good mother, and the dangerous illness of my wife, I was too distressed to give consideration to outside affairs. Now, however, my wife is better, and I am able to pull myself together once more.

Your invitation to conduct at the Chicago World's. Fair is very sympathetic to me, and I shall know in a short time if I can accept it. In order not to keep you waiting for the mail, I will cable as soon as I receive leave of absence. I could leave London, where I have to conduct six concerts, in time to reach Chicago by the 20th. One day would be sufficient for rehearsal. In regard to the programmes we shall easily agree. I will only say that unless you have made other arrangements for it, I should like to conduct the Ninth Symphony of Beethoven.

I certainly hope that I shall receive the necessary permission to go. But as I would have to return by the first of August—the opera does not begin earlier—the point in question would be whether it could be prepared in two or three weeks. My cable will probably reach you about the same time as this letter. I do not understand what living expenses cost in America, but depend on you that the sum which you have named is sufficient to cover all that I will need for the journey.

My answer to you is delayed a few days yet, because my employers of the Royal and Imperial Bureau of Censors are at present occupied with the marriage festivities at court.

With my best thanks for your friendly thought, and my colleagial greetings,

Faithfully yours,

HANS RICHTER.

This brilliant *finale* was, however, not destined to take place, for the hostile forces had triumphed before its time came, and the Bureau of Music had been destroyed by the two great blighting agencies of this world—jealousy and ignorance.

Amongst the concerts of this memorable musical exhibit, perhaps none were more interesting, in certain aspects, than the short orchestral recitals given at the noon hour every day, in the big Festival Hall. The music selected for these concerts was of the so-called " Popular " kind. There were no intermissions, but a few minutes' pause was made between each piece to allow people to come in or go out, as they were not allowed to do either while the music was going on. The audiences at these concerts were a study, for they contained every class and variety of human being. Some would come for the entire programme, others for a few numbers, and still others drifted in from curiosity, and left after one piece. But just as many came in as went out after each number, so there was always a good audience in attendance from first to last. Thomas conducted these concerts personally, as well as most of the others, for it was a little matter of pride with him that the poorest laborer who strolled in once from curiosity to hear what an orchestra sounded like, should hear the best that could be given that time, if he never heard it again. In after years we sometimes came across workingmen, in distant places, to whom this single orchestral experience was a glorified memory for life, and who expressed their appreciation very touchingly. One would often hear amusing comments made by such listeners, in the intervals of the pieces. Once, two of them seated behind me at one of these free concerts noticed on the programme an announcement of a " Wagner Programme " to be given the coming week, for which an admission was charged. " I thought Thomas was the biggest music-man they was," exclaimed one of them in a disappointed tone. " He is," replied the companion reassuringly. " Waal, then," said the first, " I don't see why he don't get nothing for his concerts when this here Waggner man gets a dollar for his'n!" On another day a Chicago woman behind me appeared to have brought with her a friend from San Francisco. She was evidently very proud of the Chicago Orchestra, and desired to have her friend duly impressed. As they sat down, the man remarked, " The last time I saw Theodore Thomas was a good many years ago, and he was playing ' End-Man ' in a nigger minstrel troupe in San Francisco." The woman indignantly repudiated this dreadful suggestion, but her protests were of no avail, and only elicited from her companion the calm reiteration, " Why, I *seen* him myself, many a time." Nor could she persuade her obstinate guest that what he had seen was a burlesque representation, and the real man had never been in San Francisco except as the conductor of great festival or operatic performances. The argument waxed so fierce between the two that I very nearly turned around to settle it in her favor, but the music began, and by the time the next pause came, I had forgotten all about it.

The attendance at the Fair during the spring and summer months was a great disappointment to its promoters, and by the time the first of August came it had fallen off so much that it was feared the whole concern would become bankrupt. In this emergency it became necessary to curtail all possible expenses, and the opponents of the Bureau of Music were not slow to point out that that foolish piece of extravagance ought now to be done away with. The Chicago Directors, who had upheld it all along, in spite of the attacks of the National Commission, were now unable to get the money to pay its expenses, and Thomas concluded that there was no use in continuing the fight any longer. He, therefore, addressed the orchestra as follows:

" *Gentlemen:*

" If when I engaged you to play here this summer I had offered you a four months' contract, instead of one for six months, you would all have accepted it, would you not? " The answer was in the affirmative, and Thomas continued: " Very well, then, you have now had nearly three months and a half. The Fair is hovering on the verge of bankruptcy and I doubt very much if I can even get the arrears of salary already owing to you, nor do I think there is any likelihood that the Exposition Company will be able to maintain the Bureau of Music for the full term of your contract. I would advise you therefore to take the following course, and authorize me to say to the Directors that if they will continue your engagement till the first of September and pay your salaries in full to that date, you will cancel the two remaining months of your contracts. We have very loyal friends on the Board, and I think they will be glad to do this for us. But if you stand out for the fulfilment of the whole term of your contracts, I think it will result in your losing not only the last two months but also that part of your salaries which is already in arrears."

At first the men were inclined to hearken to this wise counsel, but a few malcontents stirred up a spirit of dissatisfaction, and they refused to make any concession at all. Under these circumstances Thomas felt released from all obligation to remain with the orchestra, and gladly seized the opportunity to leave, for it is not pleasant for any man to have his character, his motives, his work, and his honor assailed daily in the public press, nor to hold doggedly to a position in an institution one-half of the governing body of which is using every lever to effect his removal. It was only his feeling of duty towards the orchestra which had kept him there so long, but now that he was freed from that, he lost no time in sending in his resignation in the following letter:

CHICAGO, *August* 12, 1893.

JAMES W. ELLSWORTH, ESQ., CHAIRMAN OF THE
    COMMITTEE ON MUSIC, WORLD'S COLUMBIAN
    EXPOSITION.

Dear Sir:

The discouraging business situation, which must of necessity react on the finances of the Fair and which makes a reduction of expenses of vital importance to its interests, prompts me to make the following suggestions by which the expenses of the Bureau of Music may be lessened:

The original plans of the Bureau, as you know, were made with the design of giving for the first time in the history of the world a complete and perfect exhibition of musical art in all its branches. Arrangements were made for regular free orchestral and band concerts; for festivals and choral concerts; for performances of both European and American master-works of the present day under the direction of their composers; for concerts by distinguished artists and organizations of all nationalities; for chamber concerts and artists' recitals; for concerts by children, etc., etc.; besides a general review of the orchestral literature of all times and countries in symphony and popular concerts throughout the season.

The reduction of the expenses of the Fair has obliged the Bureau to cancel all future engagements with foreign artists and organizations, and to abandon all future festival performances, thus leaving very little of the original scheme except the bands and the great Exposition orchestra, with which are given every day symphony and popular concerts. My suggestion is, therefore, that since so large a portion of the Bureau's musical scheme has been cut away, that for the remainder of the Fair music shall not figure as an art at all, but be treated merely on the basis of an amusement. More of this class of music is undoubtedly needed at the Fair, and the cheapest way to get it is to divide our two fine bands into four small ones for open-air concerts, and our Exposition orchestra into two small orchestras, which can play such light selections as will please the shifting crowds in the buildings and amuse them.

If this plan is followed, there will be no further need of the services of the Musical Director, and in order that your committee may be perfectly free to act in accordance with the foregoing suggestions, and reduce the expenses of the musical department to their lowest terms, I herewith respectfully tender my resignation as Musical Director of the World's Columbian Exposition.

Should, however, any plans suggest themselves to you in furthering which I can be of assistance, I will gladly give you my services without remuneration.

Very respectfully,

THEODORE THOMAS, *Musical Director.*

In view of the desperate financial situation, the Directors were obliged to accept the resignation of Thomas, which they never would have done for any other reason, for they felt as strongly in regard to the musical exhibit as he did, and were equally anxious that it should be completed on the original lines. Their attitude in the matter was very beautifully defined by Mr. James W. Ellsworth, the Chairman of the Committee on Music, in a letter to Mr. W. K. Ackerman, Auditor, acknowledging the receipt of the following financial statement of the total cost of the music to the Exposition Company:

FINANCIAL STATEMENT OF THE BUREAU OF MUSIC
OF THE
WORLD'S COLUMBIAN EXPOSITION

Total cost of orchestras and soloists......	$149,601.39
Less admission receipts...................	57,406.25
Net loss on the above musical features...	$ 92,195.14
Bands	$128,737.35
Total cost of music to Exposition.........	$220,932.49

My dear Mr. Ackerman: CHICAGO, *Oct.* 10, 1893.

I thank you very much for yours of the 7th instant inclosing statement of disbursements and receipts in connection with the Bureau of Music.

The Directory does not consider, however, that there has been any " net loss " in the musical features, the idea being, in the inception, that the Thomas orchestra and musical features in connection therewith were for the purpose of the exemplification of music as an art. In connection with the history of the Exposition which is to be handed down as the result of the work we are passing through, the result will justify more than the dollars and cents figure in connection therewith during the giving of the same. I hope those who disagree with this view of the matter now will ultimately acquiesce in its importance. It is the future as well as the present that I, for one, have always had in mind, as have also a number of our Directory, and I am thankful indeed that during a period of three and a half months, at least, music received the recognition that it more than deserved in connection with this great work which is about to close, and which will be acknowledged by all nations as the creation of a new period.

Very truly yours,   JAMES W. ELLSWORTH.

When it is remembered that, in addition to the operating expenses of $220,932.49 enumerated in the foregoing statement, the Exposition had spent several hundred thousand dollars on the erection of buildings for the Bureau of Music, it seems incredible that even the National Commission should have been guilty of the monumental stupidity of destroying what was, after its architec-

ture, the most unique and absolutely unprece-
dented exhibit of the entire Fair, especially as
nothing was saved thereby but a couple of months'
salaries for the musicians of the orchestra.

The short-sighted folly of the whole proceeding
was soon demonstrated, for hardly had Thomas
reached his home at Fairhaven than the financial
tide of the Exposition turned, and the people
began to flock to it by the hundred thousand, and
with them money flowed into the treasury in such
Pactolian streams that not only was past indebtedness made good, but after the Fair closed the balance sheet of its final report showed a surplus of
a million dollars, if I am correctly informed.
Unfortunately, the Bureau of Music was now
destroyed past all recall, but nevertheless, the first
act of the Board of Directors was to send an
urgent request to Thomas to return and continue
the musical exhibit in another form, offering him
a concession in the shape of the Festival Hall in
which to give daily orchestral concerts on a percentage of the admission fees.

The Exposition Orchestra, which was not yet
disbanded, had agreed to accept this engagement,
in place of the two unexpired months of their
contract, and they, too, sent to Thomas a telegram
begging him to return. But Thomas had had
enough of the World's Fair. His splendid scheme
had been ruined, and all possibilities of great art
work had vanished with it. He was worn out
physically and mentally, and did not care to return
and conduct popular concerts for the amusement

of the crowd. Nor did he think that such a series of concerts would provide the salaries of the orchestra. In reply to their telegram, therefore, he wrote the following letter, which explained his position in the matter:

FAIRHAVEN, MASS., *August 22*, 1893.
To HENRY SACHLEBEN, MAX BENDIX, AND THE OTHER MEMBERS OF THE EXPOSITION ORCHESTRA.

Gentlemen:

Your telegram I received this morning, and in answer to your request asking me to return and conduct the concerts of the Exposition, I have to say the following:

I do not ask for any thanks from you for looking after your interests as I have done this summer, but the utter lack of understanding of the trying position in which I have been placed for nearly four months, prompts me to say that if the members of the orchestra had been willing to make any concessions two weeks ago when I requested them to do so, I might still have been with them at the present moment.

When I was asked to resign the position of Musical Director last May, I did not do so because the orchestra needed my protection. In August when the financial crisis came, and I found that I could not protect the orchestra any more, and that the members were not willing to listen to any compromise, I resigned my position, and the Directors of the Exposition felt that they must accept my resignation. Now you must not blame me if I do not care to make a third attempt to continue as conductor of the Exposition orchestra, nor do I believe that arrangements to play on a percentage would be satisfactory to the orchestra, even with me as conductor. . . . I intend to return to Chicago in November, to carry out the remainder of my contract with the Chicago Orchestral Association, when I hope to meet you all again.

With love to you all, and best wishes for your prosperity,

Sincerely yours,   THEODORE THOMAS.

Thus ended Thomas' connection with the World's Fair Columbian Exposition. As had often happened before, his plans were too large, and too far in advance of the people, to be understood or appreciated, except by the cultured few, and were, in consequence, foredoomed to failure. Had he been a younger man, or had he not so recently gone through a similar experience in the American Opera and its disastrous subsequent years, he would not have felt the World's Fair fiasco so much. But he was growing old now, and the many hardships and disappointments of life had left their mark, and taken away from him the buoyant, indomitable spirit with which he had hitherto faced the world. During the early spring also, the damp walls of the newly-erected buildings in which he worked gave him a severe attack of bronchitis, which threatened to become pneumonia for a few days. Unfortunately this illness came just at the time of the first of the Festival performances, and long before he was fit for work he insisted upon leaving his sick bed and going to the Fair to conduct a heavy Wagner programme and attending to all his other duties. The result of this was that the disease fastened itself upon him permanently, in the form of a chronic catarrh of the throat, nose, and bronchial tubes, extending even to the Eustachian tubes of the ears, and threatening him with deafness. This, and the nervous strain of withstanding the siege to which he was subjected all summer, so wrought upon his physical and mental condition that he was never afterwards the man he had been before. His courage was gone, and for the rest of his life he would drop into despondency and be ready to give up at any little untoward happening, and I found it constantly necessary to buoy him up to renewed effort. " Do you want to kill me with work? " he sometimes said. But I knew that in work lay his only hope of life. He was not one who could long have endured an idle existence.

Disappointing as the summer had been, the connection of Thomas with the World's Fair had not been without some compensating features. In the first place, the daily concerts and rehearsals of the orchestra had brought it up to the very highest point of artistic proficiency, and given it an enormous repertoire of music, so that Thomas felt he now had an almost perfect instrument for the concerts of the coming winter, and that he would be ready for any emergency. This was a great relief to his mind, for he had found it very difficult to equalize the two sections of the orchestra so long as the local, or " extra," men had such a small repertoire, but now the summer's work had brought them up to an equal proficiency with the " regular " men, and he had only to keep them there.

Another pleasant feature of the Fair was that during its preliminary work Thomas had been brought into close contact with the most eminent men of other arts than his own. He was intellectually a very lonely man. His knowledge of the musical art was so far in advance of that of most of the members of his profession that nearly all musicians approached him as a master—indeed European musicians often called him " *Meister,*" or " *Maëstro.*" Now and then he would meet someone of his profession with whom he could talk on equal terms, and from whom he could gain new ideas and fresh suggestions, such as Liszt, Paderewski, Joachim, or von Buelow; but these people rarely crossed his path, and as a general rule he lived intellectually alone in a world of his own creating. It was, therefore, very inspiring to him to come into daily association with Burnham and his colleagues, and the friendship then started with the former was one of the great pleasures of his last years. Amongst the many letters received from famous musicians during the World's Fair, I have selected three from those who were unable to accept the invitation of Thomas to take part in the concerts of the Fair as being of especial interest: *

Moskow, *May* 5, 1892.
Highly honored Herr Thomas:
I have received your invitation to be on the Committee of the World's Fair in Chicago. I thank you for this and

* Translated from the German and French.

am flattered and proud, but I hardly think that it is possible to accept. I cannot go without remuneration, it is too far, and they would wish to hear only my best works. At the same time I thank you heartily.

I long to say many things to you—but it is difficult for me to write German. I know how much you have done for me and for my compositions in America, and I beg of you, dear and beloved sir and friend, not to doubt that I am truly grateful.

Sincerely yours,

P. Tschaikowsky.

Paris, *October*, 1892.

To the Director-General, World's Columbian
    Exposition, Chicago.

Dear Sir:

It is real courage on my part that has at last enabled me to write to you that I do not dare to promise positively to accept your flattering invitation to appear in the concerts of the Bureau of Music at the Chicago World's Fair next summer. And yet I expected to send you an immediate and affirmative reply. But I fear to thus make an engagement for a fixed date, for I would not dare to break my word, and yet from the moment I gave it to you it would be a source of constant anxiety to me.

You may rest assured, dear Sir, of my gratitude for the kind words in which your invitation is addressed to me, and my deep appreciation as well as my sincere regret. Accept the assurance of my highest consideration, and kindly give to the great *Maëstro* Theodore Thomas my expressions of homage.

Jules Massenet.

Mr. Theodore Thomas.   * Ischil, *Sept.* 1, 1892.

Highly honored Sir:

In reply to letters written on your behalf from your
office, allow me to repeat to you personally what I have
already explained to your representative.

First of all that I esteem very deeply and gratefully
the honor of your invitation to take part in the presentation of my works at the Chicago Exposition of 1893.
Next the frank statement that I cannot make up my mind
to accept it. I do not need to tell you in detail in how
many ways it tempts me; but it would be inconsiderate for
me to accept, for at the last moment I know that resolution would fail me and I should ask to be released from my
promise. Kindly excuse, then, the old-country man who
cannot undertake the long voyage so lightly as you do,
and turn over to another of our colleagues the honor and
pleasure of representing German music at the Exposition.

With distinguished respect,

JOHANNES BRAHMS.

Brahms must have been a very reserved and
undemonstrative man, for he was almost the only
contemporary musician from whom there is no
expression of personal gratitude to be found in
the letter files of Thomas, and yet there was no
composer of any nationality for whose music
Thomas did so much in this country, for he played
the Brahms symphonies directly against the popular will every year of his life, until the public
grew to understand and appreciate them in spite
of themselves. Something, however, even this
strange man must have felt, for when Thomas

* Translated from the German.

met him at supper on one of his European trips, a characteristic incident took place. Someone at the table reminded Brahms of the promise of a photograph. Immediately a second guest added his request for one. Thomas said nothing, but Brahms, turning to him, remarked, " I will send one also to you, Herr Thomas." The next day the three photographs were sent, and on comparing them at a subsequent meeting from which Brahms was absent, the recipients found that he had written on the first, " Promised "; on the second, " Asked for "; but on that of Thomas, " Offered."

CHAPTER XIX

1893-1896

THE third year of the Chicago Orchestral Association had now arrived, but nothing could have
been more discouraging than its financial outlook
in the fall of 1893. The World's Fair had drained
Chicago of its surplus funds, a severe financial
panic was upon the country at large, and the
winter was one of unusual severity. Chicago was
full of the flotsam and jetsam of humanity, left
by the receding tide of the Exposition—people of
every grade who had come there attracted by the
hope of working, begging, or stealing during its
continuance, and who were now stranded to be a
burden upon the community. No one had any
extra money, or if he had, the first necessity which

claimed it was the relief of these starving and freezing people, rather than the promoting of symphonic music. The financial results of the second year of the Association had been so unsatisfactory, and the deficit so large, that Thomas had come to the conclusion that its third must inevitably be the last.

It was just at this time that Thomas received a letter from Mr. Henry L. Higginson of Boston, offering him the conductorship of the Boston Symphony Orchestra. This was the one position that he had longed for for years, and which exactly suited his needs. Boston was a cultivated city, and its orchestra one of the best. There no missionary work was needed, but on the contrary, the first law of its being was " A symphony on every programme." It was near his country home and the homes of his children, its climate was less severe than that of Chicago, and life there, as in all old cities, was quiet, restful, and well ordered. Its orchestra travelled only over his own old Eastern " Highway," where railroads and hotels were comfortable, and distances short, and gave concerts only in the large cities where he best liked to conduct. His experiences at the World's Fair had bitten deeply, and his health was seriously affected by the cold, damp winds of Lake Michigan, which not only prevented him from getting rid of the bronchial catarrh contracted at the Fair, but brought back in an aggravated form the rheumatism in his conducting arm which had troubled him so much in New

York. For every reason, therefore, he wanted to go, especially as he believed that in leaving he would antedate the natural end of the Chicago Orchestra by only a single season.

But when he thought of his Chicago friends, of the large sums of money they had already given, the hard work they had done, their earnest desire to create a truly great musical institution, and, last but not least, the fact that they had come to his rescue and given him the means to restore his art, when his career had seemed ruined beyond all hope of recovery, he knew that now he could not honorably leave them until the Chicago Orchestra was either permanently established or abandoned. His reply to Mr. Higginson was, therefore, in the negative.

The season of 1893 needs little comment. The orchestra was in splendid condition, and the business routine was beginning to be better understood by the trustees. By careful pruning of expenses they managed to reduce the deficit to a little below the fifty thousand dollars provided by the guarantee fund. Nevertheless the box office receipts for the Chicago concerts were less by five thousand dollars than during the previous year. But in spite of this discouraging outlook, the trustees did not falter in their devotion to the cause, but only worked the harder to raise a new guarantee fund for the ensuing year. After this Thomas never had another written contract with the Chicago Orchestral Association. It was taken for granted that he would go on as long as the trustees were able to raise the necessary funds for the orchestra, and each year, sometime between April and July, he would be notified informally of its continuance. It was the same with the Cincinnati Festival Association, and with all the other boards with which he worked for any length of time. He used to say with satisfaction, " No one asks me for a contract who knows me. I never broke my word in my life."

This informal way of doing business was, however, often a source of trouble to him, for, if he gave no contracts, neither did he ask for any, and the result was that he never knew with any certainty just where he was going to stand financially when the current year was over. During the last decade of his life, both the Chicago Orchestra and the Cincinnati Festival Association—his two chief sources of income—were maintained simply from year to year, and it was not until each season of the orchestra or each festival was entirely over that he knew whether either institution would be continued. This uncertainty kept him continually on the ragged edge of anxiety about the future, for he was fearful that he would waste his few remaining years in the West, without establishing anything permanent, and in the end find himself stranded there, without an orchestra, when he was too old to return and make a new place for himself in the East. There seemed to be no way, however, by which either he or the trustees could forecast the future any more definitely, so there was nothing to do but take the goods the gods provided, and trust that everything would come out right in the end.

Meantime Thomas continued to make the concerts of the Association as alluring to the Chicago public as he could, and amongst the novelties of the season of 1893 was a charming Suite, " Impressions of Italy," by Charpentier, which brought the following pleasant letter from this eminent composer:

PARIS, *Dec.*, 1893.

MR. THEODORE THOMAS.

My dear Sir:

My friend Amato has written me of your performance of my work, " *Impressions d'Italie,*" in Chicago. Permit me to thank you and to add also the compliments of my publisher, M. Tellier.

I am very happy that the work has made a success, and I know all that I owe to you in the matter, for the conducting of this piece is very delicate, and demands an artist.

If you conduct choral performances, I should like to offer to you my " *Vie d'un Poête,*" but, in the meantime, permit me to send you the piano arrangement as a testimonial of my gratitude and my cordial sympathy.

G. CHARPENTIER.

The season of 1893-94 closed with the eleventh Cincinnati Festival, which still stands out in my memory as the pleasantest of all our many delightful experiences in that city, though it was not artistically the greatest. A number of intimate friends, who had come from various cities to attend the Festival, as well as most of the solo artists, stayed in the same hotel as ourselves. A private dining-room was reserved for the accommodation of all these friends, and every evening, after the concert, one or the other would give a supper and invite all the rest, and, as may be imagined, there was not a little fun going on. At last our turn came to give the supper. The concert which preceded this occasion had gone off particularly well and Thomas was in the highest spirits. After the substantial part of the meal was ended, he mixed his own particular brew of punch, and cigars were lighted. At his right hand sat his beloved friend of many years, Mrs. E. D. Gillespie, now old in years, but as young as ever in heart and brain. When all the preliminaries were settled to his liking, he arose, glass in hand, and after pledging the company, thus addressed them: " Ladies and Gentlemen, I think we cannot close this pleasant evening better than by having a little music. I therefore call upon each of the artists present to give us a song, after which I promise that my friend, Mrs. Gillespie, will sing her world-renowned aria, ' Boo, for John! ' " There was a general shout over this, and, entering into the spirit of the occasion, each artist rose in turn and sang an appropriate selection without accompaniment. As they were singing for brother-artists, each was on his mettle to do his best, and by the time Ben Davies, the famous Welsh tenor, was called upon for his number, the atmosphere was electric. He gave a short lyric, exquisitely rendered, in the English language.

As he sat down amidst the delighted applause
which followed, a slip of paper was put into his
hand by one of the waiters, which he passed along
to Thomas. On it was written, " Will not Mr.
Davies sing a Welsh song for two Welsh waiters
who have been away from home many years? "
The request was, of course, seconded by the company, and then this great artist rose again, and
sang, not as a musician in the exercise of his art,
but as a patriot in a distant land when he gives
expression to all his love and longing for home,
the wild national hymn of the Welsh. We could
not, of course, understand the words, but so powerful and impassioned was his rendering of this
strange, dramatic music, that no one who was
present will ever forget it. As he ceased the company sat spell-bound, and almost in tears, and then
Thomas relieved the tension by turning to Mrs.
Gillespie and saying, with a jolly laugh, " Now
then, it is your turn; give us ' John, for Boo! ' "
Mrs. Gillespie was equal to the emergency,
and sang the little comic song with such inimitable
drollery that she " brought down the house," and
made a very hilarious ending to the impromptu
concert.

The next day this delightful Festival ended,
and the jolly little company of friends and artists
scattered to their widely-separated homes, in
America and Europe. Thomas, of course, went
to Fairhaven, thankful for a chance to rest and
visit with his family.

The summer of 1894 was marked by another

A Snapshot of Theodore Thomas Leaving the Hall After a
Festival Rehearsal in Cincinnati

effort to draw him back permanently to the East. This time the call came from New York, where it was proposed to establish an endowed orchestra similar to those of Boston and Chicago, with Thomas as its leader. He still wanted to go passionately, for he was always homesick for New York, but the same reasons held him that had caused him to refuse the Boston offer, and he again declined.

The season of 1894-95 was virtually a repetition of the last, except that it was lengthened by a very long concert tour of nearly two months' duration, to the cities of the Western "Highway." The following extracts are from letters written while on this tour, and will give some idea of the hardships of this class of musical work in this section of the country:

Indianapolis.—"I have been trying to write for two days, but we are in the cars pretty much all day—nasty old cars—and this is as hard a trip as I ever made. I don't see how I can do this any more. Nearly all our large instruments have been broken by rough handling on the trains, and for two days we have had no dinner—only a bit of sausage and bread. This sort of traveling is not natural or right, and I cannot continue to live this way after this year."

Lincoln, Neb.—"Your letter I received yesterday, this being Thursday I will give up my walk and send you a few lines, otherwise you could hardly hear from me this week, for I had no chance to write before. Tuesday we had both a rehearsal and a concert. Yesterday two concerts. I was so fatigued from these and the two nights in the train, besides having caught some cold, that I have spent every moment I could in bed, in order to be able to do my concert work. The roads out here are too rough for me to write, even in pencil—the roads are like the general conditions, and I must say that I would like to shape the next few years somewhat differently from what the Chicago situation will probably allow. As for traveling again next year with the orchestra, I doubt if I can bring myself to make that sacrifice. I feel that I have done my share, and that the country and the people need time to develop now before we can expect an art appreciation. Consequently we must only work for the 'many-headed instrument,' the orchestra, and I fear that would be suicidal for me. In one sense I am through with my life work. The personal satisfaction of showing what I could do under favorable circumstances I will never get,—or it must come quickly,—but that may be nothing more than vanity. A man of over sixty ought not to overwork as I do and I think I must find some suitable occupation and learn to live on a smaller income."

Omaha.—" Just now it might go worse with us, but it might also go better! Everywhere we are lodged in second-class hotels, and I have even made the acquaintance of bed-bugs—it being Sunday, however, I will not swear!

" Since writing the above we have left Omaha, and have reached Des Moines, after a very hot and unpleasant journey of six hours. I still have my cold and am all used up. You see by my letters that I have nothing to say in particular, but only in general that I wish we lived somewhere and had some sort of an occupation whereby we could enjoy our existence. Neither of us really has a home;

isn't it curious? Nor is it our fault. Circumstances, and
the uncertain future of the Chicago Orchestral Association
are against us, but I think we both deserve peace, and I
swear if I am not more contented next year that I will
give up music and go into business yet. You may laugh,
but I am serious, and you will admit that I am practical
too. When I come home you can give me some advice on
the subject, and perhaps we can cut the Gordian knot of
our destiny together."

Cedar Rapids.—" I am very tired to-day from want of
sleep. I tried to get a nap yesterday but in vain, so I
walked the streets, though it was hot and dusty. I got
to bed at twelve last night, in spite of a little festivity
given in our honor by the band of Des Moines, but could
not sleep until one, and woke up again at three, after
which I could not sleep any more and so got up at five.
At seven the train started, reaching here at half-past one.
As yet we have no hotel accommodations here at all—
the hotel people, I am told, refused to make contracts. It
is nobody's fault, and I do not write to complain, but
simply to tell you how we live. Meantime while I sit in
the hotel reading-room, our manager is running about to
find beds for the men. The ' mysterious letter ' you forwarded was not an evil one, but the contrary. If you
had opened it, as you should have done, you would have
found that it was from Lang, of Boston, asking if I am
free to accept an orchestral position there beginning with
this fall. Of course I have written him that I cannot
leave Chicago under a year's notice to the trustees of the
Association, so this chance will probably slip through our
fingers like all the rest. But the fact remains that this
work is too hard for me, necessitating as it does so much
traveling in this uncultivated part of the country. As I

write the manager comes in to take forty of the men to a hotel eight miles off. But I shall stay where I am, my back aches from so much sitting in the cars. You did not say where you sent my clean clothes? But it does not make much difference, a little dirt more or less don't count at present."

Burlington, Iowa.—" Don't judge of this hotel by the picture on this paper, or you might get a very mistaken impression of it! The clean clothes came last night, after I had mailed my letter. By the time our manager had found beds for our orchestra yesterday about half of them were scattered through the town in private houses. To-day the same thing happened again here. My stomach is all out of order from the bad food. Well, I will say no more about the matter, but this traveling *must* stop for me, and I have asked Norman to notify the trustees that next year will be my last. I can see only one way to make the orchestra permanent in Chicago as long as we have no building of our own, and that is to give a long summer-night series of concerts. The time ought to be ripe for that now, and it would perhaps do away with this infernal traveling."

Davenport, Iowa.—" Just a few lines to-day, as this will be my last chance to write this week. To-morrow we start at five, and are for two days and nights all the time on the train, except when we stop to give concerts—one Friday and two Saturday. The weather here in Iowa is summer heat. Next week in Minnesota it will probably be winter cold, but at least I shall be able to find a restaurant where I can get something to eat, and then I will pick up again."

Duluth, Minn.—" Your letter is just received. Our hardships I hope are over now for a time, and it is useless to write about them. I never saw such tired men in my life, nor can I remember to have been through such a continuous strain. The basket of luncheon you sent came in just right. I had given up eating, my stomach rebelled, but your chops have cured me! The second basket came last night, but I have not opened it yet, because here we are in quite a good hotel and the manager is giving me extra attention. I went to bed at twelve last night and for the first time since leaving home I had a good sleep of seven hours, and feel like a new man again."

Minneapolis, Minn.—" Only a line to-day to let you know where I am, for I am again so tired that I can neither eat nor sleep. Even when I go to bed early, cramps in my feet—I suppose from lack of exercise—will not let me sleep. I am doing the best I can not to get sick until this miserable tour is over. But do be ready to start for Europe, as soon as I get home, and let me get away from everything and everybody for a while."

Minneapolis, Minn.—" I held a long rehearsal this morning to try and get the orchestra in shape again, but little was gained. The men are too tired, and play like machines. I thought, because they were young, they would pick up quickly, but no, they take even longer than I. The hotels here are good, and nothing is wanting in that way, so I feel better, but am still far from being rested. I am all worn out, and my body is as heavy as lead from lack of sleep. Can anyone blame me if I say that I cannot do this work any more? I feel that I must leave after next winter, and if we have no offer from Boston or New York, then we will go to Fairhaven or to Europe, and wait till something comes along. They will not leave me stranded very long in idleness. Do you agree? Your check was very thoughtful, but, Madame! you do not seem to know

me at all. I still have twenty-five dollars in bills in my
pocket, besides some change! Can you show as good
a record since I am gone?"

St. Paul, Minn.—"Yesterday I received your letter.
On reflection I consider myself a good man, and what I am I
owe to the noble impulses received from art works. But if
I were not, you would make a better man of me. I have
not made up my mind yet whether I will run home for
Sunday or not. We will be so near that I could—but I
would so hate to have to go away again the next day.
Saturday we have to travel a couple of hours, and then
play two fatiguing programmes. I shall be tired, of
course, and if I take the seven o'clock train Sunday it
means getting up at five. I will telegraph you Saturday
what I will do—probably I will come, as I do not sleep
after five anyway. I cannot tell you how intolerable the
rest of the tour is to me, it seems as if my nerves could
endure it no longer."

The letter of resignation which Thomas had
written while on this tour was never delivered.
Mr. Fay did not wish to be the intermediary in
the matter, and advised Thomas to lay it before the
trustees himself if he was really in earnest about
going. He *was* in earnest about it, not only on
account of the traveling, but on account of his
health, which was beginning to be seriously affected by the harsh climate of Chicago, and the
overwrought condition of his nerves. " I am
still in my prime as an artist," he said, " and
ripe for the best work of my life, if I can do it
under normal and satisfactory conditions. But
I am no longer able to stand the strain of pro-

longed overwork as in my younger days. If I
continue it much longer, it is simply at the risk
of ruining my health and breaking down altogether." He was, therefore, fully determined to
hand in his resignation to the trustees, at the first
opportunity. But it so happened that there was
no business meeting of the board, immediately
after his return, but after he had been at home
about long enough to get quiet and rested, and to
have forgotten some of the miseries of the tour,
the trustees gave a dinner in his honor, and on
this occasion so much good-will and affection for
himself, and such earnest enthusiasm for the
cause for which they were all working were expressed, that he did not have the heart to push his
resignation just then. Amongst the other unexpected expressions of that evening was one from
the women of Chicago, who, headed by the orchestra's devoted friend, Mrs. John J. Glessner, presented him with a large silver punch bowl. Altogether, this evening brought home to him the
serious and earnest spirit with which the Association regarded the work, and the friendship of,
not only the trustees, but the community in general, for himself, in a manner that he had not before realized. It gave him a very different feeling in regard to remaining, and he decided to
try and continue the work a while longer, hoping
that a long summer of rest in Europe would
restore his physical equilibrium, and that the work
of the association would, perhaps, be carried out
on easier lines next year.

After this Thomas ceased to plan for a return to the East, but made up his mind to stand by the Orchestral Association for good or ill, as long as he should continue his public career. He had now tried and proved the men with whom he had been so closely associated for the past four years, and had become deeply attached to them. He felt every confidence that they would not give up the work or allow its standard to be lowered so long as any effort on their part could maintain it. Having thus decided to stay in the West for the rest of his life, Thomas began to plan for ways and means of conserving the physical powers which still remained to him. With this end in view, he purchased a small estate in the White Mountains, where the air was dry and clear, and he hoped, by spending a large part of his summers in out-of-door life there, to counteract the bad effects of the cold, damp lake winds of the winter months in Chicago.

The summer of 1895 was a delightful one for us, for we went to Europe, and for four enchanted months " cast dull care away," and enjoyed the only pleasure trip we were ever able to take together. Our journey had nothing new or original about it, and we had no time for anything out of the beaten track of European travel, but every day was full of pleasant little excursions to historic places; of dreamy wanderings in wonderful art galleries; of lovely drives and walks; of cozy little tête-à-tête meals in quaint restaurants; of operas, concerts, and delightful junketings with foreign friends,—the last, perhaps, the pleasantest happenings of all, for like all musicians Thomas had, in every city, a delightful circle of musical friends ready-made, and cordially anxious to make our stay agreeable.

This little trip was of great benefit to Thomas, and by the time he returned to Chicago in the fall, catarrh and rheumatism were apparently cured, and he was in the best condition for his winter's work.

The season of 1895-96 opened auspiciously, and proceeded in accordance with the now-established routine of the Association, broken only by two short trips, described in the following letters:

" TORONTO, *Jan.* 8, 1896.

" I suppose you want to hear something from the ' Old Man,' by this time! Well, we can take it a little easy this morning and get rested, after getting up two mornings at five o'clock. We arrived here yesterday after traveling all day in a nasty hot car, and found the weather here very cold—real good winter cold, without the everlasting damp Chicago wind. The valve (brass) instruments were all frozen, and the hall cold, so it was quite a time before we got started with the concert. The hall is unsatisfactory, owing to the narrow stage. To-night we leave by special train for Cleveland, after the concert. A telegram received yesterday announces that Materna is not available for the concert of the musical club. Probably the ladies did not calculate that the prima donna would cost more than the tenor they had thought of engaging, and did not find it out till the last minute. They are learning something, poor things. Music is a rare pleasure when everything in the conditions and surroundings harmonizes, but it is only one step from the beautiful to the ugly and unsatisfactory. I hope you are having a nice time while I am gone, and I only wish that I could have it a little easier, but that is impossible, and I simply have to go on as long as this old body can stand it. The summer is, at least, a refreshing time to think of.

" How is our little new library building getting on? It will be a comfort to have an extra room for the music, and I shall enjoy having a billiard table again for a little change and relaxation.

" Now, I'm off to the hall, to try and improve the seating of the orchestra a little. My lame arm has a little needed rest to-day, as I did not rehearse because the men also need rest in order to do good work, or to work with pleasure."

" CLEVELAND, *Feb.* 15, 1896.

" Once more I am rolling about over this country, and this time the trip is not so pleasant as the last. This is the first and only moment I have had since leaving home when I could write you. The weather is mild, but the hotels, cars, and halls are all heated to meet the most intense cold, and have been simply horrible. That I am not sick is a wonder. The present hotel is better, and I am fairly comfortable, but my nerves are jumping so that I can hardly hold a pen. Our experiences on this tour have been very disagreeable all along, in other ways than physical discomfort. In Detroit there was trouble with the soloist. I did not personally exchange a word with him, but I am told that the newspapers have given a more sensational account of the matter. In Pittsburg we played to the smallest audiences of my life. For the last night some tickets were even given away, to have some people there to play to !—

a strange experience in Pittsburg, where I have played
for so many years to good houses. It seems that the opponents of the musical club which engaged us were very
active in working against us, while the club itself did nothing to counteract the opposition. In Toledo we also discovered some enemies. It is too absurd, but nevertheless
annoying. Conditions change constantly, but while the
people have now learned that there is such a thing as art,
they have as yet little use for it, and so we cannot suit
them. Beside all these unpleasantnesses I have had a
stiff back all the week, which is hard to bear, for it is
torture to stand all the evening on the platform and
conduct.

" As a compensation, our manager tells me that for the
spring engagement in New York, the Metropolitan Opera
House is already so well sold that it will probably be sold
out by the time the concerts are given. That is certainly
more than I expected. I hope that conditions will be
favorable and that we can do ourselves justice. Brooklyn and Philadelphia are also sold, so that the Eastern
trip looks promising, and I trust may turn satisfactorily.
But you know I have never felt very confident of a friendly
welcome in New York for the Chicago Orchestra, and as
for myself, I also have enemies as well as friends there."

The Eastern engagement, alluded to in the last
letter, was scheduled to come off in March, when
Thomas was to return to his old home and give a
short series of concerts for the first time since he
had moved to Chicago. The prospect of this engagement made him strangely anxious all winter,
in anticipation. The Western orchestra, although
now a splendid body of musicians, still had its old

weak spot in the discrepancy between the " regular " and the " extra " men. This was always a source of worry to Thomas, even in Chicago, and made him still more anxious about concerts in the Eastern cities, where, for the honor of the Association, he was especially anxious to have the orchestra shine. In the ordinary tours over the Western " Highway," he only took the " regular " men, so there was no difficulty of this sort then. But the Eastern concerts demanded the full strength of the organization, and there he must take the " extra " men also. Consequently, he began a special training of the whole force, on the Eastern programmes, in the fall, and kept it up continuously all winter. Every number which was to be played in the East was put on the programmes of the Chicago concerts in the course of the season, and the symphonies were played many times, there and elsewhere, until there was not a musician in the orchestra to whom every lightest shade of expression was not as familiar as household words, and on these programmes, at least, the orchestra was as thoroughly equalized as the famous old Thomas Orchestra of New York ever was in its palmiest days.

At last the winter season was over, and the time came for this important trying-out of the Western organization before the public of New York and the adjacent cities. The first concert took place on a certain Tuesday in March, and the great Metropolitan Opera House was nearly filled with an audience which seemed to be composed only

Theodore Thomas in His Study, Chicago

of personal friends, it was so enthusiastic and determined to give a warm and affectionate welcome to their old leader.

At the close of the concert Thomas was presented with a laurel wreath, and in short, the evening passed off very successfully. The second concert of the series was made memorable to him by the presentation of a large silver loving cup, on which was engraved: " To Theodore Thomas, the great conductor, the true man, and the cherished friend, in admiration and love, from Ignace J. Paderewski." Thomas, like all public men, was the recipient of a great many beautiful public gifts in the course of his life, such as ivory batons mounted in gold or jewels; silver punch bowls, loving cups, and centerpieces; engrossed testimonials, watches, and similar costly souvenirs of special events or musical organizations with which he was connected. But nothing of this kind ever came to him that gave him more pleasure than this unexpected gift. Paderewski was not in America at the time, but he knew that the first engagement of the Chicago Orchestra in New York would have an unusual significance for Thomas, and it occurred to him to aid in enhancing its festal character, by sending his beautiful personal tribute to be presented then.

A pleasant incident of another kind took place at the third concert of the series. It chanced that the Boston Symphony Orchestra was also in New York, giving concerts, and as they were to have no performance at the hour when Thomas was giving a matinée, many of them came to the box office to buy tickets for it. The relations between the two orchestras had always been of the most friendly character, and when it came to the ears of Thomas and his manager that they would like to hear the concert, an invitation was sent to the entire orchestra, to attend in a body, and was promptly accepted. They all came, attended by their celebrated conductor, Wilhelm Gericke. The Chicago Orchestra naturally felt this to be a great compliment, and never did it give a better performance. Each man was determined to do his very best. Afterwards, the Boston men came behind the scenes and the two orchestras had a pleasant half-hour together. It seemed a pity that, when the two greatest symphony orchestras of the world were on the same stage, they could not have united together in playing one splendid musical number before separating.

At the final concert still another presentation took place. This time the musicians and music lovers of New York gave Thomas a large silver centerpiece, which was brought upon the stage during the intermission, and formally presented with an appropriate speech by Mr. Gerritt Smith. For once in his life, Thomas had to say something to the audience in reply. Speech-making was not one of his specialties, and he would not attempt to do anything in public which he could not do well. Stepping to the front of the stage, therefore, he simply said: " Ladies and Gentlemen, I could never make a speech in my life, but I beg you to believe that I thank you heartily," and as soon as the long-continued applause would permit, mounted the conductor's stand and proceeded with the programme. The designer of this beautiful piece of silver, Mr. Paulding Farnham, one of the artists of Tiffany & Co., described its elaborate symbolism as follows:

" The outline and general intention of this piece represent a crown. The Greeks were the first to use a band of twisted laurel twigs to confer distinction, and sometimes oak leaves were also used, to denote strength of feeling and hospitality. In the present instance these are all intended to signify the exalted position of the recipient. The conventional form of a crown indicates a master. The violin, his favorite instrument, plays an important part in the volute of the handles. Around the base, on heart-shaped spaces, are medallions of the great musicians whose art it has been the life-work of Mr. Thomas to interpret, and one of himself in the center. Between these medallions is the torch of Hymen, denoting the marriage of the musical art and the man who represents it. The swans of Lohengrin lend their graceful outlines to the general significance of the lower section. The loops of the crown, above this gallery of masters, are strengthened by garlands of ivy leaves—denoting friendship. Topping these are oak leaves, each of which supports a triumphal *Bambino*, which lends elevation and harmony to all these attributes of genius. A Greek ornamental lyre at intervals around the top assists the whole poetic construction to form a vessel of practical dimensions for either a centerpiece for flowers and fruit, or a punch bowl. The approximate weight in sterling silver is two hundred ounces."

Taken for all in all, the visit of the Chicago Orchestra to New York was a success, and the warmth of his welcome, the large and appreciative audiences, and the beautiful tributes of one kind or another, which came to him, touched Thomas very deeply, and, as we were leaving the city, he exclaimed sadly, "Oh, New York, New York— it must be a poor sort of man who does not love his home!"

There is a good old German proverb which says: "It is so arranged that the trees do not grow into the heavens," and if Thomas experienced much that was pleasant during his New York engagement, he also had to take his full measure of criticism, for he had many bitter enemies there, In fact the majority of the press were hostile, rather than friendly towards him. Amongst those who were the latter, however, was Henry T. Finck, the eminent author and musical critic of the *Evening Post*. At the close of the engagement he summed up its results as follows:

" The results of Mr. Theodore Thomas' attempt to give seven concerts with his Chicago Orchestra in New York, in less than two weeks, may be summed up in the words that ' he got an encore '—that is to say that the concerts paid so well that it was not necessary to touch the guarantee fund, and that he has already decided to come again another year. The audiences grew larger and more enthusiastic with each succeeding concert, in spite of the virulent opposition of some of the newspapers,—an opposition which hurt its leaders much more than it did the leader of the Chicago Orchestra. . . . The enthusiastic

lovers of first-class music who attended the Thomas concerts, did not care whether Boston, New York, or London
had orchestras in which this or that individual player or
group of players was a trifle better or worse than the
corresponding ones in the Chicago Orchestra.   They knew
that with all the money placed at his disposal in Chicago,
Mr. Thomas would not lead a band of mediocre players.
But even if the players had been mediocre, the patrons
would have felt sure that he would make them play well,
and would interpret the music as they like to have it
interpreted, . . . and they flocked to the Thomas concerts
in ever-increasing numbers.   The result was that the second matinée wiped out every dollar of the heavy expenses,
and the receipts of the final concert were a net profit.
This information is official. . . . What struck me most
about this orchestra was its versatility.   It seemed to be
a different band to suit each different style of music.
Brilliant where brilliancy was called for, at other times
dignified and classic, delicate and tender, dreamy and romantic, or dramatic and thrilling, as in Mr. Thomas' own
arrangement of Chopin's ' Funeral March.'   In consequence of this versatility, which revealed the genius of
the conductor, there was a surprise in store for the audience at every concert, and it was not until the last had
been given that anyone could feel sure that he really knew
the full capacity of the Chicago Orchestra and its
conductor."

After his return to Chicago a brief interval
elapsed, and the second week in May saw Thomas
in Cincinnati, busy with the usual preliminary rehearsals for the festival of 1896.   At this festival
the two most important novelties given were Saint
Saens' " *Samson et Dalila,*" and Tinel's " Fran-

cis." Both were very elaborate and difficult compositions; that of Saint Saens, in particular, required an orchestra augmented to the largest proportions. In the ballet music there were even some instruments of percussion which are not to be found in the most complete orchestral organization, and these Thomas had had made especially, while in Europe the previous summer. We were in Paris when they arrived, and as they lay on the table in Thomas' hotel room, Saint Saens himself entered. Seeing the familiar instruments, he asked what they were for, and on being told that they were for a festival performance of his own work, he was quite delighted, and picking them up, adjusted them on his hands and proceeded to play the part for which they were designed. His performance was not lost on Thomas, and when the passage was given in Cincinnati, every shade of intonation and rhythm was reproduced to the life, exactly as Saint Saens had played it.

And now, his duties ended for a time, Thomas was free to go to Fairhaven and enjoy home life. Unfortunately, the climate of Fairhaven was even damper than that of Chicago, and the Thomas estate itself, although large and beautiful, offered him no out-of-door occupation, for it was all under the cultivation of an expert gardener. Thomas did not care to cultivate flowers or run the lawn-mower, for exercise, and longed for a bit of forest, wild and untouched, which he could trim and chop for himself. He had bought such

a little tract of land on the eastern slope of what
is now called " Mount Theodore Thomas," in
Bethlehem, N. H., two years previously, and
now decided to build a cottage there, and spend
a portion of each summer in the woods, hoping thereby to counteract the bad effects of the
Chicago climate, and get rid of his catarrh. When
July came, therefore, I was sent to Bethlehem
to superintend its construction, while enjoying the
hospitality of our kind friends, Mr. and Mrs.
Glessner. The following letters, which he wrote
me at this time, chronicle only the simple happenings of home life, but they are inserted to show
how great a change had now come over his
prevailing mood. The old bitterness had passed
away, the old anxiety was laid to rest, and, under
the new consciousness of comradeship and support
in his professional work, the naturally genial,
hopeful nature of Thomas budded and blossomed
afresh as in the springtime of youth.

" FAIRHAVEN, MASS., *July* 8, 1896.

" I hope you reached your destination at the Glessners
as promptly as I reached home yesterday. After I had
seen you safely on the train in Boston, I had to wait
until a quarter before eleven before my own train left,
but I reached New Bedford a little after twelve, walked
across the river, and, as I stepped into the house the dinner-
bell was ringing. I was very glad to be back in this restful place. One needs to go away from home sometimes
to appreciate it, but I need only half a day for that, and
I really felt as worn out as if I had been on a concert tour
—like our friend P., who was all broken up because he had

sat up two nights previously until twelve o'clock! Well, I did not sit up till twelve, but went to bed early and took the dog into my room to console him for your absence. He rewarded me by waking me up a dozen times in the night, and this morning I told Hulda.that she might have him back again.

"By this time you have probably seen our place, and decided where you are going to locate the cottage. I hope the place looks as pretty as I remember it, and that you have better weather there than we are having here to-day. It is very sultry and Dicky goes into the remotest corner of your closet and curls himself up there to sleep. I am very well; in fact, I have not felt so well for a long time—free from any ache. Perhaps the effect of rest begins to tell upon the body. I have only one complaint to make now, and that is, I fear, a chronic one with me, namely, that time goes too fast. I mean I do not accomplish enough. Mees comes to-morrow to talk over our chorus plans for next winter."

July 13.—"I have suspended work to write to you, and see if I can get into a peaceful frame of mind. Musical work is restful to me in one way, because I can do it to my satisfaction in regard to *quality*, but never in regard to *quantity*—there is so much to be done. The weather here is midsummer, no doubt about that. It is corn weather: the thermometer crawls up to near ninety degrees, but our front porch is always cooled by the sea breezes. The dog sleeps so restlessly that now he disturbs the girls, and to-night I shall open all doors and windows in the second story and let him sleep where he likes.

"I am not surprised at your experiences in building the cottage. I always thought that you could not get what you planned for the sum you allowed, for the moment one wants something pretty and harmonious, one must have better workmen, allow more time, and buy better material. However, thus it is in this world, and you will have to console yourself with the thought that it will be less trouble and expense to take care of the 'shanty,' than it would have been to look after the stone cottage with the red-tiled roof and finishings to correspond, which you first had in mind. After all, this is as it should be, for when you and I go to the mountains it is with the idea of having a ' nature spree.' We do not want household, or any other cares there.

" On account of the hot weather, I do not try to do anything out of doors, for it is not good for me to exercise in the heat of the sun. I have not even been to drive since you are gone. I cannot tell you what I have learned this summer from the dog and the horses. One can learn, of course, every day, if one only knows enough to apply it."

July 17.—" At last we have pleasant weather again, and I even had to put on an extra blanket last night. The large Braun photographs, purchased in Boston, have arrived. While they do not quite come up to my expectations, they have, nevertheless, changed the whole atmosphere of the house enough to give me much pleasure, and, since we cannot afford to buy great paintings, I prefer the photographs of master-works rather than inferior paintings. I wish we had a little money to spend on such things, for I find them not only satisfactory but very inciting. One cannot look at such a picture as, for instance, that of the Michael Angelo sculpture, without being reminded of the man who created it, and it is strengthening to the soul. How those old fellows worked, and what an age they reached!

"Studying my own nature, I believe that I have a very unhappy temperament. No one can be more conscious of this than I am, but I cannot change myself, and am afraid I shall never be able to as long as it burns in me. As Goethe says, 'Life is short, but art is long.' At all events I am good-natured and generous, fortunately. And now I think it is time for you to come home. You belong to my world, and my world is very small."

July 22.—"Do you expect me to write a nice letter to-day? Let me tell you that you can be glad if I send you any letter at all! However, I suppose it is not your fault that you are detained. What keeps you? Is it the water-works, or the contractor, or the mason? *Donner und Blitzen!!* I feel like letting the '*Walkueren-Ritt*' loose, and taking the first cloud that comes along and riding up to Felsengarten to give those fellows a ducking! Or perhaps they are on a strike, and since they have heard the outlandish name of our place, think we ought to pay more?

"Peter is getting quite crazy because you do not arrive. First he had the place, and your garden and the hedges all trimmed and fresh for last Saturday, thinking you would be home. When he heard from me that you were not coming before Wednesday he exclaimed, 'Oh, father!' Then, when I told him your coming was postponed till Saturday again, he gave up. He says 'everything will grow on him again.'

"Answering your question in regard to my system of uniform bowing in the orchestra; uniformity of bowing is, in my opinion, necessary for a good performance of orchestral music. The bow ought to be to the violinist what the breath is to the singer. But the bowing makes the phrasing of a composition, and is therefore dependent on

the conception of the conductor.   Nor is it always practical for dramatic works where singers constantly change,
and the *tempo* is influenced by the quality and expression
of the voice.   Is this what you wanted to know? " *

The little cottage in the White Mountains was
finished in time for us to go there for a few days
before returning to Chicago and try the new kind
of life we had planned to live there.   It was not
intended to be a home, but a sort of camp or
bungalow where we could go for short stays from
time to time through the summer.   Our domestic
arrangements were of the simplest.   We took no
servants with us, but cooked our own breakfast
and supper, and drove down to one of the hotels
in the village for dinner.   The time between
meals was spent out of doors, working, or perhaps
I should say, playing in the open air.   The place
was a very rough, partly wooded tract of ground,
strewn with giant bowlders, and seamed with the
outcropping crests of foundation rock.   It was
this last characteristic which suggested its name
" Felsengarten " (Rock Garden), for even before
we began the work of decoration and improvement, its open spaces were brilliant with the blos-
soms of golden-rod, asters, wild spirea, and daisies.
The place was so high on the mountain side that
the air was dry and clear, and the woods were
chiefly of the coniferous trees, so that it was an

* Thomas was the first to introduce uniform bowing into the
orchestra, and even as late as 1895 when we were in Europe, it was
not in use in the great orchestras of London, Paris, and Berlin
which we heard.

ideal place in which to conquer catarrh. Thomas
had never before lived in the real country—for
even the Fairhaven place was more of a suburban
than a country residence—and he took the greatest
delight in the work of beautifying this little spot of
ground which he felt was so peculiarly *his own*.
In winter, when he was tired or sleepless, he would
calm himself by planning what he would do to it
during the following summer, and when the summer came he would carry out his design with his
own hands. Although he had never done anything
of this kind before, his general design for the
landscape architecture of the place could hardly
be improved upon; he seemed to know by intuition
just what was the most appropriate treatment for
every corner of it, and to-day it is the Mecca to
which many tourists come every summer and
revel in its exquisite beauty.

From henceforth life brightened for Thomas, and
with the exception of one deep grief, which came to
him some years later in the death of his eldest son,
the troubles and trials of his life were over. Some
anxiety and much hard work, it is true, the future
still had in store, but nothing that made him sad
or unhappy.

CHAPTER XX

1895-1904

THE affairs of the Association looked more
hopeful, at the close of the season of 1895-96, and
the trustees thought they might now venture on
starting a chorus, similar to that Thomas had had
in New York, for the same class of musical performance. When he returned to Chicago, in the
fall of 1896, he found Arthur Mees, who had been
engaged as his assistant conductor and chorus
director, hard at work rehearsing the new chorus
and preparing it for performances to be given
during the latter part of the season. But, although
the chorus would not be ready for its official
début for some months to come, Thomas, never-

453

theless, utilized it in the second concert of the season, but in such a way that no one in the audience knew it was there. The circumstances of this concert were peculiar. It was to take place on the eve of a presidential election over which there was the most intense popular excitement. As a stimulant to the patriotism of the Chicago men, Thomas was asked to play " The Star-spangled Banner" on the Saturday night programme. It was too late to change the programme, which had already been printed, but Thomas consented to add it after the close of the concert. The last piece on the programme happened to be Massenet's quiet and almost ethereal Suite, " Les Erinnyes," and the audience, one which completely filled the great Auditorium. As no one was expecting the added number, Thomas had to do something to keep the people in their seats while he accomplished the difficult transition from the music of a Greek drama to that of an American patriotic scene. In this emergency, he bethought him of the device he had employed at the opening ceremonies of the World's Fair. His new chorus were seated in the front rows of the parquet, to lead the singing of the audience, and a drum corps was placed on the stage behind the orchestra. As the last strains of the Massenet Suite were still vibrating on the strings, the drums began a double roll so softly that it was barely audible. Louder, louder, and still louder it rose, till every heart began to beat wildly with excitement, wondering what was coming next. At last the moment of climax was reached, and then Thomas turned toward the audience, motioned to them to rise and sing, and, with the full power of the orchestra, the great organ, the chorus, and the five thousand people of the audience, all joining together in one stupendous maelstrom of sound, "The Star-spangled Banner" was given such a performance as is not often heard. Many people were in tears before it was over, and when Thomas held aloft both hands to sustain through the full measure its final glorious chord, the singing was merged in a great shout—cheer on cheer echoing through the hall. So profound was the effect of this performance that, since that night, Chicago audiences always rise, and remain standing, when "The Star-spangled Banner" is either played or sung in concert.

Meantime the financial improvement of the previous spring had evaporated, and the Association found itself as far as ever from the solution of its problem of self-support. There were not lacking people who attributed the empty seats at the concerts to the severity of the programmes, and clamored for more popular music. This was brought to the ears of Thomas, and, knowing full well the difficulties under which the trustees were carrying on the work, he decided to lay the following communication before them at one of the meetings of the Board:

"Gentlemen: In view of the recent statements of our manager, I feel it my duty to urge upon you the con-

sideration of certain points, before we make contracts, or
enter upon plans for continuing, during the coming year,
the work so nobly started by you in this city.

" First, however, let me remind you that in no city in
the world is there an annual series of forty-eight orchestral concerts of the highest class attended by so large an
average audience as that which patronizes the concerts
of the Chicago Orchestral Association. In no city in
the world is there an orchestra of the size and perfection
of ours, maintained without a large subsidy in addition to
the box-office receipts. And in no other city in the world,
except Boston, is there such an orchestra maintained
exclusively for concert purposes. Hence we may conclude
that the Chicago public has shown its readiness to support
its orchestra and attend the concerts in a ratio greater
than that shown by the people of the great European art
centers, and certainly in as great a ratio as can reasonably
be expected at the present time.

" After spending more than forty years of my life in
making orchestral programmes for the American public—
during nearly thirty of which I have given concerts in Chicago—it is my firm and unalterable belief that the better
and higher the work offered to the American people, the
more readily they will support it. And they will absolutely
not support any art work which is of inferior quality or
standard. No radical change in the programmes therefore
would, in my judgment, be of any avail in selling our
tickets, or raising our subscription fund. On the contrary, the howl which the critics of Eastern papers would
instantly raise over the inferior standard of our programmes, would react upon our guarantors and subscribers
in the most disastrous manner. Furthermore, the Chicago public is itself too enlightened now to give its support to any series of concerts of which the programmes

were made in accordance with the taste of the ignorant only. Such, at least, is my judgment after many years of experience. Nor would I be willing personally, for the few remaining years of my public career, to adopt a standard of art inferior to that which it has been the one object of my whole life to establish.

" Such being the case, it is evident that while I continue to be the musical director of the Association, no radical change in its musical policy can possibly take place. But I feel, at the same time, that I have no right to force my individual opinions upon you, knowing, as I do, the heavy financial burden its maintenance involves. This you have borne cheerfully for six years, and I therefore wish to state that if you feel that the Association can no longer be maintained upon so high an artistic plane as heretofore, I am ready at any moment to resign my position as musical director, and give you the opportunity to try the experiment of interesting the public more generally by popularizing the programmes.

" I make the above statement in all friendship and kindly feeling for all with whom it has been my pleasure and privilege to have been associated in our mutual work in this city. I know that it is your endeavor as well as my own to establish a great art institution here, and if we have not been able to make it permanent, it is because the time is not yet ripe for it. I hope you will now feel perfectly free to take any course you think best for the welfare of the orchestra. In closing I beg you to accept my grateful acknowledgments for the cordial sympathy and support with which you have honored me during the six years of our association."

To the surprise of Thomas the trustees of the Association simply scoffed at the idea of popularizing the programmes or lowering the standard of the institution in any particular, nor would they hear of his resigning. They did, however, recognize the need of some special effort to raise money for the work, and as a preliminary to this they published, toward the end of the season, the following summary of the financial history of the orchestra:

"For the information of the friends of the orchestra, the trustees herewith submit the following statement:

"It was never proposed that the orchestra should be a money-making organization, and though not extravagantly managed, it has not been carried on as such. Its necessary expenses have exceeded box-office receipts every year, and every year it has received, at first from its guarantors, latterly from its governing members (a different name for the same good friends), a heavy donation, never quite sufficient, however, to cover the loss. A deficit has, therefore, accumulated as follows:

Loss first season, 1891-2................		$53,907.99
Paid by guarantors.....................		49,000.00
Carried forward....................		$ 4,907.99
Loss second season, 1892-3..............		51,381.18
		$56,289.17
Paid by guarantors.....................		49,000.00
Carried forward....................		$ 7,289.17
Loss third season, 1893-4...............		48,972.21
		$56,261.38
Paid by guarantors...........	$49,000.00	
Paid by guarantors, extra subscription	7,261.38	56,261.38
Carried forward....................		$ 000.00

Loss fourth season, 1894-5................   34,474.02
Uncollectable accounts charged off........   1,436.80

                                              $35,910.82
Paid by governing members................   30,850.00

  Carried forward......................... $ 5,060.82
Loss fifth season, 1895-6..................   27,159.73

                                              $32,220.55
Paid by governing members................   23,700.00

  Carried forward........................ $ 8,520.55

" It will be seen that each year hitherto the loss has been reduced; yet nevertheless the orchestra commenced the current season (1896-7) over $8,500 in debt, and it is evident that the acute business depression of the last few months will result in a loss at least as great as last year's ($27,000), against which governing members have pledged about $23,000. By the end of the season, therefore, the association will owe upwards of $13,000, a debt dangerous to the life of the institution.

" The trustees believe that there are in Chicago many hundred men and women of public spirit, lovers of music and friends of the orchestra, who need but the knowledge of the emergency and the opportunity of meeting it to prove their interest and give their powerful support. To all such the trustees confidently appeal for aid in one or more of the following ways—viz.:

" By their subscriptions to and presence at the promenade concert.

" By season subscriptions to the concerts next year.

" By becoming governing members of the association."

Following this report, came the announcement of a spectacular benefit concert, which it was hoped would go far towards clearing off the little debt of

$8,000, and which would easily have done so had
it been well managed. This concert was of the
" Promenade " class, and was so beautiful in both
design and execution that it deserves a detailed
description. It was divided into three sections: the
first, orchestral; the second, choral, and the third,
devoted to the dance. The seats were taken out of
the parquet of the Auditorium and a ballroom
floor was laid. A low stage for the orchestra was
built somewhat out from the end of the hall, and
the audience sat in the boxes and balconies. The
first part of the programme served to fill up the
time while the audience was assembling, and to
prepare for what was to follow. Then came a long
intermission for conversation. The second part
was to be choral, but when Thomas raised the
baton for the March from " Tannhaeuser," there
was no chorus to be seen, nor any apparent provision for their accommodation on the stage. As
the first note of the Tannehaeuser March sounded,
however, two large doors at the opposite end of the
hall were thrown open, and through them entered a
double procession of white-robed women, followed
by an equal number of men in the conventional
" uniform " of evening dress. The two proces-
sions encircled the hall, and finally came to a stand
in front of the stage, where they sang their numbers, retiring after they were ended in the same
manner, to the strains of the March from " Lohengrin." Then followed another intermission, and
then the last part of the programme, devoted to
dancing. Like the others, it opened with a bril-

liant march, and again the doors were thrown open to admit a double procession. This time, however, it was composed of many handsome young society belles and beaux, dressed in the picturesque costume of a bygone age. Powdered hair, patches, satin, brocade, velvet, and lace shimmered into the great hall, as the dancers moved with slow and stately grace to take their places for the Court Minuet. It was a wonderfully beautiful spectacle, and exceedingly well carried out in all its details. After the Minuet Thomas did something that he never did, before or after, in his life, conducting three numbers for everyone to dance by, and for half an hour the concert was converted into a brilliant ball. This last feature was not added to the programme without some protest on the part of the orchestra, who felt that it was beneath their dignity to play for dancing. To this Thomas replied curtly: "Those who object to playing for these dances may stay away, but *I* shall be there and conduct them, whether there are any of the orchestra there to play or not." As may be imagined, after this every man was in his place when the evening came. In fact, Thomas saw nothing derogatory to the dignity of the Association or his own artistic standing, in giving an occasional spectacular programme to raise money for the cause. He did it on several occasions, and would take as much trouble to plan such a programme effectively, as any other. His innate sense of harmony and perfection would not let him slight anything that he took in hand, and he even enjoyed planning something of this sort, once in a while, just to show what he could do in a line so different from his own. The programme of the concert just described is a good example of his work of this class, and is well worth studying for its artistic completeness, the harmony of its parts, the appropriateness of its selections, and the steady crescendo of its interest, which worked the audience up to a more and more vivid excitement until it culminated in their all taking part themselves in the final numbers:

PROMENADE CONCERT
GIVEN FOR THE BENEFIT OF THE CHICAGO ORCHESTRA
April 27, 1897

Jubilee Overture..............................Weber
Dances from Suite " Henry VIII ".............German
Polonaise, op. 53, A flat.............Chopin-Thomas
Intermission
March and Chorus, " Tannhaeuser ".........Wagner
Introduction and Bridal Chorus, " Lohengrin "..Wagner
March, " Lohengrin ".....................Wagner
Chorus and Orchestra
Intermission
March, " Triumphant Entrance of the Boyards,"
Halvorsen
Minuet, " Don Giovanni ".....................Mozart
Danced by Thirty Couples in Court Costume
Waltz, " On the Beautiful Blue Danube ".......Strauss
Waltz, " Artists' Life ".......................Strauss
Polka Schnell...............................Strauss
General Dancing

The summer season was, as usual, passed between the seashore and mountain places, and the
dry clear atmosphere of the latter, with its health-
giving out-of-door work by day, and long nights
of sound, quiet sleep, again worked miracles on
both catarrh and rheumatism. The latter, indeed,
was permanently cured, and never troubled
Thomas again, but the catarrh was not so easily
conquered, and although it yielded temporarily,
and seemed to be cured every summer, a few
weeks in the Chicago climate brought it quickly
back again. At last the predictions of the doc-
tors began to be verified, and Thomas noticed,
with sad forebodings, that the hearing of his right
ear was growing dull.

A composer whose works often appeared on the
programmes of Thomas, and who was peculiarly
warm in his appreciation of it, was Massenet.
His little notes of thanks were very brief, but
quite characteristic. The following was received
from him in August, in acknowledgment of some
programmes on which Thomas had placed, for
the first time, his Suite " *Les Erinnyes* ":

Mr. Theodore Thomas.   Paris, *August*, 1897.
 Dear and great Master:
 I am touched and very, very much honored by your
attention. Accept all my acknowledgments. My thanks
also for the programmes.
           Massenet.

French music appealed very sympathetically to
Thomas, and he played it a great deal. He loved
its beauty of finish, and its masterly orchestration,

and held in the highest esteem the many French composers and musicians with whom he came in contact. It was always a source of much regret to him that he had not had time in his busy life to learn to speak their language, so that he could have had the same delightful intercourse ·with them as with the composers of other nationalities, most of whom spoke either German or English. But in spite of his very limited knowledge of French, Thomas, nevertheless, contrived to have some pleasant evenings with his French friends. One of these at which César Thomson had been his guest, was described to Paderewski by Thomson after his return home: "·What language did you and Thomas speak?" asked Paderewski with some curiosity. "*Volapuk,*" promptly replied the ready Frenchman.

Another composer who sent an appreciative word to Thomas at this time was the great Bohemian Dvořák, who was then the Musical Director of the National Conservatory of New York. Dvořák had been to Chicago and directed the Thomas Orchestra in concerts of his own works at the World's Fair, and knew that Thomas had played everything that he had ever written for many years. In 1897 Thomas wished to have him come again to the Western metropolis, and conduct his own works, and the answer was as follows:

My dear Mr. Thomas: New York, *Oct.* 21, 1897.

I sincerely ask your pardon for coming so late with my answer to your kind letter, but I have been so occupied

with my concerts and my change of residence this whole
week that I could not make the time to reply before.

Now to the point. It would please me much to be able
to direct some of my works in Chicago, but I cannot do
so without the permission of Mrs. Thurber. Please wait
a little until the secretary of the Conservatory writes you,
and then I shall be able to decide.

Meantime please accept my heartiest thanks for all that
you have done for me and my art in this important country.

Gratefully and sincerely yours,

ANTON DVOŘÁK.

This concert was not, however, destined to take
place, and Dvořák returned to Bohemia without
again visiting Chicago a second time.

The winter season of this last year of the century, like that of two years before, was full of
preparations for a second tour to the great musical
centers of the East, in March. This time, not
only New York, but Boston was to be visited,
and it was with mingled feelings of pleasure and
anxiety that Thomas looked forward to conducting in the New England musical stronghold. It
was sixteen years since he had given a concert
there; meantime, as he said: " Children had been
born and grown to a concert-going age," and the
general public—always musically cultivated—had
been trained to the nicest discrimination through
the weekly performances of a Symphony orchestra
in no way inferior to his own. In view of the
ordeal of playing there, the ordeal of New York
was forgotten.

This important concert tour was the only event

of special interest during the season of 1897-98. Thomas took with him, as before, the full strength of the orchestra, and the route included, besides New York and Boston, Baltimore, Philadelphia, Washington, and several minor places. Of course the two first-named cities were its chief objective points. As before, the welcome of New York was that of the public rather than the press. The latter were divided, some were friendly, others hostile, but the welcome of the people was not to be mistaken. It was described as follows, by the musical critic of *Harper's Weekly*:

" The Chicago Orchestra and Mr. Thomas have reason to feel proud of their welcome here. The audience at the opening concert on Tuesday evening of last week was packed with the very pith of our town's real musical culture; and along with it was a large addition of the less specially perceptive listeners. Plainly, to each class the name of Mr. Thomas was obviously a conjuring one, as ever. And what a burst of greeting—downright, spontaneous, sincere, one might write affectionate—as he came before us again!—that familiar presence, not older by an inch of girth or the loss of a hair. The veteran conductor is serene as ever in the dignity of one who seems to have decided a few years ago to grow only elderly—and to stop there once for all. It was a great welcome. No other conductor could command in New York just that sort of a reception. Does Mr. Thomas still believe that New York neglected him and drove him away? He cannot point to any rival we have better served. In any case there is none whose personal magnetism with our public abides more indisputable. The concert was what one expected—an object-lesson as to what rich ensemble-perfectness a permanent, well-balanced orchestra (even if not one of all-round exceptional material) can attain, by learning and by minding only its own business; and by doing so under a great director's continued care. Of the Chicago men have been spoken good words here before now. But when here before now the large band was less fortunate in its rank and file. Now it is strengthened by certain new members, especially. It is vastly firmer in splendid unanimity, in its solid tone, its elegance of shading—all traits to be perfected only by seasons of work. Its strings—at least the violins—often seem singularly without brilliancy and resonance—what some French musicians call " legs." Even in a fortissimo they do not stand out with authority in the body of sound. But there are many things in an orchestra far more needed than brilliancy. Yes, this Chicago band, as it is to-day, has few peers. It is a noble and expressive corps, even if the Boston Symphony Orchestra outdoes it in fiddles and fire. Would it were ours!—this said without prejudice to what we have. It is a long time since we have had so shaded, so round, so wholly Beethovenish and classic an interpretation of Beethoven's C-major Symphony. Moreover, Richard Strauss' ' Don Juan ' poem was played really magnificently. As to the conducting, it was—as in so many former years—the kind that accomplishes all its work while veiling its dominancy over every man under its spell. Mr. Thomas has not lost that sensitiveness and knowledge, that half-disguised or seemingly careless eloquence of arm and eye, which used to mean such great leading of classics that we all understood why they were immortal. The evening was a triumph for the Chicago Orchestra, and a welcome to the director of it which must have moved even Mr. Thomas at least a trifle."—*Harper's Weekly*, March 10, 1898.

But if the New York season was successful, that of Boston was a triumph. Only three concerts were given there, in the old Music Hall of happy memory—now no longer the home of the muse who was its presiding genius for so many years. Boston has always had good musical writers on its press, but at this time the musical departments of three of its daily papers were in the hands of three of the ablest and most discriminating critics America has ever known—Messrs. Wolfe, Hale, and Apthorp. The notices of these eminent writers were in the nature of a careful and thorough analysis of Thomas as a conductor; of his artistic methods and achievements, and of the orchestra under his command. Space does not permit me to give all of them, but I have selected one or two from each writer, and, collectively, they give an accurate description of the Chicago Orchestra at its best, and of Thomas as an interpreter and conductor at this the culminating period of his artistic maturity:

FIRST CONCERT

" The programme of the first of three concerts by the Chicago Orchestra, Theodore Thomas, conductor, given in Music Hall last evening, was as follows:

Symphony, G minor (Koechel 550)............Mozart
Concerto for violin, E flat (Koechel 268).......Mozart
M. Ysaye
Overture, ' Coriolanus,' op. 62............... Beethoven
Tone poem, ' Don Juan,' op. 20........Richard Strauss
Symphonie Espagnole, op. 21...................Lalo
(For violin and orchestra)
Vorspiel, ' Lohengrin '........................Wagner

" Mr. Thomas may well be proud of his orchestra, and the Chicago Orchestra may well be proud of its leader.

" The hearty and prolonged applause that greeted him when he appeared on the stage was only a slight evidence of the deep affection and respect in which he is held by the musical public of this city. Interest in him was not abated when he gave up visiting Boston as a conductor. His career has been watched, his success applauded by those who recognize what he made and what he is still making for musical righteousness in this country. It may be many years before the history of music in the United States will be written. When it is written, the most prominent, the dominating figure of the nineteenth century, so far as this country is concerned, will be Theodore Thomas.

" The years have frosted his hair, but his figure is as erect, his bearing as graceful, his quiet authority as supreme as when he first visited us. I know of no conductor who has such despotic control over his men and at the same time commands so imperceptibly. His repose is so absolute that to the careless observer the conductor seems almost indifferent, but a look at his men brings forth a nuance when another would indulge in semaphoric gesture. The secret of all this is simple: The men are thoroughly rehearsed before they appear in public. They know what they are expected to do; they do it; and they could not do it otherwise. Hence there is no frantic appeal; wild beckoning, excited glare from the leader when all are before the audience. Mr. Thomas reminds them he is there; the army is eager to follow the general.

" Now I do not propose to talk in detail to-day about an orchestra that I have heard only once. There are two more concerts, and we can all judge more clearly of merits after another hearing. It is enough at present to make a few observations concerning the performance of last night.

" I have never heard in this country or in Europe so admirably balanced, so beautifully phrased, so discreetly colored, so thoroughly musical a performance of Mozart's immortal symphony as that led by Mr. Thomas last night. There was an unerring sense of proportion; there was the subordination of wind to strings, and strings to wind whenever such subordination was in the mind of the composer; there was the fitting, the inevitable, the only pace, not a matter of experiment, but as predestinated and sure as the movement of the stars. Nor was there merely a cold, anatomical, impeccable, pedagogic spirit that set a machine agoing and then stopped it. The spirit that acted as interpreter was a lover of Mozart as well as a student of that much-abused composer; an intelligent, masterly, virile lover, whose strength was shown in delicacy, whose affection never descended to sugared compliments, and airs and graces.

" Equally admirable was the strength of the reading and the performance of the ' Coriolanus ' overture. The austerity of the opening was Roman. The entreaty of the second theme was again Roman, dignified, not hysterical.

" And I confess that the performance of Strauss' ' Don Juan,' which was first played here under Mr. Nikisch in the fall of 1891, shook mightily the prejudice I had entertained against this tone-picture of the career and meditations of the hero whose life was spent in search of the ideal woman. The opening pages of the *allegro molto con brio* were taken with great spirit, with brilliance of sonority, and at the same time with solidity of volume, so that the effect was electric. And there were details in this same performance that should call forth purple praise,

Photograph by A. Cax, Chicago

Theodore Thomas in 1898

but the night editor is inexorable, and space is limited. . ."
—*Boston Journal*, March 23, 1898.

SECOND CONCERT

" The second concert of the Chicago Orchestra in Music
Hall attracted a very large audience.   The programme
was:

Suite, No. 3, D major........................Bach
Symphony, No. 2, D major, op. 73...........Brahms
Scene and aria, ' Ah! Perfido ' ....Beethoven
Bacchanale, ' Tannhaeuser '..................Wagner
Prelude and Isolden's Liebestod, ' Tristan and Isolde,'
                                          Wagner

" The orchestra fully sustained the fine impression it
made on Tuesday evening; in fact, intensified it.   The
strings came out more brilliantly and with a larger effect,
and the wood wind was less timid.   It seemed as if both
Mr. Thomas and his players had gauged the acoustics
of the hall more thoroughly, and this better acquaintance
resulted in a more compactly solid body of tone.   The
interpretation of the interesting and singularly well-
balanced programme was splendid throughout.   Mr.
Thomas' conducting, in its ease, its unobtrusiveness, and
its repose, was again a constant satisfaction.   It was none
the less effective for the relentless self-repression that
marked it.   Nothing of warmth nor of flexibility was lost
by this method; and the enthusiasm of the players was
not damped because they were not goaded.
" The Bach suite was read with noble breadth of style
and purity of taste.   Especially beautiful was the chaste
simplicity with which the familiar second movement was
given.   The bourrée and the gigue were read with stirring
spirit.   In the gavotte the high notes of the trumpet came

out with a firmness and a precision that are rarely accorded them. The whole seemed to be the very perfection of Bach interpretation.

" The reading of the Brahms symphony in its clearness, its self-consistency, the beauty with which every point was emphasized, the keen sympathy for the work in its every phase of expression, was as perfect in its way as was the notable reading of the Mozart symphony at the previous concert. The finish was of the highest, but nothing of largeness in sentiment was sacrificed.

" The phrasing throughout was wonderful, particularly in the slow movement, where it is fairly exquisite. Beauty of phrasing seems to be instinctive with Mr. Thomas. He is never at fault here, and the charm of it makes itself steadily felt. Another striking feature in him is the skill with which he preserves the flow of the music, thus keeping its meaning always clear, instead of confusing it by hysterical spasms of pseudo-emotion. The finale of the symphony was read and played with magnificent spirit, and in the closing climax the capabilities of the wind-instrument players was convincingly shown by the precision of accent with which they acquitted themselves of their difficult task, this portion of the movement being taken at a tremendous pace. The whole work has never been more splendidly given here than it was last night, nor has a performance of it been applauded with more enthusiastic sincerity.

" The ' Tannhaeuser ' bacchanale was rendered with stirring brilliancy and richness and variety of tone color. Here, as in the ' Tristan and Isolde ' selections, the unity, the compact closeness, and the firm sostenuto of the brass were as impressive as they were unusual. There are nothing but superlatives of praise for the interpretations of the Tristan prelude and the *Isolden's Liebestod*. The climaxes were worked up to with masterly power, and when they were reached the effect was overwhelming. Mr. Thomas' crescendos are always admirably prepared; they are begun far enough back, and their growth is steady until they culminate with enormous effect. Even when his orchestra is most demonstrative the result is never noise, never confusion; it is always musical. The fire with which the Liebestod was given in its more impassioned moments almost raised one to one's feet. Its force grew like that of an avalanche. It was overpowering. And yet clearness predominated through it all."—*Boston Herald*, March 25, 1898.

" The Chicago Orchestra gave its second concert in the Music Hall, last evening. . . . The event of the evening was the playing of the Brahms symphony. Here both conductor and orchestra simply outdid themselves. Saving some few places in the last movement, which did not sound quite clear, the great work was played in a way to call for nothing but the heartiest, the most unstinted admiration. And, be it said in passing, the few passages in the last movement, the rendering of which was not perfect, are of a sort that makes a falling short of perfection quite excusable; there are some things in orchestral music which can be played with full effect only when both conductor and orchestra are in their accustomed entourage, in a hall which they are fully used to. We doubt not that, in the Chicago Auditorium, these very passages would have come out as clear as the rest of the symphony; if Mr. Thomas and his orchestra had rehearsed in our Music Hall for a fortnight, instead of a day or two, we doubt not that they would have come out perfectly clear here. . . . We could fill a column with admiring remarks about it; Mr. Thomas' reading of the score was so sympathetic, so exhaustive of its meaning, and the orchestra carried out his idea so thoroughly, that it could be called nothing less than great.   Let us expatiate only upon one point—his 'modifications of the *tempo*.' (We put the quotation-marks for reasons which will not escape some of our readers.)   Mr. Thomas' modifications of the *tempo* in this symphony of Brahms' were always in place, always to the point; not because they were sudden or gradual, strongly marked or delicate, but solely and simply because they seemed artistically inevitable, and not dictated by any mere whim of the conductor; they carried conviction with them because one felt that the music could not go otherwise, that such a passage could not be played without hurrying, that such another could not be played without holding back.   The inner necessity of the thing was always patent.   Mr. Thomas never seemed to be merely aiming at an 'effect,' nor at impressing a pet idea of his own upon the audience.   When the *tempo* is 'modified' in this way, we applaud with hands and feet, and are as ready to burn incense at the shrine of the god Rubato as any enthusiast we know. . . ."—*Boston Transcript*, March 25, 1898.

THIRD CONCERT

" Yesterday afternoon the Chicago Orchestra, under the direction of Mr. Theodore Thomas, gave its last concert in Music Hall, the programme being:

Symphony, No. 5, C minor.................Beethoven
Concerto for piano in D minor.............Rubinstein
Symphonic Poem, ' Le Chasseur Maudit '...César Franck
Two Polish Songs.......................Liszt-Chopin
Espagnole ....Moszkowski
Marche Militaire......................Tausig-Schubert

" Mr. Josef Hofmann was the soloist.

" Again are superlatives of admiration due Mr. Theodore Thomas, this time for a glorious rendering of the Beethoven symphony. There was nothing new in the interpretation, except that it was Beethoven pure and simple; Beethoven relieved of the burden of varied readings that has been foisted on him from time to time in the shape of vagaries in *tempi, rubato,* modernism generally; Beethoven, in which the individuality of the conductor was permitted to disappear and that of the composer to predominate. In this reading Fate did not knock at the door, as if it was inspired by an angry desire to batter down a portal of bronze; nor did it linger long enough between its assaults to give time for the repairing of whatever damage it might have done. Wonderfully fine was the phrasing throughout the whole of the first movement, and wonderfully clear did every orchestral device come out.

" The scherzo was perfectly read, and at a pace and with a charm of color, and, at times, with a long-missed and appropriate delicacy that did the movement every possible justice. The precision of attack and the unity of the basses in the trio were precision itself. The break into the martial, triumphant outburst of the finale was magnificently managed, and the noble strain for once was given forth with thrilling majesty of effect, owing to a proper appreciation of the large and massive dignity that was imparted to it. And these results were achieved so quietly, but so imperatively, by the conductor, that the listeners were never disturbed in their enjoyment of the music.

" The performance was as splendid as the reading, and was rewarded by as enthusiastic a tribute of applause as has ever been bestowed on the rendering of a symphony in Music Hall; to say nothing of the two hearty recalls to which Mr. Thomas was forced to respond.

" The symphonic poem by Franck was heard here for the first time. It is strong in its orchestral color, and solid and brilliant in instrumentation, but is otherwise not particularly interesting. It has overmuch of repetitions, its tonality is irritatingly monotonous, and it takes too much time in saying the little it has to say. However, it afforded a good opportunity for the display of the orchestra's virtuosity.

" In the ' Meistersinger ' overture Mr. Thomas brought out effects that have hitherto been neglected, and reversed with advantage others that have been conspicuous. There was a broad sweep in the interpretation as a whole that gave a certain ' oneness,' so to speak, to the work that made the rendering singularly interesting and satisfying. Where the several themes are combined, there was not the usual ragged and disjointed effect, the prominence given to the prize song relegating the other parts to their due subordinate places as ingenious contrapuntal accompaniments to a main theme. The result was as surprising as it was delightful.

" Under the baton of Mr. Thomas even Wagner is always sane, and the conductor is a better friend to the composer than are the most pronounced Wagnerphile conductors themselves. With something more of Mr. Thomas as an interpreter of Wagner it would not be at all wonderful if reasonable Wagnerphobists came to the conclusion that the man of Bayreuth found his worst enemies among his professedly best friends, and was a much misunderstood and undeservedly reprobated innovator. . . . These three concerts just ended have been equally important and pleasurable features in the season's music. They showed that the West is far more advanced in musical taste and art than was suspected here, and they have shown Theodore Thomas still in the plenitude of his power as a conductor, and with a ripeness of experience and of skill that makes him more worthy than ever of the laurels he has so industriously and worthily won. Chicago is to be congratulated on its splendid orchestra, and on the possession of Mr. Thomas, who has made it what it is. . . ."—*Boston Herald*, March 27, 1898.

SUMMARY

" The full force of the Chicago orchestra is 99 men, or, if you choose to add the organist, Mr. Middelschulte, 100 men.

" And they are thus arranged: Fifteen first violins, 15 second violins, 9 violas, 10 'cellos, 9 double basses, 2 harps, 3 flutes, 1 piccolo, 3 oboes, 1 English horn, 2 clarinets, 1 bass clarinet, 3 bassoons, 1 double bassoon, 4 horns, 4 tuben, 2 cornets, 2 trumpets, 1 bass trumpet, 3 tenor trombones, I bass trombone, 1 bass tuba, 2 kettledrums, 1 small drum, I bass drum, 1 cymbals.

" The concertmaster is Mr. Leopold Kramer, a Bohemian by birth, who has been concertmaster in Berlin, Amsterdam, Cologne. He, as well as Mr. Bare, the second concertmaster, joined the Chicago Orchestra last fall. Mr. Bare is Viennese, a pupil of Hellmesberger and also of Massart. He has been concertmaster, I am told, with Lamoureaux and in orchestras at Cologne and Mayence. The other principals are Mr. Kühn, second violin; Mr. Keller, viola; Mr. Steindel, 'cello; Mr. Beckel, double bass; Mr. Quensel, flute; Mr. Starke, oboe; Mr. Schreurs, clarinet; Mr. Bachmann, bassoon; Mr. de Maré, horn; Mr. Ulrich, trumpet; Mr. Gerbhardt, trombone. Mr. Loewe is the first kettledrum. Mr. Edmund Schuecker, brother of Mr. Schuecker of the Boston Symphony Orchestra, is the first harp, and Mrs. Wunderle, the second.

" The strings are of a biting tone rather than sensuous. The 'cellos are perhaps a little dry. The violins in use are probably not as fine instruments as the best in the Boston Orchestra, and indeed there are few orchestras where so many violins are of fine quality. But the string band in the Chicago Orchestra has been so carefully trained that the results in performance are admirable. The uniformity in bowing is a delight to the eye. The attack is a model, and the phrasing of each division is as though it were the work of one thoroughly equipped and temperamental musician.

" I confess that Tuesday night I was disappointed in the first flute, but he afterward showed himself competent for the position. The orchestra did not know the hall at first, and it could hardly judge of requisite degrees of force after one rehearsal in an empty chamber. Tuesday night it seemed at times as though the orchestra was feeling its way. Thursday night it played with no greater precision or beauty of phrasing, but with more ease and confidence, as though it were at home.

" Now, precision in attacking and releasing chords is often not as marked in brass and wood-wind instruments as it is in strings. This cannot be said of the Chicago Orchestra, in which precision is universal. The individual tone of the first clarinet, horn, bassoon, and trumpet is a joy, and the ensemble of wood-wind and brass is as satisfactory as it was in that wonderfully drilled Meiningen Orchestra under von Bülow. . . . The chords are sustained as though they were played by a master on organ diapasons. There is a surprising solidity to this rockbed of brass. . . . The exceeding merit of Mr. Thomas as a drill master is so indisputable that I shall not waste time in praising the precision of his orchestra. But his drill is not that merely of a military martinet. He is a master of the phrase, as well as a master of rhythm. Take any melodic passage for violins or wood-wind. If the phrase is piano, it is played piano without unmeaning expression. The beauty of the phrase makes its way without the aid of rhetorical extravagance. And with what finish and subtlety is the phrase ended! How carefully are crescendos and diminuendos made, and yet with what apparent spontaneity! How clear is the dialogue between instruments! The answer to the question proposed is always in keeping. In the stormiest passages there is the feeling of reserve strength. The repose of this orchestra is never soporific; nor is it ever feverish; it is the repose of intelligence and confidence.

"It seems to me that in the accompaniment to Mr. Ysaye's performance of the violin concerto by Mozart the discipline, strength, and beauty of this orchestra were shown as clearly as in any purely orchestral selection. And yet this praise is invidious when I recall other accompaniments he played here, as that to Beethoven's ' Ah! perfido!'

"The visit of the Chicago Orchestra under Mr. Thomas was an education, as well as a pleasure, to us all. Personally, I could well have spared the presence of any soloists. . . . The visit of this orchestra was beneficial to the cause of music. It proved to us that Bach and Mozart are not hopelessly old fashioned, that Richard Strauss is not merely an extravagant young man. And Mr. Thomas gave an object-lesson in the art of conducting that should not be disregarded or speedily forgotten."— *Boston Journal*, March 27, 1898.

In Philadelphia, Baltimore, and Washington the concerts were also successful, and when, at last the engagement was ended, Thomas turned towards Chicago feeling very happy and contented over the results of the trip,—the last he ever made to his old home.

The Cincinnati Festival of 1898 brought the season to a close. Thomas had now reached his sixty-third year. His step was as light, his spirit as fresh, and his musical powers as commanding as ever, nevertheless, time was beginning at last to undermine his magnificent vitality, and he was no longer able to sustain the great strain and fatigue that his profession constantly demanded without feeling a corresponding reaction afterwards.

This was especially the case with the Cincinnati Festivals, and for some years, already, the reaction had been very heavy after them. But after that of 1898, it was so severe that it was startling. For an entire month he would sit all day in his chair, idle, and so exhausted that every few minutes his head would drop forward in a sort of lethargic sleep. Nature seemed to be absolutely spent, and he could neither read nor write nor even work out-of-doors. Gradually the rest, and perfect quiet of Felsengarten restored his exhausted vitality, and he resumed his customary way of life, but his family thought, nevertheless, that he ought to give up festival work in future. He himself also felt very dubious about continuing it, but he was so much attached to his Cincinnati co-workers, and the institution they had created together gave him such genuine artistic satisfaction that he could not bear to give it up, and, in spite of the warnings of nature, he conducted the festivals of 1900, 1902, and 1904.

When the fall of 1898 arrived, the Orchestral Association of Chicago faced a debt which now amounted to $30,000. Anything less indomitable than the Chicago "I will" spirit, would now have abandoned the hope of making the orchestra permanent. Not so the trustees. Instead, they took a course very characteristic of Chicago men. They gave a dinner, to which they invited all the wealthy and influential men who were interested in the orchestra. Every man who accepted the invitation knew that it was like to cost him dear, nevertheless, thirty-four willing victims gathered around the festal board on the appointed evening. The occasion was a very pleasant one, and so much enthusiasm for the cause of art was aroused that before they separated, they had not only subscribed enough to pay the $30,000 of indebtedness of the Association, but had subscribed an additional $30,000 as a sinking fund against a future debt of like dimensions.

This generous assistance enabled the trustees to go on with the work on the same artistic lines as before, but although the finances of the Association were, for the time being, on a sound basis, they realized the necessity of strict economy, and the chorus was therefore discontinued. There is no cloud without its silver lining, they say, and the loss of the chorus had, for Thomas, a very important compensation in bringing into the working force of the Association Mr. Fred-

erick J. Wessels.   After this able assistant and
good friend became the practical business manager of the orchestra, Thomas had such peace and
comfort in his professional life as he had never
known before, and even traveling engagements
were robbed of much of their terror by the thought
and care with which Mr. Wessels planned and
carried out the details of the work.

In April of this year Thomas received the following invitation from Colonne, the eminent
French conductor, to conduct some concerts at
the Paris Exposition of 1900:

THEODORE THOMAS, ESQ.   *April* 15, 1899.
    Dear Confrère:
    Amongst the attractions of the World's Fair of 1900
in Paris, is a restitution of " Old Paris," built on the
right bank of the Seine. . . . Here an immense hall with
a seating capacity of eighteen hundred, and furnished
with an organ, is now in process of construction. The
organizers of " Old Paris " have invited me to give there
a series of concerts with the orchestra I have conducted
for twenty-five years, during the whole period of the
Exposition . . . and I have accepted this task. I have
accepted it with all the more *empressement*, because it will
be a new opportunity for me to show with what large
eclecticism I have always regarded the question of recognizing French compositions without distinction of school,
and foreign works without distinction of nationality. This
principle guides me in the elaboration of my programme
. . . and for this reason I have reserved certain performances for the great artistic societies, French or foreign,
capable of entering into such a scheme, whether they bring

with them their own vocal or instrumental groups, or whether they make appeal to the assistance of our orchestra and chorus.

I establish thus, the grand outlines of music of all grades without neglecting the familiar kind which has given us such charming models.

It is a vast undertaking, the difficulties of which I do not dissemble to myself, but I hope to bring it to a successful issue with the help of the high personalities, vowed by rank and taste to the protection of musical art in each country. Under this title I now solicit your moral support in the work to which I have consecrated myself during the Exposition, and I would be greatly obliged if you would be willing to give me the authority to include you among those protectors of art who ought by their high position and the authority of their names to give to the work more extension and *éclat*, and who will constitute the Committee of Patronage of the Colonne Concerts at " Old Paris."

                    Yours truly,
                                    EDWARD COLONNE,
                            With sentiments
of cordial confraternity toward the eminent Maëstro Theodore Thomas, from his Parisian colleague, who will be very happy if he may give him the opportunity to be heard during the Exposition.

This invitation Thomas declined for a reason which seems very inadequate now, but which moved him strongly at the time; namely, the trial and condemnation of Dreyfus by the French government. Thomas considered it a piece of monumental injustice, and was so indignant about it that he was unwilling to accept an invitation which came to him, even indirectly, from a gov-

* Translated from the original French.

ernmental institution. He was, of course, very
happy to authorize Colonne to place his name on
the list of the " Patrons of Art," but he would
not appear in the concerts himself. It was a pity
that he felt thus about the matter, for there was
much interest in Paris over his proposed visit with
his orchestra. A correspondent of one of the
New York musical journals took the trouble to
interview some of the most important musical
authorities of Paris on the subject and the following answers were amongst many similar ones that
he received:

Lamoreux—" I think the concerts that Mr. Thomas
means to give in Paris with his orchestra will be of deep
interest, and that the great reputation of this celebrated
leader will assure their success."

Widor—" There is no reason to doubt the hearty welcome which Theodore Thomas and his orchestra will receive at Paris. We all know that this orchestra is one of
the first. Its reputation was made long ago, and this
opinion, which has never been questioned, has been con-
firmed by all my countrymen who have heard it. Thomas
is considered one of the first orchestra leaders of our
times."

Victorin de Joncières—" I am convinced that the reception of Theodore Thomas and his orchestra in Paris will
be most cordial. For my part, I shall be most happy to
appreciate *de auditu* the worth of a conductor and a body
of musicians so renowned."

The winter season of 1899 passed uneventfully,
and the early spring found Thomas and the or-

chestra enjoying a really pleasant tour in the Southern States. The following letters were written during this tour. Mr. Wessels had provided a private car for his accommodation, and the difference it made in the matter of his comfort can hardly be overestimated:

"ATLANTA, GA., *March* 13, 1900.

"Just a few lines to tell you that we are having the most beautiful weather. The railroads are of course very rough and the noise loud and sharp. Draughts cannot be avoided, but so far I am free from cold. The catarrh is loosening, but when I swallow, my left ear (the good one) is roaring. As for my right ear, I say as Liszt did about the weather, 'I take no notice of anything which takes no notice of me!' In the stateroom of my car I have a large double bed. The first night I did not sleep much, but last night it was better. Yesterday I climbed a real mountain, and walked through pine woods to reach the road again. The car and service are pleasant, and altogether I do not see but that this trip may even do me good, although the nightly concert is of course fatiguing."

Charleston, S. C.—"I have been hunting up old places here to-day, which I remember from 1849—a long time, is it not?—The former slave market has been built over, but I nevertheless found some traces of it. This is an interesting city, I should say the most so in this country. It has nothing in common with any other American city, unless it is New Orleans. The location is beautiful and the climate matches the location. I live in the car altogether now, and do not go to the hotels. This permits me to stay in bed as late as I please in the morning. To-day I had my breakfast at eleven, then I went out and walked until nearly four in the afternoon. I shall dine early. We have been very unfortunate in the weather for the concerts, and in the halls, so far. The first three days of our trip were very warm, and I was just preparing to change to thinner clothes when we struck rain and cold weather at Montgomery, together with a newly erected building. It was very cold and damp, for there is no provision for heating in this part of the world. That day we had two concerts, and a poor hotel, and the men began to get sick, several had to go to bed even. Last night we had another damp hall, and although the weather is bright now, it is nevertheless cold for Charleston. Everyone has a cold in consequence, and even Wessels has gone to bed with a hot bottle! I am the only well person—so much for the private car, without it I would also have been sick I suppose. We have three good and willing men to look after us, and the car is not overheated. The only complaint I have made yet is too much and too good food! We have had delicious oysters and fish all along, but with so little exercise I feel heavy, and must eat sparingly.

" This morning the orchestra were taken out in carriages by the Germania Club and were much fêted. But I escaped because my car could not be found. How do things go with you since I am gone? I hope you have not taken in some old alley dog or cat to nurse! Our new library annex in the back yard would make a fine station for broken-down horses on their way to the hospital—but don't devote it to that purpose until I have taken out the music and the billiard table! The other day I saw a man maltreating his horse at a small way-station where the train stopped for a few minutes. I did not have time to get out, but I was so mad I pushed up the car window and roared at him, ' If my wife was here you would stop that pretty quick!' He was so astonished at this surprising threat that he actually *did* stop, and my wrath evaporated in a hearty laugh, as the train moved on!'"

Indianapolis, Ind.—"Here I am sitting in a large room in a hotel, experiencing quite a sensation in being away from the car, in which I have been boxed up for two weeks. Another sensation will be a bath. My room is very large, but of course overheated. I am pretty tired and have a cold and sore throat, but I am also very busy and will have no time for anything now until the season is over. The orchestra goes home to-night, but I have to go to Cincinnati first, for some final chorus rehearsals for the festival, which seems very near now. Soon that too will be over and we will be free to go home and have peace for a while. Felsengarten never appeared more attractive to my mental vision than now."

When we had built the little mountain cottage at Felsengarten it was with the idea of using it only as a sort of camping place for short sojourns. But each summer we became more and more attached to it, and spent a longer time there. In the meantime the Thomas " children " had become mature men and women, and had married or gone out into the world for themselves. The large house at Fairhaven was, therefore, empty of the young life which had made it a home for Thomas, and he now felt lonely and dissatisfied in it. " I long for a home," he said to me. " We have three houses, but not a home amongst them all. Chicago is too uncertain for me to have any home feeling here; the Fairhaven place was meant for the children, and I have never felt as if it, belonged to me; and the mountain cottage is only a ' shack.' What shall we do? " After some further discussion we decided to turn the " shack " into a good substantial house and make that our home for the rest of our lives. During the summer of 1900 this was done, and there was not a happier man in America than Thomas when it was all complete, and he was able to take possession of his cozy nest beneath the sheltering pines of Felsengarten. To him the love of home was a passion. All his life he had lived in rented houses, except for the brief summers he had spent at Fairhaven. " Home " had, therefore, hitherto meant only family surroundings, unconnected with the land. But in Felsengarten he now had a place which was peculiarly his own, for no white man had ever before lived upon its virgin soil. He was, therefore, able to design the entire place as he pleased, and afterwards to work out his design with his own hands. In like manner the cottage was planned to suit his personal needs, and so well was he pleased with both house and grounds that hereafter it seemed to him a veritable paradise on earth, and he never spent an unhappy moment there.

No one really knew Thomas who had not shared his home, for he was an entirely different person there from what he was elsewhere. In his professional life he was stern, serious, intensely in earnest, and absolutely uncompromising. His personality was so commanding that he was instantly and unquestioningly obeyed by everyone who came near him, and I have never known anyone who did not fear him. An incident illustrative of this happened at the time of the World's Fair, when his antagonists were daily printing all sorts of accusations against him. One of the newspapers sent a reporter to interview him, but Thomas did not care to be interviewed, and so it fell to my lot to receive the reporter. After he had asked me a great many leading questions I began to lose patience, and said with some heat, " If Mr. Thomas were present himself, you would not dare to put these questions to *him*." " True," replied the reporter, " and I will tell you something more: If the five men who are making these attacks on Mr. Thomas were here and he should come in, not all of them together would dare to utter one word of accusation in his presence." It is not difficult to understand why people stood so much in awe of Thomas, for his eye seemed to pierce one through and through, and he made the impression of holding, pent up within himself, some kind of tremendous force which would annihilate everything in sight if it broke loose.

Sometimes it did break loose, and then he was terrible and no one could stand against him. But this rarely happened. Ordinarily, he contented himself with mere sarcasm when he was angry or displeased, but it was sarcasm as keen and biting as the thrust of a rapier, and was almost as much dreaded as his anger. Nevertheless, in spite of these repellent qualities, it was impossible not to feel the great, warm heart, the sense of truth and justice, the sincerity and the absolute unselfishness that lay at the foundation of his character, and however much he was feared, he was loved in a still greater degree.

At home his character was reversed, and the sterner qualities were veiled, while all his warmth, tenderness, sentiment, gayety, and simplicity were uppermost. Here he was strangely dependent and even docile. He wanted to be guided and directed in everything by his family, and carried his consideration of others to an extreme. For instance, he would not eat toast when there were many people at our table, because he thought the cook had too much else to attend to; and on the occasion of the wedding of one of his daughters at Fairhaven, when the guests had gone, he returned to the dining-room, sent for all the waiters, cooks, and coachmen, and, giving them each a glass of champagne, a cigar, and a piece of wedding cake, thanked them formally for their services, and, inviting them to sit down, entertained them as guests himself for half an hour, wishing them to have some of the pleasure, as well as the work, of the day. In the summer season, when he could lay aside, for a time, the cares of his profession and enjoy his home, he was as gay and happy as a boy. My birthday he always made a little festival of and on that day he would bar the gate against all the outside world, and have a family celebration for which he would prepare a long and elaborate programme, which would be-

The Cottage at " Felsengarten," Mount Theodore Thomas, Bethlehem, N. H.

gin at breakfast and last all day. This programme was a much diversified affair, and was sure to include a procession—for which we " dressed up," and in which all the servants and animals took part—as well as a concert or two, and several substantial meals, with intermissions for rest and relaxation. On such occasions he would exert to the utmost all his charm of manner, bringing forth from the storehouse of his mind his best treasures of knowledge, thought, and experience, and talking so delightfully that the hours would glint by like minutes. To those who took part in these joyous little family festivals the memory of them is like the afterglow of sunset at the close of a summer day.

The fall brought Thomas again to Chicago, and the winter of 1900-01 passed along uneventfully, devoted to the regular work of the Chicago season and a few concert tours.

One noteworthy happening must, however, be chronicled. This was a cycle of four Beethoven Programmes, given at intervals through the season. They were as follows:

BEETHOVEN CYCLE

Chicago, 1900-1901

PROGRAMME I

Symphony No. 3, " Eroica " 1804
Piano Concerto No. 4, op. 58. 1805
Overture, " Leonore " No. 2, op. 72. 1805
Overture, " Leonore " No. 3, op. 72. 1806

PROGRAMME II

Symphony No. 4, B flat, op. 60.................1806
Violin Concerto, D major, op. 61..................1806
Overture, " Coriolanus," C minor, op. 62..........1807
Symphony No. 5, C minor, op. 67...............1807

PROGRAMME III

Symphony No. 6, " Pastoral," F major, op. 68....1808
Piano Concerto No. 5, E flat, op. 73.............1809
Symphony No. 7, op. 92.......................1812

PROGRAMMME IV

Symphony No. 8, F major, op. 93...................1812
Benedictus from Missa Solennis, D major, op. 123,
1818-1823
Symphony No. 9, D minor, op. 125..........1817-1823
Assisted by the Apollo Club

During this season Thomas made several short
tours with the orchestra, and the months of March
and April were spent in almost continuous traveling in the Southern States under conditions which
were so hard that, in spite of the private car, the
work was almost unbearable, as the following letters testify:

" MEMPHIS, TENN., *April 22, 1901.*

" Here we are in summer weather—everything is open
and we let the air blow in on us. We let the fire out the
first day and by the time we reached St. Louis it began
to be hot. I have been lame ever since leaving home, in
my back, and have suffered much pain, sometimes it seemed
as if I would drop. But it is gradually leaving me now.
I am wearing my thinnest clothing and fighting flies, and

the best thing that has happened so far is that this is
Friday. The South with its heat and dirt is not attractive, and I long to be at home."

April 29, 1901.—" The heat is simply demoralizing, and
the thermometer has stood at over ninety degrees continuously during the entire trip. To-day, thank fortune,
we have reached the first day of the last week, and see with
grim defiance the end. By the time I get home I shall
have no sense or feeling left. I think that at my age, and
with my reputation I ought not to be obliged to play to
such ignorant audiences as are found in this part of the
world. The orchestra is of course also all to pieces with
the hardships of the trip.

" Can you buy for me the works of Calderon? Try to
get an English translation, so that you can read it also,
otherwise order the German edition. It takes a long time
now to take in the world, it is so old, and so much has
happened. But one likes to learn as much as one can."

" BIRMINGHAM, ALA., *May* 1, 1901.
" This will probably be my last letter, for I simply fight
for my existence. The heat, dirt (filth), and noise are
beyond all description, and all we can do is to practice the
virtue of the mule—patience. I have nothing to write
except complaining, and as that gives no relief or help,
it is better to do without. Birmingham is a new town,
and has all the virtues of one. The business interest is
steel and iron, and I suppose it has an immense future.
The chorus here consists chiefly of Welsh people, and is
quite good for such a place. We gave half of the
' Elijah ' last night, besides some orchestra numbers. We
were brought here by the influence of my Cincinnati work.
I find many young men all over the country, who have

been under my influence there. Yesterday I went shopping for you. In every town I have amused myself looking through the hardware stores to try and find some gardening tools for you, but never succeeded until yesterday, when I bought two sets of tools, and I think they will be just what you want.

"On these tours we are doing what ought to have been done ten years ago, and play *at* the people until they catch on. Well, I believe I am laying a good foundation for what will come after me—if it is not all ruined again. But I wish the season was over, and I long for the mountains."

The most important feature of Thomas' Chicago work during the season of 1901-02, was the following:

CYCLE OF HISTORICAL PROGRAMMES

CHICAGO, 1901-1902

PROGRAMME I

* (a) Sonata, " Pian e Forte " } Giovanni Gabrieli, 1557
   (b) Canzon à 6 }

King Arthur..............................Purcell, 1658
Castor et Pollux.......................Rameau, 1683
Water Music............................Haendel, 1685
Overture No. 3, D major............J. S. Bach, 1685
Symphony No. 1, D major........C. P. E. Bach, 1714
Recitative and aria, "Diane Impitoyable," from
       Iphigenia in Aulis..................Gluck, 1714
Symphony, E flat (B. and H. No. 1).....Haydn, 1732

* The earliest known orchestral composition. The score is now in the Newberry Library, Chicago.

PROGRAMME II

Symphony, C major (K. 551)............Mozart, 1756
Concerto for violin, No. 8.............Spohr, 1784
Overture, " Der Freischuetz "...........Weber, 1786
Symphony No. 8, B minor............Schubert, 1797
Variations and March, Suite 113.........Lachner, 1804

PROGRAMME III

Beethoven

Overture, " Prometheus," op. 43.................1800
Scene and aria, " Ah perfido," op. 46...............1796
Symphony No. 3, " Eroica," E flat, op. 55........1804
Music to Goethe's " Egmont," op. 84...........1809-10

PROGRAMME IV

Wedding March and Scherzo, from " Midsummer
     Night's Dream," op. 61.......Mendelssohn, 1809
Overture, " Melusina," op. 32........Mendelssohn, 1809
Concerto for piano, No. 2, F minor, op. 21..Chopin, 1810
Symphony No. 3, Rhenish, E flat, op. 97, Schumann, 1810

PROGRAMME V

" Symphonie Fantastique," op. 14, A......Berlioz, 1803
Symphonic Poem No. 2, " Tasso "...........Liszt, 1811
Vorspiel, " Lohengrin "   ⎫
Vorspiel, " Die Meistersinger " ⎬ ......Wagner, 1813
                       ⎭

PROGRAMME VI

Symphony No. 4, E minor, op. 98........Brahms, 1833
Concerto for piano, No. 2, G minor, op. 22,
                          Saint Saens, 1835
Symphony No. 6, " Pathetic," B minor, op. 74,
                       Tschaikowsky, 1840

With the exception of this cycle of concerts, the Chicago season presented no unusual features, for the severity of the climate was steadily doing its deadly work, and Thomas was now so much weakened in health that he planned no more great musical enterprises, but was content to spend his remaining years in training both the orchestra and the public of Chicago, so that musical culture would be too deeply rooted in both to deteriorate when he was gone. He seemed to have a premonition that the end was not far off, and the naturally joyous and hopeful temper of his mind was changed to one of deep seriousness and resignation. Hereafter all the passion and struggle of this world fell away from him; he thought and spoke much of the soul, and all his art work tended towards the psychological. He was further saddened by the death of his eldest son, Franz C. Thomas, in December. Anything that affected his family touched Thomas very closely, and the loss of his son was a heavy blow to him. As in former years, work was his antidote for sorrow, and the approaching Cincinnati Festival gave him ample occupation during the season of 1901-02.

This festival, had Thomas been a younger man and able to follow it up afterwards, would have been an epoch-making series of concerts, for it marked an entirely new departure in his art, though one towards which he had long been tending. Hitherto he had sought to preserve popular interest in classic music by adapting the works of the masters as far as possible to the modern orchestra. By a thousand little devices he had enriched the classic scores and modernized them while still faithfully preserving their original spirit. Now, however, he determined that this was wrong. "I have at last come to the conclusion," he said, "that no one has a right to alter, in any particular, the work of a composer. It is the duty of the executant musician to interpret a work exactly as the composer intended that it should be interpreted, and he should not change or embellish it to suit the taste of another generation." In pursuance of this theory he cut out everything he had ever added to the classic scores and set to work to adapt the orchestra to the compositions, instead of adapting the compositions to the orchestra, as heretofore.

The most important classic work on the festival programmes of this year was Bach's great B minor "Mass," and to the preparation of this work Thomas gave two years of exhaustive study. The edition he used as the foundation of his work was that edited by Hermann Kretzmar, in 1899, for the performances of the Riedelverein of Leipsic. With this as a basis, he proceeded first to prove every note of it, and then he added everything which it lacked, and corrected whatever his own researches had shown to be wrong. There was probably not a single authoritative work on Bach or his music, in either English, German, or French, which Thomas did not study in preparing this "Mass," and the score in which the results of his

labors were annotated is unique in the world,
for it represents the consensus of the opinions of
all the great Bach experts of both Europe and
America. There was not a trill or turn in the
entire work which he did not study separately, and
write out in full, nor an instrument indicated
which was not faithfully employed, although some
of them had to be made especially and learned by
the orchestra.* In only one particular did Thomas
depart from the originals of the classic scores, and
that was in the number of musicians used in the
performances. In a hall of the size of the Cincinnati Music Hall, it was, of course, impossible
to use the small orchestra of the classic writers.
But to offset this Thomas balanced the various
choirs of the orchestra in such a way as to give
the same relative tone quality, using in the
"Mass" an unheard-of number of wood-winds
in proportion to the strings. The works of the
modern masters he had always given with the
orchestras indicated in the scores. At this festival
those selected were the very extreme of modern
scoring, and one of them, Berlioz' "Requiem
Mass," required, not only an orchestra of the largest dimensions, but four additional bands stationed

---

* Writing in this connection, the eminent musical savant Bernhard
Zieln said, "The Chicago Orchestra under Theodore Thomas has
been the only one in this, as well as in foreign countries, which
executes the ornaments of classic compositions correctly, as explained
by Quantz, Leopold Mozart, C. Ph. Em. Bach and others, and before
Thomas there was no one who did so since the classic era." The
score of the Bach Mass which contains Thomas' annotations is now
in the Newberry Library, where it is accessible to the student.

at the four corners of the main orchestral body, as well as sixteen kettledrums, tuned in chords, and ten pairs of cymbals. Those who heard this performance will never forget the perfect maelstrom of sound when all these instruments and the great chorus crashed in together in the " Tuba mirum." It expressed, in very truth, the words of its text,

> " To the throne, the trumpet sounding,
>   Through the sepulchres resounding,
>   Summons all with voice astounding.
>   Death and Nature 'mazed are quaking,
>   When, the grave's deep slumber breaking,
>   Man to judgment is awaking."

To achieve all these diverse orchestral combinations required an orchestral body of nearly two hundred performers. The subjoined table shows, in detail, how Thomas formed the orchestras for the four great masters, Bach, Beethoven, Berlioz, and Wagner:

THE BACH ORCHESTRA

Mass in D minor

21 First violins	6 Second oboes
19 Second violins	2 Third oboes
12 Violas	2 D clarinets
12 Violoncellos	4 A clarinets
12 Double basses	8 Bassoons
6 First flutes	2 Horns
6 Second flutes	6 Cornets
2 Oboes d'amour	4 Timpani
6 First oboes	1 Organ

The Beethoven Orchestra
Symphony No. 3

21	First violins	2	Oboes
19	Second violins	2	Clarinets
12	Violas	2	Bassoons
12	Violoncellos	3	Horns
12	Double basses	2	Trumpets
2	Flutes	2	Timpani

Berlioz Orchestra
Requiem Mass

Center Orchestra

21 First violins — *(listed below)*

25 First violins
25 Second violins
20 Violas
20 Violoncellos
18 Double basses
4 Flutes
2 Oboes
2 English horns
4 Clarinets
8 Bassoons
4 Horns in E flat
4 Horns in F
4 Horns in G
16 Timpani
10 Pairs of cymbals
2 Bass drums

North Orchestra

4 Cornets in B
4 Tenor trombones
2 Tubas

East Orchestra

2 Trumpets in F
2 Trumpets in E flat
4 Tenor trombones

South Orchestra

4 Trumpets in B
4 Tenor trumpets
2 Ophicleides in C
2 Ophicleides in B

West Orchestra

4 Trumpets in E flat
4 Tenor trombones

Wagner Orchestra
Vorspeil to the " Meistersinger "

21	First violins	2	Clarinets
19	Second violins	2	Bassoons
12	Violas	4	Horns
12	Violoncellos	3	Trumpets
12	Double basses	3	Trombones
2	Flutes	1	Tuba
2	Piccolos	2	Timpani
2	Oboes	1	Pair of cymbals

The year which followed the Cincinnati Festival
of 1902 was a quiet one, but it contained at least
one unusual incident in the visit to Chicago of
Richard Strauss. We have had pleasant glimpses
of this remarkable character from time to time in
the course of this narrative, and each time he
has entered the scene he has loomed larger and
larger, as a man of mark. This time it was not
he who asked for a hearing of one of his works,
but Thomas who invited him to come and conduct
a programme of them. His letter of acceptance,
and Thomas' answer to it were as follows:

CHARLOTTENBURG, *October* 18, 1903.
Highly honored Sir:

In thanking you for your charming invitation, I take
pleasure in appointing April 1 and 2 as the dates when
I shall make the personal acquaintance of your famous
orchestra. How happy I shall be, after twenty years, to
take you, who were the first to make my works known in
America, by the hand, and to thank you for all that you
have done for my art since I had the pleasure, in my old
home, to play for you my F-minor symphony at that
time.

In the pleasant hope of greeting you again, highly honored colleague and friend, and of finding you in good
health, I remain in the anticipation of a happy meeting
always, honored sir,

    Your devoted,   RICHARD STRAUSS.

Most highly honored Sir: CHICAGO, *Nov.* 11, 1903.

Your genial letter of the 18th has given me much pleasure. It will be an ever memorable satisfaction to both

myself and the orchestra to show to the greatest musician now living and one of the greatest musical pioneers of all times, our love and respect for his genius and knowledge. The name of Richard Strauss is one to conjure with in our audience, and I am delighted, dear sir, that during your visit you will find yourself surrounded by friends and admirers here.

In regard to the programmes, it would be well for me to know as soon as possible, in order to carry out your wishes, the music to be performed which is not already in the repertoire of the orchestra this year. We gave "*Tod und Verklaerung*" two weeks ago, and "*Till Eulenspiegel*" will soon follow. If you could say now whether you would prefer to give "*Zarathustra*," or "*Heldenleben*," the programme, with Madame Strauss as soloist, would be complete. The public here would probably enjoy a production of "*Zarathustra*," but it might be difficult to find four good extra horn-players. I will conduct the opening number, and the programme might stand as follows:

PART I

Overture

Zarathustra

Songs

Intermission

Till Eulenspiegel

Songs

Tod und Verklaerung

Or, do you prefer some other selections? Hoping to have a few lines from you soon, and to greet you in Chicago next spring, believe me,

Sincerely yours,

THEODORE THOMAS.

It was, indeed, a delight to Thomas when the man whose genius he had been almost the first to recognize, twenty years before, and who had now become the foremost figure in the world of music, stepped upon the stage of the Chicago Auditorium to conduct his orchestra. Thomas had prepared the programme with the utmost care, in order that nothing should be lacking to make the performance a memorable one, and to place the distinguished guest in the most advantageous light before the public. So thoroughly had he done the preliminary work that, when Strauss arrived, he found it necessary to hold only one rehearsal with the orchestra. At its close he thus addressed them:

" Gentlemen: I came here in the pleasant expectation of finding a superior orchestra, but you have far surpassed my expectations, and I can say to you that I am delighted to know you as an orchestra of artists in whom beauty of tone, technical perfection, and discipline are found in the highest degree. I know that this is due to your, by me, most highly revered *Meister*, Theodore Thomas, whom I have known for twenty years, and whom it gives me inexpressible pleasure to meet again here in his own workroom. Gentlemen, such a rehearsal as that which we have held this morning is no labor, but a great pleasure, and I thank you all for the hearty good-will you have shown towards me."

When the concert came, the Auditorium was crowded from floor to ceiling with thousands of music lovers, and as Thomas led the great composer onto the stage, this vast concourse of people

rose to their feet, cheering and applauding, while
the orchestra blazoned forth a rousing "*Tusche*"
of welcome. It was a splendid tribute of appreciation, and naturally inspired Strauss to his best
effort. No one who had the good fortune to hear
that concert will ever forget the exquisite beauty
of the whole performance.

On the day following, another pleasure was in
store for the two congenial musicians, for Strauss
spent the morning in the study of Thomas, and
together they read over and discussed his works,
especially the "*Symphonia Domestica*," which was
just fresh from his pen, and which Thomas expected soon to produce. Altogether the visit of
Richard Strauss was a very pleasant episode for
all concerned.

Another important incident of this season was
the appointment of Frederick A. Stock as the
assistant conductor of the orchestra. This relieved Thomas of some of the work at home, and
of all the traveling engagements. For thirty-three
years he had been literally tortured by incessant
traveling, and his relief at being no longer obliged
to do this class of work was inexpressible. At
the time of Mr. Stock's appointment to this important position everyone wondered that Thomas
should have selected him for the place, for he was
a quiet, modest young musician, who had had
little or no experience in conducting, and who did
not appear to have much talent for it. When
asked why he had done so, Thomas smiled that
inscrutable smile of his which indicated that he

was not going to answer any questions, and said: "I thought he could do it." Subsequent events proved that Stock was able to do it exceedingly well—so well, indeed, that when Thomas laid down the baton forever, Stock was appointed to his vacant place by the unanimous desire of the trustees, the orchestra, and the general public, and the Association never had occasion to regret that instead of importing some famous man from Europe they had confided the musical direction of the institution to a man from the ranks of their own orchestra, trained for his work under the hand of its creator.

The Association had now been maintained for twelve years, and when the spring of 1903 came the trustees once more succeeded in raising a sufficient guarantee to insure its continuance for one more year. But everyone felt that it could not be sustained in this manner much longer, and the uncertainty of its outlook, in conjunction with his own failing health, made Thomas feel a deep foreboding that this would be the last season of his public career. Such being the case, he seems to have determined that the programmes, from start to finish, should be like a necklace of pearls, each one as perfect and beautiful as the rest, having for a pendant the Cincinnati Festival of 1904, the programmes of which were composed of the largest and most priceless gems of musical art.

Already, during the previous years, Thomas had begun playing all the important works of the orchestral repertoire. During the winter of

1903-04 he completed the list, and the programmes for the two seasons represented the whole range of musical literature, and included the most important symphonies by the masters of every nationality. In looking over the programmes of these two seasons one sees that Thomas wished to play for a last time all the great compositions which it had been his life-work to teach to the new world, and to make these last years a *résumé* of his whole career. Amongst the great pianists who appeared with him in March, 1904, was the Italian master, Ferruccio Busoni, who wrote him, shortly after, the following letter:

Mr. Theodore Thomas.   Chicago, *March* 15, 1904.

Most honored Master:

It was not possible for me to call upon you personally while in Chicago, although I daily wished to do so. Please consider this only as an enforced omission.

Allow me to thank you for the two brilliant appearances which you afforded me in Chicago, and permit me modestly, but from my heart, to express my wonder at both your character and your art. Your personality commands my highest respect, and your influence is above all praise.

Continue then the friendship which you have hitherto shown me and which I have the honor to enjoy.

Yours,

Ferruccio Busoni.

The May Festival of 1904 brought the work of Thomas to a close in Cincinnati, and its programmes were of such a caliber that it was the artistic climax, not only of the long series of festivals in that city, but, perhaps, even of Thomas' own career. One colossal work was piled on another, regardless of everything but the one object of making this festival surpass, in standard and perfection, all that had preceded it.

PROGRAMMES OF

THE CINCINNATI FESTIVAL

MAY, 1904

I

Suite No. 2, in B minor..........................Bach

Mass in B minor.................................Bach

II

(Matinée)

Symphony in E flat............................Mozart

Aria, " Nie wird mich Hymen," Titus...........Mozart

Entr'acte, B minor, " Rosamunde ".............Schubert

" Ocean, Thou Mighty Monster ".................Weber

(a) Variations, op. 36.........................Elgar

(b) March, " Pomp and Circumstance ".........Elgar

Symphony No. 8, F major, op. 93............Beethoven

" The Three Gypsies "...........................Liszt

Bacchanale, " Tannhaeuser ".................Wagner

Prelude and Isolde's Love Death, " Tristan and

        Isolde " ....Wagner

III

Incidental music and Funeral March, " Grania and

        Diamid " ....Elgar

" The Dream of Gerontius ".....................Elgar

Tone poem, " Death and Apotheosis," op. 24....Strauss

Aria, " Abscheulicher," " Fidelio ".........Beethoven

Hymn, op. 26..................................Berlioz

IV

(*Matinée*)

"Alceste" ....Gluck
Overture—Aria, "Divinités du Styx."
Symphony No. 9, D minor, Unfinished..........Bruckner
Rhapsody, op. 53..Brahms
      For Soprano, Male Chorus, and Orchestra
Vorspiel, "Die Meistersinger".................Wagner
Sea Pictures, op. 37.....................................Elgar
     In Haven—Where Corals Lie—The Swimmer
Rondo, "Till Eulenspiegel's Merry Pranks"....Strauss
Hymnus, op. 33...Strauss
Overture, "1812".................................Tschaikowsky

V

"Missa Solennis," op. 123.......................Beethoven
Symphony No. 9, D minor, op. 125...........Beethoven

That Thomas, in his weakened state of health, should have been able to go through the enormous strain of such a series of performances was only another instance of his iron will-power. But even for him it was well-nigh impossible. Two circumstances, however, helped him through. First, the chorus, under the able and musicianly training of its director, Mr. Edwin C. Glover, was in splendid condition, and Thomas had nothing to correct about its performance. It was, indeed, one of the finest and best prepared choruses he had ever conducted, and inspired, instead of fatiguing him. Second, his deafness had not, as yet, affected his hearing of musical sounds. Nature had given him the most marvelous ears imaginable, and as one grew deaf the hearing of the other seemed to become only the more acute, so that to the last he was spared what would have been the worst calamity of life to him—the loss of orchestral music.   The performances at the Cincinnati Festival were, therefore, amongst the very finest that he ever gave in his life, and no one in his audience had the slightest idea of the strain under which he worked, or the nervous exhaustion which overwhelmed him the moment he reached his hotel after rehearsals or concerts.   But when the Festival was ended, and he was trying to recover from the inevitable reaction in the quiet of our mountain home, he realized that he could never do such work again.

CHAPTER XXI

1904

THE THOMAS ORCHESTRA IS PERMANENTLY ENDOWED—THE
BUILDING OF THE THEODORE THOMAS ORCHESTRA HALL
—NOTES ON THE CONSTRUCTION OF MUSIC HALLS, BY
THOMAS—THE INAUGURAL CONCERT—DEATH AND BUR-
IAL OF THOMAS

THE affairs of the Orchestral Association had
now reached a crisis. We have seen that Thomas
felt a premonition that the season of 1903-04
would be his last. Nevertheless, as it neared the
new year, he determined to make one more final
effort for the permanence of the orchestra. Both
he and the trustees recognized the futility of trying to continue maintaining it by means of an
annual guarantee. People were tired of giving
such a great sum every year to an institution
which never accomplished any permanent results,
and the trustees were doubly tired of soliciting it.

In this emergency Thomas believed that the
time was ripe for a bold stroke, which should
either win or lose the orchestra to Chicago within
the coming six months. He, therefore, said to the
trustees:

"It is useless to attempt to make an orchestra permanent without its own building. I found this to be the case
in New York, and was obliged to give up my orchestra

510

there for lack of one. Conditions in Chicago are similar
to what they were in New York when I left there. We
now have here a large and cultivated public, which demands the highest forms of music, and, I believe, would
not be willing to give up the orchestra. But what is everybody's business is nobody's business, and the people will
do nothing unless the situation is brought before them
very strongly. I therefore ask you to announce to the
general public that, unless a sufficient endowment can be
raised to provide a suitable building in which to carry on
the work of our institution during the next six months, I
shall resign my position here and go elsewhere. I take this
course because I believe it is the only way to arouse the
public to quick and decisive action, and also because if it
fails to do so, I think it is better to disband the orchestra
now, before it piles up another large debt for the Association to pay."

The trustees saw the wisdom of this course and
it was mutually decided to put the fate of the
institution " to the touch, and win or lose it all."

The Association was now in the hands of a very
strong group of men. At its head were, Bryan
Lathrop, President, a man whose name was insep-
arably connected with everything which made for
the progress of Chicago; Daniel H. Burnham, First
Vice-President, the famous architect and designer
of cities; Norman Fay, Second Vice-President,
founder of the institution; and a Board of Trustees, which included such representative names as
J. J. Glessner, Harold F. McCormick, Charles D.
Hamill, etc. The initial move in the undertaking
was made by Mr. Burnham, who interested nine

of the trustees in uniting with him in subscribing
$10,000 apiece toward securing a suitable building
lot for the proposed structure.

After this, one would have supposed that to
raise the balance of the fund would not have been
difficult, especially in Chicago, where things are
done on such a generous and magnificent scale.
But such was not the case. Hitherto the concerts
had been given in the Auditorium, an immense
theater constructed by popular subscription somewhat prior to the founding of the orchestra, for
political conventions and operatic festivals. Many
of the men who had contributed largely to this
building and also to the orchestra, not understanding the situation, felt that it was unnecessary
to invest another large sum of money in a second
hall for musical purposes. The public was also
divided on the subject, for the Auditorium was a
popular and agreeable hall for the audience, nor
could the people understand why the annual deficit
of the orchestra should be any smaller in a new
hall than in the old. All of these people, and
others, who were more closely connected with the
Auditorium, united in a common determination to
prevent the building of the new hall if it was a
possible thing, and before the trustees had gone
far, they found themselves confronted with an
opposition so strong that, for a long time, it was
doubtful if they could make headway against it.
The situation was a curious one, and the following
circular, issued by the trustees in reply to argu-
ments against the new hall advanced by the op-

position, is quoted almost in full, as showing concisely the general outlook of the Association, and the difficulties under which its indomitable trustees had maintained it for so many years:

" TO THE PATRONS

OF THE

CHICAGO ORCHESTRA

" During the last week there has appeared in the public press a communication from the Directors of the Auditorium Association regarding the use of the Auditorium by the Orchestral Association, which has evoked some editorial and other comment. This, and the necessities of the situation, make it advisable that the Trustees of the Orchestral Association should inform the public thoroughly regarding its affairs, and we now take pleasure in doing so. . . . The immediate reason for the attempt to provide a new hall, of which we shall shortly speak, is the excessive size of the Auditorium. We know by eleven years' actual experience that it is fifty per cent. too large for our average audience, and that this excess capacity prevents a sufficient season sale, which is or should be the foundation of our income. We are practically certain that the concerts cannot go on in the Auditorium without entailing a continuing annual deficit of between twenty-five thousand and thirty thousand dollars.

" We are equally certain that it is impossible to continue meeting this deficit as heretofore, by the precarious expedient of subscriptions annually solicited. Of the fifty-four original guarantors of the Association, twenty-two have died or left Chicago, or suffered financial reverses; and of the remainder only twelve continue to contribute regularly. Beside these original guarantors, ninety other individuals have contributed once or more, of whom thirteen still contribute regularly, making but twenty-five persons in all who have actually stood the strain of an annual appeal for aid. This number is not sufficient, and constantly grows smaller under the belief that the Orchestra will somehow go on.

" Recognizing the emergency, at the close of last season we formally resolved to disband the Orchestra forever at the close of the present season, unless meantime an adequate endowment should be secured. We still feel that it would be best to end its honorable career now, while it is at the very height of its perfection, before financial weakness shall bring decadence and perhaps disaster. It is almost needless to say that Mr. Theodore Thomas is in thorough accord with us in this decision. He has warned us for years that we were wasting effort and money unless our purpose was ultimately to found a permanent institution. On our part, we have waited only for a time of general prosperity to make a final attempt to do so, and that time has now arrived.

" In considering the form which an endowment, if secured, should take, we were led partly by our own experience and that of Boston, but mainly by consistency to our purpose of founding a permanent institution, to propose its investment in a simple but beautiful Music Hall, in a convenient and conspicuous situation, built for, owned and controlled by the Orchestra. Careful and conservative estimates satisfy us that the saving of the rental now paid the Auditorium, and the selling out of the greater portion of the house at our season sale, without raising prices, which would certainly result (as in Boston) from a proper relation of seating capacity to average audience, would more than prevent an annual deficit, while the rentals of the hall for other purposes would more than pay for its maintenance and operating expenses. Thus the mere fact of its ownership would permanently finance the Orchestral Association.

" But the possession of a home means much more than sound finance, important as that is, to such an institution as we contemplate. Where would be to-day Harvard University, the Cooper Union, or our own Art Institute, if they had not their own dignified and noble seats, and had been obliged to hide themselves in hired quarters? To what would affection and tradition cling, or imagination turn? Where would be their dignity and authority in the eyes of the people, or their influence and effect upon their own members? Where, indeed, would be their membership itself, or their numerous benefactors? Recognizing this tendency of human enthusiasm to center about a fixed site and a monumental building, we wish to give our Orchestra both as the best guarantee that it will endure and exercise a lasting influence upon musical art, that our people will venerate and love it from generation to generation, and that membership in it shall mean to the musicians of the world the highest professional distinction. This has been our dream.

" Sharing it, ten friends of the Orchestra a few weeks ago purchased on joint account the lot on Michigan Avenue, just south of the Pullman building, 105 feet front by 171 feet deep, for the sum of $450,000, paying $100,-000 down and giving a mortgage for $350,000, with the intention of turning it over at cost to the Orchestral Association as a site for a permanent Music Hall, provided the necessary funds to buy and build upon it can be secured within a few months. If not, it will remain their property, and they have already a chance to sell it for commercial purposes at a profit of $50,000. Messrs. D.

H. Burnham & Co. estimate that a Music Hall of great beauty, with a seating capacity of 2,500, suitable for the concerts of the Orchestra and certain public uses, can be built for between $250,000 and $300,000, so that the entire investment proposed aggregates $750,000.

" Whether this large sum can be raised is, we regret to say, as yet very uncertain. We had thought that, perhaps, some generous individual might write his name large in the annals of Chicago for the next few centuries by building and naming this Music Hall; but so far none has appeared. Many of those to whom we would naturally turn for considerable sums seem to regard the Orchestra as a mere public amusement, which should be supported altogether by its box office or allowed to fail. Others suggest that the number and salaries of the players be reduced to cut expenses, and light music given to draw the crowd, so as to put the Orchestra upon a ' business ' basis.

" While it is by no means certain that an inferior orchestra playing popular programmes would be self-sustaining throughout a long season (the experiment has been tried and failed repeatedly), it is hardly necessary to say that the Trustees and the Director of the present Orchestra have carried it on hitherto as an art and educational institution, worthy of endowment, and would courteously decline to take further interest in it, if it is to become a mere amusement enterprise. We believe our present public would repudiate us and it if we did. Broadly speaking, there seems to be no possible union of pure art or pure education and commercial profit. There has probably not been in the history of the world a single self-supporting institution devoted to the higher forms of art or learning. If self-support at the box-office must be applied to our Orchestra as a criterion of its value to

Chicago, it must be found wanting. Nevertheless, of the
$1,383,000 which it had cost up to the end of last season,
$1,012,000 was paid in at the box office by the public.

" Since the announcement of the purchase of the lot, the
officers of the Auditorium Association have courteously
protested to us against our proposed Hall as unnecessary
and injurious to the Auditorium. . . . A compromise
course has been suggested: namely, To remodel the Auditorium, somewhat reducing its size, though perhaps de-
stroying its proportion, and to raise an endowment fund
for the Orchestra, to be invested in interest-bearing securi-
ties, whose income shall meet our deficit. Our judgment
upon this is that, while alteration would necessarily be
experimental, and its result doubtful, it could not afford
a permanent solution of our difficulty, nor give the institution for which we have spent so much the character
we have so long desired and proposed. Moreover, we
doubt the possibility of raising such an endowment fund.
To put money away in bonds, whose income shall be used
to pay a deficit, does not appeal to the average imagination. Men wish something to show for their money. Some
of our best friends have declined to subscribe to such a
fund. On the other hand, we have already a response of
$100,000 to the proposition to found a home for the
Orchestra. As an endowment with us is a matter of life
and death, we naturally incline to seek it in the form men
seem most willing to give it.

" While we have determined to abandon the Orchestra at
the end of this season rather than to let it deteriorate and
come to an inglorious end for lack of money, it goes without saying that it will be a bitter chagrin to us should the
time arrive when this noble and dearly bought possession
must be thrown away in the very flower of its perfection.
Our honored Director, too, has hoped to crown a long life

of hard work for musical art in this country by leaving behind him a well-founded institution, to hand down the tradition of pure musical form and style to future generations of American musicians. We shall therefore make the best fight we can during the next six weeks, for the integrity of our Orchestra as it stands, and its perpetuation hereafter. That is all the time we have.

" The exact situation to-day is that the ten gentlemen who bought the ground have offered to head a subscription of not less than $750,000, with personal subscriptions of $10,000 each, aggregating $100,000. But it will require seventy-five such subscriptions to make up the total. We are therefore not over sanguine of success. If among those who have listened to the Orchestra all these years, there are voices to raise in its behalf, now is the time to raise them. If there is money to give, now is the time to pledge it.

GEO. E. ADAMS
JOSEPH ADAMS
D. H. BURNHAM
WM. L. BROWN
HAROLD F. McCORMICK
C. N. FAY
J. J. GLESSNER   } *Trustees.*
CHARLES D. HAMILL
BRYAN LATHROP
FRANK O. LOWDEN
ARTHUR ORR
PHILO A. OTIS
WM. B. WALKER

CHICAGO, *Feb.* 12, 1903."

After issuing this circular, announcements, advertisements, appeals and even a house-to-house canvass followed each other in quick succession, from not only the trustees, but everyone who cared for the orchestra. Never before in the history of America was the preservation of an art institution labored for by so many, or such widely diverse classes of people. When the great subscription list was finally complete, to the amazement of Thomas and the trustees, it was found to contain more than *eight thousand* names, amongst which were those of janitors, scrub-women, seamstresses, clerks, and wage-earners of all sorts, as well as those of the wealthy and cultivated.

To the firm of D. H. Burnham & Co. was intrusted the building of the new hall—a labor of love on their part, it is needless to say—and when Thomas left for his summer vacation in the mountains, he was assured that it would be completed and ready for use by his return in the fall.

After giving ten thousand concerts, and more than twice ten thousand rehearsals, in the best halls and theaters of every city in America, it may be supposed that Thomas had a very accurate knowledge of what was necessary for the planning, building, and equipment of a hall for orchestral purposes. It is, therefore, of interest to insert here his ideas in detail. I am able to do this in his own words, owing to the following circumstance. In 1897 Thomas was asked by the eminent architectural writer, Mr. Russell Sturgis, to supply him with an article on the construction of music halls, for a Dictionary of Architecture which he was at that time compiling for the Macmillan Company.   Thomas did not like to write for publication, saying, " I have been so long before the public as an expert in my own profession that I do not care to come before it now as an amateur in another."   On this Mr. Sturgis asked for notes on the subject, which he could embody in an article of his own.   Thomas agreed to supply them, but in the end he wrote the desired information out so fully that Mr. Sturgis was able to use it almost *verbatim*.   It is reprinted here by the kind permission of Mr. Sturgis and the Macmillan Company:

NOTES ON THE CONSTRUCTION OF MUSIC HALLS

By THEODORE THOMAS

I. Soft wood should be used to cover, or line, the walls of a music hall throughout, replacing plaster.   Under no circumstances should there be anywhere a brick wall not so covered.   Nor should the wall facing the stage be of brick.   The hall should be a separate structure, built within and separated from the outer walls and roof of the building, the spaces between being used for foyers, staircases, etc., as is customary.

II. It is necessary that the walls and ceiling should be connected by a continuous curve which will allow the sound waves to move unhindered and fast enough not to be caught by new waves.   A similar, if not the same curve should be used to connect the side walls with the ceiling, as well as that facing the stage.   It is often good to have

The Theodore Thomas Orchestra Hall, Chicago

the ceiling of the entire hall slope gradually down towards the stage. The height of the highest point of the auditorium is not important, but the point where the ceiling joins the wall back of the stage should not exceed thirty-five feet in a large hall, and should be even less in a small one. The object of limiting the height of the hall above the stage is to preserve the integrity of the tone. If the ceiling is too high the tone loses something before it reaches the audience; also, in orchestral performances, the various choirs cannot blend. A stage should never have the form of an alcove, with a semicircular wall having a half-dome for a ceiling.

III. A music hall should not be built on a rock foundation, nor should it have another hall beneath it, as the large empty space below causes too much vibration and acts on the principle of a drum. An ordinary cellar, without flooring, and on a soft soil is better.

IV. A modern orchestra has a large choir of brass instruments, and one of percussion. These can only be placed behind the string and wood choirs. For this reason, and in order to be in communication with the conductor, their seats must be on raised platforms. Now, neither a brass instrument nor a drum expresses its true character unless played with a certain freedom. In order that the wall at the back of the stage shall not give too great resonance for these instruments, these platforms must be set at some distance in front of that wall. Other means for diminishing the too great brilliancy of the brass and percussion instruments may be employed; thus, a permanent chorus stage, or series of platforms with seats rising one above the other may be constructed. Or, if chorus seats cannot be established here, there may be an opening between the orchestra and the rear wall of the stage, above, or on each side, or both, to reduce the superfluous force of the brass and percussion choirs, and to enable them to blend with, instead of overpowering the other instruments. Resort to this method has been found necessary when, as in the Chicago Auditorium, or any ordinary theater, the orchestra played on a stage cased with canvas scenery and ceiling. Here the drop scene at the rear of the stage had to be moved back from six to ten feet behind the orchestra, and the canvas ceiling also cut away from over the same space. When such expedients are necessary, care must be taken that no draught can come through these openings, as the effect of draughts on the instruments makes a good performance impossible.

V. The sounding board is only useful in the open air, or in a very large building or theater. Its purpose is to throw the tone directly toward the auditorium. Apart from this it is objectionable, for it affects the tone quality by forcing it. The summer concerts in Chicago, from 1879 to 1890, given in a vast building two blocks long, were very satisfactory, although we had an orchestra of only fifty or sixty musicians, because of a sounding board, made of thin wood.

VI. An escape for the sound through the roof is not practicable because the tone waves from the stage should travel undisturbed through the whole building. A high and deep gallery is good because the tone waves can run out and disappear gradually, as the Rhine loses itself in the sand. It must not be forgotten, however, that the seats under the gallery are never good for hearing music, consequently the upper gallery should be a continuation of the hall, built over the foyer of the second story. The bare wall above this gallery is, however, very apt to throw the sound back into the parquet, even as far as the stage, causing confusion. This space might, perhaps, be covered with some soft material, but this is the only place where such material could be used to advantage, as the audience itself usually absorbs the sound as much as is necessary. Certainly no hanging should be put over the stage, where it would influence the life and quality of the tone.

VII. A hall may be good for vocal music, or for instrumental solos, and yet be absolutely bad for orchestral music. The modern orchestra has endless resources in color and rhythmical combination partly in consequence of its numerical strength. Where Mozart, and even Beethoven used only one or two flutes, the modern composer uses three or four, thereby establishing an independent choir of flutes alone, enabling him to give the full harmony of instruments of the same tone quality. It is the same with all the other instruments. It can be seen that when a separate choir can be formed of each individual kind of instrument, there must be many distinct tone-colors, independent of the mixtures produced by combining the different choirs. This possible independence of the choirs, each of the other, allows many different rhythms to be used at the same time, giving a certain undercurrent of life. Too much vibration will prevent the rhythmical combinations from being audible. The modern orchestra represents polyphony, as opposed to the homophony represented by the soloist.

VIII. An empty hall should have much resonance, but no echo. It is advisable to have a number of aisles in the parquet, the floors of which should be covered with a thin carpet, and which should always be kept unoccupied by the audience. There is scarcely anything which takes so much from the brilliancy of the tone, as a packed parquet without open passages.

IX. To the above considerations should be added the historical distinction between the instrumentation of the time of Mozart and Beethoven, and that of the present day. It is probable that nothing could be done more instructive for music, in the best sense, than the building and careful preparation of a small music hall, and the organization of a small orchestra exactly such as Mozart is known to have used. To this orchestra should be intrusted the rendering of the classical music exactly as it was first composed. The performance of the works of the great eighteenth-century masters by the full modern orchestra, is of necessity a translation from one language into another, although a kindred language. A similar change in the interpretation of music is made, when that which was written for the spinet is performed on a grand piano.

The new "Orchestra Hall," as it was at first named, was built just after the terrible burning of the Iroquois Theater, and the consequent enactment of the most stringent ordinances in regard to the building and management of all halls and theaters. The architects were very much hampered by those ordinances, which forbade the use of wood for floors, walls, or ceilings. The lot on which the hall was built was also too short to allow them to carry out all of the ideas of Thomas. Nevertheless, the hall was an almost ideal place for concert purposes when it was finished, and a brief description of its chief features will therefore be of interest, and also serve to show what are the needs of a great orchestral institution, and why it is essential to its permanency to own and control its especially constructed building.

In its general plan the hall followed, as nearly as the conditions just mentioned would permit, the suggestions of Thomas. The stage was not an inclosed space behind a proscenium arch, although an ingeniously contrived ornamental molding gave it somewhat that appearance. Instead, it extended across the full width of the hall, and its walls and ceiling were united by unbroken planes with those of the main body of the house, having just the right curves, so that the tones of the various choirs could blend and expand in the proper proportion, and permeate the whole auditorium equally, like smoke or vapor, while against this soft, iridescent background, special effects, like bursts of flame, could be introduced at the will of the conductor. The height over the stage was moderate, but as the hall receded from it, the ceiling rose, and was slightly broken by arched mouldings each a little higher than the one before, preventing echoes, or the interference of returning tone waves. To counteract the hard quality of tone which Thomas feared might result from the use of iron and cement in the interior finish of the hall, he had the long ornamental panels over the stage filled with wire netting covered with cloth, instead of with the solid steel plates originally designed. He also had as much wood as permission could be obtained for, built on the stage in the form of platforms for chorus and orchestra, etc., etc., and by these devices the acoustics of the hall were made very satisfactory in spite of the obstacles put in the way by the city fathers.

Behind the stage were a number of private dressing-rooms for solo performers and conductor, as well as lockers in which to store the harps, timpani, and other large instruments when not in use. Under the stage was a commodious room for the use of the orchestra. Here each man had his own locker in which he could keep his dress suit, extra strings, small instruments, or anything else that he might need in connection with his work. To one side of this was a small room with deadened walls in which a solo violinist could "warm" (practice on) his instrument and prepare it for performance while a concert was in progress, without being heard by the audience. Another very large room was fitted up as a cloak-room for a chorus. Still others, which were kept at a uniform temperature, and free from dampness, were devoted to the storage of the 'cellos, double basses, and instruments not provided for above, such as the *schellenbaum,* bell-piano, tam-tam, piano, church bells, and many others, as well as the large cases for instruments and music used in traveling. Into these rooms no one had admission but the librarian and his assistant, so that the valuable instruments stored here were always safe from careless handling, or the still more disastrous injuries of steam heat or dampness. Other large rooms were provided for the storage of the orchestra chairs, music racks, extra platforms, and paraphernalia of all sorts. Finally, there was a completely appointed library, 100 feet long by 20 feet wide, where Thomas' great col-

The Stage of the Theodore Thomas Orchestra Hall, Chicago

lection of music could be stored in inclosed cases, and furnished with long tables and desks where it could be sorted and repaired, and where librarians and copyists could work comfortably. The storing and care of this great library had always been one of the most difficult problems to Thomas, for its size, and the fact that a large portion of it was in constant use, and therefore had to be accessible at all times, made it almost impossible to manage in a private house, besides necessitating the transporting of a great mass of music back and forth between the hall and the house every day. Every nook and corner of his house which would hold a music case was filled with it, and, in addition, an extra building was erected in the rear and packed with the overflow. Some idea of the size of the library can be gained from the fact that Thomas never had less than two librarians and a copyist to take care of it, and it required the whole time of these three men to attend to simply that part which was in use in the regular orchestral concerts. Besides the orchestral music there was everything imaginable in it for choral and operatic performances and chamber concerts, together with all the great concertos for every instrument, and much vocal and piano literature. It contained, also, collections of the programmes of other orchestras, librettos, books of reference, and—last but not least—a complete collection of his own ten thousand programmes. Thomas valued these programmes more than anything in the library, not merely because they were his own work, but because they represented the history of music in America during its first half-century. When he had begun his career, music was in a hardly more than embryonic state. He was the pioneer to blaze the trail for those who came after, except in two or three cities, and even in these he raised the standard far higher than it had been before. As he went on, it was his principle to play the current, as well as the old and tried literature, especially American works, and to engage every worthy soloist who could be obtained, year by year. If, therefore, one wishes to know what music was played at any given time, or in any given city, or when any particular artist was before the American public, he has only to look it up in these programmes and he will find both music and artist enrolled there in their due order. As Thomas continued this from 1855 to 1904, the historical value of his collection of programmes is important, in addition to their artistic worth.*

Hardly less agreeable to Thomas than the foregoing artistic facilities of the new building, was the prospect of a pleasant office in which to transact the business part of his profession. Hitherto he and his manager had had to discuss all the innumer-

* After his death the widow and heirs of Thomas divided his library between the Orchestral Association and the Newberry Library of Chicago: to the Orchestral Association were given all the orchestra " parts," and most of the modern scores ; to the Newberry Library were given the classic scores, and those of modern writers in which the annotations of Thomas were especially valuable to musical students. The books of reference, and the collection of Thomas programmes were also placed here, where they are now accessible to the public.

able business details of the orchestra, seated on a couple of dirty wooden chairs, behind the scenes of the Auditorium stage, in a light too dim to read by, and with scene shifters noisily at work around them preparing the stage for the next performance. After thirteen years of this kind of inconvenience, the prospect of a clean, quiet, well-appointed office, where he could be alone and undisturbed with his manager and other officials, was not the least of the anticipated pleasures of his new orchestral home. Nor were present necessities all that were provided for in this unique building. It contained, in addition to the large hall, a small one, in which Thomas planned to give performances of classic music with the exact orchestra of the classic writers, as well as chamber concerts, which last, he often said, were the foundation of all musical culture. There were also in the building several stories of fine offices, so arranged that at any time they could be easily converted into classrooms, when the money should be raised for the musical university Thomas had so long planned for. In short, everything looked bright and hopeful for the future, and for the first time in his long and arduous career Thomas was able to rest serene in the knowledge that his work was at last assured beyond the current year, and to plan for its development on permanent lines.

But alas, *it was too late*. Already he felt within himself the approaching end, and said sadly, " I have sown, but others will garner the harvest." All through the summer of 1904 he was rapidly breaking down. One ear was now entirely deaf, and one eye nearly blind. Both heart and nerves were in bad condition, and the catarrh of the throat was so deeply seated that even the air of Felsengarten no longer gave him any relief. For the first time a cloud hung over our home-life—a cloud that we could neither forget nor dispel.

I have just spoken of the value Thomas placed upon his programmes, because of their historical importance. He had for some years been anxious to have them published, in order that they might be preserved and made accessible to the public. His old friend, Mr. Upton, now came forward and consented to undertake the arduous task of editing them, and at his request Thomas wrote a short autobiographical sketch to serve as an introduction to the volumes. All through the summer of 1904 he sat in a darkened room, writing this little sketch, or committing to memory new scores to be played in the concerts of the coming season, in order that he need not be dependent on the notes in public. The heart trouble from which he suffered made it impossible for him to work out of doors as in former years, and he could only walk quietly about, saw in hand, and do a little light pruning. It was pathetic to see the old, sick lion, wandering slowly through the woods where he had been wont to roam in all the glory of abounding health and strength, or trying to spur his jaded energies on to meet the tasks of the coming winter,—the more so that he did not murmur or repine, but wore his customary cheery face, and seemed to feel the same deep and quiet content that always pervaded his spirit at Felsengarten.

Just previous to leaving Chicago in the spring, Thomas had received the following letter from Mr. E. Francis Hyde, of New York, written on the part of the Philharmonic Society of that city:

Dear Mr. Thomas: NEW YORK, *April* 18, 1904.

The Philharmonic Society of New York, following the plan adopted by them during the last winter, expect next winter to have a number of conductors to preside over the eight concerts of the season.

A Committee has been appointed to make engagements, and all the members of it agreed with one accord that we should be delighted to have you conduct one of the concerts with its public rehearsal. It was also unanimously agreed that, before undertaking to engage any other conductor for any concert of the season, the Committee should make its request to you, leaving it to you to decide, if you accept its invitation, which concert you would prefer to conduct. . . . It would be very delightful if you could open the season for us, but we should be only too glad if you could appear at the head of the orchestra at any concert of the season, at your choice. You are first in all our hearts, and we trust that you will give us the supreme pleasure of seeing you once more in the place where for so many years we loved to see you,—at the conductor's desk of the Philharmonic Society of New York.

Sincerely yours,

E. FRANCIS HYDE, *Chairman.*

This invitation was very highly valued by Thomas, and yet he could not at first bring himself to accept it, because he no longer had the courage

to face the unrelenting hostility of the press which
a public appearance always brought out against
him in New York. Had it been a question of
taking his own perfectly trained orchestra and
giving concerts there, he would not have minded
so much, but would have "fought it through,"
conscious that the public would recognize the
standard of his work, even if the press did not.
But to conduct an orchestra which had not come
under his hand for so many years, with only a
few hurried rehearsals, was another matter, and
if it showed any shortcomings under his leadership he knew full well that his enemies would
instantly say, "Thomas is growing old," and that
was the one thing which, in his present sensitive
condition, he could not bear. He therefore declined the invitation. But the Philharmonic
Society was not to be put off. Its members had
set their hearts on being conducted once more by
their old leader, and meant to make this the
great gala occasion of his life. So, when they
received his refusal, they simply put the *Concert-
meister,* Mr. Richard Arnold, on a west-bound
train and sent him to Chicago, to see what a personal interview would accomplish. Of course after
this Thomas could no longer withhold his consent,
and commissioned Mr. Arnold to appoint March
24 and 25 as the dates when he would once more
stand in his old place and conduct his New York
colleagues and friends.

Great rejoicing hailed the return of Mr. Arnold
with this information, not only on the part of the

Philharmonic Society, but also on the part of the hundreds of friends, known and unknown, who had made up the Thomas audiences in former years. There was a general desire throughout the musical world of the city to make the concerts a royal demonstration of honor and affection for him. On behalf of the Society Mr. Hyde wrote:

Dear Mr. Thomas: New York, *May* 31, 1904.

We hail with great pleasure your consent to conduct the last concert and rehearsal of the Philharmonic Society on March 24 and 25. Your conducting will be a great event in the musical season of next year. While we were arranging a list of those whom we should like to have conduct, the public here were suggesting your name, as you see by the inclosed clipping from the *Evening Post,* of March 19. You need not fear anything but the most enthusiastic reception, and your appearance at our last rehearsal and concert will make a splendid close to the season.

All of the Committee are delighted that you have accepted, and we are all looking forward to your appearance as to a great and extraordinary occasion.

Sincerely yours,

E. Francis Hyde.

In former years Thomas would have made the programme for this concert during the summer, for it was his custom to prepare for all the important concerts of the coming season before leaving the country, and he generally worked about eight months in advance of any given event. But this year he planned for nothing, and gave even this great and unusual concert no thought.

On September 28 we started on our westward journey, and as he passed out through the gates of his beloved mountain home he knew that he would never return. He did not put this presentiment into words, but all his actions during the journey showed what was in his mind. Instead of going directly to Chicago, with only a brief sojourn with his children in New York *en route,* as was his wont, he visited also all his old friends, in Boston, New York, Farmington, and Philadelphia;—even going to spend a day in the old Fairhaven homestead with his faithful gardener Peter McLaughlin; while, at his request, I went out to the beautiful cemetery of Mount Auburn, in Cambridge, to select our last resting-place.

On reaching Chicago at last, Thomas was much disappointed to learn that the new hall was not yet ready for use, and the first few concerts would have to be given as heretofore, in the Auditorium. He had a very impatient streak in his character, although he generally held it under stern control,— and after working and waiting for this building for thirty years, the last few days of waiting seemed perfectly intolerable to him, and his nerves were so on edge that the most trivial happening would make him almost hysterical. At last, however, the new hall was ready for use, and one day after a Friday matinée at the Auditorium, he said to me, "Now I will take you to see our hall, if you want to go with me!" I had not seen its interior before, nor had he, as we wanted to wait till it was finished, and we could go to-

gether. We walked the short distance which separated it from the Auditorium, and just as we neared
it and were about to turn in at its main portal, two
nuns, their long black veils fluttering back almost
over us, stepped before us and preceded us into
the building, and even the length of the aisle to
the very stage. To me, anxious and alarmed as I
already was about his health, it seemed a sinister
omen that Thomas should make his first entrance
into the hall in the wake of these black-robed figures.
He, however, was not superstitious, and his delight
over the new building and relief when he had tested
it and found that it had no serious acoustic defects,
soon banished the incident from my mind. He
had been so anxious over the latter question that
he would not allow me to be present at his first
trial of its quality with the full orchestra. The
piece he selected for this test, was the " Tannhaeuser " Overture,—a composition which is calculated to bring out any defect in acoustics which
a building may have. After it was over he turned
to the boxes at the other end of the hall, in one of
which were seated Mr. Lathrop, Mr. Fay, and one
or two others, and shouted triumphantly, " Your
hall is a success, gentlemen, a great success! "
After which he sent the following telegram to Mr.
Burnham, who was at that time in Manila:

D. H. Burnham: CHICAGO, *Dec.* 7, 1904.

   Hall a complete success. Quality exceeds all expectations.

THEODORE THOMAS.

In saying that the hall was satisfactory Thomas did not, of course, mean that there was nothing to improve about it, for the hall was never built that did not have to be adjusted to the music to be given in it, just as an instrument has to be tuned. He meant that it had no structural defect which could not be remedied by the proper adjustment of orchestra and stage to the new conditions. The orchestra and its belongings were now moved into their new home, and Thomas set about energetically to accomplish this important work. It was no easy task, for there could hardly be two halls more different in construction than the Auditorium and the Orchestra Hall. During the thirteen years of his work in the former, he had never ceased to experiment with sounding-boards, platforms, and the arrangement of the musicians. The timpani traveled all round the semicircle, and back again—the double basses collected in the middle, divided on either side, strung themselves out in a row and finally bunched together at the left— the violins advanced out on to extra platforms built over the front rows of seats in the parquet, and retreated again behind the proscenium arch; while the wood-winds, brasses, and harps were equally restless in their wanderings over the stage. As for sounding-boards; sometimes the stage was inclosed tightly, at others a space six feet wide would be left open at the back; again, a broken sounding-board, made like great slats, with an open space between each one, would be used. The orchestra sat on two sounding-boards besides the

regular flooring of the stage, and Thomas was incessantly tinkering at the varying heights at which
each man should be elevated above the floor level.
In short, the fine effects achieved by the orchestra
in the Auditorium were due quite as much to the
work of Thomas in adjusting the orchestra and
stage, as to the good acoustics of the theater
itself. The same problem had now to be worked
out in a new and strange hall, with the added
difficulty that the popular ear was tuned to the old
place, and the popular affection anchored there.
The antagonists of the new hall were also ready to
pounce upon anything imperfect that could be
found in it, and Thomas realized the importance
of getting his orchestra adjusted to it before their
criticism had done it any appreciable injury. Unfortunately circumstances forced the Association
to use the hall before it was really finished. The
cement and plaster were still damp, doors and
windows were only half fitted, the air was charged
with dust from the recently removed scaffolds, and,
to counteract the draught and dry out the walls, a
fierce heat was turned on, making an atmosphere
like that of a tropical greenhouse. Under these
circumstances it is not strange that Thomas caught
a severe cold, and by the time the opening concert
took place he was already far from well.

One of the features of the new building was,
as I have said, a small hall for recital purposes.
This room connected with, or rather formed a
part of the main foyer of the large hall. Here
the orchestra members had planned—so soon as

Thomas should be well and everything in good order—to give a banquet in his honor. On this occasion they wished, also, to present him with a testimonial of their affection, and passed a series of resolutions which were beautifully engrossed by the artist Rascovitch, and elaborately mounted and cased. They were worded as follows:

TESTIMONIAL TO THEODORE THOMAS

FROM

THE MEMBERS OF HIS ORCHESTRA
Chicago, 1905

Resolved, That we place on record the gratitude we owe to you as our revered and respected leader in our own campaign of education, for your patience so untiringly displayed, for your help so freely given, for the vigilant watchfulness with which you have always guarded our interests.

Resolved, That we place upon record our admiration of the high musical standard you have maintained and of your straightforward, unswerving course, and of our love for the man who never trifled with his gifts, and who never sacrificed the honor of his art to gratify personal ambition or further personal ends.

Resolved, That now your reward has come, and leader and players are in their own home, given them by lovers of music, that we extend to you our heartiest congratulations. Fifty years of honest work have not been wasted. You have come to your own, nobly striven for, nobly won. You are recognized and will be remembered for your self-sacrificing, courageous devotion to the highest in our noble art. None recognized it sooner, none will remember it longer than those who have worked with you.

Resolved, That as a token of our admiration for you as a musician, of our loyalty to you as our leader, and our affection for you as a man, we ask you to accept this tribute with the wish that we may have many happy and useful years together in the new home, which stands as a testimonial of the popular love and respect for an honored leader under whose baton we have served so long and so pleasantly.

(Signed by all the members of the Orchestra.)

Could Thomas have lived to receive this testimonial from his " boys " it would have given him one of the happiest experiences of his life, and would, taken in connection with the Philharmonic testimonial in March, have brought home to him, as nothing else could have done, the comforting assurance that his work had been understood and appreciated at its true value by his professional colleagues, in East and West. But, alas, this was not to be, and he never read these loving words of his orchestra.

Wednesday evening, December 14, 1904, was the fateful night which saw the fruition of that for which Thomas had worked for nearly half a century—the establishment of his orchestra, permanently endowed, in a building of its own, where he hoped it would be the foundation upon which would rise an art institution of the noblest and broadest character, which should not only maintain the highest standard in executive art, but should, in time, develop a musical university and set an equally high standard in educational work. Such was the institution which Thomas saw with his mind's eye as he stepped upon the stage of the new hall and raised his baton for the first number of its inaugural concert.

The programme was a strange one for a gala occasion, and in the light of subsequent events it might be called his *" Morituri Salutamus."* Four of its five numbers were deeply psychological in character, and the sequence in which they were performed was very dramatic. First came Wagner's stirring salutation to the building, " Hail, bright abode," sung by the Apollo Club. This was followed by the Overture to " Tannhaeuser," a composition which represents the struggle of a passionate and sensuous soul against material sin, and its final purification. Then came the terrible tone poem of Richard Strauss, " Death and Apotheosis," which portrays with frightful realism the physical agony of dissolution, and the passing of the soul through bodily suffering into the eternal repose of the hereafter. This, in turn, was followed by Beethoven's Fifth Symphony— a composition which, more than any other, was associated with Theodore Thomas, and of which he said: " The first movement represents a conflict, and the will-power of a great soul. The second represents the emotional side of the same soul, and is a temporary rest. The third renews the conflict again and leads to a final triumph of unusual strength and happiness in the fourth." The last number of the programme, Haendel's inspiring, " Hallelujah Chorus," was a thrilling climax to this extraordinary sequence of master-works.

Coming, as it did, at the close of an evening which had been devoted to the serious contemplation of the soul, its struggles here, and its triumphs hereafter, the famous chorus seemed to have even more than its customary significance, and its great and solemn strains carried the mind irresistibly up to the heavenly vision which was its inspiration:

" And I heard as it were the voice of a great multitude, and as the voice of many waters, and as the voice of mighty thunderings, saying:

" ' Hallelujah! For the Lord omnipotent reigneth!' "

After such a programme as this, performed on the night which had placed the laurel crown of success upon his artistic career, it was fitting that Thomas should have found an unusual company of friends waiting at his house to offer him their congratulations. They were the friends of many years' standing, who had spontaneously gathered from, not only Chicago, but Boston, New York, Cincinnati, Washington, and other cities, to witness the happy consummation of his life-work. There were so many that our dining-room would not accommodate them all, and we had supper served in the parlor, where, seated around a big, jolly table, this reunion of so many life-long friends from his old fields of labor, was as delightful to Thomas as it was unexpected.

The evening was not one, however, which was calculated to recuperate his waning strength, and within a day or two the cold from which he was

suffering, became the "grippe." He was now
really ill, but could he have rested quietly at home
and taken care of himself for a few days, he might
still have recovered. In his anxiety to adjust
the orchestra to the new hall, without delay, he
would not do this, but arose from his sick bed
every day to go and conduct rehearsals and concerts, and returned to it again as soon as he
got home. In spite of this suicidal course, when
Christmas Eve came he seemed to be somewhat
better. We had planned to have a little Christmas supper by ourselves in his study, after the
concert—there was always a concert to be conducted before Thomas could think of pleasure—the
servants were sent to bed, and we roasted oysters
in the shell over the coals of the open fire. "How
good these taste!" he exclaimed. "It is the first
time anything has tasted good to me since we
got into the new hall. Come, we must drink
'*Brüderschaft*' together, German-fashion, to cele-
brate the day, and the well-cooked oysters, and my
recovered appetite, for I believe I begin to feel
better at last." So we went through with the
quaint little ceremony, and opened the Christmas
boxes from his absent sons and daughters, and for
an hour he was his old, genial self, and as gay and
happy as a boy. All at once he seemed to wilt.
His laughter died, and his buoyant spirits fell.
"I am so tired, so tired," he said wearily, "I must
go to bed."

All the next day he was very ill. Monday he
once more tried to drag himself down to the

rehearsal, but could get no further than the front door, and had to go back to bed again. The rest is soon told. By Thursday pneumonia had set in, and after a few days of torturing illness, borne without a murmur, it became apparent that the end was near. A few hours before his death the lamp of life flickered up for a moment, and as I sat beside him he murmured: " I have had a beautiful vision—a beautiful vision——" and seemed to want to tell me what it was, but was too weak to frame the words. It was given to me, in this supreme moment, to divine his thoughts, and I said: " I know what you have seen. It was our lovely Felsengarten at the sunset hour, with its flowers, rocks, and trees; its great, silent mountains showing blue and purple against the golden sky, and the quiet cattle grazing in the valley below." He smiled a dreamy assent, and with this happy thought of home in mind drifted off into unconsciousness, and never wakened more. A few hours later, in the early morning of January 4, 1905, he died, quietly and painlessly, surrounded by those he loved best, in the seventieth year of his age.

The death of Theodore Thomas was regarded as a national calamity, and memorial services and musical performances were held in his honor in nearly every city in the land. His funeral was very simple, and the only music was the rendering of a few stately German chorals by a choir of twenty trombones, as the funeral cortège entered and left the church where the services were held. Later in the day the orchestra held a musical memorial service for the regular attendants of the Symphony concerts, which was repeated on the following Sunday for the general public. The last named performance was given in the Auditorium on account of its large seating capacity, but so great was the concourse of people who desired to attend that not only was it taxed to its utmost limit, but many thousands, unable to get in, stood silently in the wintry blasts of the streets without, while it was in progress. The interment took place a few weeks later in the presence of only the family and a few intimate friends, in accordance with the oft-expressed wish of Thomas. There was no music at this brief ceremony, but as the casket, which contained his mortal part, sank slowly into its last resting-place, twelve solemn strokes were tolled upon the silent air by the bell of a distant church.

After this manner was the passing of Theodore Thomas. Hundreds, nay thousands, of letters and testimonials came to us from all parts of the world, after his death, expressing the universal love and honor in which he was held. Amongst them was one from his devoted friend, Paderewski. Let me close, in his words, this simple record of a beneficent life:

" The entire musical world joins in deepest sorrow over this terrible bereavement. The passing away of the illustrious Theodore Thomas is an irreparable loss to our art, for scarcely any man

The Theodore Thomas Cross at Mt. Auburn Cemetery,
Cambridge, Mass.

in any land has done so much for the musical education of the people, as did he in this great country. The purity of his character, the firmness of his principles, the nobility of his ideals, together with the magnitude of his achievements, will assure him everlasting glory in the annals of artistic culture."

APPENDIX

WHEN a man passes away who has devoted his life to any national cause, it is customary for his contemporaries to sum up the results of his labors, and give public expression to their verdict before writing the final " *Requiescat in Pace* " upon his tomb. It had been the life object of Theodore Thomas to create the highest standard of art in music throughout America, to educate the nation to understand and love that standard, and to found a permanent musical institution which should serve in a special sense to guard and conserve it to future generations. After his death his work, like that of others, was weighed in the balance of public opinion, and the popular estimate of its value was printed far and wide in the editorial columns of the world. Could he but have known, while still living, how truly his aims were appreciated, his character understood, and the object for which he had worked achieved, it would have glorified and inspired his declining years. But very little of all this came to his knowledge, for, while he was the recipient of many honors during his life, they came chiefly from special sources, and of the popular reverence and love he realized comparatively little. After his death there was a very general outpouring of affection, grief, and honor for the departed musician, and from the mass of resolutions, memorials, essays, sermons, editorials, etc., which were printed then, the following have been selected as representative of the estimation in which the man and his work were held by those who were co-laborers in his larger schemes; by the press, the pulpit, and the musical profession.

Memorial of
The Chicago Orchestral Association

" We, the Trustees of the Chicago Orchestral Association, wish it were possible to place upon its records a fitting tribute to the memory of our friend and leader, Theodore Thomas. We feel how inadequate any formal expression of regard and regret must be. The world knows what Theodore Thomas has done to inspire the American people with love of the highest form of the most spiritual of all the arts. Only those who came nearest to him knew the difficulties of his task and the wisdom and patient courage with which he overcame them.

" We deplore his death as our own personal bereavement, and an unspeakable loss to the higher life of our country; but we rejoice that such a man has lived and labored, and so far as in us lies we resolve that his labors shall not have been in vain.

" THE CHICAGO ORCHESTRAL ASSOCIATION."

[As a public memorial in his honor the Association decreed that the name of the " Chicago Orchestra " should henceforth be changed to the " Theodore Thomas Orchestra," and that of " Orchestra Hall " to the " Theodore Thomas Orchestra Hall " and that the said name should be carved on the two stone panels of its façade.—R. F. T.]

From the University of Chicago " Record ":

" As an indication of the sense of almost irreparable loss felt by the University of Chicago over the death of Theodore Thomas, the *Record* publishes the following tribute from President W. R. Harper:

" ' The sense of sorrow caused by the death of Theodore Thomas is universal throughout the city of Chicago. His work has been done for all classes and conditions of people. There is no element of our population but what has been delighted again and again by his music, and his fame has truly been a pride to the whole city. Members of the University, therefore, in common with the whole city, pay their tribute to him as a matchless musician and a noble benefactor of Chicago. At the same time, as an institution which aims at higher learning, the University has peculiar reason to feel thankful for his influence in elevating musical taste and his steadfast adherence to the highest ideals of art. We shall always remember with special gratitude his kindness during the last year in bringing his orchestra to Mandel Hall and thus putting the best music at our very door. Words can express only a small part of what we feel; but no one who knew Mr. Thomas, or knew the devoted following that he had at the University, can doubt that his memory will be long cherished among us. The loss to all is very great, one which we cannot now fully appreciate.

"'WILLIAM R. HARPER, *President*.'"

Memorial of
The Cincinnati Musical Festival Association

" The directors have met to-day for the purpose of recording on the minutes of the association their acknowledgment of the services of the great leader, Theodore Thomas, to the cause of music in Cincinnati, and of expressing their sense of personal bereavement at his death.

" Mr. Thomas has been the conductor of these festivals from the beginning. He conducted the first concert of the first festival on Tuesday, May 6, 1873, and every concert of every festival thereafter until he laid down his baton after the memorable performance of Beethoven's Ninth Symphony, with which he brought the sixteenth festival to

a glorious close on Saturday, May 14th, 1904. What
he accomplished for the education of the public and for
the cause of music in this city during those years of
service is not recorded in any written annals, and cannot
be: it is part of the history of Cincinnati and of the lives
of her citizens, which he enriched and made better, purer,
and happier by inspiring them with an appreciation of
the highest and best forms of music, and by revealing to
them the ineffable beauties of the art to which he devoted
his life with noble and unselfish purpose. His upright
character, his high ideals, his sound judgment matured
by years of study and labor, his indefatigable energy,
his courage and patience in times of trial, his catholic
spirit, his faith in the people and his confidence in the
ultimate triumph of his appeals to their intelligence and
of his efforts to raise the standard of art in their midst,
are the qualities of heart and mind which have endeared
him to his associates, and have laid the foundation of his
enduring fame as a benefactor of mankind.

"He came to us when he was a young man; he gave us
a large part of his life; he has gone full of years and
honors. He fought a good fight and kept the faith. We
deplore the loss of our leader and mourn the death of our
friend. In the shadow of his death we pledge ourselves to
continue the work which he began, and to maintain the
Cincinnati festivals on the plane of excellence where he
placed them, and in the spirit of conscientious endeavor
and high artistic purpose with which he endowed them.

"THE CINCINNATI MUSICAL FESTIVAL ASSOCIATION."

[As further tribute to the memory of Thomas, the Association has placed a statue of him in the great foyer
of the Cincinnati Music Hall, at the unveiling of which,
during the first concert of the festival of 1910, the Presi-

Statue of Theodore Thomas, Unveiled in the Cincinnati
Music Hall, May 8, 1905, at the First Concert
of the Nineteenth Festival

dent of the United States made the dedicatory address.—
R. F. T.]

The Memorial of Boston

(From the Boston " Transcript ")

" King's Chapel has very naturally, through all its associations with old Boston, come down to us as the place of
all civic and public ceremonies—the little Westminster
Abbey of Boston—most appropriately, therefore, it was
chosen for the memorial service on Sunday afternoon in
honor of the great American musician and educator of
the American people in music, Theodore Thomas. The
writer can imagine nothing more moving to reflection on
the noble figure that has gone in his prime—the embodi-
ment of dauntless power in character, and matchless refinement in art, a rare and splendid illustration of perfect
union between music and morals—than the hush of this
occasion in King's Chapel, broken only by the perfect
music one hears there always, and the fitly spoken word.
First the burial service was read by the minister of King's
Chapel, followed by an address by the vice president of
the Harvard Musical Association. A choir of forty professional singers, conducted by Mr. B. J. Lang, sang
' *Ein' Feste Burg*,' and the ' Burial Chorus ' from the ' St.
Matthew Passion Music ' of Bach."

The New York Memorial

Metropolitan Opera House, Jan. 8, 1905

Programme

Nahan Franko, Conductor

Symphonic Poem, " Les Préludes ".............Liszt
Metropolitan Opera Orchestra

Aria, " Pro Peccatis " from " Stabat Mater "....Rossini
Mr. Marcel Journet

"Pardon Me," from "Passion Music"............Bach

Mme. Louise Homer

Aria from "Iphigenie".......................Gluck

Mr. Andreas Dippel

Aria di Chiesa.......................... Stradella

Mme. Marcella Sembrich

Funeral March, Orchestrated by Theodore Thomas,

Metropolitan Opera Orchestra   Chopin

Aria, "Il Re Pastore".................... Mozart

Mme. Marcella Sembrich

Largo............................... Haendel

Mr. Max Bendix

"Les Rameaux"........................ Faure

Mr. Marcel Journet

Aria, "And He shall feed His flock," "Messiah,"

Mme. Louise Homer   Haendel

Funeral March, "Goetterdaemmerung".......Wagner

From the Aschenbroedel Verein:

New York

" MRS. THEODORE THOMAS,

"WERTHE FRAU THOMAS,

"Der Aschenbroedel Verein * von New York spricht Ihnen, geehrte Frau, hierdurch die tiefempfundenste, aufrichtigste Theilnahme an Ihrem Gerechten Schmerz aus welchen das Ableben Ihres Gatten, unseres hochgeschaetzen Ehrenmitgliedes Ihnen verursacht hat.

"Wir sind ausser Stande Trost zu spenden; nehmen Sie aber die Versicherung dass in aller unser Herzen eine aufrichtige und dauernte Verehrung fuer Ihren geliebten

---

*The Aschenbroedel Verein includes in its membership all the orchestral players of the first rank in New York and vicinity.

Gatten, den Ersten und Besten Gruender guter—und nur guter—Musikauffuehrungen in America wohnt; und dass wir ihm ein bleibendes, seiner wuerdiges Andenken bewahren werden bis auch wir zu den Entschlafenen zaehlen.

"Moegen diese wenige Worte der Anerkennung, Wuerdigung und Verehrung aus den Herzen von Berufsgenossen kommend, ihren Zweck nicht verfehlen und Ihnen einige Linderung Ihres von uns vollauf gewuerdigten Schmerzes geben.

"Der mit Ihnen trauernde

"ASCHENBROEDEL VEREIN."

Memorial of the Brooklyn Philharmonic Society

"The Board of Directors of the Philharmonic Society of Brooklyn desire to place upon the minutes of the Society their sense of personal loss in the death of Theodore Thomas, who became their conductor in 1873, and terminated his engagement in 1891.

"To us of this Board he was more than the peerless conductor and tireless educator, who by being true to his lofty ideals brought the musical taste of this community up to an appreciation of the best and highest in musical art. To us he was our cherished friend, who mingled with his duties as musical director a rare personality, that attracted us to him by its charming nature and by its invariable evidences of friendship. . . . Our minds revert with delight to his many brilliant successes in the superb work which his orchestra rendered in our concerts, under his inspiring leadership, and also to the notable performances of great choral works, which will be long remembered. We can see, even now, the grace and dignity with which he wielded the baton, and the magic effect upon every member of his orchestra, and our thoughts dwell lingeringly upon the recollection of those occasions when we met him socially, and when his warm-hearted and genial nature brought joy to us all. Our minds are full of memories of our dear friend and conductor, for his strong nature impressed us with admiration, and we found that to know him better was but to love him the more.

" A life so full of noble work, so true to the highest and best, so persistent in its efforts, and fashioned in such a heroic mold, is rarely met with in this world, and the memory of Theodore will be lovingly cherished in all our hearts. The members of this Board, appreciating his great life work, and the fact that it was their privilege to be associated with him for twenty years, hereby express their keen sorrow at his death, their sincere sympathy with his bereaved family, and offer this tribute to their beloved conductor and their personal friend.

" JOHN S. FROTHINGHAM, *Secretary.*
HENRY N. WHITNEY, *President.*"

Resolutions of the
Contemporary Club of Saint Louis

" The Contemporary Club, of St. Louis, representing the widest range of interests in art and education, at a meeting held on January 5, 1905, when the subject for consideration was ' Toward American Music,' and on a day when the American people had been saddened by the death of one who had been such a pervading influence in all that pertains to true art, passed a resolution that a committee be appointed to give expression to the feelings of its members because of the loss of Theodore Thomas.

" In accordance with this resolution we desire to extend our sympathy to the family of Theodore Thomas and to the people of Chicago.

" We believe we are speaking not only for this Club

but for the whole City of St. Louis in expressing our appreciation of what this man has done by his heroic career in the art to which his life was consecrated.

"The loss is not only to his family and to the cities where he has resided, but to the whole United States of America. The misfortune falls not simply upon the art which he represented but upon all the high arts without distinction.

"We feel that he has been a world educator and in the realm of eternal ideas and ideals has led the minds and souls of generations.

"We honor those who have upheld him in his great work and we wish to express to them, as well as to his family, our sorrow that he could not have been spared much longer in order to add still greater glory to the art of music and to be still for us a higher inspiration.

"Yet we feel that nothing could have added to his fame and we are grateful to his memory for his exalted work.

"By devout and masterly genius he ennobled the world in which he lived and his influence, incalculable in extent, will be imperishable.

"WALTER L. SHELDON,
JOHN W. DAY,
WILLIAM M. CHAUVENET,
Committee."

From the New York "Times":

"It is hard to estimate the debt that this country owes to Theodore Thomas. It is the debt of a pupil to a teacher; or it is the debt of a people led out of a wilderness to the prophet who has shown them a sight of the promised land. To him more than to any other single force is due the present state of musical culture in this country. To an amazing persistency in the face of

piled-up difficulties he joined the fine and catholic taste
and, most of all, the willingness to make his propaganda
gradually, that were precisely the qualities that were necessary to make his success.   He knew that there were many
kinds of good music; and that the love and appreciation
of the greatest kinds were best attained by a gradual
uplift through the lesser. . . . The immediate loss is
Chicago's, but the whole country, and New York in particular, will not let the western city mourn alone."

From the " Nation ":

" The most remarkable characteristics of Theodore
Thomas as a musician were his catholicity of taste and
versatility.   No one interpreted the oldest masters—
Bach, Haendel, Gluck, Haydn, Mozart—more impres-
sively than he, or with keener insight into the antique
spirit of music.   Beethoven and Schubert he worshiped,
and made propaganda for them every week of his life.
He did missionary work for Wagner, Liszt, and Berlioz
at a time when it meant money out of his pocket and the
incurring of critical censure.   And he kept his interest
in the new music until the last moment, his latest *protégés*
having been Richard Strauss and Elgar. . . . Attention
may also be called to the fact that he did more for American composers than any other conductor has done.

" Thomas was a born commander.   His stubborn determination to carry out his plans and wishes frequently got
him into trouble, and he made many enemies: but they
were for the most part enemies to be proud of.   He was
not without jealousy, and when Anton Seidl came to New
York he looked on him, unfortunately, as a rival rather
than a helper.   But when he became more familiar with
Seidl's admirable work (when he conducted the Thomas
Orchestra in Grau's operatic performances in Chicago),

he cordially offered his colleague his friendship and praise."

From the Boston " Transcript ":

"In these days of endowed symphony orchestras in America it is difficult for younger generations to understand the honor in which the name of Theodore Thomas has been held by his contemporaries. Nowadays it is merely a matter of setting aside a million and issuing a fiat and an orchestra exists. In Thomas' day the taste and desire for good music had to be built up in the first place. It was his destined life work to create the broader popular base for musical culture on which alone it can have any vital relation to or influence on the national character and refinement. . . . All of Thomas' efforts to make a financial surety of fine music in America were, one after another, year by year doomed to disappointment. It is this pathetic and heroic struggle, during all of which it never occurred to him to give up, that accounts for his being held by those who witnessed it all, one of our American heroes, a man to be ever remembered and looked up to as a public character and benefactor. Of course there were in him the usual defects of his qualities. A born leader, fit for such a struggle, must be made of the sternest stuff, and Theodore Thomas, though personally modest to shyness, was a dictator in matters of music, and a hard taskmaster to his players. . . . He has died in harness, as he would have chosen, and with his place in art and share in the evolution of American culture honorably recognized, and the great work of his planting in full bearing."

From the Chicago " Tribune ":

"One of the few really great orchestral conductors of the world, and the foremost leader of musical progress in America, has passed away after fifty years of honorable,

dignified, consistent, and uncommercial service. Theodore
Thomas was a musician with great gifts, which he never
degraded, and with which he never trifled. Music was never
an amusement to him, but the highest expression of æsthetic
possibility, and his work for it was always of an educational character. . . . His life work was singularly complete. It reached half a century, and in that period was
comprised a successful growth, with a future promise such
as few musical leaders have ever achieved. He lived to see
the accomplishment of his purpose, and to receive his
reward in such a popular gift as no other musician but
Wagner has ever received, and no other American city
has attempted to make. Grand in his ideals, unswerv-
ingly honest and honorable in his career, splendid in
musical gift, and noble in manliness of character, with
a great loving heart behind his austere seeming, he has
gone, and thousands will mourn for him."

Resolutions of the Chicago Press League

"With feelings of profound sorrow we, the members of
the Chicago Press League, wish to express our appreciation of and high respect for the life of the great musician
just deceased.

"Theodore Thomas was the high priest in the temple
of music which he builded for Chicago and the American
people. On its holy altar he consecrated the powers of
his strong and noble manhood. At this sacred shrine the
hearts of the people were uplifted into the realms of the
most beautiful on earth, and in this temple, be the creed
or nationality of its votaries what they might, all were
made to feel their kinship with the divinity.

"That harmony which is the culmination of life's highest ideal was here realized, and his preaching of sounds
sunk deeper into hearts than that of words.

" With the sacred hope that his family will feel consoled in the thought that his great uplifting work will live forever, we bid farewell to the great soul who has entered where peace and rest abide forevermore."

From the " American," New York and Chicago:

" Theodore Thomas died just as he had realized the dream and goal of his long and splendid life. . . .

" There is something pathetic and moving beyond words in the blind fate that takes from the laboring hands the fruit of so many years of thought and sacrifice and conscientious effort. The house is built and the builder may not dwell in it. The noble end is attained and the man that wrought it may not stay to enjoy it.

" We shall not see again this earnest and inspired figure leading his artists through the intricate colors and shades of the great tone poems, but his work remains, his true work is less perishable than statues of marble or buildings of stone.

" After all, it is the effect of a man's life that endures. After all, it is a question of the impress he has left upon the contemporaneous mind.

" In the long story of the world even the most solid creation of human hands is as transitory as a breath. The effect of a great life goes on from generation to generation as long as the race exists.

" Few men in our time have made this impress deeper than Theodore Thomas.

" He was the father of classical music in America. When he began his work the orchestra was practically unknown here. There was no taste for the thoughtful and satisfying forms of music. There was scarcely a vestige of a discerning and appreciative musical public.

" It was his service to change all that. He introduced

to America every great composer who now has a following here. He made classical music popular. He interpreted Wagner and made those wonderful sound structures as familiar in American homes as the songs of childhood. He strove for higher ideals with a kind of strenuous and buoyant faith that no adverse criticism could daunt. He created musical taste where none was before; he set a standard; he inspired a widely dispersed army of enthusiasts, and through him light, new ideas, and new ideals, and broader culture came into the lives of millions who never saw him.

"Greater and more honorable achievement can hardly be. Soldiers and politicians fill the world with noise, and pass and leave no mark. The man that affects thought and ideals and the inner life of a people is the tremendous power to whose work all the rest is sound and fury, signifying nothing.

"Theodore Thomas was undoubtedly the greatest interpreter of orchestral music who has so far lived on this earth. He had a mind abnormally sympathetic with the most subtle musical moods. He was an orchestral genius. The innovations and improvements he wrought have gone around the world. He was recognized wherever music is played from scores as the greatest of directors. His influence is imperishable.

"The greatest lesson of his life is that true success, enduring success, the only success that is worth having, comes and can come only from uncompromising adherence to the highest ideals. Mr. Thomas never made the slightest concession from the standards of his faith. He never compromised with his artistic conscience, never considered expediency, never temporized, never tolerated error that good might come of it. There is no other lesson so important to the world. The substance of this man's life was that right is right and right will win. Time was when a host of critics poured upon him a virulent wrath for adhering inflexibly to his conceptions, for playing Wagner when nobody wanted to hear Wagner, for insisting always upon the best as eventually the most popular. He lived to see every adverse criticism overwhelmed and the music that he introduced become the favorite of the people.

" He was a great man, a great soul, a great inspiration and leader. He drew men to him by the sheer strength of his character and the innate kindness of his heart, and of all the tributes that will be paid to him none will be more heartfelt than the grief of the men that he has led and instructed and inspired so many years.

" The blow to Chicago, to the orchestra that is Chicago's pride and glory, and to the cause of good music everywhere is heavy, for a great and helpful light has gone out."

From the " Standard," Chicago :

" When a man not only cherishes and preaches great ideals but in difficulty substantiates them, this man the world calls great. Happy are we if we know our great while yet they are with us. A great man has gone out of the music realm of two hemispheres. Theodore Thomas, of Chicago, is dead. We have our awe and homage for soldiers, statesmen, divines, and captains of industry. Let us not fail to know that it is one of the world's transformers, a maker and master of musicians, who has joined the stately company of leaders of the race. Mr. Thomas and his orchestra had become institutional. He was the energizing force in a city which is one of the musical centers of the world. When his passing is noted, and his services are estimated by people remote from this metropolis, the error of judgment should not be made that this remarkable man was at best but a successful entertainer. As well confound the University of Chicago with a lyceum bureau. Mr. Thomas was orchestral organizer and conductor, teacher, leader, prophet all in one. No such commanding personality as his survives in the world of music in the United States or Europe. . . . Mr. Thomas was a leader in every great sense, and the thousands that mourn him, that sustained him with money and sympathy, are leaders too, some in very large ways, some in smaller, but all devotees of the art that most effectually of all the arts bridges earth and heaven. However approximate one's appreciation is of the services of this man to the humanizing of the American people the kind of a man he was and the kind of work he sought should not be overlooked. Profoundly educated in music himself—in younger years a violinist—strong of will and clear of purpose, he was a discoverer, importer, and developer, as the case might be, of true masters old and new. He not only disciplined his musicians but he disciplined the public, educating it sometimes perhaps against its will. It may have casually remonstrated; but now lamenting the departed it finds all well. Mr. Thomas passed in honor, love, and glory, an orchestra for his legacy, a temple for his monument."

From the Boston " Herald ":

" THE MUSICIAN AS PROPHET AND PRIEST

" The tributes paid to the late Theodore Thomas by musicians have been notable and deeply suggestive. But they were to be expected. It was not so certain that the spiritual value of his work would be recognized as fully as it has been by men who are set apart distinctly in the community as spiritual guides, but who now and again are wont to define the limits of spiritual influence in terms of ecclesiasticism.

" The comments of the clergymen of Chicago on Theodore Thomas' service to humanity are very suggestive. They frankly recognize that he was both priest and prophet, and not only a great spiritual force by reason of his gifts as a conductor and the effects he produced on men's higher being by his orchestra's rendering of great masterpieces, but also a great spiritual force because he was an idealist whose standard was the best, and who would be content with nothing else.

" Such appreciation from a poetic, beauty-loving spirit like Rev. Dr. Gunsaulus might have been expected, who said, ' We have said good-by to a priest and prophet. It makes no difference that Theodore Thomas never acknowledged his divine call to a high noble ministry. Music is the soul's expression of that irrepressible desire for harmony and aspiration after concord which is the heart of true religion. It is, perhaps, the sublime unconsciousness in which such a man works his transformation upon our less-gifted natures that witnesses most to his finest quality.' But hearty recognition of Mr. Thomas' high service to society as a spiritual guide came from some of the most conservative and most practical of the city's preachers.

" Of course the intimate kinship between religion and music in all their infinite gradations of mood and conceptions of life is something long since seen and declared, and the praise of Mr. Thomas as a great spiritual factor in Chicago's life by the Protestant and Jewish clergy, only registers the fact that this kinship is seen by men of to-day in a city devoted to the material aspects of life. . . . The point is that there has been a tribute to a priest and prophet of one sort, by priests and prophets of another sort. No doubt the very contrast between the materialism and the emphasis on the things of the outer man, accentuated, both in Mr. Thomas' mind and in the minds of those who now praise him, the value to society of that refining, quieting, consoling, illuminating quality of music, which might not have been so profoundly appreciated because less needed, in a city less given to strife for those commodities which keep the body alive and in comfort but do not minister to the soul.

"In Massachusetts also tributes to the life work of the late Theodore Thomas were paid from several pulpits yesterday, and the lessons of his devotion to high ideals and lofty ambitions were enforced upon the minds of the congregations. At the Crombie Street Church, Salem, the Rev. Dr. A. A. Berle, preaching on the subject, 'The Faith That Makes Power,' referred to Theodore Thomas as follows:

"'The multitudes who to-day enjoy the musical feasts which are spread before us with so lavish a hand can hardly realize what a howling wilderness it was musically to which Theodore Thomas came with his magnificent power and with his wonderful faith, and how steadfastly he adhered, with great loss and often utter lack of appreciation, to his high and catholic standards of musical interest and appreciation. The so-called upper circles, as is often the case, were the last to come around to his support and understanding. Men still living can remember when the only place where one could hear his orchestra and have the inspiration and benefit of the great delight and spiritual uplift he was giving to the American people was a beer garden, and when the people who crowded delightedly around him were the foreign population, chiefly the immigrant Germans and their children.

" ' His was a work of faith which has had a mightier impress upon American life than much of the legislation which has been passed in the same period. It has had a vaster influence upon the public mind and character than much of the more formal instruction. There is not a school or church or theater or concert hall or home in the land but is richer and of finer type because of the work of Theodore Thomas. The pioneer who had to begin his work of the musical culture of America in a beer garden ended in persuading the newest and the most turbulent metropolis in the world to erect a beautiful home for his orchestra, and saw in his own person his art receive a crown, which will be held in everlasting remembrance among those to whom the glory of America is not in its colossal fortunes, but in its magnificent idealisms carried to the sumptuous fulfillment, which America can provide as no other country in the world can.'

" In a prelude to his sermon last night at People's Temple, the Rev. Charles A. Crane said of Theodore Thomas: ' He was a master in affairs as well as in music. A strident and discordant civilization blustering in the metropolis of the West—Chicago—he so far changed that musical people, the musical trade, the standards of music and musical taste were strengthened, broadened, and elevated. He never catered to the public. He called them up to the heights. Two generations have been educated by his masterful hand. . . . Who can name his limitations? He was a priest and a prophet in the temple of music and that most beautiful of all arts was adorned by his devotion to it.' "

From Musicians:

" LEIPSIC, January, 1905.

" Theodore Thomas was the pioneer of music in America. We younger composers must always be especially grateful to him, for he often brought out our works in the United States before they were given here in Europe. His memory will never be forgotten.

"FELIX WEINGARTNER."

"BERLIN, January, 1905.

"Not only Americans, but we all owe Theodore Thomas enormous thanks. Without his indefatigable pioneer work we musicians of the Old World could never have had such success in the United States.

"ARTHUR NIKISCH."

"VIENNA, January, 1905.

"It is impossible to exaggerate the great loss the death of Mr. Thomas means to the musical world. His position was unchallenged; *the greatest orchestra conductor in the world.* He had no equal. There is none to take his place.

"WILLIAM GERICKE."

"BERLIN, January, 1905.

"I confess the death of Theodore Thomas has shocked me in the highest degree. Art loses in him a musician of the rarest purity and strength of character. I myself mourn the deceased great Master as a faithful friend. What he signified for musical development in America is well known. What we Germans owe him shall be held in everlasting remembrance.

"RICHARD STRAUSS."

"BERLIN, January 7, 1905.

"MY DEAR MRS. THOMAS,

"I am more than sad to-day. You have lost a wonderful husband, I a dear, dear friend, and America—no, Music, Art,—has lost more than can ever be expressed. Mr. Thomas did all for it with his manhood, and his will power, and worked with his high and earnest valor more than could a thousand others.

"Beside yourself, dear Mrs. Thomas, there are few people who appreciated him, his character, and all that he did, so highly as I. I never met a musician who equaled him, and I was, and will be ever proud that he called me his friend. I am more than ashamed of New York when I think that it was not possible for him to establish his orchestra there—a city where thousands and thousands of dollars are spent every year for nothing—flowers, cloaks, races, and the Lord knows what.

"You know that Mr. Kalisch and I have always thought of him and you with all the love we could bear to such dear friends, and we, especially I, will always remember him as a Master such as we seldom met. I hope he was buried like the King that he was, and that his death was a peaceful one.

"Most affectionately yours,
"LILLI LEHMANN KALISCH."

"PARIS, February 7, 1905.

"Vincent d'Indy desires to convey to Madame Thomas the expression of his profound sympathy for the cruel loss which the art of music has suffered in the death of the celebrated conductor, Mr. Theodore Thomas, to whom all French composers, and Mr. d'Indy in particular, owe the highest gratitude."

"BOSTON, January 5, 1905.
"MY DEAR MRS. THOMAS,

"I cannot begin to describe to you the sense of desolation and irreparable loss which the death of Mr. Thomas has caused to me and to all of us here. His services to this country and to the cause of art were well known and valued, for his fame was national, and international. But what he was to us younger musicians of Boston, and what his influence meant to us, will never be known except by those who were fortunate enough to belong to our circle.

"For myself, as 'Deacon' of the group (as he called me), I can truly say that I have never had any other teacher or friend in my whole career, from whom I absorbed so much in knowledge, in stimulation, or in courage to fight for a high standard and for an ideal. It was impossible to come into his presence without feeling his magnetism and the force of his great personality.

"Every word that he uttered carried conviction with it—one felt at once that here was a *man*, and that he was intolerant of everything that was against the principles of eternal truth and beauty.

"It will always be my pride that it was through me that he learned to know and respect our younger Boston composers, and that through me they got a share of the inspiration which his friendship brought. He alone, of all the American conductors, has treated American composition as a dignified and serious effort. Not, on the one hand, as the work of incompetent amateurs to be scoffed and sneered at; nor, on the other, as an infant industry to be coddled and shielded from all opposition. He produced the works of American writers side by side with the classic, and also the modern masters, so that they could be compared with their contemporaries, and could stand or fall by their own intrinsic value—the only position that a real artist cares to occupy.

"Now that he is gone there is no one on whom his mantle can fall, and there will not be until an American is raised up who takes some interest and pride in the work of American musicians. . . .

"Sincerely yours,

"GEORGE W. CHADWICK."

" Cambridge, January 12, 1905.

" My dear Mrs. Thomas,

" I cannot tell you how shocked I was to hear of the death of your beloved husband. The whole world mourns with you. . . . You know how much I honored and loved him, both as friend and musician. No one ever did so much for me professionally, and I have always felt deeply grateful to him; and what he did for me he did for many others. The world will not see his like again. . . .

" Yours sincerely,
" John K. Paine."

" Des Moines, Ia.

" For a quarter of a century Theodore Thomas has been an uncrowned king among the musicians of this country. He ruled with an authority that compelled recognition, with an autocracy that vied with sovereignty, and received homage from us as to an emperor. His throne has been our art which he established in the West upon the very highest standards. We in this part of the country have lost a man whose individuality and ideals have been an inspiration and whose place will never be filled in exactly the same way. The general public cannot appreciate what a leader he has been to us, yet they know how we have looked up to him. On whom will his mantle fall? I hope from the American ranks. Memorial services and addresses will be given, requiems will be sung in his honor, biographies written. A great hall is erected and will embody his memory in stone and mortar, but his greatest monument is the unseen tribute of all musicians, who in their hearts hold his name sacred and live for ideals such as he would commend.

" Frederick Howard."